~~AN

THE HOUSE OF COMMONS
IN THE EIGHTEENTH CENTURY

THE
HOUSE OF
COMMONS
IN THE
EIGHTEENTH
CENTURY

BY

P. D. G. THOMAS

CLARENDON PRESS · OXFORD

1971

Oxford University Press, Ely House, London W.1

GLASGOW   NEW YORK   TORONTO   MELBOURNE   WELLINGTON

CAPE TOWN   SALISBURY   IBADAN   NAIROBI   DAR ES SALAAM   LUSAKA   ADDIS ABABA

BOMBAY   CALCUTTA   MADRAS   KARACHI   LAHORE   DACCA

KUALA LUMPUR   SINGAPORE   HONG KONG   TOKYO

PRINTED IN GREAT BRITAIN
BY WILLIAM CLOWES AND SONS, LIMITED
LONDON, BECCLES AND COLCHESTER

PREFACE

This book is a study of the practice and procedure of the House of Commons in the eighteenth century, that 'classical age of the constitution' when the King's government needed but in an era of non-party politics could never be assured of a majority in the Commons. This political background, first depicted by the late Sir Lewis Namier, gave real meaning to the decisions of the House and importance to the views of individual members.

The chief sources have been the Parliamentary and other diaries of M.P.s, and, despite their imperfections, the contemporary printed reports of debates in the years from 1714 to 1784. The law of diminishing returns soon came into operation. I have not read every report of every debate in that period, and the political correspondence and press of the age have both merely been sampled. Any historian studying British politics in the eighteenth century or periods before or after that time may find information that supplements or corrects what has been stated here.

The errors and omissions of this study would have been much more numerous but for the help I have received from many people. Sir Lewis Namier suggested the subject to me, and gave unfailing guidance and help during my first years of research into it. The book has grown from a University of London Ph.D. thesis on 'Debates of the House of Commons 1768-1774', and has benefited from comments made by Professor Ian R. Christie on that work and his subsequent interest in the project. Dr. James Tumelty read nearly the whole of the book in typescript, and it has been improved by his many suggestions. Professor Henry Horwitz also made helpful comments after reading the greater part of the work. I have received assistance on various points from Mr. John Brooke, Dr. E. L. Ellis, Mrs. Sheila Elton, Mr. R. S. Lea, and Dr. A. N. Newman. The History of Parliament Trust has afforded ready co-operation, and the published volumes and unpublished drafts of that *History* have been the unacknowledged source of much political and biographical information about M.P.s. Positive and courteous help has been received from the staffs of many libraries and repositories, and especially from those of the British Museum, The National Library of Wales, the House of Lords Record Office, the Institute of Historical Research, and the Library of the University College of Wales. All this practical assistance has been supplemented by the encouragement of my wife, who must feel that she has lived in St. Stephen's Chapel for the last few years.

This book has owed much to the generosity of owners of manuscripts, and I am grateful to the following for permission to cite and quote from manuscripts in their possession or in public repositories: the Marquess of Cholmondeley, Earl Fitzwilliam, the Earl of Harrowby and the Harrowby MSS. Trust, the Earl of Malmesbury, Sir Francis Dashwood, Mr. W. L. Clinton-Baker, and Mr. Humphrey FitzRoy Newdegate.

CONTENTS

I

INTRODUCTION

And thus I now, for the first time, saw the whole of the British nation assembled in its representatives, in rather a mean-looking building, that not a little resembles a chapel. The Speaker, an elderly man, with an enormous wig, with two knotted kind of tresses, or curls, behind, in a black cloak, his hat on his head, sat opposite to me on a lofty chair; which was not unlike a small pulpit, save only that in the front of this there was no reading desk. Before the Speaker's chair stands a table, which looks like an altar; and at this there sit two men, called clerks, dressed in black, with black cloaks. On the table, by the side of the great parchment acts, lies an huge gilt sceptre, which is always taken away and placed in a conservatory under the table, as soon as ever the Speaker quits the chair. . . . All round on the sides of the house under the gallery, are benches for the members, covered with green cloth, always one above the other, like our choirs in churches; in order that he who is speaking, may see over those who sit before him. The seats in the gallery are on the same plan.

The chamber of the House of Commons, so described by the German traveller Carl Moritz in 1782, was St. Stephen's Chapel in the royal Palace of Westminster.[1] Other buildings in the Palace included the law courts of Westminster Hall, the House of Lords, and the Painted Chamber, which was the meeting-place for conferences between representatives of the two Houses of Parliament. St. Stephen's Chapel served as the meeting-place of the Commons from about 1547 until the destruction of the old Palace by fire in 1834. A screen had divided it into a chapel and ante-chapel, which became respectively the debating-chamber and the lobby of the House of Commons. The chamber measured only 57 feet 6 inches by 32 feet 10 inches, the lobby through which it was entered being 28 feet by 30 feet.[2] As Moritz observed, the chamber

[1] Moritz, *Travels*, pp. 52–3. The following account is based on M. Hastings, *Parliament House*, pp. 80–4, 105–15.

[2] O. C. Williams, *The Topography of the Old House of Commons*, p. 2. This corrects

retained the internal arrangement of a church. The stalls had become the benches, four along each side, extending behind the Speaker's Chair towards the back or east wall, with some cross-benches by the entrance at the west end of the chamber, on each side of the Bar. The House had long been found inadequate in size, even before membership swelled to 558 after the union with Scotland in 1707. Dissatisfaction in the later seventeenth century led to alterations by Sir Christopher Wren, completed in 1707. The height of the ceiling was lowered from 45 feet to 30 feet, with consequent complaints now of heat rather than cold, at least on crowded occasions. Three round-headed windows in the east wall behind the Chair gave the chamber a distinctive character. The most important of Wren's alterations, intended to provide additional room for members and not accommodation for strangers, was the introduction of galleries. They were inserted at a height of 15 feet along the side walls and at the west end of the House, being supported on columns. Wren's chamber survived until the beginning of the nineteenth century, when Sir James Wyatt made further alterations after the arrival of 100 new members from Ireland. Wyatt then provided an additional row of seats along each side of the chamber by reducing the thickness of the walls.

From its initial foothold in St. Stephen's Chapel the House of Commons obtained possession of an ever-increasing proportion of the Palace of Westminster, for use as Committee rooms and for the work of the officials of the House.[1] The Speaker early acquired a withdrawing room, to which he often retired when the House was in Committee. The Speaker's Room was on the north or right-hand side of the House. A door at the back of the chamber gave access to it through a passage constructed behind the back wall and known as 'Solomon's Porch'. In 1660 the House had only one Committee room, above the lobby and known in the eighteenth century as 'the old Committee room'

the dimensions of the chamber given by Hastings as 60 feet by 28 feet, op. cit., p. 84.

[1] The following account is based on O. C. Williams, *The Topography of the Old House of Commons*. A copy of this unpublished monograph is available in the House of Lords Record Office. Appended to the text are reproductions of contemporary diagrams and sketch-maps. Others may be found in M. Hastings, *Parliament House*, pp. 108–9, 119.

or 'the smoking room'. From 1693, however, the place designated for the first meeting of every Committee was the Speaker's Chamber. This was situated above the cloisters in the angle of the House of Commons and Westminster Hall, and was entered by a stair from the back of the lobby. It comprised two rooms, each about 20 feet square, and was the place for most Select Committee business in the earlier part of the eighteenth century. Such accommodation proved inadequate for the growing volume of Committee work, and the House gradually obtained more Committee rooms by conversions and additions to the Palace of Westminster. Contemporary references to such rooms are vague and confusing, and instructions given by the House were not always carried out promptly: but by 1780 there were at least six and perhaps a dozen or more Committee rooms.

Even more numerous were the rooms provided for the officials of the House. A residence within the Palace was built for the Clerk of the House in 1760, although not until 1794 did the Speaker acquire the house of the Auditor of the Exchequer as his official residence; and it may not have been until the same date that the Speaker obtained possession of his dining-room below the chamber of the House. The location of the offices of the various under-Clerks is difficult to trace, and frequently changed. By 1718 two rooms had been partitioned off in the Court of Wards, one of them becoming the Journal Office by the reign of George III. Other offices were scattered in the main building of the Palace, and new rooms were built on the outside walls of St. Stephen's Chapel; one of them was the Votes Office, which was entered through the lobby.[1] By 1780 the chamber of the House was surrounded by offices and the Speaker's Room. The only entrance was through the lobby, which itself led into a small outer lobby.

Another impression noted by Carl Moritz was that 'the members of the House of Commons have nothing particular in their dress. They even come into the House in their great coats, and with boots and spurs.'[2] By the time Moritz visited St. Stephen's Chapel the period of the American war had seen a sharp decline in the sartorial elegance of the House, and

---

[1] *London Evening Post*, 2 Mar. 1771.
[2] Moritz, *Travels*, p. 53.

especially in that of Charles James Fox.¹ Here is diarist
Nathaniel Wraxall's comparison of Fox in 1774 and 1781:
'At five and twenty I have seen him apparrelled *en petit Maitre*,
with a Hat and Feather, even in the House of Commons;
but in 1781, he constantly, or at least usually, wore in that
Assembly, a blue frock Coat, and a buff waistcoat, neither of
which seemed in general new, and sometimes appeared to be
threadbare.'²

The Speaker wore a gown and full bottom wig. Such wigs
were also worn by the chief law officers, and other members
wore ordinary wigs with or without hats.³ Leading ministers
and a number of other officeholders appeared in full court
dress with swords, perhaps because their duties or inclinations
often caused them to visit the court beforehand, perhaps from
convention or personal choice.⁴ Bubb Dodington in 1730
privately ridiculed Sir Robert Walpole 'for having such a
passion to the House of Commons, because he shined so well in
the debates, that he dressed himself out every morning to
appear there, as if it were to see his mistress'.⁵ Lord North was
also meticulous in his dress, and often resplendent in his
Garter ribband after 1772; being short-sighted, he one day
when walking down the chamber impaled the wig of Welbore
Ellis on the point of his scabbard, to the hilarious delight of the
House.⁶ Opposition leaders and other members were usually
attired in ordinary coats and boots, and often carried sticks.
Wraxall therefore recorded as a curiosity the scene when the
House re-assembled on 8 April 1782 after Lord North's long
ministry had been succeeded by the second Rockingham
administration: 'Never was a more total Change of Costume
beheld, than the House of Commons presented to the Eye.'
Lord North and his friends were 'wrapped in great coats, or
habited in Frocks, and Boots. Mr. Ellis himself, no longer
Secretary of State, appeared for the first time in his Life, in an

---

¹ Townsend, *House of Commons*, II, 421–3.

² Wraxall, *Memoirs*, II, 229. Blue and buff were the colours worn by the American rebels.

³ *Erthig Chronicles*, I, 326. Moritz, *Travels*, p. 53. The dress of members can be seen in contemporary illustrations of the House.

⁴ See, for example, Wraxall, *Memoirs*, II, 126–8, 214; III, 48.

⁵ *H.M.C. Egmont Diary*, I, 31–2.

⁶ Wraxall, *Memoirs*, II, 127.

Undress. To contemplate the Ministers, their Successors, emerged from their obscure Lodgings, or from Brookes's, having thrown off their blue and buff Uniforms; now ornamented with the Appendages of full Dress, or returning from Court, decorated with Swords, Lace, and Hair Powder; excited still more astonishment.' It so happened that about this time one of the resigning office-holders, Lord Nugent, was robbed of some court clothes; and his mock accusation of theft against Charles Fox and Edmund Burke was a joke that attained wide circulation.[1]

Visitors to St. Stephen's Chapel were dismayed by the behaviour of members as well as disappointed by their attire. Carl Moritz was amazed at the lack of attention to business: 'It is not at all uncommon to see a member lying stretched out on one of the benches, while others are debating. Some crack nuts, others eat oranges, or whatever else is in season.'[2] Members could eat or sleep in the chamber, but they were not allowed to read or to smoke.[3] Noise was the impression noted by James Boswell on his first visit to the House on 11 March 1763: 'My respect for it was greatly abated by seeing that it was such a tumultuous scene.'[4] Both inattention and noise were permanent features of the Parliamentary stage, and in 1843 this reflection was recorded by a contemporary observer:

Public morals have been improved immeasurably within the last century; the manners of public men have been subdued, and chastened, and refined, yet the balance in favour of modern decorum is not, perhaps, so great as might have been anticipated from the increase of civilisation . . . discord in all its varieties of inharmonious sounds—the loud buzz of conversation and laughter, as at a club, carelessness in dress and demeanour, render St. Stephen's Chapel more disorderly than becomes the first assembly of gentlemen in Europe.[5]

The House of Commons was more than 'the best club in Europe'. It was becoming the centre of the political state, with the King's government dependent on its goodwill for the

[1] Wraxall, *Memoirs*, III, 26–8.
[2] Moritz, *Travels*, p. 53.
[3] A resolution of 1694 extended the ban on tobacco to the gallery and to Committees. *Commons Journals*, XI, 137.
[4] J. Boswell, *London Journal*, p. 236.
[5] Townsend, *House of Commons*, II, 437.

passage of business and his ministers for their survival in office. Speaker Arthur Onslow wrote with pride in the middle of the century that 'a court has less power than ever it had to pursue measures, or preserve ministers, against the sense and inclination of parliament, or of the house of commons alone.'[1] Support for government was nearly always forthcoming, but no ministers could assume it or appear to do so. The key to the procedure and practice of the House of Commons in the eighteenth century was the presence in the House of a majority of members who were in varying degrees independent of administration. This was the permanent political situation until the evolution of a two-party system in the next century. It explained the moderate tone in politics, with opposition to government an accepted part of Parliamentary behaviour; the real significance of debates in a House where there were votes to be won; and the survival and development of a procedure that had originated as a means of defence against the Crown.

Opponents of ministers were able to exploit Parliamentary rules and conventions, and they did not suffer or fear imprisonment for words spoken in the House. Characteristic of the changing atmosphere of politics were such incidents within the chamber as the famous bet of 1741 between minister Sir Robert Walpole and opposition leader William Pulteney,[2] and this conversation on 18 November 1777. After Charles James Fox had made a vehement attack on Secretary of State Lord George Germain he went over to talk with First Lord of the Treasury Lord North, who said to him, 'Charles, I am glad you did not fall on me today, for you was in full feather.'[3] Symbolic of the more modern approach to politics was the decline in the number of duels arising from altercations between opponents in debates. From time to time during the century Speakers forbad various members to pursue quarrels further, when their attention was drawn to the possibility of a duel. On 20 May 1717 the House unanimously passed a resolution that Speaker Compton should interpose between the two leading men in the Commons, Robert Walpole and head of the

---

[1] Burnet, *History*, IV, 280N.   [2] See *infra*, p. 131.
[3] This instance of open personal friendship in the House between political opponents may be misleading, for North and Germain were then on bad terms. H. Walpole, *Last Journals*, II, 76.

ministry James Stanhope.[1] Usually the initiative of individual members prevailed on the Chair to act.[2] Actual duels caused by Parliamentary quarrels or remarks were extremely rare; but duels between William Adam and Charles James Fox in 1779 and between William Fullarton and Lord Shelburne in 1780 seemed to presage a revival of the practice, and Sir James Lowther raised the matter in the House on 24 March 1780: 'If this was to go on, and the House did not interpose its authority, there would be an end to the freedom of debate and an end of the business in Parliament . . . If free debate were to be interpreted into personal attack, and questions of a public nature which came before either House were to be decided by the sword, Parliament would resemble a Polish diet, and the members would do better to give up all ideas of Parliamentary discussion.'[3] The House came to no resolution on the subject, but this public ventilation of the problem apparently led to a greater restraint in debate that produced fewer pretexts for challenges.

The practical importance of debates in the House of Commons was deduced by Sir Lewis Namier from his analysis of the contemporary political system.[4] Arguments needed to be persuasive and not merely formal, and had to be expressed in language simple enough for an assembly often inattentive and for the most part ill-educated. 'The general rate of understanding in the House of Commons is not very acute', Lord Rockingham commented to Edmund Burke in 1773;[5] and most speakers took account of this circumstance, although seldom Burke himself. This need for comprehension has been overlooked by writers impressed with the cultural background of the age, who have often assumed that debates were liberally adorned with classical quotations. That is a myth. Extracts from Latin verse and prose do occur in speeches, but they are rare, and were not a device calculated to win the support or sympathy of the House. The practice of leading politicians of

---

[1] Chandler, *Debates*, VI, 134–5.
[2] See, for example, *Knatchbull Diary*, pp. 74–5; *H.M.C. Egmont Diary*, I, 221, 263; H. Walpole, *George II*, I, 19, 112; H. Walpole, *Letters*, V, 400; Almon, *Parl. Reg.*, IX, 239–41.
[3] Almon, *Parl. Reg.*, XVII, 407–8.
[4] Namier, *Structure of Politics*, pp. 7–8.
[5] *Burke Correspondence*, II, 402.

the later part of the century was recorded by Nathaniel Wraxall:

> Mr. Pitt, who well knew how large a Part of his Audience, especially among the Country Gentlemen, were little conversant in the Writings of the Augustan Age, or familiar with Horace, always displayed great Caution in borrowing from those Classic Sources. In the lapse of near fourteen years that I have heard him almost daily address the House of Commons, I question if he made in all, more than eight or ten citations. Fox and Sheridan, though not equally severe in that Respect, yet never abused, or injudiciously expended the Stores of ancient Literature that they possessed. Burke's Enthusiasm, his exhaustless Memory, and luxuriant Imagination, more frequently carried him away into the Times of Virgil and Cicero: while Barré usually condescended, whenever he quoted Latin, to translate for the Benefit of the County Members.[1]

Speakers who wanted to win support paid more attention to legal and constitutional precedents than to classical quotations; and in particular they sought to exploit the attachment of members to the forms and privileges of the House. Many discussions arose from points of Parliamentary procedure, and many tactics and arguments were based on precedents. Here members were to a large extent dependent for their ammunition on the officials of the House, for few rivalled the Clerks in their knowledge of the *Journals*. Procedure was already becoming too complex a matter for all but a small number of members to master: Lord Barrington, seconding the proposal of Sir John Cust as Speaker in 1761, expressed regret that 'too few in this Age have applied themselves to what used to be the highest ambition of an English gentleman, that of being a knowing Parliament man.'[2] Two of the Clerks were notable authorities on the law and custom of Parliament. Jeremiah Dyson, Clerk from 1748 to 1762, was probably the author of the only contemporary manual of procedure, since published as the *Liverpool Tractate*;[3] and John Hatsell, Clerk from 1768 to 1820, compiled four volumes of *Precedents* which appeared in various editions from 1776 to 1818. When Dyson became a

---

[1] Wraxall, *Memoirs*, III, 317–18.

[2] *Commons Journals*, XXIX, 7.

[3] Namier thought that Dyson was the author, but no evidence on the point has been found. The editor, Catherine Strateman, tentatively suggested George Grenville. *Liverpool Tractate*, pp. xii–xviii.

member himself in 1762, he soon won a reputation as a formidable expert on procedure.[1] Ordinary members were reduced to obtaining information from the under-Clerks of the House, as when the opposition leaders in 1769 employed several of them to collect all the precedents of votes of incapacity and expulsion appropriate to the Middlesex Elections case.[2] It was not usually possible to anticipate the need for such information. During debates the Clerk and Deputy Clerk, who sat at the Table, were apparently expected to produce appropriate precedents, but members who knew what to ask for enjoyed an obvious advantage. When on 19 February 1771 Dyson called for a precedent of 1746 William Burke's only rejoinder was to question, 'is that the last order?' Speaker Norton then intervened. 'If the honourable gentleman will be so good as to point out any other it shall be fetched. No man's opinion I would sooner take than the Clerk's.'[3] This method of debating often became artificial and sterile, and sometimes provoked criticism. Thomas Townshend caustically described Jeremiah Dyson and Edmund Burke as being 'both armed to the teeth with precedents' on 28 April 1774;[4] and lawyer Alexander Wedderburn made this protest on 19 February 1770: 'Is there no rule to govern an assembly by but that of precedents? Is there no rule that results from the reason of the thing?'[5]

Discussion of Parliamentary precedents arose from political conflicts, and motives of political advantage led to the continuous evolution and refinement of Parliamentary practice. The basic forms of Parliamentary procedure had already developed by the end of the seventeenth century; but only in this general sense is there validity in the opinion of that foremost authority on the subject, Joseph Redlich, that 'the period from the Revolution to the Reform Bill is, as a matter of fact, that in which the least change in the rules of procedure took place.'[6] When the House of Commons became the main political battlefield the rules of Parliamentary warfare became ever more intricate, as government and opposition sought

[1] See *infra*, pp. 238–9.
[2] B.M. Add. MSS. 30870, fos. 95–6.
[3] B.M. Eg. MSS. 225, p. 28.
[4] B.M. Eg. MSS. 256, p. 62 (shorthand).
[5] B.M. Eg. MSS. 220, p. 192.
[6] Redlich, *Procedure of the House of Commons*, I, 54.

tactical advantages that could win support for themselves or cause difficulty for their rivals. Periods of bitter political conflict saw the evolution of new procedural devices. Here is Speaker Arthur Onslow's comment on the reign of William III: 'The opposition to the government in these Parliaments afforded precedents of many useful checks upon courts and ministers, to the confirming of the rights and privileges and powers of Parliament, especially in the house of commons'.[1] The adaptation of procedure for political purposes continued throughout the eighteenth century, and especially during the long ministries of Sir Robert Walpole and Lord North, when seemingly permanent alignments proved to be hothouse conditions for political developments of all kinds.

The multiplication of opportunities for discussion of and resistance to legislation and other decisions of the House led Redlich to designate the rules of the Commons at this time as 'the procedure of an opposition.'[2] Two qualifications need to be made to this famous judgement. The almost invariable administration majorities in the House enabled ministers and their adherents to thwart opposition moves and to create precedents in cases of dispute; it was ministerial henchman Jeremiah Dyson who was the 'master of order' under George III, not an opposition member. Moreover, although opportunities for the obstruction of business certainly existed, in the right of every member to make motions on any subject without notice and to move any number of blocking motions without any restrictions, they were rarely exploited. The contemporary conventions of political decorum, indeed, had a wider interpretation than mere avoidance of any manipulation of the forms of procedure: it was also understood that members should not take unfair advantage of such habits as the irregularity of the time for the start of business, or the frequently poor attendance of members at the House; the quorum, fixed in 1640, was only 40 members. Opposition leader William Pulteney, accused by Sir Robert Walpole on 12 May 1738 of introducing business at an unusual time, made this indignant reply:

If I had been capable of acting as the honourable Gentleman who spoke last has suggested, I might have had many opportunities of

---

[1] Burnet, *History*, IV, 280N.
[2] Redlich, *Procedure of the House of Commons*, I, 57.

taking the advantage of a thin House, either to bring in or throw out bills of the greatest consequence. I appeal to every gentleman who hears me, if it has not been many times in my power to have dropt in, even upon a land tax bill, with half a dozen of my friends, and to have thrown it out. But, Sir, I have always disdained these arts.[1]

The absence of obstruction was one reason why in the eighteenth century there was no formal alteration of a procedure that was becoming increasingly antiquated and impracticable. Another was the absence of any real pressure of time. Ministers were usually able to arrange government business as they wished, and they realized the impolicy of claiming formal priority for official matters. Encroachments on the rights of ordinary members to make any motions whenever they chose would have been contrary to tradition and would have offended independent opinion in the House. All members remained equal, except that only the King's ministers could propose public expenditure and taxation; and not until 1835 was there to be any formal and procedural distinction between government business and other business.

The importance of the individual member helps to explain not only the survival of the old procedure but also the continuing emphasis on the privileges and prestige of the House. Privilege had evolved as a means of defence against the Crown. By the Hanoverian era the Commons was conscious of its power and less concerned with its formal dignity, but nevertheless continued the practice of giving deliberate priority over current business to any matters of privilege that arose. Cases of privilege were of two kinds. It was customary for the House itself to hear those in which the issue was whether the otherwise illegal action of a member or his servants was covered by his Parliamentary privilege, as in the case of John Wilkes and his libel in the *North Briton No. 45* in 1763. More frequent were complaints by members of breaches of privilege by other persons, and these were always referred to the Committee of Privileges and Elections. It was a common idea that matters of privilege invariably took precedence over other business. Horace Walpole stated in 1771 that 'it is a standing order of the House that breach of their privileges must supersede all

---

[1] Chandler, *Debates*, X, 296–7.

other considerations.'[1] Walpole was wrong. No such order was
cited by John Hatsell in his discussion of the point.[2] Custom did
not remove the decision about priority for matters of privilege
from the discretion of the House, and this right was exercised
in 1767 when the administration found a complaint politically
embarrassing. On 25 November George Grenville raised, as a
matter of privilege, 'a treasonable American paper', an issue
of the *Boston Gazette*. Grenville contended 'that, if any member
complained of any book or paper, as containing matter which
infringed on the privilege of the House, he had a right, without
any question put, to deliver it in at the Table, and to have it
read'. The claim that any single member had the right to
insist on action by the House was so absurd when clearly stated
that Jeremiah Dyson and other members objected to it. The
debate on the subject was postponed until 27 November, when
George Onslow moved to adjourn it for six months, 'which the
House, with a laugh, approved of'. Horace Walpole thought
Grenville had complained only 'in form'; but Grenville
himself remarked afterwards to diarist James Harris that the
ministry had 'postponed it contrary to the uninterrupted usage
of Parliament through all the time of the present and the late
Speaker, and with no precedent to the contrary but a single
one 75 years ago.'[3] In 1771 vain protests were made about
the dislocation of other business caused by the proceedings
against the newspaper printers. On 14 March William Burke
pointed out that this matter of privilege had no formal precedence, and that it had earlier twice been postponed to allow
time for other business, on 11 and 14 February. Speaker Norton
confirmed that it was in order for the House to postpone
questions of privilege. The administration, however, insisted
on priority for the newspaper case, and members who had
attended for other business walked out.[4]

Apart from questions of privilege much of the House's time
was taken up by other matters affecting Parliament itself.
Points of order were always accorded priority over other

---

[1] H. Walpole, *George III*, IV, 195.
[2] Hatsell, *Precedents*, II, 121.
[3] Hatsell, *Precedents*, II, 165. *Commons Journals*, XXXI, 427, 432. H. Walpole,
George III, III, 84. Harris Diary, 29 Nov. 1767.
[4] B.M. Eg. MSS. 226, pp. 85–101.

business.[1] Proceedings were interrupted at once whenever a member was waiting at the Bar to be introduced and sworn after his election.[2] The first session of a new Parliament was always concerned with the hearing of election cases, to an extent delaying other business, until George Grenville's Election Act of 1770 transferred the duty to Select Committees of members chosen by ballot. The hearing of election cases often continued into the second session of each Parliament and sometimes longer, as late as 1746 after the general election of 1741.

Only when such matters had been disposed of or postponed, as often happened to election cases, could the House take up or resume consideration of the nation's business. There was no limit to the competence of Parliament, save any matter that encroached on the royal prerogative. Even that qualification was largely nominal. The sovereign, through need of money or desire for support, often invited the House of Commons to discuss such topics as the civil list or foreign policy that were by tradition the concern of the Crown. Virtually any subject might come before Parliament, to form the field for political conflict or the pursuit of private interests. For constitutional purposes, however, the business of the House of Commons as the representative body of the nation can be divided into three functions—inquiry into grievances, action by legislation, and the provision of finance for the government of the country.

[1] Hatsell, *Precedents*, II, 121.
[2] Debrett, *Parl. Reg.*, XII, 353.

THE BUSINESS OF THE HOUSE:
I. 'THE GRAND INQUEST OF THE NATION'

BY TRADITION Parliament fulfilled a general role as 'the grand inquest of the nation', remedying individual grievances and keeping a jealous eye on the government of the country, both on matters of general policy and on details of administration. Much of the political conflict took place under the guise of this function, which was asserted by opposition members and accepted by ministers. When on 23 January 1730 William Shippen said that 'it was for the benefit of the Ministers to find fault, for the more they were rubbed, the brighter they would be', Sir Robert Walpole made this answer: 'If so, he must be the brightest minister that ever was.' Pulteney replied that he knew nothing was the brighter for rubbing but pewter and brass, alluding to Sir Robert's nickname of "Brazen Face"—'ribaldry unfit for the House', so Lord Perceval thought.[1] During his Budget speech of 18 May 1774 Lord North made this comment on the role of the opposition: 'In this House I am sure every indulgence, every degree of gratitude, I think are due to those gentlemen who undertake the very difficult, the very painful, the very meritorious task of watching our Ministers; of reprehending them; of blaming and calling them daily to account; they, Sir, deserve the indulgence of this House ... the whole of their intention is to put the administration to an answer.' Edmund Burke made this humourless reply: 'The noble lord ... has given a great deal of indulgence to those who he says have great merit in finding fault with government. We are (I take the word we) intitled to a great deal of merit, and ought to have a good deal of indulgence; as to merit I think there is some to stand up against power to its face.'[2]

[1] *Knatchbull Diary*, p. 99. *H.M.C. Egmont*, I, 9.
[2] B.M. Eg. MSS. 258, pp. 79–80, 127–8.

The only challenge to this consensus of constitutional opinion that has been found was an extraordinary remark by Welbore Ellis, Treasurer of the Navy, on 25 May 1778: 'He did not think the House of Commons an assembly calculated for the discussion of state affairs; it was the business of Parliament to raise supplies, not debate on the measures of government. The one was the proper object of legislation, the other of executive power.' Opposition members pounced on this indiscretion. Thomas Townshend condemned the doctrine as 'calculated to crush all enquiry at all times, and as depriving the House of one of its first privileges', while Charles James Fox declared that 'he, as a member of this House, had, with other persons in it, been insulted by what the right honourable gentleman had said . . . The privilege of this House was certainly to enquire into, and to censure the conduct of those who were entrusted with the executive power.' The incident ended with an assurance from Lord North, the head of the ministry, that he would welcome any inquiry at a proper time.[1]

This constitutional function of the House, despite the general agreement on its principle, was inevitably subordinated in practice to political considerations—a consequence deplored by responsible members on both sides of the House. On 22 November 1770 administration supporter General Conway, though opposing a motion for papers concerning the Spanish seizure of the Falkland Islands, made this declaration: 'It is not a question upon the merit or demerit of administration . . . Every question is made a private or a public question . . . the single question with me is this now a time to enter into this?'[2] A week later, on a similar motion for papers, opposition leader William Dowdeswell complained bluntly: 'Of all the doctrines I ever heard in this House, the most preposterous is this, that we will not stir, because we have confidence in administration . . . We can go into nothing if that shall be a reason: we shall never see the time, when there will be fewer than 350 members who will not have confidence in administration, let who will be ministers. We pride ourselves on being the grand inquest of the nation.'[3]

[1] Almon, *Parl. Reg.*, IX, 210–2.
[2] B.M. Eg. MSS. 222, p. C. 171.
[3] B.M. Eg. MSS. 223, p. 7.

Attacks on government under the pretext of inquiry rarely produced results, because of the almost permanent majority enjoyed by ministers in the House. This circumstance was deplored by John Hatsell: 'The controul, which the independent Members of the House ought to have over the conduct of Ministers, is entirely lost; and the direction and detail of the measures of Government are left, without attention or examination, to those in whose official department they happen to be.'[1] Hatsell was being pessimistic and superficial; and ironically it was Speaker Arthur Onslow, so venerated by Hatsell, who recorded his belief that the House of Commons fulfilled this purpose:

This constitutional check upon power, by the house of commons, is one of the most beneficial advantages the people receive by frequent parliaments. It has such an effect upon all counsels and offices whatsoever, that the being barely named there for any misfeazance creates a terror to everybody concerned in it. A majority for them is not a sufficient security for wrong doing; and I have known the smallest minority there, by the freedom of speech only, keep the ablest and boldest ministers in awe. If parliaments sit annually, which they may always secure to themselves now, if they will, and should never depart from, it is almost impossible that any exorbitancy of power should subsist long enough to do much mischief. No person can stand it, unless supported by violence, if the abuse be great and glaring. He may be acquitted by a corrupt majority; but he is undone, notwithstanding that.[2]

The inclination of Speaker Onslow to emphasize and even exaggerate the importance of the House of Commons might be held to render his opinion suspect: but testimony to the effectiveness of the House in this role is provided by a shrewd contemporary observer who was often critical of Onslow's pomp, Horace Walpole:

Every topic is treated in Parliament as if the liberty and fate of the country depended upon it: and even this solemnity, often vested on trifles, has its use. The certainty of discussion keeps Administration in awe, and preserves awake the attention of the representatives of the people. Ministers are, and should be suspected as public enemies: the injustice arising to them, or the prejudice to the country by such jealousy, can hardly ever be adequate to

<hr/>

[1] Hatsell, *Precedents*, II, 101.   [2] Burnet, *History*, V, 278N.

the mischief they may do in a moment, if too much is left to their power, if too much trust is reposed in their integrity.[1]

'Public fame' might be urged as sufficient ground for inquiry and action by the House, as in several attacks on Sir Robert Walpole in 1742: but almost always members recognized the need for prior information. It was obtained in a variety of ways. The attention of the House could be directed to specific matters from outside, by petitions; these were often instigated by members themselves. Within the House the demand for an inquiry might also be founded on information supplied directly by members or obtained from witnesses and papers; and the century also saw the development of the modern practice of Parliamentary questions.

Petitions were an obvious weapon for opposition to utilize or arrange against administration. One on 25 April 1771 from William Allen, father of a man killed in the riots of St. George's Fields three years earlier, was merely a contrived excuse for reviving the old complaint of the Middlesex Elections.[2] Undoubtedly petitions were often a political expedient or viewed in a political context. But the procedural device of petitioning did serve a useful purpose in bringing the genuine desires and grievances of individuals, communities and corporate bodies to the notice of the House. Petitions might be for specific legislation, or for other action by the House. Petitions against actual or intended decisions of the House were also frequently submitted. Petitions were often received against proposed or existing legislation. They were also allowed against existing taxes, but not against any intended new taxation. The right of 'subjects' to petition even against resolutions of the House itself was confirmed by Speaker Cust on 26 January 1769, after William Beckford had raised the point.[3]

Each petition had to be presented by a member of the House. James Harris has left a description of the usual practice of introducing a petition, 'an account of which you give the Speaker, who enters it with other matters in his paper; you sit in your place with the petition in your hand. When he beckons, you rise and say, I have a petition which I beg leave

---

[1] H. Walpole, *George II*, II, 156.
[2] B.M. Eg. MSS. 230, pp. 110–20.
[3] B.M. Eg. MSS. 216, p. 105.

to present. The question being put, you are ordered to bring
it up. You go down below the Bar, and there in a few words
set forth its contents. You bring it up. Then the Committee is
named, and sit.'¹

The duty and discretion of a member in submitting petitions
to the House was a question debated but not resolved during
the century. The absolute nature of an obligation to present all
petitions was expressed by Sir John Barnard when producing
one on 13 March 1741: he then asserted, 'I am equally with
the other members a stranger to what it contains, for it is my
opinion that a representative is to lay before the House the
sentiments of his constituents, whether they agree with his own
or not, and that therefore it would have been superfluous to
examine the petition.'² This declaration, however, appears to
have been contrary to tradition and practice. On 24 November
1768 the matter came under discussion during one of the debates
on the petition of grievances submitted by John Wilkes. Speaker
Cust observed from the Chair, 'Every person ought to present
a petition, but the person ought to answer for the contents of it.'
Jeremiah Dyson remarked, 'It is of great consequence, that no
petition should be presented to the House, without the presenter
of it be responsible for it, whether the petition was decent. The
petitioner was formerly called upon to own the contents of the
petition. That method is laid aside.' George Onslow supported
the Chair: 'Every member is bound to present a petition.'
Hans Stanley disagreed with the Speaker, who evasively
ended the discussion by this explanation: 'It dont follow,
because a petition is presented, that it is to be brought up.'³

Certainly the point was in this sense academic. The House
was free to reject petitions outright, if unfounded or outrageous.
Sir Roger Newdigate noted in his diary on 7 March 1751, 'a
petition rejected *nem. con.* The Speaker threw it over the
table.' It was deemed improper, however, to reject a petition
recommended by the sovereign: on 20 April 1725 Speaker
Compton therefore insisted that Arthur Onslow should withdraw his motion to reject a petition from Lord Bolingbroke
that had been recommended by George I.⁴ Immediate rejection, indeed, was rare, the usual way to kill a petition being a

---

¹ Harris Diary, 17 Feb. 1762.   ² Chandler, *Debates*, XII, 286.
³ B.M. Eg. MSS. 215, pp. 239–40.   ⁴ *Knatchbull Diary*, p. 48.

motion to leave it lie unread on the Table. This was a common method of countering unwelcome petitions, a tactic used, for example, by Walpole's ministry on 4 February 1734 to dispose of a petition against the tea excise.[1] Even if later action on a petition was intended, it might be ordered to lie on the Table as 'a mark of dislike', the treatment accorded to the petition of John Wilkes when it was presented by Sir Joseph Mawbey on 14 November 1768.[2] A favoured petition might result in the immediate introduction of a bill: but the usual practice was for a petition to be referred to a Select Committee before any decision was made. A notable exception to many of the rules concerning petitions lay in the privileged position of the City of London. The sheriffs of the City could themselves present petitions directly to the House: and Speaker Cornwall on 11 June 1783 was avowedly declaring the ancient practice when he stated that the House always received any City petitions without previous intimation of contents, even if they were petitions against proposed taxation.[3]

Whether their case was before a Committee or at the Bar of the House, petitioners could be heard either by themselves or by counsel, but not by both methods. Speaker Onslow reminded members of this rule on 3 March 1738, after a petition from West India merchants complaining of Spanish attacks on their ships had asked that they might be 'heard by themselves and counsel'. As soon as the petition had been read, the Speaker intervened: 'Though my Office, while I am in the Chair, deprives me of having any Share in your Debates, yet it obliges me to declare what are the Forms of the House. As I conceive this to be a point of form, it is my duty to acquaint you, that so far as I have yet observed, it never was the method of this House to admit parties to be heard by themselves and counsel.' After a brief debate the House accepted this ruling of the Chair.[4]

Information provided by members themselves could not derive from their personal knowledge. On 9 May 1765 George

[1] *H.M.C. Egmont Diary*, II, 19–22.

[2] H. Walpole, *George III*, III, 175.

[3] Debrett, *Parl. Reg.*, X, 135. See also the Clementson Diary, p. 15; and for a debate of 10 April 1733 on this privilege see *H.M.C. Egmont Diary*, I, 358–9, and *infra*, p. 70–1.

[4] Chandler, *Debates*, X, 96–102.

Onslow said that he had heard a Secretary of State had omitted the name of the Princess Dowager of Wales from the Regency Bill then before the House. 'This occasioned his being called to order. Sir John Rushout, as the ancient oracle of the House, declared that Onslow might say what he had heard from common fame, but might not say he had heard it himself.'[1] This rule was evaded on 14 January 1784 by the device of one member informing the House that another member had been the subject of an attempt at bribery by the Duke of Portland's ministry in the previous year. An argument ensued until Speaker Cornwall ruled that the House should adopt the usual procedure when information was submitted by members. It was customary, he said, to proceed by recording the general information before them, on which any subsequent motion would be founded.[2]

Petitions and facts given by members usually led the House to further inquiry rather than to immediate action. Whether this was conducted in the House itself or in Committee, witnesses and papers constituted the main sources of information; and an elaborate series of conventions and rules existed to obtain, examine and utilize both.

Before any member could suggest witnesses it was necessary for the House to decide that an inquiry should be held: and no witness could be produced without prior notice to and leave from the House. Speaker Onslow told Hatsell that this rule had been enunciated by Speaker Compton.[3] The occasion of this pronouncement may have been 28 April 1721, when Compton intervened in a debate about witnesses to declare that a separate motion was necessary for each witness. The only exception was that 'when a cause was depending before the House he could issue his warrant for any person without a particular question. (So might a Chairman of Committee)'.[4] This rule concerning witnesses was confirmed on 3 March 1779, when an attempt was made by Charles James Fox to question Admiral Keppel 'as a member in his place'. Lord North appealed to Speaker Norton, 'who said that no question

---

[1] H. Walpole, *George III*, II, 103–4. Sir John Rushout had been an M.P. since 1713.

[2] Debrett, *Parl. Reg.*, XIII, 565–6. *Commons Journals*, XXXIX, 864.

[3] Hatsell, *Precedents*, II, 137N.   [4] Dashwood MSS. D 1/2, fos. 1–8.

could be taken down in writing, in order to frame a motion upon the evidence, unless the House was in a previous inquiry'. After this opinion from the Chair the House negatived without a division a motion made earlier by Sir William Meredith 'for taking down the questions and answers in writing'.[1]

A serious defect in the method of obtaining information from witnesses was that they could not be examined in the House on oath, although there did exist the anomaly that oaths were sometimes administered to witnesses in Committees appointed by the House. The reliance placed on such evidence given before the House therefore depended entirely on the credibility of individual witnesses, and often this was suspect. On 12 March 1729 Sir Charles Wager declared that evidence given by some merchants 'yesterday at the Bar was impossible to be true, and as they were not on oath, they might say what they pleased'. An argument was ended by the contention of William Clayton that 'if there was any difference to be made in people's asserting things, he thought for the honour of the House a merchant's word at the Bar ought by no means to stand in competition with a member of the House; and everybody thought he put it on a right foot.'[2] Attempts to remove this difficulty were unsuccessful. On 13 February 1722 members were informed that witnesses to a charge against Sir Francis Page of bribery in a Banbury by-election had been told beforehand that their evidence would not be on oath. Archibald Hutcheson therefore moved that the witnesses should be 'examined in the most solemn manner', a proposal defeated by only two votes by the ministry.[3] A decade later, on 17 April 1732, the whole matter was exhaustively discussed when an opposition motion was made to hear on oath witnesses on a bill for the resumption of estates confiscated from the Jacobite Lord Derwentwater.

The arguments for not swearing the witnesses were that the House of Commons has not a right to do it; that it is erecting our House into a Court of Record; that the House of Lords will not suffer it . . . That the House never practised it but once, and that

[1] Almon, *Parl. Reg.*, XII, 34–7.
[2] *Knatchbull Diary*, p. 91.
[3] Dashwood MSS. D 1/2, fos. 1–8. For the political background see Plumb, *Walpole*, I, 371–3.

was threescore years ago in the case of the Popish Plot, which was an extraordinary occasion; that the not using it since shows the House did not look on it as a right in them, and custom of Parliament is the law and constitution of Parliament. That every part of the Legislature ought to keep itself within its proper bounds . . . It may also provoke the Lords to revive their pretensions to add pains and penalties to our bills and interfere in our right of giving money.

It was argued on the other side that the House has the right to examine witnesses upon oath, as appears many ways. There is an Act of Parliament of Henry 8, declaring that none should demand their wages for serving in Parliament, but such whose attendance is recorded in the Journals of the House, which implies that the journals were a record, or they could not be given in evidence. We have the precedent of the Popish Plot, which the Lords did not object to. The reason of the thing also showed it, for it is undisputed that we have a right to order Committees to examine upon oath. We have constantly practised it . . . it is absurd to say that we can delegate a right that we have not ourselves . . . There is, 'tis true, a tacit sort of compromise between the Lords and us that we should have the sole giving of money, and they be a Court of Judicature, but their right of judicature was till within the memory of men contested by the Commons, which shows it was not always allowed to be inherent in them, at least not solely in them.

These constitutional arguments for the motion were reinforced by the practical point, 'what security can we have to form our judgments unless the witnesses are on their oaths?' But Walpole's ministry defeated the proposal by the device of the previous question.[1] Although the House had come to no positive resolution on the matter, the effective decision had been taken. When the same issue was raised in a debate of 19 January 1764, Jeremiah Dyson declared that he could remember no examination of witnesses on oath by the House during the previous seventeen years, and recalled that the Jacobites John Carnegy and Thomas Forster had been expelled after the Fifteen Rising 'by evidence, without oath, that proved them in open arms'.[2] John Hatsell later concluded from an exhaustive examination of precedents that the House had 'not, at any period, claimed, much less exercised, the

---

[1] *H.M.C. Egmont Diary*, I, 257–9. See also Chandler, *Debates*, VII, 242–3; and, for discussion of the previous question, *infra*, pp. 178–82.

[2] Harris Diary, 19 Jan. 1764.

right of administering an oath to witnesses; not even in cases of Privilege or of controverted Elections'.[1]

Even the established practice of examining witnesses on oath in Committees was abandoned in the second half of the eighteenth century. A comment by James Harris in 1764 clearly reflected doubt as to the efficacy of the procedure: 'This had never been done but in Committees, and then a Westminster justice sat without the door and swore them—an oath hardly justifiable in him to administer, and clearly not subjecting a man, if he broke it, to the pain of perjury.'[2] Hatsell found evidence of Committees being empowered to examine on oath, and of members who were J.P.s for Middlesex and Westminster administering such oaths, only between 1678 and 1757. He thought that the practice had been dropped as illegal, and it was not used in the later extensive inquiries into the affairs of the East India Company.[3]

Witnesses stood at the Bar of the House, although a chair was provided within the Bar for any peer.[4] The strict rule of the House was that only the Speaker could interrogate witnesses, but this was usually ignored. Hatsell recorded both the rule and the practice of the House.

> When a witness, not in custody, or in custody without the Mace standing by him, is at the Bar to be examined, the House supposes the Speaker to ask him all the necessary questions; and these questions may, by the rules of the House, be proposed, at the time of the witnesses standing at the Bar, by the Members to the Chair; and the Speaker is to put them to the witness. This is the rule; but the practice, for the sake of convenience, often is, that the Members themselves examine the witness without the intervention of the Chair; this practice however is irregular, and seldom fails to produce disorder.[5]

Many reports of proceedings in both the House and in Committees confirm that individual members did question witnesses themselves. Discussion and argument often arose

---

[1] Hatsell, *Precedents*, II, 158.
[2] Harris Diary, 19 Jan. 1764.
[3] Hatsell, *Precedents*, II, 155–7.
[4] Harris Diary, 5 Mar. 1765. For the procedure for the examination of ordinary witnesses, witnesses in ill-health, judges, and Scottish peers, see the Clementson Diary, pp. 13, 42, 43, 68 respectively.
[5] Hatsell, *Precedents*, II, 141.

over proposed questions, as on 12 February 1773 when Speaker Norton declared, 'I cant hear this irregular debate . . . if there is a question give it me.'[1] Such conduct was disorderly unless the witness had previously been ordered to withdraw. The rule was that this should be done whenever an objection to a question was made by a member or the person at the Bar, for no motion could be put in the presence of witnesses or counsel.[2]

This practice of direct questions by members to witnesses was not possible on the rare occasions when a witness was brought as a prisoner in custody, with the Serjeant standing beside him at the Bar with the Mace: for when the Mace was thus 'off the Table' no member could speak at all, not even to suggest questions to the Chair. In such cases members had to write down proposed questions and give them to the Speaker before the prisoner was brought in.[3] This rule was invariably observed, despite the inconvenience: instances included the interrogation of Jacobite William Kelly in 1723, and that of the mayor of Chipping Wycombe in an election case of 1726.[4] A notable later case was that of John Horne, summoned before the House on 18 February 1774 for an alleged libel on the Speaker. Norton's request for members to submit written questions to him beforehand gave rise to a hot debate by members accustomed to less formal proceedings, until the House realised that the Speaker was adopting the correct procedure.[5]

The power of the House of Commons to send for witnesses appears to have been unlimited, except with respect to peers: the permission of the House of Lords had to be obtained by such of its members as wished to give evidence before the Commons. Similarly the House was able to demand from corporations, companies and their officials papers relevant to any inquiry: but attempts to send for state papers often threatened to encroach on the royal prerogative, particularly in the field of foreign policy. The correct procedure in such

---

[1] B.M. Eg. MSS. 244, pp. 6–7.
[2] Hatsell, *Precedents*, II, 144.
[3] Hatsell, *Precedents*, II, 141–2.
[4] *Knatchbull Diary*, pp. 19, 56.
[5] B.M. Eg. MSS. 252, pp. 81–6. See also H. Walpole, *Last Journals*, I, 294; Hatsell, *Precedents*, II, 142; and Clementson Diary, pp. 46–7.

cases was an Address to the sovereign for the papers desired. Members often asserted in general terms the right of the House to any papers it required. It was a politician in office, Lord of the Treasury Sir William Yonge, who on 23 January 1734 referred to 'the power which this House has of calling for whatever papers they may think necessary, to give them proper lights into any affair they are going to take under consideration. That the House has such a power is what I believe no gentleman will deny.'[1] Such statements were misleading. Papers even on matters of foreign policy were often obtained by the House, but an important restriction was observed. No motion could be made for state papers, James Oswald reminded the Duke of Newcastle in 1761, 'except some foundation had been given for it from the Crown'. Such a pretext that the opinion of the House had been requested might be as slender as the word 'advice' in the King's Speech, but there must be some excuse.[2] Accordingly a motion on 11 December 1761 for papers on Anglo-Spanish relations could be opposed by Colonel Isaac Barré on the ground that it tended, 'by bringing the Power of making peace and war into this House, to lower the King's prerogative'.[3] Parliament, however, was entitled to receive certain papers, such as declarations of war and some treaties: and other official papers might be produced without an Address by royal command when the active co-operation of Parliament in government policy was required.[4]

When papers were laid before the House or referred to Committee, any member had the right to have the papers read aloud once by the Clerk at the Table. There are instances of this process occupying several hours of the time of the House: but it became increasingly the practice for only the titles of papers to be read unless a member asked for the whole or part of a paper to be read out: on 9 February 1725, for example, some papers were read out and the others left on the Table for the perusal of members.[5] This may already have become

[1] Chandler, *Debates*, VIII, 15.   [2] B.M. Add. MSS. 35421, fos. 139–40.
[3] Harris Diary, 11 Dec. 1761.
[4] Sheila Lambert, 'A Century of Diplomatic Blue Books', *Hist. Journal*, X (1967), p. 126. Papers from different departments or offices had to be delivered to the House separately, even when brought by the same person. Clementson Diary, pp. 13–14.
[5] *Knatchbull Diary*, p. 38.

the habit even before 1714: for on 25 January 1718 former
Speaker John Smith felt the need to remind the House, concerning the reference of papers to Committees, that they 'used
formerly to be first read, but of late only the titles, unless a
Member insisted they should be read, and then nobody could
oppose it'.[1] Reference could subsequently be made to any
paper in the possession of the House or Committee, whether or
not it had actually been read out. In any later proceedings,
however, no member had the right to insist on a paper being
read: if an objection was made the Speaker had to take the
sense of the House on the point.[2] This was the rule as stated by
Clerk John Hatsell: but a possible modification of it, at least
in the case of papers submitted by witnesses, is suggested by an
incident on 27 November 1783. Before the debate that day on
the second reading of Fox's East India Bill, Sir James Lowther
asked that the accounts of the Company delivered in at the
Bar of the House should be read. 'The Speaker said, that in
point of order, all papers delivered in at the bar by witnesses,
were considered as evidence already given to the House, and
therefore it was not necessary that they should be read, except
pro forma, and every member might argue from them as if they
had been read. He called on the old members of the House to
set him right, if he was wrong in his opinion.' None did so,
but Lloyd Kenyon commented that the practice could not be
reconciled with reason or common sense. Speaker Cornwall
then amplified his statement. Any counsel at the Bar of the
House could have read what evidence he pleased, but it was
not the custom of the House to read out all evidence, as too
much time would be lost. Any member, however, Cornwall
said, might refer to these papers in debate or ask for any part
to be read.[3]

There was one category of papers literally on the Table to
which members could not refer—those petitions that had been
ordered to lie there unread. This procedural point was highlighted by an incident on 13 March 1741. Sir Robert Walpole,
speaking on a bill to increase the number of sailors, was
criticizing one such petition from London against it when he

---

[1] Hatsell, *Precedents*, II, 164N.
[2] Hatsell, *Precedents*, II, 163–4.
[3] Debrett, *Parl. Reg.*, XII, 127–8.

was interrupted by Sir John Barnard. 'The petition was not ordered by the House to be placed in the Right Honourable Gentleman's hand but on the Table; nor has he a right to make use of it or any other means for his information, than are in the power of any other member. If he is in doubt upon any particulars contained in it, he may move, that the Clerk should read it to the House.' Walpole, who had evidently taken advantage of his front bench seat to pick up the petition, then put it back on the Table; but a few minutes later he leaned forward to read the petition as it lay there, and Barnard again spoke to order: 'I insist that henceforward he obey the rules of this House with his eyes as well as with his hands, and take no advantage of his seat, which may enable him to perplex the question in debate.' Speaker Onslow at once confirmed this objection: 'It is undoubtedly required by the orders of the House, that the petitions should lie upon the Table, and that any member, who is desirous of any further satisfaction, should move that they be read by the Clerk, that every member may have the same opportunity of understanding and considering them.' Walpole then proposed that the Clerk should read the petition, and, after this had been done, continued his speech with the observation that he had sat over forty years in the House and had never before been called to order.[1]

If verbal evidence given to the House suffered from a credibility gap consequent on the absence of solemn oaths, written evidence also lacked any complete guarantee of authenticity. Papers laid before the House were copies or extracts: when William Pulteney demanded original papers concerning Dunkirk on 19 February 1730, 'Sir Robert Walpole said as long as he has been in Parliament he never knew originals given.'[2] Moreover, from the reign of George I all papers laid before the House had to be in English. Protests were made in 1718 when Latin copies of international treaties were laid before the House, and translations were speedily provided.[3] The practice of translation soon became so uniform that on 27 February 1730 Speaker Onslow had to rule that

---

[1] Chandler, *Debates*, XII, 292–4.

[2] *H.M.C. Egmont Diary*, I, 53–4.

[3] G. C. Gibbs, 'Parliament and the Treaty of Quadruple Alliance', *William III and Louis XIV*, p. 301.

members were entitled to see the original documents, after John Norris complained of mistranslation from French of papers then before the House.

Mr. Norris therefore desired the original might be read, which was peevishly opposed by the Court ... It was said by Sir William Wyndham that anciently papers were communicated in their original language only, and that it is a late practice to have translations given and the originals denied; but the Speaker said that translations are only to be read except when any member did not understand the original, or doubted of the translation, and in that case the original should be produced. Accordingly, Mr. Norris was at liberty to call for it ... that we are a British House of Commons, and owe that to our own honour that what passes under our consideration ought to be in our own language, yet pieces in their original language may be called for when doubts arise.[1]

The debate reveals that translation of papers from Latin or foreign languages was then a recent development, within living memory: but thereafter members would not accept papers in foreign languages unless they were accompanied by an English translation. On 29 January 1762 the House refused to receive papers concerning Hessian soldiers on this ground, demanding prior translation. James Harris noted that ''twas admitted French papers could not lie on our table, not being translated'.[2]

Papers on the Table were in the possession of the House. Even members could not take them to other parts of the chamber while the House was sitting. On 4 May 1728 Speaker Onslow ordered Edward Vernon to stop copying a paper he had removed from the Table into the gallery. Vernon returned the paper, but later again removed it. 'The Speaker told him positively he must not do it, for, if he wanted a copy, he must come before the House sat, and averred a standing order to the contrary.'[3] Such free access at other times to papers on the Table gave rise to the danger that the evidence might be altered or removed. On 3 May 1780 Lord Beauchamp made a formal complaint that this had happened. Speaker Norton said that it was 'a matter of a very important nature', and the House at

[1] *H.M.C. Egmont Diary*, I, 73–4.
[2] Harris Diary, 29 Jan. 1762. *Commons Journals*, XXIX, 133.
[3] *Knatchbull Diary*, p. 78.

once voted to appoint a Select Committee to inquire into the circumstance. The report of the Committee next day proved an anti-climax. Alterations had been made, but 'out of sport not malice'. The culprits were not known, and the House contented itself with a resolution that such papers should never be removed from the House.[1]

The period during which the House remained in possession of any papers that had been laid on the Table was at first only the same session: but this was extended in the eighteenth century to an indefinite period. On 15 February 1726 Speaker Compton ruled that the House was not in possession of papers laid on the Table in earlier sessions, after Samuel Sandys had moved for some papers relating to court salaries that had been laid before the House the previous year.

It was objected it was unparliamentary, for that, if you designed any use of them by proceeding originally upon them, you must move for them afresh this year, but that you might make any other use of them as being part of the journals, which is always supposed to lie on the table, so you never order it to lie on the table, but call only for it and turn to it, and that if you could proceed on papers laid before the House the last sessions there would be no end, for you might go back to the beginning of Parliament for papers and the Chair declared they never knew it done.[2]

Four years later, on 22 January 1730, this decision was attacked in debate.

It was objected the difficulty gentlemen would lie under if the doctrine laid down from the Chair in the late King's time upon the paper of pensions being asked for should prevail, which was that, if a paper was delivered in the former session and the same paper asked for in the next session, that paper could not be made use of by the rules of the House, unless it was readdressed for and laid before you, although it was in the possession of the House before; this doctrine was exploded, but not settled one way or other, until the case shall again happen.[3]

The House may have been reluctant to come to any formal resolution contradicting the decision of a Speaker, and the question was tacitly and indirectly solved the next month. On

[1] Almon, *Parl. Reg.*, XVII, 622–3, 638–9. *Commons Journals*, XXXVII, 835, 838.
[2] *Knatchbull Diary*, p. 51.
[3] *Knatchbull Diary*, p. 99.

11 February 1730 papers that had been in the possession of the House in earlier sessions were explicitly obtained without new motions being made for them.[1] In 1783 this practice had become sufficiently the custom to receive endorsement from the Chair: for on 29 January 1783 Speaker Cornwall informed the House 'that the papers moved for had been laid before the House two years ago, and were now on the table'.[2]

Examination of witnesses and papers was a slow and cumbersome method of obtaining information. A quicker and more convenient way was found in the verbal interrogation of ministers. The eighteenth century saw the evolution of the Parliamentary question.[3] This new practice apparently began first in the House of Lords, where procedure was less formal than in the Commons: and little evidence of it in the House of Commons can be found before the reign of George III. On the contrary, formal motions were still being used for what was later to be the main purpose of informal Parliamentary questions—to obtain information about administration decisions or intentions. On 6 February 1734 Sir William Wyndham moved an amendment to the army estimate avowedly to obtain information about the ministry's policy concerning the War of the Polish Succession. Paymaster-General Henry Pelham answered that 'gentlemen are not obliged to say more than what is necessary for their present argument; nor are they bound, upon every occasion, to satisfy the private curiosity of other men.'[4] Pelham was later Leader of the House for over a decade before his death in 1754: and his hostility to the principle of direct questions might well have delayed the innovation. As late as 26 January 1756 George Grenville moved an Address to ask the King to inform the House on what grounds he had been advised to appoint no fewer than three Joint-Vice-Treasurers of Ireland: the motion was negatived, and his purpose might have been better served by a verbal question.[5]

Procedural difficulties over questions were twofold. Members were only permitted to speak to a motion, and they had to

---

[1] *Knatchbull Diary.* pp. 104–6.

[2] Debrett, *Parl. Reg.*, IX, 192.

[3] For a general discussion, based only on William Cobbett's *Parliamentary History*, see Patrick Howarth, *Questions in the House*, pp. 11–46.

[4] Chandler, *Debates*, VIII, 71–7.

[5] Newdigate Diary, 26 Jan. 1756. *Commons Journals*, XXVII, 405.

address the Chair: an exchange of questions and answers between individual members was therefore strictly out of order. Moreover, a clear distinction could be and often was drawn between a decision of the House to request information, by a motion, and the desire of a single member to satisfy his own curiosity. This was the basis of Pelham's objection: and the right of individual members to obtain answers to Parliamentary questions was not to be conceded even when the practice was firmly established.

These obstacles were less effective in Committee, and the custom of Parliamentary questions may well have begun in the Committee of Supply. Procedure was more informal: members were able to speak more than once, and there was less stress on the rule of relevance. The spending of public money aroused general concern and specific interest, and was a valid and natural subject for investigation; in particular, the relation of military and naval expenditure to future policy was an obviously fertile field of inquiry. Questions on this topic were asked in 1744 and 1745, during the War of the Austrian Succession.[1] Lack of military success increased the incentive, and in the War of American Independence members frequently interrogated office-holders on proposed expenditure, both in Committee and in the House proper: a few examples must suffice. On 16 December 1778 'Lord Newhaven put a variety of questions to the gentlemen belonging to the board of ordnance upon the different heads of their estimates for the service of the ensuing year ... Sir Charles Cocks and Sir Charles Frederick rose alternately, and answered these interrogaries with great candour till at length Colonel Barré said that it would be endless for the House to sit and hear a perpetual conversation, consisting merely of questions and answers.'[2] Yet on 1 February 1782 it was Barré who informed a new Ordnance official, John Kenrick, that it was usual for members of the Ordnance Board to offer only a general explanation of the estimates he was presenting, and then to sit down to give the Committee of Supply an opportunity to ask questions: and many questions followed.[3] Such inquiries could

---

[1] P. Howarth, op. cit., p. 28.
[2] Almon, *Parl. Reg.*, XI, 181–2.
[3] Debrett, *Parl. Reg.*, V, 285–98.

range widely. When the annual navy estimates were under the scrutiny of members in December 1780 Lord Lisburne of the Admiralty Board was asked why certain admirals were unemployed and what officials were still at Rhode Island.[1] Members also began to ask questions about proposed taxes.[2] By the end of Lord North's ministry in 1782 questions had become commonplace in both the Committee of Supply and the Committee of Ways and Means.

Questions in the House proper may well have been established practice long before the first instance found of a question put to and answered by a minister. This inquiry was made by Henry Fox of Chancellor of the Exchequer Henry Legge on 21 March 1757, and noted by Sir Roger Newdigate: 'Mr. Fox called upon Mr. Legge to say that if at any Board of Council where he sat any proposal had been made to send British troops to defend Westphalia. Mr. Legge said he had not heard any.'[3] The next known example was on 17 December 1765, when George Grenville asked Jeremiah Dyson of the Board of Trade what information had been received from the American colonies, receiving the reply that all news was 'immediately sent to government and must be sought for from the ministers'.[4] More consistent evidence of the practice is available after 1768 in the very full diary of Henry Cavendish. A notable instance of an early question occurred on 9 January 1770 when Colonel Barré addressed himself to the First Lord of the Admiralty, Sir Edward Hawke: 'I here call upon that gallant Admiral to tell the House, whether he knows of any order, given directly or indirectly, to the captains of the fleet to give up the right of the British flag?' Barré was alluding to a recent incident in the Channel, and Sir Edward Hawke gave an account of the episode: British naval honour had been upheld, for a French ship had struck her pennant after two shots had been fired near her.[5]

By the early years of Lord North's administration the custom of Parliamentary questions had developed to such an extent

[1] Debrett, *Parl. Reg.*, I, 203–6, 232–3.
[2] See, for example, Debrett, *Parl. Reg.*, VI, 412.
[3] Newdigate Diary, 21 Mar. 1757.
[4] Harris Diary, 17 Dec. 1765.
[5] B.M. Eg. MSS. 3711, pp. 40–1. For some other instances of questions to ministers see B.M. Eg. MSS. 223, pp. 381–2; 231, p. 205; 244, p. 10.

that ministers were sometimes obliged to remind the House of their right to refuse an answer. On 4 February 1771, after Lord North had declined to answer questions from opposition members concerning alleged French interference in the Falklands Islands dispute, Sir Gilbert Elliot rose to defend his attitude:

> It is well known, that no member has a right to call upon members to make answer to any question at all. It is destructive of the freedom of debate. If such a right did subsist, not only the freedom of debate but the freedom of silence itself would be destroyed . . . I may be asked if questions are not usually put? I answer, nothing is more usual. He either says, or is understood to say, in order to save a deal of trouble in calling for papers; in that case the Minister would give an answer on the spot.[1]

Lord North himself made a general complaint on 18 May 1774: 'I have been from the beginning of the session to this moment constantly answering questions, six, seven, eight or nine times. If a question is asked twenty times, am I obliged to answer it every time?' He had repeatedly answered questions about the navy, America and other matters. Was he expected to have at hand information 'to answer upon the spot any question any gentleman may ask any day? . . . I hope, therefore, I am acquitted by the House for not answering questions which are not the business of the day.'[2] As late as 18 April 1777 Paymaster-General Richard Rigby condemned the whole practice of individual members questioning the minister.

> He was astonished how the noble Lord could waste his time in answering all the trifling and irrelative questions which had been put to him in the course of the evening. For his part, were he in the noble Lord's situation, he would make it a rule never to answer a question put by an individual member in his place. The minister had no occasion to waste his time so idly, and to so little purpose. If, on the other hand, the House, or the majority of it, as binding the minority, asked questions or demanded explanations then indeed it was incumbent on the minister to give such answers as were not inconsistent with his duty to his sovereign, and to a true and faithful discharge of the particular office which he filled. It was proper to answer the House, but not otherwise.[3]

[1] B.M. Eg. MSS. 224, pp. 72–4.
[2] B.M. Eg. MSS. 258, pp. 162–3.   [3] Almon, *Parl. Reg.*, VII, 120.

When ministers declined to answer questions, members were obliged to revert to the old method of a formal motion. In May 1776, after repeated administration refusals to answer questions from General Conway on American policy, he gave notice that he would put them in the form of a motion: and on 22 May he unsuccessfully moved for an Address to the King to inform the House of the peace conditions of the Howe mission to the colonies.[1] Usually, however, evasion rather than blank refusal was the tactic of a minister reluctant to reveal information. When Barré asked North a question on this very same subject on 31 October that year, North gave an answer, though not one that satisfied Barré.[2] Lord North became an expert Parliamentarian in this respect. Here is Wraxall's description of his reply on 14 December 1781 to questions from Charles James Fox and General Conway on the ministry's intention to continue the American war: 'He underwent a species of cross examination. But such was his Ability and Address in eluding or evading the precise Questions put to him, that little additional information could be extracted from his answers. The House remained, if I may say so, *at Fault*.'[3] By that time North was experienced in such matters, for throughout the period immediately before and during the War of American Independence the ministers were subjected to frequent interrogations on the colonial situation.[4] One of the most devastating Parliamentary questions of all time was put on 3 December 1777, when Colonel Barré called on Lord George Germain, as Secretary of State for the Colonies, 'to declare upon his honour what was become of General Burgoyne and his brave troops; and whether or not he had received expresses from Quebec, informing him of his having surrendered himself, with his whole army, prisoners of war?' Germain reluctantly gave official confirmation of this rumour.[5] Extremely damaging to the Rockingham ministry was the question by which on 22 May 1782 John Rolle forced Secretary of State Charles Fox to admit that Admiral Rodney had been

[1] H. Walpole, *Last Journals*, I, 551–2.
[2] Almon, *Parl. Reg.*, III, 79–81.
[3] Wraxall, *Memoirs*, II, 469–70.
[4] See, for example, Almon, *Parl. Reg.*, I, 16; III, 79–81. H. Walpole, *Last Journals*, II, 129.
[5] Almon, *Parl. Reg.*, VIII, 96–7.

recalled, when news had just arrived of his victory at the Battle of the Saints.[1]

The next year endorsement of the new practice of Parliamentary questions came from the Speaker's Chair. The background to this circumstance was a notorious public scandal, the unwise re-appointment by Paymaster-General Edmund Burke of two officials, John Powell and Charles Bembridge, who had been previously dismissed for peculation. On 21 May 1783 Burke was questioned by Rolle on this matter, and an angry scene developed. Speaker Cornwall then intervened.

The Speaker said he had often repeated, and wished to impress it on the mind of the House, that conversations were disorderly; but any member had, in his opinion, a right to put a question to a Minister, or person in office, and that person had a right to answer or not to answer, as he thought proper, and, if he pleased, to explain and enter into a justification of his conduct, and give his reasons before he gave his answer to the question.[2]

Such a pronouncement was anathema to conservative members like Richard Rigby; and when on 2 June Rolle raised the matter again and Burke refused to reply, the following exchange ensued:

Rigby. He must deny the doctrine which he saw gained ground, and which had lately received countenance from the Chair. He could not allow that it was parliamentary for any individual member to put a question to another, whether a Minister or not, and insist on an answer. . . . If the practice prevailed, what would be the consequence? Their time would be taken up with asking questions of each other, and instead of the great national business going on, the best part of the session would be spent in questions and answers. No man had a right to insist upon an answer to any question he chose to put; in many cases Ministers would act imprudently if they gave any answer.

Speaker. The doctrines he had laid down went no further than that when an honourable member put a question to a Minister, that the Minister ought to be heard in reply, or in assigning his reasons why he chose to decline giving any direct answer. Such a deviation from the strictness of the general rule of order, the Speaker said, had been at all times allowed, as a means of obtaining the

---

[1] Wraxall, *Memoirs*, III, 122–3.
[2] Debrett, *Parl. Reg.*, X, 49.

House material information, which might, as it had in many instances, throw a light upon the business before them.[1]

Parliamentary questions had thus become an established custom before the end of the American war: but for some decades they were to remain infrequent; days and even weeks would pass without any. There were other differences from more modern practice. Questions were asked without notice, and nothing like a formal question-time existed. Questions were put at the beginning of public business, but also when it was over, and during or between debates. As yet, too, questions were concerned only with matters of political importance: petitions still formed the method of bringing individual grievances to the notice of the House.

Information was intended to be the precursor to action, although Parliamentary action might be taken against servants of the Crown or other persons whether or not evidence had been obtained. The Hanoverian period saw a marked change in the modes of procedure: in this respect the most significant development of the eighteenth century was the virtual, though not the actual, end of the traditional procedure of impeachment. This was the formal indictment of a minister or other accused person, lodged before the House of Lords 'in the name of all the Commons of England' by a Committee of M.P.s appointed to manage the case. It had one technical advantage: an impeachment, once commenced, was not ended by the close of a session or even a dissolution.[2] But the House of Commons acted merely as prosecutor, the House of Lords as judge. Moreover, the whole process was complex, time-consuming, and unsuited to an age when incompetent or unpopular politicians no longer risked the loss of life, liberty or property. Immediately after the Hanoverian Succession Whig ministers used this weapon, with varying success, against Oxford, Bolingbroke and other ministers of Anne's reign.[3] Thereafter it ceased to serve such political purposes, and was retained primarily for use against rebels, traitors, and men accused of misuse of public funds. The same function explained the survival of the two methods

[1] Debrett, *Parl. Reg.*, X, 100–3.
[2] *Knatchbull Diary*, p. 51.
[3] Chandler, *Debates*, VI, 26–32.

of direct punitive action by Parliament against individuals, Bills of Attainder and Bills of Pains and Penalties. The latter method was used against the leading Jacobite plotters of the 1722 conspiracy: less demanding in respect of proof, it could not include the death sentence.[1]

As a political weapon used by Parliamentary oppositions against the King's administration impeachment was abandoned in favour of votes of censure on policy or votes of no confidence in the King's ministers. In a debate of 13 January 1730 regret at this change from the formal and dignified procedure of impeachment was voiced by Edmund Bacon, who complained that the method of Parliamentary criticism was unfair to ministers: 'If bad, why are they not impeached? This would be a conduct becoming the House of Commons, but to rail continually at them as we see some members every day to do . . . was unworthy the character of any who have the honour to sit in this House, and what he thought the dignity of it could not suffer.'[2] This was a solitary and eccentric protest at the changing character of politics: but the argument of encroachment on the royal prerogative could still be advanced against Parliamentary censure of ministers. Sir Robert Walpole contended on 13 February 1741 that the proposed opposition Address to George II to remove him 'from His Majesty's presence and counsels forever' was unconstitutional.[3]

If a minister or other member was accused in a charge of which previous written notice had been given, the correct procedure was for that member to make a statement in his own defence and then to withdraw before the House came to any decision. Lord North did this when accused in March 1780 of corrupt interference in the Milborne Port constituency by one of the sitting members, Temple Luttrell. While the House discussed the charge North was 'sometimes in the Speaker's chamber and sometimes in the gallery', returning to thank the members after he had been acquitted.[4] The motion against Walpole in 1741 was made without previous intimation of the exact charge, and the House therefore held that he should not

[1] Chandler, *Debates*, VI, 301–2, 307.
[2] *H.M.C. Egmont Diary*, I, 5–6.
[3] Chandler, *Debates*, XII, 121.
[4] Almon, *Parl. Reg.*, XVII, 210–13, 346–71.

withdraw until every other member had spoken, so that he would be able to answer all accusations.[1]

By the reign of George III, direct motions of censure or of no confidence were becoming common, although motions for papers often themselves formed the excuse for criticisms of ministerial policy. The only debate over the French seizure of Corsica took place on a motion for papers on 17 November 1768. To some extent this tactic was involuntary, when opposition members knew or suspected that ministers would not disclose any papers: but there was also the calculated realization that a demand for information was a more favourable ground for winning the votes of independent members than formal motions of censure. Even George III conceded that 'a question for papers . . . might naturally catch many.'[2] In 1769 Sir Roger Newdigate, though a firm supporter of government, voted for William Dowdeswell's motions for papers on the Civil List debt.[3] Opposition speakers could use such arguments as those put forward by Alexander Wedderburn during the debate of 22 November 1770 on Dowdeswell's motion for papers about the Falkland Islands dispute: 'Motions of this kind have been frequently made. Your Journals are full of them . . . I take it to be the absolute right of this House to call for the intelligence of office upon any material subject of national concern . . . The particular inconvenience is always made the ground for opposing the generality of such motions.' Richard Rigby, although speaking against the motion, conceded the principle: 'I agree with the honourable gentleman who spoke last, in all the doctrines he has laid down with regard to calling for papers. It is undoubtedly the business of every parliamentary man to be jealous of administration, particularly in dangerous times.'[4] Motions for papers had evolved as a common opposition tactic by the administration of Sir Robert Walpole, who affected scorn of 'this sort of parliamentary play'. But the device put ministers on the defensive: information, valuable as opposition ammunition, was often obtained from the debates or from the papers themselves, if the demand was conceded, while refusal enabled the published

[1] Harrowby MSS., Doct. 21.   [2] Fortescue, *Corr. of George III*, IV, p. 62.
[3] Newdigate Diary, 28 Feb. and 1 Mar. 1769.
[4] B.M. Eg. MSS. 222, pp. C 212–18.

Votes to be a vehicle of opposition propaganda, branding administration with the stigma of secrecy.[1]

It was natural that this function of Parliament as 'the grand inquest of the nation' should be exploited primarily by opposition. But it also provided a convenient means by which ministers obtained Parliamentary approval of their policies. This took the form of an Address of Thanks to the sovereign for intimation of such important decisions as peace, war, or alliances that had been communicated to Parliament in a royal speech or message: or an Address promising support for such proposed business as the various Regency Bills of the century or other items of intended legislation announced during the course of a session.

One such vote of confidence was an annual institution, in the opening debate of the session, on the Address of Thanks in reply to the King's Speech. The occasion was one of formality as well as political significance. The members of the House heard the Speech, read by the sovereign himself or the Lord Chancellor, in the House of Lords: and after they had returned to their own chamber, the Speaker read it out twice again.[2] An Address of Thanks was moved and seconded by members selected beforehand by the administration. The proposer, who indicated 'the heads of the address' in his speech, subsequently became Chairman of the Select Committee appointed to draw up the Address. It was also customary to include in the Committee any members who had spoken in support of the motion. Certain rules were observed in the preparation of the Address. Every part of the Speech had to be answered, and when the Address of 1727 omitted one aspect of it diarist Knatchbull observed, 'I believe it the first instance in many years when the Speech was not answered in every particular.'[3] Conversely, it was improper for the House to mention any subject not included in the Speech.[4]

---

[1] Cobbett, *Parl. Hist.*, IX, 205–13.

[2] Harris Diary, 6 Nov. 1761 and 25 Nov. 1762. The formal procedures at the opening of a new Parliament, and of each session, are given in the *Journals* of the House. Further details on the ceremonial and procedure can be found in the Clementson Diary, pp. 19–21, 48–54; the Harris Diary for 3 Nov. 1761 and 1–3 Nov. 1780; and the *Knatchbull Diary*, pp. 1–3, 72.

[3] *Knatchbull Diary*, p. 60.

[4] *H.M.C. Egmont Diary*, II, 336. H. Walpole, *George III*, I, 68.

When the Address was reported, usually on the next day, the King appointed a time to receive it at St. James's Palace. The Speaker was attended there by such members of the House as chose to be present. James Harris has left a note of the scene on 16 November 1761: the King sat 'under his Canopy of State in the great Drawing Room, attended by his great officers, and on each side up the room a kew [*sic*] of the Gentlemen-Pensioners'. A year later Harris, as the mover of an Address, had an excellent chance to observe the whole procedure.

The ceremonial is that when we are called in, the Speaker walks through the first apartments with the Mover of the Address on his right, and the Seconder on his left. Just as we enter the Presence-Chamber, the Lord Chamberlain meets us, who then takes the Speaker's right and the Mover goes round to the left, taking the Seconder then on his left. Thus we walk up to the King, making three bows, which the King returns by taking off his hat each time. We stop within a yard of the King, and then the Speaker reads our Address, and kneeling puts into the King's hand, who gives it the Lord Chamberlain. The King then reads his answer and we bow back, as we had advanced, after which the King rises.[1]

The initial proceedings in the House of Commons were a set piece of formality: on 13 November 1755 the mover of the Address, Lord Hillsborough, even arrived too late to hear the Speech that he answered.[2] Both the Speech and the Address, indeed, were known to many members beforehand. It was the usual practice for the leading minister in the House to summon a private meeting of the twenty or thirty most important supporters of the administration in the Commons, two days before a session began. The next day saw a general meeting of the ministerial supporters in the House at the Cockpit, a government building in Whitehall: the Earl of Egmont knew it as 'the new Treasury' in 1735.[3] Both meetings had become customary by 1722; the purpose of the first meeting was to prepare for the anticipated debate, that of the second was to inform supporters of the King's Speech and the proposed reply

[1] Harris Diary, 13 Dec. 1762.
[2] H. Walpole, *George II*, II, 49.
[3] H. Walpole, *George III*, I, 18N. *H.M.C. Egmont Diary*, II, 144. The Cockpit was the former Cockpit of the old Palace of Whitehall.

to it.[1] Nathaniel Ryder recorded this account of the 1758 Cockpit: 'The whole ceremony is that the leading man in the House of Commons . . . reads the King's Speech twice over, and then reads the heads of an address of thanks twice over likewise, after which he declares who are the persons who are to move for it and who is to second it, which concludes the whole.'[2] In 1761 the two meetings heard the Address in full.[3] This may have been an innovation by George Grenville, for in the ensuing Commons debate on the Address George Dempster attacked 'the Cockpit method of a minister's bringing an Address thither in his Pocket; that it should be the act of a Committee for that purpose appointed.'[4] Criticisms of the Cockpit meetings as detracting from the dignity of the House were made throughout the century. During Walpole's ministry Lord Perceval always ignored invitations to attend, noting his reason in 1730: 'I look on such meetings as precluding the judgment, which for honour sake at least ought to have the appearance of being determined by the debates of the House.'[5] In 1777 Temple Luttrell, an opposition member who had received a Cockpit invitation by mistake, remarked in the debate on the Address that 'it seems the supreme sovereignty is now transferred in fact to the Cockpit, and we . . . meet here for no better purpose than to confirm and register the acts of that more august assembly.'[6]

The Address was usually proposed and seconded by office-holders, or members aspiring to office. Such a custom did not reflect the role of the Address as ostensibly the independent opinion of the House: and there is evidence of criticism even from administration supporters when the growth of the practice in the earlier eighteenth century culminated on 21 January 1729 with the Address being moved by a Lord of the Treasury and seconded by a Paymaster of Pensions. 'A pretty choice to open the debate', commented Sir Edward Knatchbull, while Lord Perceval noted that 'formerly County Gentlemen, for the better appearance, did it; of late years they

[1] *Knatchbull Diary*, p. 115. Harrowby MSS., Doct. 7P, 26 Jan. 1734.
[2] Harrowby MSS., Doct. 44.
[3] Harris Diary, 6 Nov. 1761. H. Walpole, *George III*, I, 68.
[4] Harris Diary, 13 Nov. 1761.
[5] *H.M.C. Egmont Diary*, I, 2.
[6] Almon, *Parl. Reg.*, VIII, 25.

are gentlemen of employment.'[1] Ministers doubtless preferred to enlist independent members for the task, and sometimes did so; but those willing to undertake it were few, and office-holders continued to perform the duty on most occasions throughout the century.

The King's Speech surveyed the past policies, present problems and future plans of his administration. John Wilkes described it in 1777 as 'a kind of ministerial chart, which the House may adopt, or reject at pleasure, and pursue the same, or a course directly opposite'.[2] Certainly the occasion was thought to provide a good test of the political temperature of the forthcoming session. William Dowdeswell observed to Lord Rockingham on 24 December 1771, 'I know several members who conjecture from what passes the first day upon the operations of the session.'[3] The mere fact that a division took place might portend a stormy time for ministers. Voting on the Address was uncommon. Only nine divisions took place in the period between 1714 and 1742, and they remained infrequent until the War of American Independence.[4] There were two reasons for this. Opposition members were seldom mustered in strength at so early a date, and there had evolved the convention that the Address was merely an empty compliment: the administration majority on the Address therefore tended to be deceptively large. Such trials of strength as took place were on amendments to the Address, not on a direct negative. It was now established Parliamentary practice that there should be some reply to the Speech. This would appear to be the explanation of a ruling by Speaker Onslow on 16 January 1733 when Sir Thomas Aston announced that he could not support the Address. Here is Lord Perceval's unclear account of Onslow's statement: 'The Speaker told him he could not speak against the address in general, because that was already resolved, but he was at liberty to propose any amendment he pleased.'[5]

Sometimes there was not even a debate on the Address: but

[1] *Knatchbull Diary*, p. 80. *H.M.C. Egmont Diary*, III, 330.
[2] Almon, *Parl. Reg.*, VIII, 5.
[3] Wentworth Woodhouse MSS. R1-1391.
[4] Foord, *His Majesty's Opposition*, pp. 99–100, 176, 353–4.
[5] *H.M.C. Egmont Diary*, I, 308.

the usual tactic of opposition members was to voice criticisms without forcing a vote. By mid-century custom had made the debate 'a day of conversation when all things usually discusst, without regard to a particular subject'. Thomas Townshend was explaining the practice on 10 January 1765 to a member attempting to enforce relevance: and after a similar objection on 14 January 1766 Speaker Cust 'being applied to, declared that on the day of discussing the speech and address such digressions had usually been admitted.'[1]

Apart from particular matters of policy, there was one general aspect of the Address procedure liable to arouse protests from opposition members during the early decades of the Hanoverian period. This arose from the contention that detailed approval of administration policy in an Address would restrict freedom of debate during the remainder of the session. On 23 November 1719 William Shippen recalled 'that the House had formerly been reflected on, for approving the measures of the ministry by the Lump', but withdrew his amendment that only part of the Speech should be approved after John Hungerford had asserted 'that Addresses of this Nature were but customary Compliments, but he hoped that in the course of this session they should have opportunities enough to inquire into the grievances of the nation, and the conduct of the ministry'.[2] Shippen made similar protests in almost every debate on the Address for over a decade, stating his general objection at length on 13 January 1732:

It has, Sir, upon such an occasion, been the ancient custom of this House, to present an Address of Thanks to his Majesty, for his most gracious Speech from the throne, but such Addresses were in former days always in general terms; there were in them no flattering paragraphs, no long compliments made to the throne, for transactions and successes which had never been laid before the House, and of which, by a necessary consequence, the House must have been supposed to have been entirely ignorant. It is true, Sir, we have of late years fallen into a custom of complimenting the throne upon every such occasion with long Addresses, and this custom has been followed so long, that I am afraid it may at last become a vote of course, to vote an Address to his Majesty, in such

---

[1] Harris Diary, 10 Jan. 1765 and 17 Jan. 1766.
[2] Chandler, *Debates*, VI, 200–1.

terms as shall be concerted by those very men, whose measures are approved of by the compliment made to the throne . . .

When such Addresses have been proposed, it has been promised, and we have been assured, that no advantage should afterwards be taken of any words contained in the complimentary part of such Address; but every member in this House knows, that when the House had an opportunity of examining things more particularly, and debates ensued thereupon, they have then been told that they could not censure any of the past transactions, because they had approved of them all by their Address of Thanks to his Majesty for his most gracious Speech from the throne.[1]

Shippen was not alone in his protests. William Pulteney on 13 January 1730 had 'proposed to give thanks in the old Parliamentary way'.[2] The previous year, on 21 January 1729, Pulteney had announced that 'he would have the Address go unanimously and be looked on as words of form that did not bind the House.' Sir Robert Walpole had then agreed that 'he was far from thinking it ought to tie up gentlemen's hands from debating these matters.'[3] There is no evidence, indeed, that members felt inhibited from later discussing any subject mentioned in an Address, and contentions to this effect were merely debating-points.

Parliamentary inquiry, or even the mere threat of such action, often itself served the purpose of those who invoked it; but it was usually the prelude to legislation. Permanence could be given to Parliamentary decisions only by their enactment into statute law, and legislation had long ago emerged as the distinctive form of Parliamentary action.

[1] Chandler, *Debates*, VII, 91–2.
[2] *Knatchbull Diary*, p. 97. See also *H.M.C. Egmont Diary*, I, 3–4.
[3] *H.M.C. Egmont Diary*, I, 330–1.

3

THE BUSINESS OF THE HOUSE:
II. LEGISLATION

'THE chief business of Parliament is to make new laws, revive or abrogate old ones', wrote the anonymous contributor of an article on 'The Forms of Parliament' in the *London Magazine* for 1770.[1] This was a contemporary statement of fact; but the old idea that the common law rendered new legislation unnecessary died hard. Colonel George Onslow was arguing against such a concept as late as 16 May 1774. Speaking in support of a Copyright Bill, which was designed to reverse the effect of a recent judicial decision, he declared, 'What is all the statute law, but an amelioration of the common law of the land? Do we sit here for no other purpose but to tax the people? I think the most glorious privilege, the most glorious power the House have is that of redressing the grievances of the people wherever we can.'[2]

Legislation is designed as a remedy for long-standing evils or as a solution of more immediate problems, and served the same purposes in the eighteenth century: but there were important differences from more recent practice. In the eighteenth century, legislation was not based on explicit political ideology. Nor was it especially a matter for the ministers of the Crown. There was little government legislation apart from routine financial measures, except for such emergencies as the War of American Independence. Opposition and independent members could introduce and often carry public legislation of national importance, such as the Nullum Tempus Act of 1769 and George Grenville's Election Act of 1770. The great mass of legislation was personal and local in scope, largely consisting of enclosure bills, turnpike and canal bills,

[1] *London Magazine*, 1770, p. 622.
[2] B.M. Eg. MSS. 259, p. 116. For further details and documentation of what follows see my 'Debates of the House of Commons 1768–1774' (Ph.D. thesis. London. 1958), pp. 78–81.

and naturalization bills: much of this legislation, indeed, was concerned with subjects that would now be regarded as questions for executive rather than Parliamentary decision. Private matters might engross the attention of individual members even to the exclusion of important public business. Lord Folkestone's Parliamentary Diary contains no references at all to America in March and April 1774, a period of significant legislation on the colonies. His concern was with other matters, particularly two private bills he was endeavouring to steer through the House of Commons.

By the eighteenth century there was a clear procedural distinction between such private business and public legislation: and the old rule that all legislation had to be initiated by petition still applied to private bills. In practice this distinction between public and private business was sometimes fine enough to require definition from the Speaker's Chair.[1] Procedural restrictions and other disadvantages of private bills often led members to introduce their legislation as public bills, perhaps by widening their scope from the relevant particular instance to a general rule. A common motive was evasion of the fees payable on private bills, but this reason in particular sometimes aroused opposition to the bill in protest against the unfairness of the tactic.

A distinction was only possible at all because by now each item of legislation was concerned with one specific purpose, and any divergence from this custom might incur criticism. There was, however, one regular exception to this practice. Towards the end of the session it was customary to bring together a number of miscellaneous and unrelated items into the same bill, which was therefore known as the 'Hotch-Potch Bill'. This was the explanation given by one member to another in a debate of 1782.[2] The origin and antiquity of this custom are unknown: the only other reference to it that has been found is the description by James Harris in 1764 of 'the hodge-podge bill: this contains all the appropriations of the

---

[1] See, for example, a ruling by Speaker Norton on 24 May 1773. B.M. Eg. MSS. 249, p. 5. For an attempt in 1751 to define a private bill with respect to fees see *Commons Journals*, XXVI, 277–8. Total fees amounted to at least £14 for each private bill or enacting clause. O. C. Williams, *Clerical Organisation of the House of Commons 1661–1850*, pp. 300–4.

[2] Debrett, *Parl. Reg.*, VII, 275.

money voted by Parliament, and other matters foreign such as prolonging the time for qualifications, lengthening the terms of expiring laws etc.'[1]

Bills could be introduced first into either the House of Commons or the House of Lords, except for certain categories of bills: all finance measures necessarily originated in the House of Commons; and it was the privilege of the Lords that all acts of grace should begin in their House. Most legislation, both public and private, began in the Commons, for reasons of convenience, decorum and expediency: but from tactical motives even important government measures were sometimes introduced in the Lords; the Septennial Act of 1716 and the Quebec Act of 1774 both began there.

In the Commons the process of legislation changed very little over several centuries between the reigns of Elizabeth I and Victoria: and the modern basis of the procedure has always been that any bill should receive three readings, with a Committee stage for detailed examination of the measure after the second reading. But during this long period the ingenuity of members gradually multiplied the potential occasions of discussion and opposition, by taking advantage of many hitherto formal motions that occurred during the progress of a bill. This development was possible because of the strict Parliamentary rule stated by John Hatsell: 'Every stage of a bill submits the whole and every part of it, to the opinion of the House, and this being the known order of the House, there can be no surprise upon any person whatsoever.'[2] By the middle of the eighteenth century, debates and divisions might and did arise at a possible maximum of fourteen questions put during the passage of any public bill originating in the House of Commons, and twelve on bills that came down from the House of Lords. This total does not include a number of stages that were apparently still a formality.[3] Opposition might occur also at the Committee stage, and by way of amendments, motions of adjournment and other subsidiary motions.

[1] Harris Diary, 12 Apr. 1764.   [2] Hatsell, *Precedents*, II, 135.
[3] See the Appendix to this chapter for a list of the stages of legislation. By 1848 the number of stages where divisions might occur had risen to 18. Redlich, *Procedure of the House of Commons*, I, 65 N. For a contemporary account of the procedure for public bills see the *Liverpool Tractate*, pp. 5–19.

The initial motion was for leave to introduce the bill, unless it had come down from the Lords: this was necessary even for bills that had been before the House in a former session.[1] This stage was by no means a formal one, and debates often arose. Reluctance to waste time on measures doomed to failure outweighed any courtesy due to the members initiating legislation; throughout the century, for example, bills for 'shorter Parliaments' were always rejected at this point. Divisions were quite frequent, and more than half the bills taken to a vote at this stage were defeated. After successful motions for leave, the practice was to appoint a Select Committee to draw up the bill: but a discussion over this point was provoked by Samuel Sandys on 31 January 1733. Instead of making the customary motion for leave to bring *in* the same Pension Bill that had been defeated in the Lords in the previous session, he moved instead for leave to bring *up* the bill, declaring he had a copy in his hand. Thomas Winnington at once put forward two objections: 'That the constant practice of the House, for an hundred years past, has been to move for a Bill to be brought in, and not for leave to bring it up to the Bar: that should this laudable method be broke into, and the ancient custom revived for each member to present what he pleased, they might be surprised into things very improper and inconsistent with the dignity of the House.' Sir William Wyndham attempted to apply common sense to procedure: 'We certainly ought in general to observe the usual method of proceedings; but surely, we ought not to observe any customary method, when the observing it appears to be in itself absurd.' But precedent was sacred in the eyes of the ministerial majority. Even Speaker Onslow's opinion was interrupted by shouts of 'No, No' when it seemed to be favouring Sandys. He concluded by strongly advising adoption of 'the usual method'. Sandys withdrew his motion, and complied with Onslow's specific request not to bring in the bill immediately after the House had given him leave to do so: 'decency' was observed by the prior dispatch of other business.[2]

Debate was rare at the next stage, the first reading. When on 1 June 1781 Henry Bankes asked whether it was in order to

---

[1] Luttrell Diary, II, fos. 10–11.   [2] Chandler, *Debates*, VII, 260–7.

speak his opinion at this point, 'the Speaker informed him, that if he intended an opposition to the bill, he was perfectly in order to speak in this, or any other stage, and there could not be a more proper time than on the reading of the title of the bill, to state his oppositions to the foundation and intentions of it.' After Bankes had duly spoken, Lord North felt obliged to reply, although commenting that it was 'an unusual stage' for debate.[1] Speaker Cornwall had undoubtedly been so scrupulous in respecting the right of a member that he had encouraged a break with conventional practice. Sixty-five years earlier, on 19 April 1716, Lord Guernsey was not allowed to move the rejection of the Septennial Bill sent down from the Lords without the House having read it: 'because that would have been an unprecedented method of proceeding, the House would not agree to it, but read the bill the first time'. The first debate on that measure therefore took place on the third stage, the motion to appoint a date for the second reading.[2]

The fourth question, the second reading itself, was already the customary stage for the main debate on the principle of a bill. That is evident both from current practice and from statements of contemporary commentators. The political observer writing in the *London Magazine* in 1770 remarked that 'the speaking for or against a bill' usually took place at this point:[3] and a few years earlier the author of a contemporary manual of procedure, the *Liverpool Tractate*, made the comment that 'if any Gentleman has any Objection to the Whole of the Bill 'tis proper to debate it on the Second Reading.'[4] The second reading also came to be the usual occasion for the hearing of counsel on a bill. Speaker Cornwall was confirming a long-term trend when he intervened on 1 June 1781 over a request for counsel against the first reading of a bill, remarking that 'it surely could not be a question, but that the counsel ought to be heard upon the second reading of the bill.'[5]

The particular importance attached to the stage was shown by the rule that once an order had been made for the second

---

[1] Debrett, *Parl. Reg.*, III, 472–3.   [2] Chandler, *Debates*, VI, 68.
[3] *London Magazine*, 1770, p. 623.   [4] *Liverpool Tractate*, pp. 6–7.
[5] Debrett, *Parl. Reg.*, III, 472.

reading of a bill, it was 'contrary to the Order of Proceeding in the House, to appoint an earlier Day'. This was clearly intended to prevent unfair tactics, and was strictly observed. On 3 December 1770 the second reading of a bill on the import of provisions was ordered for 24 January 1771. Three days later the House was informed that such a delay would cause great public inconvenience. The order was therefore discharged, the bill withdrawn, and leave given for another in its place. The new bill passed through all its stages by 13 December.[1] On 22 March 1784 William Hussey asserted that 'when a dissolution was expected, the orders were relaxed, and bills suffered to proceed sooner, with the greatest dispatch', but the House took no action over his request that the second reading of a bill fixed for 26 March should be brought forward.[2]

The importance of the second reading arose from the need for approval by the House of the principle of a bill before detailed examination of its provisions was made in Committee. This purpose could be achieved equally well by a debate on one of the next three motions: that this bill be committed on a named day; that this bill be committed; and that the Speaker do now leave the Chair, for the Committee. Sometimes, for tactical or other reasons, opponents of a bill would allow it to have a formal second reading and then force a debate at one or more of these stages instead. On 2 March 1780 Lord North did not oppose the second reading of Edmund Burke's Establishment Bill, a popular measure in the campaign for economical reform; and the motion to commit the bill was carried by 211 votes to 91: but the eventual fate of the bill in Committee, when it was so altered that Burke withdrew the measure, was foreshadowed by the administration success in postponing the Committee from 3 March to 8 March, after a ministerial victory of 230 votes to 197 on the point.[3] George III drew this conclusion, for he wrote to his first minister on the next day, 'Lord North must see the propriety of having rather divided on the day for holding the Committee, than against the Second reading of the Bill.'[4] Such a manoeuvre was deemed perfectly

---

[1] *Commons Journals*, XXXIII, 46–8, 57, 59, 61, 62.
[2] Debrett, *Parl. Reg.*, XIII, 300.
[3] *Commons Journals*, XXXVII, 687.
[4] Fortescue, *Corr. of George III*, V, p. 25.

proper: when on 8 May 1780 intended opposition to a bill was announced not for the second reading but on the motion to leave the Chair, Speaker Norton confirmed that this behaviour was orderly.[1]

Public bills were usually considered by Committees of the Whole House. Contemporaries recognized that the Committee stage was the time only for detailed examination of the bill, for amendment but not total rejection. Sir George Yonge declared in 1780 that 'the second reading was the only fit time for debating the principle of any bill: that in the Committee the wording of the clauses and subordinate matters might be altered and amended, but not the principle'.[2] Emund Burke made the same point of order on 7 June 1774 in the Committee on the Quebec Bill: 'I did conceive that we do admit the principle of the bill when we are arguing in the Committee. That the time for debating the principle of the clause was when the clause was finished.'[3] This distinction implied that only the House itself could throw out a bill, and also that the House should not concern itself with details. On 24 February 1730 Sir Robert Walpole, replying to detailed criticism of a bill, declared that such objections were 'more proper for the Consideration of the House, in a Committee of the Whole House, where every paragraph would be debated; where every member might reply as often as occasion required, and fully pursue the inquiry'.[4] It was because details of bills were examined in Committee that members were allowed to speak more than once.[5]

A Committee usually postponed to the end the preamble of the bill, which stated the principle or purpose of the measure. Otherwise a Committee would go through a bill systematically, taking each clause in turn. This was the time for 'filling in the blanks', the insertion of the detailed provisions of the bill, and the most suitable opportunity for members to suggest amendments.[6] Once a clause or any part of it had been approved, either explicitly, or implicitly by attention to later words of the bill, members could not return to it.[7] They could speak,

[1] Almon, *Parl. Reg.*, XVII, 683–4. [2] Almon, *Parl. Reg.*, XVII, 61.
[3] B.M. Eg. MSS. 259, p. 293. [4] Chandler, *Debates*, VII, 60–1.
[5] B.M. Eg. MSS. 262, pp. 59–60. [6] Luttrell Diary, I, fo. 19.
[7] H. Walpole, *Last Journals*, I, 62.

indeed, only on the clause or phrase then under consideration, and not about any other, whether earlier or later.[1] Additional clauses, however, could be proposed after the Committee had disposed of all the existing ones.[2]

Contemporary practice often rendered difficult any clear distinction between amendment and opposition. There might be a case for opposition to the entire bill in Committee, for members introducing legislation were not obliged to provide the full text to the House.[3] Often the precise details of a bill, that might make it objectionable to members previously in support of the general principle, were not disclosed or decided until the Committee. The Earl of Egmont believed that the Walpole ministry should have used this pretext to defeat the Place Bill of 1734 in Committee rather than on the second reading: 'I think it had been more decent, popular, and wise, if the ministry had given way to a committal . . . the throwing the Bill out upon a second reading, before the limitations intended to be proposed were known, is a stretch of insolence of power.'[4]

Even if no such excuse existed, members sometimes flouted the convention. When on 24 February 1769 Charles Yorke protested that members were going into the Committee on the Nullum Tempus Bill with the intention of debating against the whole bill, Attorney-General William De Grey retorted, 'If I dont like the bill, I will oppose it both there and at the third reading.'[5] The ambiguity of contemporary attitudes was illustrated by the behaviour of the Rockingham group on the Royal Family Marriage Bill. Although strongly critical of the measure, they supported the Order of the Day on 11 March 1772 for going into Committee. This action was explained by Edmund Burke. After conceding that many members held the opinion that now was the last correct stage to oppose the bill, he claimed that the question whether to oppose on the first, second or third readings, or at any other point, was merely a matter of prudence. This particular bill, he said, was best opposed in the Committee, for it could there be made the object of detailed criticism.[6] George III interpreted this

---

[1] H. Walpole, *George II*, I, 133. [2] Luttrell Diary, II, fo. 403.
[3] H. Walpole, *Last Journals*, I, 21. [4] *H.M.C. Egmont Diary*, II, 38.
[5] B.M. Eg. MSS. 218, pp. 2–4. [6] B.M. Eg. MSS. 236, pp. 166–7.

behaviour as a tacit admission that some legislation on the question was necessary, and his constitutional point was correct:[1] but contemporaries did not regard acceptance of the principle of a bill as imposing any restraint on amendments in Committee. The *reductio ad absurdum* of Committee procedure was attained during a Committee of 8 March 1774 on a bill to prevent vexatious removals of the poor. Sir Cecil Wray then moved to leave out the whole bill except the title, in order to substitute another.[2]

When the Committee stage had been completed, and not before, the Chairman would make his report to the House. It was not customary for bills to be reported on the same day that the Committee finished, unless the members were unanimously in favour. The usual practice was for the Chairman to announce that his report was ready, and for the House then to appoint another time for the report.[3] Altogether four questions were put at this point in the progress of a bill: the first was that the report be received on a named day. On that day the Chairman made his report 'according to Order', and three further stages followed: that the amendments be now read a second time; that the House agree with the Committee in the said amendments; and that the bill be engrossed. This last motion was intended to put the bill in a final form. The Clerk of the House had to write up the text, as amended up to the report stage, on a parchment roll: any subsequent alterations by either House were made by deletions from or additions to this basic text. The motion for engrossment was not put on bills sent from the House of Lords, for they were already engrossed. Convention usually made the whole process of the report a formality. There was a strong feeling in the House against renewed debates on matters that had already been decided: when on 11 April 1763 the House refused to agree with one of the amendments made in the Committee to a bill concerning Irish butter imports, diarist James Harris noted the decision as 'a bad precedent, which the Speaker much disapproved'.[4] Few amendments were challenged, either because of this convention or because they had been agreed as compromises

---

[1] Fortescue, *Corr. of George III*, II, p. 328.
[2] B.M. Eg. MSS. 253, pp. 247–9.   [3] Luttrell Diary, II, fo. 336.
[4] Harris Diary, 11 April 1763. *Commons Journals*, XXIX, 628–9.

or desirable alterations. The formal questions on them were put quickly, and quietly. Speaker Cornwall explained the practice on 3 June 1783 when answering a complaint by Samuel Estwick, that alterations to a bill had been made secretly. 'As he understood that the parties concerned were all agreed, and that no opposition was to be given, he had put the question in a low voice, merely loud enough to be heard by the parties themselves, who were at the time round the chair, attending to what was going forward; in a word, the question had been put just in the same manner, as in all cases, where the parties were perfectly agreed.'[1] Even this formality was not always carried out. At the report stage of the East India Regulating Bill on 8 June 1773, Speaker Norton remarked, 'I presume gentlemen will not have me put the question upon every amendment. They will be so good as to tell me when they come to any part to be objected to.'[2]

New amendments could be offered at the report stage, as at any other time. When Thomas Gilbert moved some amendments after the report of his Poor Bill on 16 May 1782 Speaker Cornwall suggested that 'the most orderly method would be to recommit the bill', hinting that he wished to speak in Committee himself. Gilbert, fearing the loss of the bill so late in the session, refused to accept this advice from the Chair and the question was then put on the amendments in the House.[3]

The engrossed bill had now to receive a third reading, a stage comprising two questions: that the bill be read a third time on a named day, a motion often put at the report; and that the bill be now read a third time. Sometimes the main opposition to a bill was deliberately reserved until this point. On 25 April 1774 William Dowdeswell, leader of the Rockingham group in the Commons, informed the House of his wish to have one full debate on the ministry's American measures of that session, and announced that he would take the opportunity of the third reading of the bill to regulate the government of Massachusetts Bay, which was ordered for 2 May. Henry Cavendish rose to ask whether it was 'usual to debate the principle of the bill after the Committee', and Colonel Barré declared that the

---

[1] Debrett, *Parl. Reg.*, X, 112. For the background to this incident see Wraxall, *Memoirs*, III, 432–4.

[2] B.M. Eg. MSS. 250, pp. 36–7.   [3] Debrett, *Parl. Reg.*, VII, 165.

second reading was 'the usual stage to oppose the principle of the bill'.[1] These comments from other opposition members produced no change of plan, and the main debate on the American legislation took place on 2 May. Opposition on the third reading was often regarded as unfair: that is apparent from remarks made on 17 February 1777, when Attorney-General Thurlow protested at an opposition amendment to the third reading of a bill to suspend habeas corpus in America. 'He observed that it was a very unusual thing to debate a bill in this stage: that many opportunities had presented themselves since its first introduction into the House; on the second reading, in the committee, and on the report; but all these opportunities were partly passed over, and administration were now called on to defend and amend a bill in a stage, in which, if debated at all, it is scarcely or ever offered to be amended.' Thomas Townshend replied that 'it was neither unusual nor uncommon to debate bills on the third reading: nay, even to add clauses, by way of rider, after the principle of the bill had received the approbation of both Houses. He could not therefore conceive on what ground the learned gentleman could seem surprised, at what, which if not every day's practice, was nevertheless the constant practice and usage of Parliament.'[2] Amendments could be offered even after the third reading. Speaker Cornwall told Lord Surrey on 25 April 1782 that as the bill under consideration was engrossed and the question put for the third reading, he could not add a clause then, but might add it afterwards; and he did so.[3] Any significant alterations at this point, of course, would undermine the procedural safeguard of the whole legislative process: hence the contemporary criticism of those members who on 19 March 1725 introduced an important amendment to a bill after the third reading. 'This was thought very irregular but on the question carried.'[4]

Finally, often on the same day as the third reading and sometimes confused with it by reporters, there came the question put by the Speaker in this form, 'is it your pleasure that the bill do pass?'. Lord Perceval commented on 19 March 1730

---

[1] B.M. Eg. MSS. 256, pp. 8–10 (shorthand).
[2] Almon, *Parl. Reg.*, VII, 259.   [3] Debrett, *Parl. Reg.*, VII, 79.
[4] *Knatchbull Diary*, p. 42.

that 'it was a surprise, and not a fair procedure, though strictly Parliamentary', when a division was called for at this stage.[1] In fact divisions on the motion to pass were fairly common, although bills were seldom defeated at this point. One that did suffer this fate was the hitherto unopposed Qualification Bill of 1732, rejected by surprise administration resistance in a thin House.[2]

As soon as a bill was passed it had to be carried up to the Lords, by the member responsible for its introduction. This was usually done the same day, unless the member was absent. In February 1732 Speaker Onslow privately criticized Samuel Sandys for not attending the House to take up his Pension Bill, 'for that as soon as ever a Bill is passed our House, it ought to be carried to the Lords; that in old time it used to be carried the very day of its passing, and if Mr. Sandys did not speedily appear, he should himself be obliged to move the House to appoint some other member for that office'.[3] For greater solemnity on formal or other occasions an order would be made that the whole House should attend the Speaker to the Lords with a bill. This was a rare occurrence, for both this step and such other proposals as an official message to the Lords that the Commons had a particular concern for the passage of a bill would certainly be resented by the peers as undue pressure.[4] Complete unanimity on a bill, however, was recorded in the published *Votes* of the House. John Wilkes remarked on 26 November 1778, 'When a bill of great importance passes with unanimity, I believe, Sir, that you think it your duty to give it a further weight by the addition of a *nemine contradicente* in the Votes.'[5]

The total number of possible divisions on a bill was a purely academic matter to contemporaries. Never was there sustained resistance to a measure throughout every stage of its progress, and even determined opponents of a bill did not necessarily choose to challenge it on many of the fourteen stages where convention permitted opposition. There were twenty-one divisions on the controversial Royal Family Marriage Bill of 1772. Only two of the six that took place in the House itself

---

[1] *H.M.C. Egmont Diary*, I, 81.   [2] *H.M.C. Egmont Diary*, I, 244–5.
[3] *H.M.C. Egmont Diary*, I, 222.   [4] *H.M.C. Egmont Diary*, I, 80–1, 140–1.
[5] Almon, *Parl. Reg.*, XI, 24.

occurred on any of these fourteen formal stages, one on the question to leave the Chair for the Committee, the other on the final motion to pass the bill. Four were on such subsidiary questions as a motion to print the bill, a motion that the royal right asserted in the bill had no legal foundation, an adjournment motion on the second reading, and a limiting clause on the report. Of the fifteen divisions in Committee, five were purely obstructive and not on details of the bill, three being to leave the Chair and two to report progress.[1] To contemporaries the various stages of legislation represented alternative rather than continuous opportunities for discussion and opposition. This choice was becoming limited by convention to such stages as the second reading; but the number of points at which it might be exercised was still increasing.[2]

Private legislation was subject to far more stringent regulation than public bills.[3] First of the several safeguards against malpractice was the rule that a preliminary petition was still obligatory for private bills under a standing order of 1685, 'that for the future, no private bill be brought into this House, but upon a petition first presented, truly stating the case, at the peril of the parties presenting the same, and that such petitions should be signed by the parties, who are suitors for the bill'. Nor was this a mere formality. No subsequent bill could go beyond the terms of the petition, and this rule was strictly observed: on 14 March 1765 Speaker Cust declared a bill to be irregular after an objection to it on this ground, and his opinion was accepted by the House.[4] The usual practice was therefore to draw up a petition in very general terms, to avoid later problems and expense. Each petition had to be presented

---

[1] *Commons Journals*, XXXIII, 549–612. B.M. Eg. MSS. 234, pp. 230–8; 235, pp. 1–227; 236, pp. 2–174, 178–247; 237, pp. 1–283; 238, pp. 6–291; 239, pp. 1–161.

[2] For conventions restricting the number of divisions on legislation, and for the incidence of divisions on bills see *infra*, pp. 261–2.

[3] For a more detailed survey of private bill procedure in the eighteenth century see O. C. Williams, *History of Private Bill Procedure*, I, 23–40. For contemporary summaries of procedure see the Clementson Diary, pp. 16–18, and the *Liverpool Tractate*, pp. 20–7.

[4] Harris Diary, 14 Mar. 1765.

by a member, who would then take charge of any ensuing bill throughout all its stages. Such a member was usually connected with the enterprise or sitting for a constituency in the area concerned, and this task of conducting local legislation through the House was accepted as a conventional obligation by the great majority of members.[1] The usual practice was for a petition for a private bill to be referred to a Select Committee before any decision was considered. An order of 13 March 1717 made this obligatory for any petitions for bills involving the levy of public tolls or duties; this regulation covered proposals for turnpike roads or canals, but not bills for enclosure or naturalization.[2] The practice of referring private petitions to a Committee was so customary, however, that it was often assumed to be invariable: as early as 16 December 1724 Speaker Compton had to remind members that each such decision was the choice of the House.[3]

The method of appointing Select Committees was the same for the examination of petitions, the consideration of bills, and the prosecution of particular inquiries. The practice was for individual members to rise in turn and make two nominations: the alternative method of a ballot was never used for private business. When the number was felt to be sufficient, the Speaker asked the Clerk to read out the names, and then, for private business, he usually added several general categories—all the members for constituencies deemed to be affected, and perhaps also all merchants or lawyers or other relevant groups. The advantage of personal, local or professional knowledge was clearly held to outweigh the danger of bias or jobbery arising from such connections, especially as other stages of legislation contained safeguards against unfair practice.

The Chairman of the Committee was usually the member sponsoring the petition. He arranged the dates of meeting with the other members nominated, for no public notice of such meetings had to be given. The Committee examined the statements in the petition, and also until 1773 any counter-petitions that

---

[1] The diaries of Sir Roger Newdigate and James Harris show how conscientiously they undertook this task.

[2] *Commons Journals*, XVIII, 496. A Committee had to consist of at least eight members. Clementson Diary, p. 16.

[3] *Knatchbull Diary*, p. 35.

might have been presented to the House: on 5 May 1773 an order was made that no petitions against a petition would be heard until the Committee had reported to the House.[1] The procedure at that point was for the Chairman to make his report from the Bar of the House, saying 'The Committee appointed to report upon the petition relating to . . . have examined the allegations of the same, and found them to be true, and have ordered me to report the same.'[2] After the Clerk had read the report, which summarized the evidence, the same member would move for leave to bring in a bill, and he would head the small Committee appointed to prepare it. When this had been done, he then presented it in the manner described by James Harris from his own experience in 1762:

The Speaker being acquainted with your purpose, takes a note of it on his paper, then calls on you in your order, as you stand in that paper. You go to the Bar, to be so called. When called on, you stand with the Bill in your hand and say, 'The Committee appointed to prepare a Bill for . . . have prepared the same, and have ordered me to . . .' Then present it. You are then to stay, till you are ordered to bring it up, which you do by three bows, leaving the Bill on the right hand side of the table. When the Speaker has it, you move to have it read the first time.[3]

Thereafter the stages of private legislation were the same as for public bills, except that the Committee was a Select Committee and not a Committee of the Whole House. It was customary for private bills to receive a first reading immediately after presentation, even though there existed an order of 12 November 1705 that they should be printed beforehand.[4] This safeguard had clearly been devised because the general phraseology of the petition might make it impossible to anticipate the particular contents of the bill: yet it was apparently ignored, unless bills were printed before their presentation to avoid delay. Nor was any heed paid to a further safeguard, an order of 1698 that on the first reading of private bills a time should be appointed for the second reading. Standing orders of 1699 did ensure that there should be three

---

[1] *Commons Journals*, XXXIV, 300.
[2] Harris Diary, 17 Feb. 1762.
[3] Harris Diary, 17 Feb. 1762.
[4] *Commons Journals*, XV, 18.

clear days between each reading of all private bills, to prevent surprise; and that there should be a week's notice between the second reading and the commitment.[1] These regulations were generally observed, but even standing orders were not sacrosanct. On 23 March 1784 William Hussey asked that the date for a Committee on a private bill should be brought forward. 'The Speaker stated to the House that it was contrary to their Order so to accelerate it, but said, they had it in their power to do it if they thought proper.' The House then empowered the Committee to sit on the next day.[2]

Petitions against the principle of a bill, as contained in the preamble, had to be heard in the House, usually on the second reading, although there was no procedural objection to a later stage: petitions for amendments or restrictions were heard in the Committee. Opposing parties almost always employed counsel, and the objectors were heard before the promoters. Committees on private bills had a duty not only to consider the detailed provisions, as on public bills, but also, under a standing order of 1699, to report on the allegations of the bill and any agreement or disagreement between different parties. After the Committee the subsequent stages of private legislation appear to have been exactly the same as on public bills, without further restrictions.

The eighteenth century saw a steady rise in the number both of bills introduced and of bills successfully completed as legislation. The increase in the items designated as public bills was larger than that for private bills. To some extent this trend reflected the greater responsibilities of government and the growing complexity of social and economic conditions; but much of this comparative change was technical, the designation as public bills of local measures that early in the century were introduced as private bills.[3]

There were no specified intervals between the various stages of legislation on public bills.[4] A bill might pass rapidly through the House of Commons at times of crisis; in 1722 and 1745

---

[1] *Knatchbull Diary*, p. 33. Clementson Diary, p. 17.
[2] Debrett, *Parl. Reg.*, XIII, 307. *Commons Journals*, XXXIX, 1048.
[3] The totals are taken from Townsend, *House of Commons*, II, 379–80.
[4] Clementson Diary, p. 18.

Reign	Public Acts	Private Acts	Average Number Per Session
William III (1689–1702)	343	466	58
Anne (1702–1714)	338	605	78
George I (1714–1727)	377	381	58
George II (1727–1760)	1,447	1,244	81
George III (1760–1820)	9,980	5,257	254

bills to suspend the Habeas Corpus Act both passed in two days, and one in 1744 for the detention of suspected traitors took only three days. Government legislation usually took less than a month, and little attention should be paid to such partisan remarks as the opinion of diarist Wraxall that Charles James Fox pushed his East India Bill of 1783 with 'indecent Ardor. Scarcely three weeks elapsed, from the time of his moving for Leave to bring in the Bill, on the 18th of November, to his Appearance at the Bar of the House of Peers, on the 9th of December; when he presented it in Person ... An ordinary Turnpike, Canal, or Enclosure Bill, if opposed in its Principles or Progress, might have taken longer time.'[1] Wraxall's comment is unfair. During the century much important government legislation had passed in comparable periods of time; the hotly contested Royal Family Marriage Bill of 1772 got through the Commons in twenty days. His comparison with opposed private or local legislation, moreover, was misleading. Such business normally took longer to pass through the Commons than government measures because ordinary members lacked an administration's control of Parliamentary time. Ministers may in theory have been equal with other members; but in practice they were almost always able to arrange the timetable of official business to suit their own convenience. Every year, however, some public bills sponsored by individual members failed to complete the legislative process before the end of the session. Private bills were often lost in this way, even though the last day for petitions for such legislation was usually fixed for February or early March, at least three months before the expected close

[1] Wraxall, *Memoirs*, IV, 558.

of the session. An administration, when finally deciding on the annual prorogation of Parliament, could take little account of the state of legislative progress of all the measures, public and private, introduced by individual members.

A bill usually came before the House of Commons on at least seven different occasions, quite apart from the Committee stage.[1] Breaches of this accepted practice led to complaint. On 16 February 1731 it was Leader of the House Sir Robert Walpole who objected when an opposition motion was made to receive at once the report of the Committee on a Pension Bill, instead of the customary proposal to fix a future day. Walpole complained of 'the unparliamentariness of huddling a matter of such consequence so fast, and the ill consequence of it in future times; what would those gentlemen have said if other matters which had been carried by majorities against them, had been passed in like manner.'[2] Such complaints were often formal. Contemporaries knew that no pressure could deprive members of the House of Commons of the opportunity of debating any bill at indefinite length at over a dozen stages— if any demand for such a discussion existed.

---

[1] These were on the motion for leave, first reading, second reading, beginning of the Committee, end of the Committee, report, and third reading.

[2] *H.M.C. Egmont Diary*, I, 133.

APPENDIX

Stages of Public Legislation

1. That leave be given to bring in the bill.
2. That the bill be read a first time.
3. That the bill be read a second time on a named day.
4. That the bill be now read a second time.
5. That the bill be committed.
6. That this House will resolve itself into a Committee on a named day.
7. That the Speaker do now leave the Chair.
8. That the report of the Committee be received on a named day.
9. That the amendments be now read a second time.
10. That the House agree with the Committee in the said amendments.
11. That the bill be engrossed.
12. That this bill be read a third time on a named day.
13. That the bill be now read a third time.
14. That the bill do pass.

These are the stages at which debates and divisions are known to have occurred during the century. Debates never arose on more than a few of these stages on any single bill, and for most bills stages were taken together, so that a bill would pass through the House on six or seven scattered days, apart from the Committee stage. Stages 2 and 3 were often taken on the same day, also stages 4 to 6: after the Committee, stages 9 to 12 on a single day would be followed by a final day on 13 and 14. If the Committee took only one day, stages 7 and 8 would both occur then.

There were also a number of other stages, at this time apparently formal. Four are listed by J. Steven Watson in his total of 13 stages of legislation,[1] which omits numbers 6, 7, 9, 10 and 12 of those given above. They are as follows.

(a) A motion to put the bill on the Table (after 1 above).

[1] 'Parliamentary Procedure As a Key to the Understanding of Eighteenth Century Politics', *Burke Newsletter*, III (1962), 118–19.

(b) That the report of the Committee be received now (after 8 above).

(c) That the title of the bill be agreed.

(d) That the bill be sent to the Lords (both come at the end).

4

THE BUSINESS OF THE HOUSE:
III. FINANCE

IT was in the later seventeenth century that the House of Commons had finally obtained the exclusive power of granting finance to the sovereign. Thereafter the House was always concerned to ensure both the observance of this privilege by the Crown and its defence against the House of Lords. The first was a mere formality. The Crown's request for supplies in the Speech from the Throne at the opening of each new session of Parliament was always made in a paragraph addressed specifically to the 'Gentlemen of the House of Commons'. Other royal requests for money were likewise addressed exclusively to the House of Commons. The only adverse comment on this practice was made by an unknown member in a Committee debate of 11 February 1740 on a royal message for an extraordinary supply, and met immediate and severe censure from Speaker Onslow: 'I think myself obliged to rise up on this occasion, when somewhat has been thrown out that seems levelled against the great and most important Right of this House, that of granting Money. It is a Right, Sir, that never ought to come into doubt; it is a Right which we cannot part with the sole Exercise of, without giving up our own Power, without betraying the Liberties of our Constituents.'[1]

No minister ever allowed his sovereign to make the elementary mistake of any application for money other than one solely to the Commons; and in the eighteenth century the defence of this exclusive privilege of finance always centred on relations with the House of Lords. In formal matters great care was taken to avoid the issue, as when Speaker Onslow reminded the Commons on 29 March 1756 that no Address from the House mentioning money was ever communicated to

---

[1] Chandler, *Debates*, XI, 294–5.

the Lords.[1] But the question often arose over legislation on three points—the introduction of money bills, alterations to money bills, and amendments to financial provisions in other bills. That money bills could not begin in the Lords was accepted constitutional doctrine: and it was for this reason that opponents of the Quebec Bill asked the Chair on 26 May 1774 whether it was a money bill. Speaker Norton declined to give his opinion on the matter.[2] How zealously the Commons defended this privilege can be seen from a note made by Sir Dudley Ryder in 1742: 'The Lords cannot send a bill to the Commons that imposes a fee with the levying money on the people, and though it is only said that no greater a sum than so much shall be taken, that makes it a money bill.'[3] Nor did the Commons accept amendments by the Lords to financial legislation, for these implied participation in such business. In 1783 Speaker Cornwall quoted to the House a written opinion of Speaker Onslow, 'from which it appeared that the extension of the powers of a money bill, by the Lords, was contrary to the exclusive privilege of the Commons, of originating money bills'.[4] Complete rejection of the bill was the practice on such occasions, and sometimes with vigour. After a motion to reject such a bill had been carried in February 1752, 'the Speaker threw it on the table, and the Clerk threw it on the floor.'[5] On 11 June 1779, when Speaker Norton put the question to reject another such amended bill 'the House seemed unanimous in saying Aye. Upon which the Speaker threw the bill over the table upon the floor, and Mr. R. Whitworth kicked it down to the door.'[6] Amendments made by the Lords to an acknowledged money bill would not be accepted by the Commons even if they were thought desirable. The procedure to be followed in such a case was outlined by Speaker Cornwall on 8 May 1783. The method was to postpone consideration of the amended bill, and to order in a new bill framed according to the amendments. Such a bill would pass all its stages within a few days.[7]

[1] Newdigate Diary, 29 Mar. 1756.   [2] B.M. Eg. MSS. 260, pp. 136–8.
[3] Harrowby MSS., doc. 21, 29 June 1742.
[4] Debrett, *Parl. Reg.*, X, 1–2.
[5] Harrowby MSS., doc. 21, 25 Feb. 1752.
[6] Almon, *Parl. Reg.*, XIII, 349–50.
[7] Debrett, *Parl. Reg.*, X, 1–2.

By the middle of the century the House of Commons, at the instigation of Speaker Onslow, was attempting to extend this privilege to include any clause, whatever the bill, that involved any charge upon the public. On 13 April 1743 the Commons considered amendments by the Lords to a vagrancy bill that attempted to clarify the method for ascertaining rates to be levied by local magistrates. 'The Speaker told the House this amendment was trifling on their sole privilege of granting money, which extended to all impositions on the subject, not merely such as were granted to the Crown. But allowed that penal bills and others granting money which were not mere grants of aids to the Crown the Lords might amend in anything but those parts by which the money was granted.' Many members thought that Onslow's claim was 'ridiculous': but the House adopted the tactic of throwing out the amendments *nem. con.*, and returning the bill to the Lords with reasons other than privilege for their rejection.[1] The rejection of a bill on the same ground in February 1752, after Speaker Onslow had said 'in strong terms' that it encroached on the privilege of the House, was contrary to many precedents, so Lord Chancellor Hardwicke informed Sir Dudley Ryder.[2] The next month Hardwicke decided to attack this extension of privilege by the Commons when a similar incident occurred over a bill to suppress unlicensed houses of entertainment and music. The Lords geographically extended the power to finance independent prosecutions out of the poor rate from the London area to the whole country. When this amendment was reported in the Commons 'the Speaker said it was trifling on the Commons privilege who had the sole power of giving money or laying taxes on the people, which he said was founded in this, that those who pay only could give and those who give only could regulate the payment.' The House accepted this interpretation and decided on a conference with the Lords, adopting the usual tactic of giving reasons based on the merits of the amendment without mention of privilege. Since the attempted extension of privilege was not explicit, rejection of the claim was possible without a quarrel between the two Houses. Lord

[1] Harrowby MSS., doc. 21, 13 Apr. 1743. Sir Dudley Ryder says that the bill was rejected, but it was lost in this way. *Commons Journals*, XXIV, 476–81.
[2] Harrowby MSS., doc. 21, 25 Feb. 1752.

Chancellor Hardwicke took the opportunity to declare that there was no privilege in the case, 'as being addition of penalty or increase in which he said had been determined by the Commons themselves not to be privilege'. The Lords gave up the particular amendment, but adopted the view that the Commons had conceded the point of privilege.[1]

This was a clash on a marginal point. There was never any challenge by the Lords to the principle that the Commons had exclusive control over money bills, even when assertion of this privilege led that House into an unduly comprehensive interpretation of what constituted such financial legislation. In practice it came to mean any bill involving government expenditure: in 1760, for example, Speaker Onslow defined as a money bill a measure that made militia costs payable by the Exchequer.[2] Such a wide interpretation sometimes posed problems for ministers over legislation, and it was for this reason that a more limited one was substituted by Lord North on 2 July 1779. John Dunning asked the Chair whether a militia bill amended by the Lords was not a money bill. Speaker Norton repeatedly refused to give any answer, declaring that 'he conceived the House would take care of their own privileges; and the matter was then entirely in their hands.' Lord North feared the loss of the bill, a government measure: and administration put forward a procedural definition of financial legislation that was much narrower than the previous practice. This contention was that, to qualify for this privileged immunity from alteration or rejection by the Lords, a money bill must have originated in the Committee of Supply. The new interpretation was implicitly established by a majority decision, the amendments by the Lords being carried after two divisions.[3]

The House of Commons had won financial power for itself, not for its constituents. Supply bills were never printed, to minimize discussion and protest outside the House. The Walpole ministry refused to allow printing of the Excise Bill in 1733, despite the administration's own argument that

[1] Harrowby MSS., doc. 21, 20 and 24 Mar. 1752. *Commons Journals* XXVI, 501–14.
[2] H. Walpole, *George II*, III, 281.
[3] Almon, *Parl. Reg.*, XIII, 539–49. Cobbett, *Parl. Hist.*, XX, 968–1008.

opposition to the bill arose merely from ignorance of the proposals.[1] The reason then put forward was that any tax known in advance would meet opposition and the task of taxation would therefore become virtually impossible: but such arguments were soon abandoned in favour of the simple contention noted by Sir Dudley Ryder in 1748, when a motion to print a finance bill was rejected because it was 'the rule not to print money bills'.[2]

That the House of Commons was determined to prevent any encroachment on its financial powers from below as well as from above was shown by the evolution during the early decades of the century of a rule that the House would accept no petitions against money bills imposing new taxes. This was a deliberate reversal of previous practice, for many precedents for such petitions existed from before 1714. The habit of prohibiting any such petitions began without any formal standing order, as a result of the great and growing number of petitions arising from the multiplicity of new taxes in the period after 1688.[3] On 15 February 1693, for example, a petition against some proposed new duties was rejected as 'wholly irregular, for if you will receive petitions against the taxes you raise, you will never have done; their representatives are here, and their consent is sufficient.'[4] By the reign of George II the ban on such petitions had become sufficiently routine for Speaker Onslow to make this pronouncement on 27 January 1730, over a Bristol petition against the existing duties on soap and candles:

Mr. Speaker declared the order of the House to be that, where petitions were offered against laying a new duty, the House would not receive them, the House being the most competent judges of what was for the advantage of the nation, which they represent. But against duties already laid the petitions are always received, because the particular people who suffer under that experiment are most capable of informing the House of the grievance which is felt in consequence of the duty.[5]

[1] *H.M.C. Egmont Diary*, I, 354.
[2] Harrowby MSS. doc. 21, 17 Mar. 1748.
[3] Harris Diary, 15 Feb. 1765.
[4] Luttrell Diary, II, fo. 360.
[5] *Knatchbull Diary*, p. 145.

Onslow therefore suggested that the correct procedure would be for the petition to lie on the Table, since the Committee of Ways and Means was not yet in existence for that session. The petition, however, was rejected outright on a division, the House taking the view that 'at this rate we should be pestered every day with petitions against all the duties that were appropriated, for they were all grievances in some respect or other.'[1]

If administration failed to accept Onslow's dictum that all petitions against existing taxes should be heard, opposition refused to give up the weapon of petitions against new tax proposals. The whole question was ventilated in 1733. On 8 March administration speakers claimed twenty years of invariable practice as precedent for the rule, a contention denied by opposition members. This discussion was over a Rhode Island petition against the Sugar Bill, but the colonial protest was merely an opposition stalking-horse; the real aim was to prepare the way for later petitions against Walpole's Excise Bill. The manoeuvre failed, for the ministerial majority refused either to hear the petition or to appoint a Committee to look into precedents.[2] The opposition then turned to exploit the belief of the City of London in its own 'peculiar right to petition against Money Bills'.[3] The City petition against the Excise Bill was presented on 10 April, and the debate centred on the request to be heard by counsel. Opposition claimed two precedents, and the general right of the subject. The administration reply was summarized by Lord Perceval:

It was said on the other side, that not one precedent for allowing petitioners to be heard by their counsel against a Money Bill, appeared on our journals. There were two instances indeed that came near the point, which were the brass wire petitioners, and the potmakers, but theirs is not the present case. All the precedents quoted (of which there were above thirty) were to be relieved of duties already enacted, not of duties about to be enacted; that if it be suffered to petition against a Money Bill to be enacted, there would no taxes be laid at all, for taxes must press somewhere. That

---

[1] *Knatchbull Diary*, pp. 100–1.
[2] Chandler, *Debates*, IX, 309–15. *H.M.C. Egmont Diary*, I, 340–1.
[3] *H.M.C. Egmont Diary*, I, 357. For this privilege see *supra*, p. 19.

if any other than the City of London had petitioned, their petition had been rejected, but the City having a peculiar privilege to be treated in a civiler manner, namely, that their petition delivered in their corporate capacity should be received without opening it, when delivered by their Sheriffs, this petition has been read and ordered to lie on the table, as a decenter way of disregarding it. That by very many precedents (which Mr. Winnington quoted) it appeared petitions against Money Bills, and even from the City, had been rejected.

Political allegiance rather than constitutional argument was responsible for the endorsement by the House of this administration view, by the narrow margin of 214 votes to 197.[1] Sir Robert Walpole had already resolved to drop the Excise Bill, but he deliberately concealed this decision until after these debates so that no right to petition against new tax proposals would be established.[2] In this sense Walpole emerged even from the Excise Bill crisis with a minor success. No evidence of further controversy on the point has been found until the second reading on 15 February 1765 of what was to be George Grenville's Stamp Act. Petitions from several colonies against the measure were offered by various members. Grenville at once quoted the precedent of 8 March 1733, and later denied the opposition claim that the year's delay of the stamp duties had been intended to give the colonies time to petition. Procedural expert Jeremiah Dyson admitted the rule to reject such petitions was 'not antient', but urged that 'practice made the rule, and tis dangerous to break it.' The petitions were rejected without a vote.[3] By the later part of the century it was the established rule that no petitions, apart from any from the City, could be accepted against money bills imposing new taxes.[4]

When the authority of the House of Commons in financial matters had become fully established in the later seventeenth century, there had soon become apparent the danger that this power might be abused by individual members. The number

---

[1] *H.M.C. Egmont Diary*, I, 358–9.   [2] Plumb, *Walpole*, II, 268–9.

[3] Harris Diary, 15 Feb. 1765.

[4] See, for example, Almon, *Parl. Reg.*, XVII, 630–1. Debrett, *Parl. Reg.*, X, 116–17, 135.

6—H.O.C.

of private grants petitioned for and often obtained by members led to this decision on 11 December 1706: 'Resolved that this House will receive no Petitions for any Sum of Money, relating to publick service, but what is recommended from the Crown.' This resolution was made a Standing Order on 11 June 1713.[1] The consent of the sovereign thereafter had to be signified to the House by a minister before consideration of any application for money: but Speaker Onslow informed Sir Dudley Ryder in 1750 that this rule had not been scrupulously observed. 'Speaker told me that it had been the regular custom to have the King's consent whenever his money is to be disposed of by bill either by bringing it or some time during its passing, but some instances have been where it has not been done.'[2] Usually the observance of this rule was strict, and the interpretation broad: when Sir Herbert Mackworth presented a petition from the holders of ordnance debentures on 24 June 1782, he was told by Speaker Cornwall that a recommendation by the Crown was necessary![3] Almost invariably royal consent was given at once for private measures designed in the public interest, but Lord Perceval's account of the relationship of the Georgia trustees with Sir Robert Walpole in the 1730s shows how a minister could use it as a means to remind members of his power.[4]

The inability of private members to propose charges on public funds without royal consent was a notable safeguard against extravagance by the House of Commons. More important, and in accord with the traditional role of the House as a check on the royal executive, was the elaborate system of procedure devised to prevent too easy a grant of money even for the routine purposes of government. There were formal preliminaries before any step could be taken. The Address in reply to the King's Speech always included a promise of supply, in response to the request in the Speech. Motions would soon follow in the House to consider the Speech and to grant a supply. When the Committee of Supply met, the first business

---

[1] *Commons Journals*, XV, 211; XVII, 417. For a contemporary account of finance procedure see the *Liverpool Tractate*, pp. 59–66.

[2] Harrowby MSS., doc. 21, 16 Jan. 1750.

[3] Debrett, *Parl. Reg.*, VII, 261.

[4] *H.M.C. Egmont Diary*, III, 102, 178–80. The rule is discussed in the *Liverpool Tractate*, pp. 30–2.

was always a resolution to this effect. Not until this decision had been reported to the House could Addresses be made to the Crown for the necessary papers to serve as the foundation for detailed proposals. Any intended expenditure then had to pass under the scrutiny of the Committee of Supply and the Committee of Ways and Means before the necessary financial legislation could be introduced: for a standing order of 18 February 1668 laid down that any motion for supply must be referred to a Committee of the Whole House.[1] Even the Civil List duties, granted to each new sovereign for life on his accession, were subjected to separate and formal consideration in the two Committees before being incorporated in a general bill. This stipulation that every tax must go 'through the whole form of parliamentary form' did not apply to the reduction or repeal of taxes.[2] On 10 February 1764 William Dowdeswell accordingly asked leave to introduce a bill for the repeal of the cider tax, citing precedents for his action. Even so, Speaker Cust himself spoke to order, doubting 'whether a motion can be made either to lay or to impose a tax without going previously into a Committee'. The Chair was contradicted by procedural expert Dyson, who thought 'otherwise as to repealing, but not to laying on a tax'. The debate on Dowdeswell's motion then continued, but it was defeated on a division.[3]

It was the duty of the Committee of Supply to vote money for the various purposes of government, and the task of the Committee of Ways and Means to raise the amounts required. Contemporaries sometimes referred to both as the Committee of Supply or 'Committee of Supplies': but that this distinction of function was maintained in practice was shown by the care taken to correct a mistake on 21 March 1728. A resolution that £30,000 be voted for 'the deficiency of the general fund' was reported in error from the Committee of Ways and Means: when the House realized that the matter was one of supply, the resolution was ordered to lie on the Table, so that the question could later be referred to the Committee of Supply.[4] This difference between the respective functions of the two Committees was of comparatively recent origin. In the seventeenth

---

[1] *Commons Journals*, IX, 52. [2] Harris Diary, 29 Mar. 1764.
[3] Harris Diary, 10 Feb. 1764. [4] *Knatchbull Diary*, p. 76.

century the distinction appears to have been that the Committee of Supply raised money by the imposition of recognized taxes, whereas the Committee of Ways and Means was created for the purpose of devising new ways of raising money. When the House of Commons won the exclusive right of levying taxation, the authorization of expenditure became clearly distinguished from the imposition of taxation. The function of the Committee of Supply then came to be the voting of estimates, that of the Committee of Ways and Means to raise money by taxation to cover the amounts voted in the Committee of Supply: until the institution of the Consolidated Fund in 1787 the proceeds of each tax were directly assigned to particular services.

The custom had developed for the two Committees to meet on Mondays, Wednesdays and Fridays. During the greater part of the session one or both were usually ordered for each such day. This was a procedural precaution, and the Committees met only as financial business required or other business of the House permitted. Administration was not always able to obtain priority even for taxation. In 1780, when illness prevented Lord North from introducing some new taxes on 9 March, the insistence of opposition members on consideration of the bills already allocated to the next two sitting days meant the postponement of the financial measures until 15 March.[1] They were not standing or permanent Committees, and always adjourned from day to day, the Chairman on each report asking the House for leave to sit again.[2] Even if he neglected to do so, any other member could move for a Committee of Supply.[3] In practice both Committees sat at the discretion of ministers, and they were closed for the session with the completion of Treasury business: indeed, Lord Barrington in 1771 described this step as 'the signal that the session is at an end.'[4]

The two posts of Chairman of the Committee of Supply and Chairman of the Committee of Ways and Means had already become a recognized position, held together and permanently

---

[1] Almon, *Parl. Reg.*, XVII, 280–1, 294. *Commons Journals*, XXXVII, 713, 717, 724.
[2] Harris Diary, 12 Apr. 1764.   [3] *Knatchbull Diary*, p. 68.
[4] B.M. Eg. MSS. 230, p. 196.

until the incumbent died, resigned, or lost his Parliamentary
seat. The holder also took the Chair in the Committee stages
of the subsequent financial legislation. The arduous nature of
the duties of the 'money chair', as the Duke of Newcastle
called it in 1761, was recognized by an unofficial salary of
£500 a year from the secret service fund; this was being paid
from at least the seventeen-fifties, and perhaps much earlier.
In 1777 Jeremy Bentham believed that it had risen to £800, and
that a sinecure at the Customs or Excise Boards was 'the usual
retreat for a superannuated Chairman'.[1] The post, like the
Speakership, was filled by a nominee of the ministry in office
at the time of a vacancy. Only one contested election is known,
on 15 February 1765 to replace the deceased Marshe Dickinson.
Administration nominated John Paterson and opposition
Charles Whitworth, 'both good men' in the opinion of James
Harris. Paterson was chosen by 165 votes to 84; but he lost
his seat in 1768, and Whitworth became Chairman for the
next decade.[2]

Both Committees had always to be Committees of the Whole
House, under a standing order of 29 March 1707, 'that this
House will not proceed upon any petition, motion, or bill, for
granting any money, or for releasing or compounding any
sum of money owing to the Crown, but in a Committee of the
Whole House'.[3] Speaker Compton therefore intervened on
16 February 1727 after a motion for a private Committee to
consider a petition from the commissioners for the duties on
hawkers and pedlars, that asked permission to compound
debts left by their defaulting cashier: the Speaker insisted that
under the standing order of 1707 it was a matter for a Committee of the Whole House.[4] A Committee of the Whole House,
however, did not prove a satisfactory method of detailed
scrutiny of government estimates: and the period of Sir
Robert Walpole's ministry saw three unsuccessful attempts by
opposition members to return to the former practice of small
Committees. Daniel Pulteney proposed on 16 April 1729 that

---

[1] See the biographies of the Chairmen 1754–90 in Namier and Brooke, *The House of Commons 1754–1790*, where they are listed, I, 537. *Bentham Correspondence*, II, 11–12.
[2] *Harris Diary*, 15 Feb. 1765.   [3] *Commons Journals*, XV, 367.
[4] *Knatchbull Diary*, pp. 63–4.

the Civil List account should be referred to a private Committee instead of the Committee of Supply, but his motion was defeated by 181 votes to 106.[1] On 23 January 1730 Samuel Sandys moved to have the navy estimates referred to a Select Committee instead of the Committee of Supply, a proposal defeated by 230 votes to 122 after opposition members had contended that 'as the business of a House of Commons was to look narrowly into the demands of the Ministers, the only way was to have a select committee as the old way: it was answered there could be no fruit of such a committee any more than a Committee of Supply, and this having been the usual way for 40 years, why go out of it.'[2] Six years later a proposal that the navy estimates should be referred to a Select Committee was again made, by William Pulteney on 28 January 1736. He argued the case for returning to the old practice of a detailed scrutiny of each item, but his motion failed by 256 votes to 155.[3] No later attempt was made to change the decision of 1707.

After the formal resolution of principle in the Committee of Supply that a supply should be granted, it was customary for one day each to be devoted in turn to such important matters as the navy or army estimates: precedence was invariably accorded to the naval supply. Each supply would be moved by an appropriate office-holder. The naval supply was always proposed by the First Lord of the Admiralty or, if he was a peer, by the next senior Lord of the Admiralty: John Buller performed this task under Lord Sandwich in nine successive sessions until his promotion to another office in 1780. Army estimates were moved by the Secretary at War, the Paymaster of the Forces, or his Deputy: and Ordnance estimates by one of the officials of that department. Some members believed that navy and army officers should not take part in the discussion of their own service estimates; diarist Knatchbull thought in 1730 that General Ross spoke 'very improperly, being an officer where the troops were concerned':[4] but such officers were speaking frequently in appropriate supply debates by the second half of the century.

[1] *Knatchbull Diary*, pp. 94–5.   [2] *Knatchbull Diary*, pp. 99–100.
[3] Chandler, *Debates*, IX, 121–30.   [4] *Knatchbull Diary*, p. 102.

The rule that any member could speak as often as he liked in debates in Committee was intended to allow detailed examination of any proposals: but this theory was greatly abused in practice. The Committee of Supply on the Ordnance on 11 February 1784 was described by a reporter as 'a most tedious conversation, in which the same members, availing themselves of the privilege of Committees, were up ten times'.[1] Similar complaints could have been made about many debates in the Committee of Supply: for, by convention, they were not restricted to discussion of the motion for a specific sum of money. Hume Campbell was privately informed by Speaker Onslow in 1755 'that everything might be said there with impunity'.[2] Certainly it is evident that Supply debates were often concerned with general issues rather than matters of detail, even though direct questions to officials also became a characteristic feature of the Committee. During the Committee of Supply of 7 December 1770 on the army Colonel Barré commented on the contemporary practice: 'This, I presume, is a day of conversation, as no one is inclined to give serious opposition: but everybody will agree that it is right there should be a conversation, and that that conversation should be extremely liberal.'[3] Lord North stated in the Supply debate on the navy on 29 January 1772 that 'the consideration of this day may very properly and very Parliamentarily take a course wide from the immediate question upon your table.'[4] This is what happened on many occasions: the debate of 5 March 1763 on the army estimates, for example, was concerned with the National Debt; in that of 25 November 1768 the radical member William Beckford attacked the need for a standing army at all; and that of 24 January 1770 centred on the location of the army units.[5]

Motions made in the Committee of Supply were subject to certain rules. One obviously designed to curb expenditure was a resolution of 3 November 1675 that 'all lesser sums proposed must be first put.'[6] Moreover, if a motion specifying a certain

---

[1] Debrett, *Parl. Reg.*, XIII, 107.   [2] H. Walpole, *George II*, II, 125–6.
[3] B.M. Eg. MSS. 223, p. 204.   [4] B.M. Eg. MSS. 232, p. 30.
[5] Harris Diary, 5 Mar. 1763. B.M. Eg. MSS. 215, pp. 245–7; 3711, pp. 100–6.
[6] *Commons Journals*, IX, 367. For contemporary references to this rule see *Knatchbull Diary*, p. 1, and Hatsell, *Precedents*, II, 111.

amount of money for a particular purpose was unsuccessful, it was out of order for a smaller sum to be proposed instead: and so Jeremiah Dyson informed the Committee on 16 March 1764 that the defeat of a vote of £19,000 for London Bridge made impossible an alternative motion for £7,000.[1] In accordance with a rule applying to all Committees of the Whole House, no motion to be reported to the House could contain any opinion or reason for any sum voted. The report merely informed the House of the decision.[2] Since all grants had to originate in the Committee of Supply no resolutions could be altered on report by an addition. When William Hussey moved an amendment to this effect on 6 December 1781 Speaker Cornwall informed him that the correct procedure was to recommit the report.[3]

In the Committee of Ways and Means the entire task of proposing revenue measures fell on the Chancellor of the Exchequer, who was always a member of the House. If that post was vacant, as in the ministerial interregnum of 1757, taxes were proposed by one of the other Lords of the Treasury.[4] In this Committee, too, there was a customary order of proceeding; and the land tax, whenever Parliament met before Christmas, was usually voted before that recess. Proceedings were governed by a general rule that the total of taxes and other income voted by the Committee of Ways and Means should never exceed the total of expenses already approved by the Committee of Supply.[5] But this safeguard against executive abuse was sometimes disregarded: it was in vain on 7 March 1780 that David Hartley objected on this ground to a report of the Committee of Ways and Means. Lord North admitted that the rule was being broken, but urged the need to provide for the public service, and the report was accepted without a division.[6]

The highlight of the Committee of Ways and Means, and often of the whole session, was Budget Day. In 1777 John

---

[1] Harris Diary, 16 Mar. 1764.

[2] *H.M.C. Egmont Diary*, III, 106. This was the opinion of Speaker Onslow in 1740.

[3] Debrett, *Parl. Reg.*, V, 116.   [4] H. Walpole, *George II*, III, 11.

[5] Liverpool Tractate, p. 62. This was the opinion of Speaker Cornwall in 1782. Debrett, *Parl. Reg.*, VI, 308.

[6] Almon, *Parl. Reg.*, XVII, 224–5.

Wilkes gave the House this account of what happened on such an occasion: 'On that day, the minister submits to the House his state of the finances of this kingdom, an account of the various sums voted during the session, the ways and means he proposes of raising the supply, the certain and probable expenses of the year, the new taxes, and in general the revenues and sources of the empire.'[1] Many of the taxes would already have been voted by this date, for usually it was late in the session. The Chancellor of the Exchequer would then explain the whole balance of the national income and expenditure for the year, and propose the final taxes and perhaps any loans or other devices, such as lotteries, that were required to complete the revenue necessary to meet the expenses previously voted in the Committee of Supply. It was clearly essential that the total burden of the supplies should be known. Hence the denunciation by Edmund Burke in 1779 of Lord North's decision to proceed before such expenses as the army extraordinaries were known. 'To talk, or pretend, therefore, to open a budget, without having the whole of the debit and credit side of the account under the inspection of those who were to pass it, was improper, unprecedented, and delusive.' North commented that Burke was describing the usage customary in peacetime, and Burke retorted that no minister had departed from this practice until North himself had done so the previous year.[2]

The origin of this great Parliamentary occasion is obscure. No reference to Budget Day has been found for the first half of the century. The first contemporary use of any appropriate phrase was a note by Sir Dudley Ryder on 5 February 1753, 'Pelham opened the budget'[3]: but it is mere conjecture unsupported by direct evidence to suggest that the institution of an annual day of accounts may have been one of the financial reforms initiated by Henry Pelham. From the seventeen-fifties contemporary references occur frequently, and a general remark by Richard Rigby in 1769 implied that there had been a regular Budget Day since at least the time of Pelham's ministry.[4]

[1] Almon, *Parl. Reg.*, VIII, 5. [2] Almon, *Parl. Reg.*, XII, 4–5.
[3] Harrowby MSS., doc. 21, 5 Feb. 1753.
[4] *Bedford Papers*, III, 408.

Ambiguity of reference arose from the novelty of the practice. 'The opening of the budget' was a phrase used sometimes to denote only the beginning of the Committee of Ways and Means: and the confusion is heightened by the custom of some Chancellors of the Exchequer of then giving members a broad indication of their future proposals.[1] The actual Budget Day might afterwards be described as 'closing the budget',[2] although 'opening the budget' was the usual phrase for the occasion. The lack of consistency in contemporary terminology is shown by the statement of a reporter that Lord John Cavendish 'moved the Budget' on 22 May 1782, when he was merely proposing some taxes additional to those already raised that session by his predecessor Lord North.[3]

A temporary departure from the custom of a single Budget Day arose out of the financial problems of the War of American Independence. In 1778 Lord North adopted the expedient of dividing the budget into two days. On 6 March, 'the day for opening the budget', he proposed only the loan for that year, leaving the new taxes for 9 March.[4] He continued this practice for the last four years of his ministry, and Lord John Cavendish did the same in 1783.[5]

Budget Day, Horace Walpole commented with reference to 1765, was 'an occasion that generally produces applause to the Head of the Treasury, who must possess more lights on that subject than other men'.[6] In 1774 opposition member Isaac Barré ruefully remarked beforehand, 'That day is marked as the triumph of the Minister. It is looked upon not only as unfashionable, but foolish to get up and dispute what is in the Budget.'[7] John Wilkes in 1777 referred to 'the important day towards the close of session, which is regarded as the day of his triumph, and called the opening of his budget'.[8] It may have been George Grenville who began the practice of a lengthy exposition of the state of the nation's finances: his

---

[1] See, for example, Harris Diary, 14 Dec. 1761.
[2] Newdigate Diary, 19 Mar. 1762.
[3] Debrett, *Parl. Reg.*, VII, 191.
[4] H. Walpole, *Last Journals*, II, 128. Almon, *Parl. Reg.*, IX, 1–7.
[5] Harris Diary, 24 Feb. and 1 Mar. 1779. Almon, *Parl. Reg.*, XVII, 200, 280. Debrett, *Parl. Reg.*, II, 179, 240–1; VI, 412; IX, 608.
[6] H. Walpole, *George III*, II, 61–2.
[7] B.M. Eg. MSS. 257, p. 291.   [8] Almon, *Parl. Reg.*, VIII, 5.

budget speeches of 1764 and 1765 were timed respectively as two and three-quarter hours and two and a quarter hours.[1] Lord North continued this custom, his speeches averaging about two hours. Financial ability as well as superior knowledge combined to make Budget Day a satisfying occasion for men like Grenville and North. Nathaniel Wraxall, who heard North's last two budget speeches, left this judgment: 'In opening the Budget, he was esteemed peculiarly lucid, clear and able. On that Account it constituted a Day of Triumph to his Friends and Supporters . . . But Lord North could sustain no comparison with the late Mr. Pitt.'[2]

Resolutions of the two Committees of Supply and Ways and Means were internal decisions of the House that had to be subsequently converted into legislation. A succession of supply bills enacted the resolutions of the Committee of Ways and Means for taxes and duties. Since only a Committee of the Whole House could vote money, the detailed clauses in these bills were left blank until the Committee stage. It was out of order for a supply bill to be introduced with 'blanks or summs filled up': when this happened in 1691 the bill was ordered to lie on the Table and a new one was brought in.[3] Similarly, at the report stage of a supply bill, there could be no amendment to add further duties or taxes. Such a proposal in 1693 was 'opposed as irregular, because in the house which have no power to raise money: ought to come from a Committee of the whole house'. It was quite in order, however, for the House to reject any tax in a supply bill.[4]

This financial legislation was related to the resolutions of the Committee of Supply either by appropriation clauses or by the last supply bill of the session—in the form that, for example, 'there may be issued a sum not exceeding so much towards the naval service hereinafter mentioned . . . and after all the particulars are specified, it concludes with enacting that the said supply shall not be applied to any use whatsoever other than the uses before mentioned.'[5]

---

[1] Harris Diary, 9 Mar. 1764 and 27 Mar. 1765.
[2] Wraxall, *Memoirs*, II, 137–8.
[3] Luttrell Diary, I, fo. 59. *Commons Journals*, X, 558–9.
[4] Luttrell Diary, II, fo. 371.
[5] Harrowby MSS., doc. 21, a note by Sir Dudley Ryder in 1744.

All this elaborate procedure of estimates and detailed appropriation was largely a matter of Parliamentary form. The House of Commons had little control over government expenditure, especially in wartime. The 'extraordinaries' voted for the army or navy had usually been spent beforehand; and even the specific appropriation of sums of money for particular purposes was often ignored. This was openly admitted in the House in 1778. In a Committee of Supply on the navy on 13 February Temple Luttrell complained that money voted to repair several named ships had not been spent on them. One of the Lords of the Admiralty, Lord Mulgrave, agreed that this was so, 'but said the money was applied to other naval purposes ... that the estimate was the usual mode of raising money, but never meant to state the purposes the money was to be applied to; that if it was a crime, it was one that had been often practised ever since the reign of James II'. Edmund Burke rose in anger, 'expressed his astonishment at what the Admiralty had dared to acknowledge: and in the warmth of his indignation, threw the book of estimates at the Treasury Bench; which, taking the candle in its way, had nearly struck Mr. Ellis's shins; Mr. Burke exclaiming, that it was treating the House with the utmost contempt, to present them with a fine gilt book of estimates, calculated to a farthing, for purposes to which the money granted was never meant to be applied.' This was a mock Parliamentary storm. Burke's attack on the first public avowal of what many members must have already known as the customary practice evoked no response in the House.[1]

The traditional strategy of the House of Commons, a demand for the redress of grievances before the grant of money to the sovereign, had now been outmoded by constitutional and political developments. Opposition was never made to the formal principle of giving supply, except by hot-headed members. On 17 November 1742 Jacobite John Philipps, entirely on his own initiative, raised the old constitutional cry by demanding that a Committee on the State of the Nation should meet, on 17 January next, before any Committee of

---

[1] Almon, *Parl. Reg.*, VIII, 373–4.

Supply. The House rejected the motion, both the suggestion and the delay being quite impractical.[1] Even more eccentric was the action of radical John Sawbridge in the Committee of Supply on 30 October 1775. He then rose to oppose the formal motion by Secretary of the Treasury Sir Grey Cooper that a supply be granted. Sawbridge's contention was that the ministers were too 'weak and wicked' to be trusted with any money, a view that received no support.[2] Responsible politicians knew that no opposition could behave in this way. The tactics of Charles James Fox against the minority Pitt administration in early 1784 were merely to delay taxes, not to refuse them. Public avowal of the strategy may have helped to defeat its purpose, but Fox had no alternative. The House could no longer use against the King's government the age-old weapon of denying supply.

Opposition over finance was therefore confined to points of detail. In the Committee of Supply particular items of proposed expenditure might arouse criticism, and an administration sometimes deemed it wise to allow a reduction in estimates: on 1 February 1727 the Ordnance estimate was cut by £23,000.[3] Opposition often occurred on army estimates, for it was with reluctance that the House came to accept a permanent army. The hire of foreign soldiers was almost certain to incur opposition, and the votes for Hanoverian troops were a regular cause of political controversy under the first two Georges. But by the reign of George III no serious opposition on supply was expected: and a division of 223 votes to 130 in February 1778 brought this comment from a reporter: 'So large a minority upon a question of supply was thought extraordinary, it having been commonly observed, that questions of supply are usually carried unanimously, or but weakly resisted.'[4]

Opposition was more common in the Committee of Ways and Means. Taxes new or old were often liable to arouse contention. For much of the century the land tax was the centre of taxation disputes: but divisions were infrequent, and only once did opposition defeat administration on the issue. This famous occasion was on 27 February 1767, when a motion to reduce the tax from 4s. to 3s. was carried by 206

---

[1] N.L.W. MSS. 1352, fos. 128–9. [2] Almon, *Parl. Reg.*, III, 77.
[3] *Knatchbull Diary*, p. 61. [4] Almon, *Parl. Reg.*, VIII, 347.

votes to 188.[1] Taxes on articles of popular consumption were often the subject of Parliamentary opposition, but only one occasion has been found when a minister suffered the inconvenience of defeat: sectional interest caused Henry Pelham to lose his sugar tax on 20 February 1744.[2] Otherwise ministers carried even unpopular taxes. Dashwood's cider tax of 1763 survived three divisions in Committee, and also one on the subsequent supply bill.[3] Dowdeswell's window tax of 1766 was carried by 162 votes to 112 on Budget Day, and by 179 to 114 on the report.[4] Opposition to taxation merely to harass ministers, to men rather than measures, was rare and unsuccessful, and usually occurred in Lord North's administration. On 22 March 1780 an attempt to postpone until 7 April a report from the Committee of Ways and Means of new taxes was heavily defeated, and an opposition attempt on 7 March 1781 to omit the proposed lottery also failed.[5] A fleeting success came on 9 March 1778. After North had explained the taxes in his Budget speech, a motion by opposition member Thomas Gilbert to add a 25 per cent tax on all official salaries was carried by 100 votes to 82: but this snap victory was reversed on the report next day by a ministerial majority of six votes, 147 to 141.[6]

By the time of Lord North's ministry opportunities for opposition on finance were limited to the two Committees and the reports of their resolutions: for the eighteenth century saw the growth of a convention that the supply bills should not be opposed. This had not been so in the earlier part of the century:[7] but the last known division on a supply bill occurred on 17 March 1763 over a motion appointing a time for the second reading of the Cider Bill. In 1779 Colonel Barré remarked during a debate 'that a doctrine has for years prevailed in this House, no matter whether well or ill-founded, that it is not orderly to oppose a money bill in any stage of its

---

[1] Other divisions took place in 1751 and 1770. Ward, *The English Land Tax in the Eighteenth Century*, pp. 66–85.

[2] Cobbett, *Parl. Hist.*, XIII, 652–5.

[3] Harris Diary, 7 to 17 Mar. 1763.

[4] Harris Diary, 18 and 21 Apr. 1766.

[5] Almon, *Parl. Reg.*, XVII, 415. Debrett, *Parl. Reg.*, II, 201.

[6] Almon, *Parl. Reg.*, IX, 1–7.

[7] A. S. Foord, *His Majesty's Opposition*, pp. 99, 176, 296.

progress; and that the forms of proceeding of this House bind, or affect to bind every member, to urge whatever he has to offer in the committee, or on the report'.[1]

The elaborate procedure of raising money had been devised as a check upon the executive, and the Parliamentary forms were strictly observed, even though they failed to ensure either any detailed scrutiny of the estimates or any exact appropriation of the money voted. Opposition members were quick to attack any apparent breach. William Pulteney on 2 March 1732 objected to the insertion of a clause in a Salt Tax Bill for a tax on salted white herring, since there had been no resolution to this effect. Sir Robert Walpole answered that the duty was covered by the general resolution in the Committee of Ways and Means, and members accepted this interpretation: but none disagreed with the principle asserted by Sir William Wyndham. 'The ancient Orders of this House ought most punctually to be observed. Some of them may perhaps seem to be of little consequence. But if we fall into a way of breaking through them upon slight occasions we shall soon fall into confusion: then indeed we may probably discover, that those orders which we now think to be trivial, were of the utmost consequence; but then it will be too late.'[2] In 1733 one opposition objection to the Excise Bill was that it affected existing financial legislation, 'which is irregular, and if the forms in passing or repealing Money Bills, or in altering them, is not observed, there is an end of Parliaments'. Attorney-General Sir Philip Yorke denied that there had been any such infringement, agreeing that 'forms in passing Money Bills are sacred'.[3]

Although the House was agreed on the principle of proper procedural safeguards in finance, two important exceptions did exist in practice, arising from respect for the Crown and from the pretext of national emergency. Messages from the sovereign informing the Commons that there was a debt on his Civil List account opened a breach in the strict form of Parliamentary control of finance. They were always referred at once to the Committee of Supply, as in 1725, 1729, 1769 and 1777: and the opposition demand for a prior inquiry into the accounts,

[1] Almon, *Parl. Reg.*, XIII, 221–2.   [2] Chandler, *Debates*, VII, 222–34.
[3] *H.M.C. Egmont Diary*, I, 347.

as being more Parliamentary, was never conceded.[1] The other loophole was the device of votes of credit. The first instance occurred on 8 April 1717, in a Committee of the Whole House to consider the King's request for a supply to take precautions against a possible Swedish attack. Opposition spokesmen urged that 'it was unparliamentary to grant a supply before the occasion was known, and an estimate of the expence was laid before the House'. Widespread concern among members at the innovation was reflected in the small size of the administration majorities, fifteen votes in the Committee and four on the report.[2] When another royal message for an extraordinary supply came before the House on 24 March 1726, Shippen unsuccessfully moved for an account of the £250,000 granted in 1717.[3] Votes of credit soon became common, and in 1730 Walpole's ministry sought to gain support by the mere announcement that none would be requested that session.[4] As early as 1728 Samuel Sandys had to remind the House that there had been no precedents for them before the previous decade. Walpole then explained why the practice had begun at that time: 'Money given without account is no new thing, for in King William's reign it was all given, even the whole year's supply, till in 1696 the custom of appropriation came in . . . That in succeeding times all our supplies being appropriated, and no provision made for contingencies and sudden occasions, Parliament thought it more expedient to give a vote of credit to be paid the following year than to open again the Committee of Supply'.[5] The innovation had been due to emergency needs, and was soon routine practice in times of war and crisis: a vote of credit on 24 February 1744 was opposed by only one M.P., Sir John Philipps.[6]

The constitutional objection to votes of credit was not only that money was being granted without estimates, but also that they had to be for an unspecified amount. On 26 March 1726 Speaker Compton explained to the House that though it was unparliamentary to vote a limited sum without an estimate

---

[1] *Knatchbull Diary*, pp. 42, 94–5. B.M. Eg. MSS. 218, pp. 181–225. Almon, *Parl. Reg.*, VII, 55–95.
[2] Chandler, *Debates*, VI, 117–20. [3] Chandler, *Debates*, VI, 369–70.
[4] *H.M.C. Egmont Diary*, I, 98. [5] *Knatchbull Diary*, pp. 126–7.
[6] N.L.W. MSS. 1352, fos. 215–17.

an unlimited one might be so voted, 'which is odd', commented diarist Knatchbull.[1] Similarly, no sum could be mentioned in any motion asking the King to authorize the payment of money for any purpose in advance of an Act of Parliament. In 1732 Speaker Onslow therefore altered a motion, before its introduction, for an Address intending to request George II to give a sum not exceeding £10,000 to assist emigration to Carolina: 'it was contrary to form and order that the House in their address should mention a sum to his Majesty, which ought to be left to him'.[2]

The development of votes of credit is a reminder that the safeguards against the extravagant or unwise use of money for private or public purposes had been devised by the House itself, and might be disregarded by the majority opinion in the House at any time. Customary modes of proceeding could be bypassed, and standing orders suspended. The power of a ministry to ignore rules and precedents was shown on 3 June 1766. On receipt of a message from George III about the forthcoming marriage of his sister Princess Caroline Matilda to the King of Denmark, the Rockingham administration introduced a motion 'to assure his Majesty, that this House will enable His Majesty to give ... a Portion with Her Royal Highness'. Jeremiah Dyson objected that this prompt promise was contrary to Parliamentary rules of procedure, citing the resolution of 18 February 1668 that laid down that any motion for public expenditure must be referred to a Committee of the Whole House, and that no immediate decision could be made. An opposition amendment was proposed, to substitute the words 'to enter into the immediate consideration of this important affair'. This copied exactly a resolution of the House on 8 May 1733 concerning the marriage of the Princess Royal, but the original motion was carried by 118 votes to 35.[3] This incident occurred in a thin House near the end of a session on a formal matter of little importance: no member opposed the principle of that supply. Its only significance is to underline a characteristic feature of the contemporary constitution. The

---

[1] *Knatchbull Diary*, p. 57.   [2] *H.M.C. Egmont Diary*, I, 273.
[3] *Commons Journals*, XXII, 142; XXX, 842. Fortescue, *Corr. of George III*, I, p. 353.

real check on the power of administration in the field of finance did not lie in procedural formalities: it arose from the practical concern of ministers for the pride and self-respect of the House that politicians would flout at their peril. For the great majority of members subscribed to the doctrine laid down by opposition spokesman Thomas Townshend in a debate of 22 May 1777 on army extraordinary estimates: 'It was one of the prime privileges of that House, and became an essential part of its duty, as connected with the power of granting money, to watch the minister in the disposal of it, and check its expenditure. It was a part of their business in that House, and the leading object of their assembling, to call the minister to an account for the treasure committed to his charge.'[1]

[1] Almon, *Parl. Reg.*, VII, 219.

5

THE ARRANGEMENT OF BUSINESS

DURING the eighteenth century the Parliamentary session became longer and more formalized. In the early part of the Hanoverian period Parliament usually sat only during the first few months of each year. Sixteen of the twenty-three sessions between 1717 and 1739 began after Christmas.[1] This practice virtually ended with the onset of a long era of wars and uneasy peace. Only six subsequent sessions began after the start of the year.[2] In theory the summoning of Parliament before Christmas remained an unusual expedient, at least in times of peace, and until well into the reign of George III the King's Speech would contain a formal apology for such 'early' meetings. Yet by the period of the War of American Independence an autumn meeting had become so customary that in the debate of 27 November 1781 on the Address, opposition member Isaac Barré complained that postponement of the start of the session to that late date was a ministerial device to dissuade members from coming to town before Christmas.[3]

For most of the century the annual session therefore lasted from the last quarter of one year to the second quarter of the next, usually from November to May. The session was divided into three periods, by adjournments for four or five weeks at Christmas and for about ten days at Easter, a custom deplored as 'modern practice' by Speaker Onslow in 1759.[4] The duration of each session lay within the discretion of the ministry, which had to balance the requirements of official business against a politic reluctance to detain independent members in town longer than was necessary. This perennial dilemma was shown by an incident in a debate of 17 March 1773. Lord North,

---

[1] The session beginning in March 1715 lasted until June 1716. There were short extra sessions in the summers of 1721 and 1727.

[2] 1751, 1753, 1765, 1770, 1772, and 1774.

[3] Debrett, *Parl. Reg.*, V, 42.   [4] Burnet, *History*, VI, 214N.

aware of East India Company business ahead, chanced to remark that the session would be almost at an end in three months. 'Here some of the country gentlemen showing a dislike of this piece of information, his lordship corrected himself by saying two months.'[1] North's concession was purely verbal, for the House was not prorogued until 1 July. Administration had to consider not only official business but also the anxiety of individual members about their own private and public legislation, much of which was left uncompleted at the end of each session. The expeditious conduct of such matters was one task of the Speaker. Sir Fletcher Norton in March 1770 boasted that he 'had taken more than ordinary pains to get the private bills forward'.[2] George II learnt of this role of the Speaker in 1731 when pressing Walpole to end the session by 28 April.

Sir Robert replying it was impossible, the King asked why. Because, answered Sir Robert, of the quantity of business before them. "I know of none", replied the King, "what is it?" "I cannot tell your Majesty all", replied Sir Robert, "but I will ask our Governor" (meaning the Speaker). Whereupon the King replied. "Governor! I thought you was Governor." Sir Robert finding the King so earnest, told his Majesty the House of Commons should be up by the time he desired.[3]

Each session also nominally included a few days during the summer and autumn, for Parliament was rarely prorogued more than two months at a time. The meeting on such days was a complete formality. The rule requiring the presence of a quorum, being established by the members of the House only as a restraint on their own conduct, did not extend to occasions when Black Rod knocked on the door with a message from the King.[4] There was no need for a single member to be present. The *Journal* for 4 October 1771 records, 'The House being met ... and Mr. Speaker being in the country, ... the House, with the Clerk Assistant, went up to the House of Peers': but the Clerk, John Hatsell, remarked in a letter to a friend that not one member had been there.[5]

---

[1] *The Gazetteer*, 19 Mar. 1773.
[2] Malmesbury MSS., Memo. of 17 Mar. 1770.
[3] *H.M.C. Egmont Diary*, I, 176. Parliament was prorogued on 7 May.
[4] Hatsell, *Precedents*, II, 176.
[5] *Commons Journals*, XXXIII, 406. Ley MSS., 7 Oct. 1771.

When Parliament was in session, the House of Commons normally sat from Monday to Friday. After late sittings it often adjourned over the following day. The criterion for this step was usually the continuation of a debate after midnight: in the debate of 9 March 1772 Speaker Norton, as a matter of course, reminded the House that 'we, having been got upon a new day, adjourn over that day.'[1] From the outbreak of the War of American Independence, however, the House no longer adjourned over the next day merely because of a midnight sitting.

The normal pattern of a five day week was also broken by observance of certain formal occasions. After George I's reign Parliament did not sit on the birthday of the sovereign, nor on that of George III's mother, 30 November, until her death in 1772. Parliament also respected the anniversary of two historic events, 30 May for the restoration of the monarchy in 1660, and 30 January for what Horace Walpole described as 'the commemoration of what is ridiculously termed King Charles's Martyrdom'. Walpole's dislike of the act enforcing this day of mourning was shared by many contemporaries. Henry Fox in 1755 and Lord Strange in 1763 both moved that the House should sit on that day, and Frederick Montagu proposed the repeal of the act on 2 March 1772: all the protests were unsuccessful.[2]

The weekend adjournment became customary under George II. The House never met on Sunday during the century, except for the taking of oaths on the death of a sovereign in 1714 and 1760.[3] The period of the Walpole administration gave rise to the permanent habit of adjourning also over Saturday. Speaker Onslow recalled the reason in 1759: 'this ... was begun by Sir Robert Walpole for the sake of his hunting, and was then much complained of, but now every body is for it.'[4] The invention of the 'five day week' was not the least of Walpole's contributions to the betterment of humanity! This custom did not begin with the precision suggested by John Hatsell 'in about 1732';[5] but it had become usual by the middle of the century.

---

[1] B.M. Eg. MSS. 235, p. 226. For the number of times this happened see *infra*, pp. 164–5.
[2] H. Walpole, *George II*, II, 3; *George III*, I, 190; *Last Journals*, I, 39–40.
[3] Hatsell, *Precedents*, II, 113N.   [4] Burnet, *History*, VI, 214N.
[5] Hatsell, *Precedents*, II, 209N.

The House did still meet on a few Saturdays each session. Sometimes this was accidental: Saturday was still technically a day of business, and a simple unqualified motion to adjourn on a Friday could result in an unintentional Saturday sitting.[1] When such meetings were deliberate the *Journals* show that Saturdays were used only for private business, such as the receiving of petitions, and for formal transactions, especially those connected with the passage of routine financial measures. Often it was difficult to procure the attendance of the forty members required for a quorum. On 15 January 1774 'the patience of the Speaker was exhausted before a sufficient number of members could be collected to constitute a House. His Majesty's answer to the Address was reported, and the House broke up.'[2] No other attempt at a Saturday meeting was made that session! Since Saturday was not a day for important business, the motion by George Onslow of the Treasury Board on Friday, 14 April 1769, that the poll in the fourth Middlesex election of John Wilkes should be taken into consideration on the following day met with protests. 'The Opposition opposed Saturday, as contrary to the custom of Parliament, which never did any thing of consequence on that day; that Saturday was dedicated to other business, or pleasure.'[3] William Beckford complained, 'It has been the usage of Parliament not to sit upon Saturday . . . Sitting on a Saturday is only usual in carrying on matters of form.'[4] The ministry nevertheless insisted on the point, and Colonel Luttrell was voted the seat on the next day.

Although the average session comprised under a hundred days, there is little evidence of any problem of insufficient time for business during most of the eighteenth century. On a considerable number of days the House found no business to detain it after four o'clock, and therefore broke up.[5] Sometimes on such occasions a member might take the opportunity of introducing unexpected business. On 31 January 1733 'the House having no immediate Business before them', Samuel Sandys stood up and, after remarking that 'the House seems

---

[1] See, for example, B.M. Add. MSS. 32955, fo. 360.
[2] *Gentleman's Magazine*, 1774, p. 244.
[3] Almon, *Debates*, VIII, 146. [4] B.M. Eg. MSS. 219, p. 214.
[5] The House always had to sit until four o'clock, for the swearing in of new members: see *infra*, p. 155.

at present to be at Leisure', he moved to bring up the Pension Bill defeated in the Lords the previous session.[1] The late sittings that did occur were the result of lengthy debates rather than the volume of actual business. Indeed, there was a strong feeling that the House should not proceed to important new business late in the day. On 18 May 1773 anticlimax came when General Burgoyne announced that he would not make his expected motion on the abuses of the East India Company, as members had already been fatigued with a preceding debate.[2] When on 15 April 1774 the House went into a Committee on American affairs, Governor Johnstone rose to protest that it was then seven o'clock, and too late to start important business. Other members called out 'Go on! Go on!', so Lord North made his motion for the introduction of the bill concerning the administration of justice in Massachusetts Bay.[3]

Towards the end of a session, however, congestion of business might occur. Difficulties were sometimes experienced in arranging time for all the legislation in progress. On 5 April 1769 Thomas Townshend spoke against the committal of a Westminster Paving Bill, on the ground that it was then too late in the session to find time to pass the bill.[4] Lord Folkestone on 13 May 1774 opposed a motion to postpone the Copyright Bill, for the same reason. 'We have at present an open day, and we know by experience the difficulty of finding one at this time, for we sat, I believe, last night a full hour and a half on this very question.'[5] His allusion was to a debate on fixing the date of a Committee on the linen trade.[6] On 16 May allegations were made in the House that the opponents of this Copyright Bill were deliberately trying to postpone the various stages of the bill so that it would 'fall by delay'.[7]

Despite the inconvenience that individual items of legislation were lost through sheer lack of time, the only formal restriction on the amount of business that could come before the House was in the field of private legislation. Early in every session a resolution was passed that the House would receive no petitions for private bills after a certain day, usually in February or

---

[1] Chandler, *Debates*, VII, 260–1.   [2] B.M. Eg. MSS. 246, pp. 291–3.
[3] B.M. Eg. MSS. 255, p. 107 (shorthand).   [4] B.M. Eg. MSS. 219, p. 140.
[5] See my 'Debates of the House of Commons 1768–1774' (Ph.D. thesis. Univ. of London. 1958), p. 96.
[6] B.M. Eg. MSS. 257, pp. 279–86.   [7] B.M. Eg. MSS. 259, pp. 81–2.

early March, and often a Saturday. This precaution was obviously intended to reduce the congestion late in the session. The *Journals* show a rush of petitions just before the closing date in each year, many being received on the last day itself. On 7 February 1782 it took three hours for the Clerks, 'one relieving the other', to read through all the petitions.[1] This order was disregarded 'very rarely and in cases of absolute necessity'.[2] A petition for a Durham Yard Lottery Bill was accepted as late as 24 May 1773 on this pretext, and the bill was passed that session.

Members were not yet prepared to accept the need for any rigid timetable, and business was seldom arranged more than a few days in advance. Lord North was clearly announcing an unusual pressure of business when he said on 27 April 1780 that 'there was no open day for a week to come'.[3] Dates were claimed for individual items of business either officially by Orders of the Day, or informally by notice of motions. Orders of the Day were usually confined to public business, but any Parliamentary activity might form an Order. Orders could only be made for business that had already obtained the approval of the House, such as Committees and bills. It was customary for Orders to be made to assign the various stages of legislation to particular days: a time was always appointed for the second reading of important or opposed bills; Orders were often made for the Committee and Report stages, and for the third reading of bills that were still disputed.[4]

Orders were made for virtually every day that the House met. The sequence for a particular day was apparently that of their chronological seniority of appointment for the day. This was irrelevant to the relative importance of or interest in the various items of business, and the custom tended to give automatic preference to routine items of business. The sequence was therefore often altered to suit the occasion, as on 7 March 1783, when the House decided to postpone the first Order, for a Committee of Supply on the Ordnance, in favour of the second Order, the more urgent matter of a Committee on the American Trade Bill.[5] The order of Orders could itself become a subject

[1] Debrett, *Parl. Reg.*, V, 406.   [2] *Liverpool Tractate*, p. 33.
[3] Almon, *Parl. Reg.*, XVII, 588.   [4] *Liverpool Tractate*, pp. 6–7, 11, 16.
[5] Debrett, *Parl. Reg.*, IX, 429–31.

of debate between individual members or between government and opposition: it was after a division, and by 204 votes to 143, that the House decided on 9 March 1730 to read the last Order fixed for that day in place of the first one.[1] In this way ministers could obtain priority for their business over matters previously arranged by other members, but they needed to exercise their power with discretion: usually the methods available to all members were sufficient for the Parliamentary management of government business.

Items of business were frequently ordered for the morning or for particular hours. This was not interpreted literally. The intention was that the matter should be the first business on that day.[2] If such an Order had been made, the business could not be commenced before the appointed time even though the House might have nothing else to do. On 22 January 1762 the members remained idle for half an hour before four o'clock, the time appointed for consideration of the Lichfield election.[3] Moreover, this tactic could secure only moral priority, since the determination of preferences between different Orders on a particular day lay entirely with the House.[4] On 21 February 1774 William Graves made an attempt to ensure that the second reading of his bill to prevent vexatious removals of the poor would be the first business on 2 March, by an Order that it should be read at twelve o'clock, for the second reading had been postponed four times since 3 February. His move did secure a second reading for the bill on 2 March, but only as the last business of the day.[5]

When, as often happened, there was not time to proceed on all the Orders for a particular day, this was usually because one or more debates arose, rather than because of the mere volume of business: on 1 April 1765 the House was able to dispose of 'no less than ten orders of the day, and many of great consequence'.[6] Henry Seymour vainly objected on 19 May 1773 to a motion ordering East India Company business for 21 May, because an Order had already been made for the report on that day of the Committee on a Selby Canal Petition.[7] As he

[1] *Knatchbull Diary*, pp. 111–2.   [2] See *infra*, p. 158.
[3] Harris Diary, 22 Jan. 1762.   [4] B.M. Eg. MSS. 227, pp. 1–2.
[5] *Commons Journals*, XXXIV, 416, 424–5, 446, 465, 471–2, 527. *St. James' Chronicle*, 22 Feb. 1774.
[6] Harris Diary, 1 Apr. 1765.   [7] B.M. Eg. MSS. 247, p. 117.

had feared the report was postponed, by the great debate on Lord Clive, until 24 May.[1] Even important legislation introduced by the administration was liable to this delay. When on 24 March 1774 a debate developed over the Copyright Bill, Lord North informed the House that the third reading of the Boston Port Bill, ordered for that day, would be postponed to the next day.[2]

No new business could be introduced after the House had begun to read the Orders of the Day, until all the Orders had been disposed of. On 20 January 1741 a petition from the Georgia trustees for money could not be presented because Sir Robert Walpole, who was to announce George II's consent to the proposal, did not arrive at the House until after the Order of the Day had been called for.[3] The rule explains the great anxiety on 25 February 1757 of Horace Walpole, who was seeking to save Admiral John Byng from the courtmartial death sentence consequent on his failure to save Minorca. Walpole, temporarily out of the Commons when changing constituencies, was unable himself to move for a bill to permit Captain Augustus Keppel to give evidence to Parliament by absolution from his court-martial oath. 'The time passed, the Speaker was going to put the question for the Orders of the Day, after which no new motion can be made.' Walpole therefore persuaded Sir Francis Dashwood to interrupt Speaker Onslow and raise the matter, an action which resulted in the introduction of the proposed bill, and the postponement of Byng's execution.[4] Members desirous of proceeding to the Orders of the Day were apparently expected to give way to those with other business to propose. On 25 April 1780 a motion by Lord North for the first Order of the Day, for a Committee on the Grenada Trade Bill, was interrupted by Sir George Yonge on the ground that he had a motion to make. 'Sir G. Yonge could not give up his point, as he said, it was customary for motions to come before any order of the day.' The House supported 'the justness of this remark' and Yonge made his motion.[5]

---

[1] *Commons Journals*, XXXIV, 329. B.M. Eg. MSS. 248, pp. 1–375.
[2] B.M. Eg. MSS. 255, p. 17 (shorthand). *Commons Journals*, XXXIV, 591.
[3] *H.M.C. Egmont Diary*, III, 179.　　[4] H. Walpole, *George II,*, II, 328–32.
[5] Almon, *Parl. Reg.*, XVII, 567.

The opinion of members on the procedural point is quite clear: yet the *Journals* in the eighteenth century show that unordered business, both public and private, was frequently interposed between Orders of the Day. It is only possible to reconcile this evidence by a distinction between new business, forbidden once the Orders of the House had been begun, and other business already in progress or of which notice had been given: the simple alternative explanation is that the House did not always follow its own rule.[1] It was not until 1811 that Orders of the Day were accorded preference over motions for which advance notice had been given, and then only on Monday and Friday.[2]

When all the ordered business had been finished, any new motions could be made: but the leave of the House was necessary after two o'clock, a qualification now made invariable by the hours of business. Members were clearly expected to stay for the business appointed for the day, and the rule was intended to prevent motions being made afterwards by surprise in a thin House.[3] The *Journals* show that such leave was granted as a matter of course. Urgent matters were thus introduced after the ordered business of the day had been completed. George III feared that a debate on the third reading of the Ayr Bank Bill, ordered for 28 March 1774, would oblige Lord North to postpone the motion he intended that day for leave to introduce the Massachusetts Government Bill. The debate finished at half past six o'clock, and North was able to make his motion.[4]

Orders of the Day could not be made for individual motions on new business. It therefore became increasingly the practice for members to give advance notice in the House of motions that they intended to make.[5] This notice was sometimes given at the end of the day, but usually at the beginning of public business. The notice might be merely a general intimation that a particular motion or bill would be introduced:

---

[1] For most of such business there is no evidence as to whether or not notice had been given.

[2] *Commons Journals*, LXVI, 148.

[3] Hatsell, *Precedents*, II, 183–4. B.M. Eg. MSS. 259, p. 73.

[4] Fortescue, *Corr. of George III*, III, pp. 86–7.

[5] Notice of motions was also a tactic to secure the attendance of members. See *infra*, p. 118.

on 10 May 1773 Sir Edward Astley gave notice that in the next session he would move for a bill to make Grenville's Election Act permanent.[1] Usually, however, such notice took the form of an announcement by a member that he would make a motion on a stated day, although the subject might not be specified. The normal convention for the introduction of a new subject was to take the first open day, so as not to interfere with previously arranged business.[2] In the more leisurely sessions care was even taken to avoid a clash with other activities that might engage the attention of members. When Henry Fox moved on 22 March 1757 that the House should consider the papers on the case of Admiral Byng on 19 April, Sir Francis Dashwood mentioned the Newmarket race meeting. Fox pointed out that there were, in fact, two meetings, and a debate ensued on this topic during which a preference emerged for the date suggested by Fox.[3]

In general only one important item of business, likely to occasion a debate, would be arranged for any day. On Thursday, 17 February 1774, Sir Edward Astley announced that he proposed to make his long-heralded motion on the following Monday. Lord North thereupon rose to point out that the naval estimates were already fixed for that day.[4] On the next day Astley was one of three members who then gave notice of bills, announcing that his motion would be postponed to the following Friday: a fourth member, William Graves, moved to discharge one order for a bill and to make a new one for Monday, and Lord North reminded the House of the navy estimates on the same day.[5] Such preliminaries to the actual business of the day had become commonplace by the reign of George III.

The arrangement of important business might even be discussed on a date itself decided in advance. On 4 February 1771 Richard Sutton, as Under-Secretary to Lord Rochford, presented to the House papers relating to the Falkland Islands agreement with Spain. Lord North suggested that a day should be fixed for taking them in consideration, the occasion that would be the main debate on the treaty. Opposition member

[1] B.M. Eg. MSS. 246, pp. 104–5.　　　[2] B.M. Eg. MSS. 226, pp. 26–7.
[3] B.M. Add. MSS. 32870, fo. 309.　　[4] B.M. Eg. MSS. 252, pp. 72–4.
[5] *St. James' Chronicle*, 19 Feb. 1774.

Isaac Barré expressed the hope that the point would not be settled until the House was fuller, and administration speakers accepted this suggestion. Sir Gilbert Elliot remarked, 'A common way has been to let the papers lie upon the table, and some days after name a day for taking them into consideration.' Taking up this idea Lord Beauchamp announced, 'As it is usual to fix a day for taking into consideration the proper day for considering the papers, I rise to give notice that on Wednesday I shall move to fix that day sevennight.'[1]

Administration normally gave a few days' notice of official business. The task of arranging and announcing it usually devolved on the Leader of the House. In 1773 it was Lord North who gave notice on several occasions of motions concerning the East India Company, and on 17 May he outlined the proposed order of business on that subject.[2] Similarly, on 25 April 1774 North told the House of the timetable planned for the two Massachusetts bills, and on 29 April he informed members that there would be a Committee on the corn trade on Monday, 9 May, with the Budget on the following Monday.[3] On 8 December 1779 Barré asked North to outline to the House next day the Irish proposals he intended to move on 10 December, and North complied with this request.[4] Departmental business, however, was apparently arranged as well as introduced by the official concerned. When on 7 December 1770 Barré asked whether the ordnance estimate would come on that day after the army estimates, he was answered by General Conway as Lieutenant-General of Ordnance. Conway replied that although it was usual to refer the ordnance and vote it the same night, the matter would be postponed until Monday, 10 December, if the army estimate took up much time. Lord North then rose to say that in that case the consideration of the land tax, arranged for Monday, would be put off to the Wednesday.[5]

The practice of giving notice of motions led to the unparliamentary habit of informal discussion, a development soon

[1] B.M. Eg. MSS. 224, pp. 45–6.
[2] B.M. Eg. MSS. 244, pp. 147, 246; 245, pp. 185–6; 246, pp. 221–33.
[3] B.M. Eg. MSS. 256, pp. 10 (shorthand), 89.
[4] Almon, *Parl. Reg.*, XVI, 163–4, 168–9.
[5] B.M. Eg. MSS. 223, pp. 186–8.

deplored from the Chair. On 2 April 1778 Speaker Norton even criticized the whole practice of notice on this ground: 'if gentlemen will continue to converse when notice of a motion is known, he begged the House would revert back to the old rule, and not give any previous intimation, but accompany the notice with the motion itself.'[1] Speaker Cornwall reaffirmed the rule on 28 January 1782, when he declared that it was disorderly to debate merely on notice of a motion, as there was no question before the House.[2]

Notice of a motion by a member gave him the right to speak first: and so, in a discussion on 10 February 1784 over the arrangement of business for the next day, Lord Beauchamp could claim 'that he was already in possession of the House for tomorrow, as he had given notice of an intention to move on this day some resolutions'.[3] This procedural point explains the long wrangle on 20 March 1782 before Lord North was able to announce his resignation, 'Lord Surrey, who had given notice of a motion for that day, being consequently in possession of the right to speak first and having likewise risen'.[4]

The growing practice of giving notice of motions led to the idea that there was something unfair or irregular in introducing motions on important political matters without notice. This was clearly not the case in the earlier eighteenth century, when surprise opposition motions were a recognized weapon in Parliamentary warfare. Here is Lord Perceval's account of an opposition motion about the Treaty of Seville on 21 April 1730: 'It was a surprise on the House, and none of the Ministry to speak against the motion present, but they were sent for in a hurry, and the debate maintained by Sir William Strickland and Sir George Oxendon till Mr. Walpole, Sir Robert Walpole, and Pelham, Secretary of War, came in.'[5] As a matter of courtesy Samuel Sandys did give Sir Robert Walpole two days' private notice of the famous censure motion against him on 13 February 1741. 'Sir Robert paused a little upon so unexpected a Compliment, but thanked him very politely for the Information, and said, he desired no Favour, but fair Play.'

---

[1] Almon, *Parl. Reg.*, IX, 98. [2] Debrett, *Parl. Reg.*, V, 264–5.
[3] Debrett, *Parl. Reg.*, XIII, 90. [4] Wraxall, *Memoirs*, II, 599–600.
[5] *H.M.C. Egmont Diary*, I, 95. For another important surprise motion see *ibid.*, III, 278.

Sandys intended no favour, for, deeming surprise less important than publicity, he announced his intention to the House immediately afterwards.[1]

Little information on the custom of advance notice has been found until after the accession of George III, when public and private notice became common. Diarist James Harris, for example, recorded that Charles Bunbury gave two or three days' notice of a motion on an important subject for 12 February 1762, and 'being asked to explain on what, he replied on recalling the German troops': and that on 25 February 1765 Nicolson Calvert gave notice of 'a great constitutional motion which he proposed to make this day sevennight: another of the same stamp was expected this day from the Cavendishes, but deferred (as was said) on account of the Chancellor of Exchequer's absence, who was ill.' In the previous month opposition member Sir William Meredith had kept the head of the ministry, George Grenville, informed of the changing date of his motion on general warrants.[2]

Within a generation ministers came to regard almost as a right the courtesy Sir Robert Walpole in 1741 had deemed a favour. When on 17 November 1768 Henry Seymour moved for papers about the French seizure of Corsica Henry Cavendish noted in his diary that 'this motion, though acknowledged to be parliamentary, was objected to by some gentlemen, as being made without any previous notice: for though Mr. Seymour gave notice that he would make a motion, he did not acquaint the House with the object of it.' Cavendish clearly had in mind the remarks made by General Conway and Lord North. Conway had commented that 'it would have shown more attention to Parliamentary dignity to have given a little previous notice'; and North, who had succeeded Conway as Leader of the House, had complained, 'When a motion comes into the House without intimation, as an Opposition motion, I call that roasting a minister.'[3] On 3 December 1770 Serjeant John Glynn gave notice of a motion for 6 December, but refused to reveal the subject when asked by several members. Richard Rigby conceded that Glynn was

[1] Chandler, *Debates*, XII, 63N.
[2] Tomlinson, *Additional Grenville Papers*, pp. 241–2.
[3] B.M. Eg. MSS. 215, pp. 163, 185–6.

perfectly in order in not declaring his motion. He affirmed that 'this was a new custom, to declare motions, and that gentlemen used to make them without any previous notice.'[1] Lord North on 12 February 1773 asked Thomas Townshend to disclose the nature of the motions he intended to make on 15 February concerning the recent expedition to St. Vincents. 'The honourable gentleman will at least give us some information of the grounds upon which we are to be accused of a crime.' Townshend refused, remarking that Wilkes in 1769 had not received prior information of the motions against him, and North admitted, 'I did not put it as a claim'.[2] Nearly a decade later, on 12 December 1782, an unexpected opposition motion on Gibraltar gave rise to administration complaint, and this opposition retort. 'Lord Mahon said, that it was candid to attempt to take Ministers by surprise, or to bring on a consideration of so much moment, without a previous notice. Lord George Cavendish thought this idea of previous notice entirely unparliamentary; he was an old member, and never had heard the idea started till of late years; and it was mostly urged by young members; but Ministers held up this shield, whenever an attempt was made to touch upon a delicate spot.'[3]

Throughout the closing decades of the century opposition members resisted administration demands for invariable prior notice of Parliamentary attacks. Any such innovation could be portrayed as an encroachment upon the rights of individual members. William Dowdeswell on 9 March 1772 made a point of denying that there was anything unfair about his sudden motion concerning George III's message on the Royal Family Marriage Bill. He attacked the practice of giving notice of every motion, 'so that if a gentleman comes into the House, and makes a motion at the time he thinks proper, he is to be understood as offering something irregular in point of sense'.[4] Surprise motions remained a tactical weapon to be deployed on suitable occasions. In February 1768 the opposition leaders deliberately kept secret their intention of bringing in a Nullum Tempus Bill, Rockingham remarking, 'I think it would perplex them much, if they have but little time to decide in.' The manoeuvre nearly succeeded, for the ministry had to use the

[1] B.M. Eg. MSS. 223, pp. 45–6.   [2] B.M. Eg. MSS. 242, pp. 266–8.
[3] Debrett, *Parl. Reg.*, IX, 104.   [4] B.M. Eg. MSS. 235, p. 211.

evasive device of a previous question to obtain a small majority of twenty against the bill.[1]

Members did not even concede to the Chair the right of advance notice of motions. Speaker Norton's notorious quarrel with Sir William Meredith on 16 February 1770 was caused by his complaint that Meredith had displayed 'a lack of candour' in not giving the Chair advance notice of his motion that complicated questions should be divided. Lord Belasyse formed the impression that the Speaker was 'seeming to carry with him a power not to be allowed of by the House, which was, that he expected whenever any member had a question to propose he should first be acquainted therewith'.[2] Norton's indignation, however, probably stemmed from the ensuing appeal, without prior warning, to his opinion on an important point of procedure. When Meredith protested that he had given notice of the motion in Committee of the Whole House, the Speaker explicitly declared, 'I did not say it was the duty of the member. I know my duty too well. I did say, I thought in candour the gentleman should have told me.' The constitutional point was clarified by George Grenville: 'I think every possible respect due to the Chair. I have always thought so. At the same time, I must say, I did not think it the duty of any member to communicate to the Chair any motion he intended to make.'[3]

This cherished Parliamentary right, that any individual member could propose a motion at any time he chose, did not long survive the eighteenth century. There were already signs during Lord North's ministry that the practice of giving notice of motions was becoming formalized. By 1780 all notices of motions were being entered in the Order Books of the House, together with the Orders of the Day.[4] Voluntary written notice of some motions evolved into compulsory prior notification of every motion. In 1806 Speaker Abbot gave a ruling to the effect that notice of all important or controversial motions should be given not later than the day before: this was not a

---

[1] B.M. Add. MSS. 32988, fos. 331, 369–70.
[2] For details of the incident see my 'Debates of the House of Commons' (Ph.D. thesis, Univ. of London, 1958) p. 96.
[3] B.M. Eg. MSS. 220, pp. 123–42.
[4] Almon, *Parl. Reg.*, XVII, 64. Debrett, *Parl. Reg.*, III, 475–7.

8—H.O.C.

formal death-blow to the old right, but thereafter members had to provide convincing excuses for motions without notice.[1]

Throughout the century the ratio of Parliamentary time to Parliamentary business was gradually worsening. The steady rise in the amount of business can best be demonstrated from the growth of legislation. The number of successful bills rose from an average of under one to over two a Parliamentary day.[2] The evidence of the increase in Committees, debates, petitions and inquiries is less susceptible to statistical evaluation, but suggests that other aspects of Parliamentary business expanded in similar proportions: in 1810 the number of items of business a session was said to have risen from 2,348 in 1760 to 6,381 in 1800.[3] Along with this growth of business there took place a reduction in Parliamentary time that was not compensated for either by the greater length of sessions towards the end of the century, or by the increasing duration of the Parliamentary day itself—for this was caused and taken up by longer debates. Many days a session were now lost by the long Christmas and Easter adjournments and by the new custom of not sitting on Saturdays. In 1759 Speaker Onslow condemned these developments as 'a great delay of business, and of the sessions . . . these things want reformation.'[4] The solution that began to emerge in the following half-century, however, was not any return to old Parliamentary ways, and not one that Onslow envisaged or would have approved. The decisions of 1806 and 1811 involved in practice more deliberate priority for government business, which had hitherto in theory and sometimes in fact taken its chance among other business; and they meant the first curtailment of the freedom of individual members.

[1] P. Fraser, 'The Growth of Ministerial Control in the Nineteenth-Century House of Commons', *Eng. Hist. Rev.*, 75 (1960), pp. 449–50.

[2] See *supra*, p. 61.

[3] Fraser, op. cit., p. 446N.

[4] Burnet, *History*, VI, 214N.

6

THE ATTENDANCE OF MEMBERS

THROUGHOUT the eighteenth century the *Journals* of the House of Commons solemnly recorded that leave of absence was being given to individual members, usually for stated reasons and for specified periods. This constitutional theory bore no relation to political practice. Each session some members never went up to London at all, and many of those who did so visited the House on infrequent occasions. Only a small number of conscientious members made this punctilious application to the House to leave town; even in the earlier part of the century attempts to revoke such orders of leave were unsuccessful; and the empty formality of the whole procedure is shown by a casual reference by Sir William Meredith on 2 March 1774 to this practice as 'the manner of our ancestors'.[1] Political leaders were therefore faced with the twofold and perennial problem of securing the presence of their friends in London, and their subsequent attendance in the House.

Official machinery for the purpose had existed since at least 1549 and continued to be used until 1836. This was the Call of the House, a roll-call of members.[2] In theory an order for a Call was made whenever attendance was markedly poor: but every motion for a Call seems to have been made explicitly in anticipation of some particular business. The period of notice to members became longer during the century: at first it was a fortnight or even less; but on 20 December 1781 Lord North remarked that a month or six weeks was 'customary', and on 19 February 1783 he declared that six weeks was the notice 'required to be given by the rules of the House'.[3] The purpose was not to detect the absentees, but to procure their attendance: and, at the time a Call was ordered, the Speaker would usually be directed to write circular letters to the sheriffs,

---

[1] *Knatchbull Diary*, pp. 41, 95. B.M. Eg. MSS. 253, p. 101.
[2] Hatsell, *Precedents*, II, 96. H. Walpole, *George III*, III, 9N.
[3] Debrett, *Parl. Reg.*, V, 205; IX, 294-5.

and the Lord Warden of the Cinque Ports, instructing them to summon the members to attend. This direction was also some-times given alone, as an alternative to a Call.

On the day appointed for the Call the Serjeant-at-Arms would be sent with the Mace into Westminster Hall and other places in the vicinity of the House, to summon the members. The names of the members were then called out in the order of their constituencies. English counties were taken first, in alphabetical order, including the boroughs they contained: then followed the Welsh counties and lastly the Scottish ones. Each member rose and answered to his name, bowing to the Speaker and being bowed to by him: he could then leave the House if he wished. Many members did so, for the whole proceeding lasted about two hours.[1]

The names of defaulters were then called over again, and excuses of illness or other unavoidable absence were offered on their behalf. Such excuses were sent beforehand either to other members or direct to the Speaker.[2] Each order for a Call was accompanied by a resolution that all members who failed to attend should be taken into the custody of the Serjeant-at-Arms, and in the earlier eighteenth century it was usual for the House to order that some or all of the members for whom no excuses were provided should be taken into custody. On 21 February 1723, for instance, there were nine such defaulters: two were excused on divisions, and seven committed to the Serjeant, two after divisions.[3] The number of absent members with excuses was usually large: at the Call on 13 March 1733 Lord Perceval noted 'not so many as I thought we should be'; but only one absent member on this occasion lacked an excuse and was ordered into custody.[4] The number of members without excuses was always very small, and the practice of committing such members for mere lack of foresight or respect to the House gradually lapsed. The last instance known to

[1] Brief accounts of Calls were noted by five diarists. (a) Nathaniel Ryder on 24 Feb. 1758. Harrowby MSS., doc. 43. (b) James Harris on 20 Feb. 1765. (c) Henry Cavendish on 5 Feb. 1771. B.M. Eg. MSS. 224, pp. 95–7. (d) Matthew Brickdale on 5 Feb. 1771. Brickdale Diary, II, 20–30. (e) John Clementson on 5 Feb. 1771 and 11 Feb. 1779. Clementson Diary, pp. 31, 62.

[2] See, for example, Debrett, *Parl. Reg.*, V, 281–2.

[3] *Knatchbull Diary*, pp. 13, 119–20. *Commons Journals*, XX, 145.

[4] *H.M.C. Egmont Diary*, I, 342. *Commons Journals*, XXII, 87.

John Hatsell when he became Clerk of the House in 1768 had occurred on 18 January 1743, when three members were committed and three other absentees ordered to attend in a week's time, which they did.¹ It became the custom for the House to order a separate Call of defaulters a week or more later, by which time reasons had been found by all. In the first edition of the second volume of his *Precedents*, published in 1781, Hatsell made the fair comment that 'every trifling excuse' was allowed; and he then clearly regarded the practice of taking members into custody for non-attendance as obsolete.² But to later editions he had to add the case of John Roberts, M.P. for Taunton. At a Call of defaulters on 15 February 1781 no excuse was offered for Roberts: and Sir Joseph Mawbey, disclaiming any personal motive and criticizing the usual lenity of the House, moved that he be taken into custody. Lord North opposed this 'severity . . . long relaxed . . . with a young member' who had attended before the Christmas recess, but the motion was carried on a division. Ironically the absence of Roberts was due to genuine illness, and when four days later the House learned of this circumstance and of his return to town his discharge was at once ordered.³ This was the last instance: the very next year two members were absent without explanation at the Call of defaulters; one was excused as having been in the lobby a few minutes before, and the other was ordered to attend the next day.⁴

Another development of the century also weakened the efficacy of the Call as a summons to members, the increasing proportion of Calls that were never carried out. Instead they were often repeatedly postponed until the orders were discharged or allowed to lapse. In the period between 1714 and 1790 the *Journals Index* lists ninety-five Calls as having been ordered, but only thirty-two as taking place. Nevertheless, even though an order for a Call might be a false alarm to absent members, the procedure did retain some value in securing their attendance. Diaries and correspondence show that many members came to town because of news of a proposed Call of the House: and the attendance of members at a Call

¹ N.L.W. MSS. 1352, fo. 107. *Commons Journals*, XXIV, 383, 392.
² Hatsell, *Precedents*, II, 99–100.   ³ Debrett, *Parl. Reg.*, I, 480–1, 506.
⁴ Debrett, *Parl. Reg.*, V, 283–4.

seems to have been always higher than that at any debate of the same session. Details of attendance at Calls were never officially recorded, but information on the Call of 5 February 1771 is provided by diarists John Clementson, Henry Cavendish and Matthew Brickdale. 474 members were present. Forty-nine members were granted exemption as 'ill and excused', and a further nineteen as being abroad. Five members had not then taken their seats. The remaining eleven were ordered to attend in a week's time.[1] The Call of defaulters was postponed to 19 February, when seven of them apparently attended; the House found it necessary to excuse only four, one as abroad, another as ill, and two as in town.[2] Altogether, as the result of the Call, 483 members were known to be in London. Twenty were abroad, so only fifty had been excused through illness or spurious reasons.

Since a Call of the House brought the independent members to Westminster, it formed a tactical weapon for opposition use. Hardly a session passed without at least one and often two or even more Calls being proposed, and almost every Call was moved by opposition or independent members. When doing so they mentioned the particular business that was expected, such as the Peerage Bill of 1719 or Fox's India Bill of 1783.[3] This tactic usually secured a good attendance for the occasion, though rarely success for the opposition. A typical instance occurred when a settlement with Spain over the seizure of the Falkland Islands was announced on 22 January 1771. Edmund Burke promptly asked when the matter would be taken into consideration, in order that he could move a Call of the House for the same date. Lord North proved evasive, and Burke therefore moved for the Call that took place on 5 February and resulted in the attendance of 483 members in London.[4] All but ten were available to attend when the main debate on the settlement was held on 13 February. 437 members were present at the division, and thirty-six paired off.[5] Individual

[1] B.M. Eg. MSS. 224, pp. 96–7. Brickdale Diary, II, 30. Clementson Diary, p. 31. At the Call on 11 Feb. 1779 470 members were present, 74 were excused, 12 were ordered to attend, and 1 had not taken his seat. Clementson Diary, p. 62.

[2] *Commons Journals*, XXXIII, 142, 157, 184.

[3] Chandler, *Debates*, VI, 196. Debrett, *Parl. Reg.*, XII, 51–5.

[4] B.M. Eg. MSS. 224, p. 1.

[5] Wentworth Woodhouse MSS., R 1–1361.

or indiscriminate employment of this weapon could defeat its purpose, however: during the North ministry the radical member John Sawbridge regularly proposed a Call to coincide with his annual motion for shorter Parliaments; but members assumed that such Calls would not be carried out, and attendance was never high on this subject.

Administrations rarely challenged this political use of an accepted constitutional practice: but in 1729 a motion for a Call was evaded by a previous question; and on 18 December 1739 one was openly negatived.[1] This event caused opposition leader William Pulteney to initiate a debate on the subject on 31 January 1740. Administration speakers refused to concede his claim that any member had a right to obtain a Call whenever he chose: but there was general agreement on the desirability of the House being called over at least once every session.[2] A first motion for a Call in any session usually passed as a matter of course: but on 7 December 1770 Lord North found a particular reason to answer a threat of a Call with regard to a proposed increase in the land tax. 'That notice is not practised upon any tax', he replied, and no motion for a Call was made.[3]

Ministers, however, usually professed to welcome the attendance of members, and Leaders of the House sometimes seconded opposition motions for a Call. Henry Fox did so in 1755, and George Grenville in 1765.[4] Such motives of propriety even caused ministers themselves to move for a Call. Sir Robert Walpole took this step before the introduction of his controversial Excise Bill in 1733, the only precedent remembered by contemporaries when on 7 April 1773 Lord North moved for a Call after the Easter recess, on 26 April.[5] Edmund Burke commented to John Cruger, 'It is very unusual for a Minister to move a call of the House'. Speculation about North's motives varied from payment of the Civil List debt to a French alliance, but Burke correctly guessed 'the desire the Ministry have of securing the sanction of a full house' for the legislation on the East India Company.[6] Thomas Bradshaw of

---

[1] *Knatchbull Diary*, p. 95. *Commons Journals*, XXIII, 407.
[2] Chandler, *Debates*, XI, 246–64. [3] B.M. Eg. MSS. 223, p. 188.
[4] B.M. Add. MSS. 32861, fo. 55. Harris Diary, 6 Feb. 1765.
[5] B.M. Eg. MSS. 245, p. 272. Malmesbury MSS., Memo of 9 Apr. 1773.
[6] *Burke Correspondence*, II, 429.

the Admiralty Board explained to Sir Robert Murray Keith that 'Lord North has moved a call of the House for the 26th, wisely thinking that the Blue Sky will otherwise carry all the Country Gentlemen home, and that it will not be proper to carry important Questions respecting the future regulations and management of the East India Company, by a small number of Placemen'.[1]

As a political weapon the Call of the House could be used only at infrequent intervals. Moreover, once it had taken place, members were free to return home. Motions for subsequent Calls in the same session were unpopular, often opposed and sometimes defeated. The tactic had therefore evolved by the period of the Walpole ministry for a Call to be deliberately postponed to keep members in London: and in 1738 a reporter gave this explanation of a postponement to his readers. 'It was rightly judged, that when the Call was over, many members would drop off, whereas, if it was delayed from day to day, it would be a method to detain them in Town.'[2] Repeated postponements became a regular opposition tactic, at intervals of a week or more for periods of one or two months. Lord North himself in 1773 postponed his Call weekly from 26 April until 9 June.[3] This step can never have been popular with independent members, and routine use of the expedient during the War of American Independence evoked increasing protests. The period from 1780 to 1783 saw frequent divisions over postponements of Calls, and in 1781 and 1783 the objectors won the day. John Rolle, M.P. for Devonshire, led this campaign, arguing both that the custom lessened 'the respect due to the House' and that if there was the threat of a Call 'members who lived at a great distance from the capital, were obliged to come to town, while many of those who live near town, though absentees from their duty, were not treated as if they had neglected it'.[4]

The constitutional method of summoning members was inefficient and unpopular. Direct contact with individual

---

[1] B.M. Add. MSS. 35504, fo. 170.   [2] Chandler, *Debates*, X, 107.
[3] *Commons Journals*, XXXIV, 284, 296, 306, 321, 326, 356, 364. *General Evening Post*, 3 June 1773.
[4] Debrett, *Parl. Reg.*, I, 377; V, 281, 283, 420; VI, 374–5, 446; IX, 137, 160, 204–5, 294–6.

members was a far more certain method of ensuring their presence in London. From at least the time of Sir Robert Walpole's administration it was the practice for each ministry to send out circular letters to supporters throughout the country, requesting their attendance at an eve-of-session meeting at the Cockpit.[1] This was the meeting where the King's Speech was read, and the policy of the administration explained: the beginning of each new Parliament saw two Cockpit meetings, for one concerned with the appointment of a Speaker preceded the usual gathering to hear the King's Speech.[2] It was the Leader of the House who presided, often a point of political importance if there was a struggle for power within a ministry: after his resignation in 1742 Sir Robert Walpole advised Henry Pelham to preside at the next Cockpit, even though he was only Paymaster-General and Samuel Sandys was Chancellor of the Exchequer, and Pelham did so. John Roberts had this coup in mind when in 1765 he warned the new First Lord of the Treasury Lord Rockingham that 'whoever took the lead by such a mark of the royal confidence would be looked upon as future, if not the present minister.' In 1755, Henry Fox, although not yet officially Secretary of State, deliberately took over from Henry Legge, who had presided the previous year as Chancellor of the Exchequer. Nor was the claim to do so forfeited by a minister who had temporarily vacated his seat on appointment to a new office: as John Roberts observed in 1765, 'there can be no impropriety in a Person's presiding there, who is not at that time, in Parliament; the work of that evening being a private and confidential communication from the Crown.'[3]

The circular letters were drafted and signed by the Leader of the House himself: but in 1777 Temple Luttrell, complaining of the practice, told members that his invitation had been anonymous, a discourtesy due to carelessness or increasing

---

[1] For a discussion of mid-century practice see L. B. Namier, 'The Circular Letters: an Eighteenth Century Whip to Members of Parliament', *Eng. Hist. Rev.*, 44 (1929), pp. 588–611. For fuller information on the Cockpit meetings see *supra.*, pp. 40–1.

[2] See *infra*, pp. 331–2.

[3] H. Walpole, *George II*, I, 391; II, 47. Wentworth Woodhouse MSS., R 1–536. This letter was printed and discussed by J. E. Tyler, 'John Roberts, M.P., and the first Rockingham Administration', *Eng. Hist. Rev.*, 67 (1952), pp. 547–60.

formality.[1] The letters were sent, either directly or through leaders of political groups, to all supposed friends of government. Many members, however, although willing to support the ministry, refrained from committing themselves openly by going to the Cockpit. Lord Perceval, who gave independent support to Walpole, made this comment on such meetings in 1732: 'They have an air of servileness I dont like, and if a member should happen to vote against anything recommended in the Speech, he is not well looked on by his friends for doing so, after having appeared among a number of gentlemen who were resolved to approve all.'[2] Attendance at the Cockpit therefore never represented an administration's voting-strength in the House. It was usually about 150, and that of 289 in 1755 was a record.[3] No more than 179 members went to the Cockpit meeting of 8 January 1770, at a time of political crisis: yet 256 voted for the ministry over the Address on the next day.[4] The real advantage to ministers of these pre-session circular letters was not a general approval of policy at the Cockpit, but simply that the friends of administration were informed when a session was beginning. Uncertainty about the date was one factor in the reluctance of independent members to travel to London early in the winter: as Lord Chesterfield complained in 1741, 'fox-hunting, gardening, planting or indifference' kept opposition members in the country until the known eve of the session.[5]

Administration was always at a great advantage over opposition in sending for members. Government facilities provided an organization to hand, of secretariat, postal service, and funds: opposition leaders had to improvise from their own resources.[6] Independent members, too, would rarely be offended by a request to support the King's government even if they had no intention of doing so. But opposition leaders could not summon the independents on whom they relied for most of their votes in the same manner. On 12 December 1770 Sir Edward Astley, a county member who usually voted in the

---

[1] H. Walpole, *George II*, II, 63. Almon, *Parl. Reg.*, VIII, 25.
[2] *H.M.C. Egmont Diary*, I, 214.
[3] Newdigate Diary, 13 Nov. 1755. Namier, op. cit., p. 595.
[4] *Chatham Correspondence*, III, 390. *Commons Journals*, XXXII, 456.
[5] Coxe, *Walpole*, III, 580–1.   [6] Foord, *His Majesty's Opposition*, p. 34.

minority, answered a remark by Stephen Fox that the opposition leaders might have sent for their friends with these proud words: 'Will any man say, that an independent gentleman, who may think perhaps with those who are more generally declared to be in opposition, would obey the summons of that party? Would he not be provoked? If anybody took that liberty with me, I should have taken it ill.'[1] Well might Edmund Burke in 1772 bemoan the fact that 'the spirited but undisciplined Troops of an Independent opposition, will never make such a figure in an early Muster, as the well formed and well paid Bands of the Court.'[2] Various expedients were used from time to time to offset this disadvantage. A notable one was an opposition circular letter of 1743, signed by twenty-two members of a wide range of political opinions.[3] A more permanent method was attempted at the height of the controversy over the Middlesex Elections of 1768–9. Seventy-four of the minority, at the general invitation of William Dowdeswell, dined at the Thatched House tavern on 9 May 1769, at the close of the session: Dowdeswell was the Commons leader of the main opposition group headed by Lord Rockingham.[4] A similar meeting there was arranged for the beginning of the next session, and eighty members met at a dinner on 8 January 1770, held simultaneously with the Cockpit meeting of administration supporters.[5] Thatched House dinners were held for several years, but they never developed into a rival institution to the Cockpit gatherings.[6]

Resort to the Call of the House was therefore the only way opposition could hope to muster a respectable vote in the many sessions when there was no sense of national crisis and no sensational or controversial issues of debate. Even in such circumstances administration had an advantage—the ability to despatch messages to those supporters who remained out of town, and to receive such replies as Sir Roger Newdigate sent in answer to Lord North's circular of 25 February 1770: 'I most sincerely wish to support his Majesty and to see the Lord North enabled to do all that good which the best part of the

---

[1] B.M. Eg. MSS. 223, pp. 328–30. [2] *Burke Correspondence*, II, 398.
[3] Newdigate MSS., B 2550. [4] *H.M.C. 12 Report, Part X*, 294.
[5] *Chatham Correspondence*, III, 390.
[6] *Burke Correspondence*, II, 388. Wentworth Woodhouse MSS. R 1–1478.

nation expects and hopes for from the administration.'[1]
Already on 30 January Newdigate had received at his Warwickshire home a letter by Treasury messenger from Lord
North, requesting his attendance at an important debate on
the next day. Newdigate made the journey in sixteen hours,
arriving in time to vote.[2] Not all independents were as conscientious as Sir Roger Newdigate; but on very few absent
members could opposition leaders make any such demands.

It was within the context of such summonses to members
out of town that the first known Parliamentary instance of the
use of the term 'whip' occurred. In the debate of 8 May 1769
on a petition from some Middlesex freeholders against the
seating of Henry Luttrell instead of John Wilkes, Edmund
Burke mentioned that the ministry had sent for their friends
to the north and to Paris, 'whipping them in, than which, he
said, there could not be a better phrase'.[3] Although Burke's
particular emphasis on the expression implied its comparative
novelty, the hunting term had been used in this political
context for at least a generation: on 18 November 1742
Heneage Finch remarked in a letter to Lord Malton that 'the
Whigs for once in their lives have whipped in better than the
Tories.'[4]

'Memorandum. 510 members sworn before the debate of
the Suspension Bill, and but 441 at the division. Q: what
became of the others that did not appear.'[5] This sardonic note
by Sir Edward Knatchbull, after a debate on 16 October
1722 over the suspension of the Habeas Corpus Act immediately
followed the swearing of members at the beginning of a
Parliament, highlights the real problem of attendance con-
fronting political leaders—not to bring members up to London,
but to secure their presence in the House. The custom of a
London season was well established, and members did come
to town for the winter as a matter of course.

For a short period in 1772 detailed information on the location of members is available in lists compiled in connection
with the Royal Family Marriage Bill by John Robinson, one

---

[1] Newdigate MSS., B. 2023.   [2] Newdigate Diary, 30 and 31 Jan. 1770.
[3] B.M. Eg. MSS. 219, fo. 404.   [4] Wentworth Woodhouse MSS. M 3–122.
[5] *Knatchbull Diary*, p. 3.

of the Secretaries to the Treasury. Robinson's first 'State of the House', dated 27 February, shows that 492 members were then in London, of whom ten would not be able to attend because they were 'sick'. Twenty-seven of the absent members had been sent to or might attend, five were marked as 'sick', and the other thirty-one were discounted as incurably absent. Two seats were vacant. The attendance of members in London must have been near the maximum, for the position was remarkably similar on 8 March, despite the efforts of administration and opposition to rally their followers. Robinson listed 499 members as being in town, of whom fifteen were 'sick'. Twenty-one of the fifty-eight absent members might attend, and nine were 'sick'.[1] Correlation of the information in these lists compiled by John Robinson in 1772 with that revealed by the Call of the House in 1771 provides some basis for a tentative estimate of the usual distribution of members in the middle of a session. About a score would be abroad, for pleasure, on business, or as diplomatic envoys. A further dozen or more, whether in London or in the country, would be prevented from attendance by ill-health or age. One or two seats were normally vacant. At the height of a session, nearly 500 members would be in London at the same time.

Attendance at the House of Commons was quite another matter. On 27 February 1772 only 320 out of the possible 482 listed by John Robinson were at the division on Sir George Savile's motion for a bill to safeguard the rights of electors—yet that was a popular subject, arising from the Middlesex elections controversy.[2] Even on the Royal Family Marriage Bill itself no more than 412 members were present at the biggest division, and fewer than 300 voted in eleven out of the twenty-one divisions during the passage of the bill.[3] By 23 March 1772 Robinson was basing his calculations on the belief that a maximum of 433 members might attend: in fact, no more than 287 voted on the passage of the bill next day.[4]

[1] B.M. MS. Facs. 340 (3), fos. 66, 72–3.
[2] *Commons Journals*, XXXIII, 524. Both totals exclude the Speaker.
[3] *Commons Journals*, XXXIII, 553, 579, 584, 608, 612. B.M. Eg. MSS. 236, pp. 193, 195; 237, pp. 84, 270, 273; 238, pp. 68, 149, 157, 163, 205, 209, 245, 282, 291.
[4] *Commons Journals*, XXXIII, 612. B.M. MS. Facs. 340 (3), fo. 55.

Ministers and their opponents could not leave the attendance of supporters in town to the enthusiasm, conscience or even self-interest of individual members. Here, too, an official method did exist to summon members to attend the service of the House. The Speaker would send the Serjeant-at-Arms with the Mace into Westminster Hall and other places nearby.[1] The original motive behind this practice, which went back to at least the sixteenth century, was to summon those members who were lawyers practising in the courts situated in Westminster Hall.[2] The order to the Serjeant was given at the request of individual members on the pretext of forthcoming important business, but the consent of the House was necessary.[3] Wraxall thought this use of the Serjeant on 17 December 1783 an 'extraordinary mandate from the Chair':[4] but the measure was not uncommon, and usually undertaken at the behest of opposition members. The Serjeant was also sent out to fetch members on certain customary occasions—when a quorum was needed, almost always when the House was called over, and, after Grenville's Election Act of 1770, before the consideration of any election petition. The Serjeant, however, could summon for any purpose only those members who were already in the Palace of Westminster. There is no evidence that politicians placed any reliance on this largely formal procedure. More effective methods were to hand.

Ministers had always used unofficial pressure to secure the attendance of members at the House for the vote at the end of important debates. Such requests and instructions were given by word of mouth or note of hand. Political decorum made necessary the employment of members of the House themselves in this task. One such member in the earlier eighteenth century was Thomas Brereton, of whom Lord Perceval observed that as soon as he was elected for Liverpool in 1724 he 'gave himself to be entirely to be the slave of Sir Robert Walpole, and was made use of in the little job works of the House, such as carrying and bringing messages and whispers to and from the members, for securing their votes on particular

[1] Hatsell, *Precedents*, II, 99.
[2] Townsend, *House of Commons*, II, 368. Luttrell Diary, II, fos. 93, 307.
[3] B.M. Eg. MSS. 225, p. 54. Debrett, *Parl. Reg.*, XII, 420.
[4] Wraxall, *Memoirs*, IV, 599–600.

questions'.[1] The hold of an administration on many supporters was closely connected with patronage, as the independent opposition member Sir Edward Astley scornfully observed in 1770. 'Everybody knows, where there are dependencies, they are in the nature of demands. "Come, Sir, or I will turn you out."'[2] The leading role in the organization of Parliamentary support had therefore devolved on the two Secretaries of the Treasury, one of whom was almost entirely and the other partly engaged in this task: the distinction between patronage and financial Secretaries was not absolute. Only occasional glimpses of this work have survived, perhaps because for much of the century it was seldom required. James West, a Secretary to the Treasury for fifteen years under Henry Pelham and the Duke of Newcastle, had little cause for concern during most of the period: but he was spurred into action when a motion for the second reading of a government bill on 17 March 1756 received an unexpectedly narrow majority of nine votes, 129 to 120. He warned Newcastle, 'Our friends are of opinion it will be very tight work to go through with it. I speak to every one, but I submit there should be some large meeting on the necessary steps to be taken.' Five days later the danger was over, the bill being committed by a majority of 245 votes to 142: for no further opposition was made after this triumph of organization.[3] The papers of John Robinson, patronage Secretary to the Treasury under Lord North from 1770 to 1782, testify to his key role in the maintenance of a Parliamentary majority.[4] Growing pressure threw the emphasis less on personal contact and more on circular letters. Here is a typical one signed by Robinson on 27 February 1779: 'Public business of most essential consequence being fixed to come on on Monday next and for several following days perhaps ten days or a fortnight, I hope you will permit me most earnestly to entreat your attendance in the House during that time.'[5] Sometimes Robinson scribbled notes during debates to summon absent members.[6] On 8 May 1781 George Byng gave a general

---

[1] *H.M.C. Egmont Diary*, I, 87.   [2] B.M. Eg. MSS. 223, p. 230.
[3] B.M. Add. MSS. 32863, fo. 332; 35877, fo. 244.
[4] B.M. MS. Facs. 340 (1–4). *Parliamentary Papers of John Robinson 1772–1784*, ed. W. T. Laprade (1922).
[5] Harris Diary, 27 Feb. 1779.   [6] B.M. Add. MSS. 38212, fos. 279–80.

description of the activities of such adherents of 'the minister: ... when the issue of a debate was doubtful, what were the arts, and what the industry of his creatures to collect his hands from the coffee-houses, to make them leave their dinners and their bottle, and come staggering into the House to decide on the fate of their country.'[1]

Byng was replying to a reference by Lord Fielding to himself as 'the ablest political muster-master', a designation he accepted in the debate and that may have become fixed to him: for Wraxall soon afterwards described Byng as 'the "Master Muster-General" of Opposition, as he was denominated'.[2] Certainly George Byng during the last years of the North ministry did his utmost to fulfil for the opposition the function Robinson performed for the administration. It was Byng who organized the Calls of the House, arranging their postponement or enforcement as he judged expedient: and it was to Byng himself that many absent members sent their excuses.[3] Byng often acted as an opposition teller in divisions: and it was he who in June 1781 made a general request to opposition members to attend early in the next session.[4] George Byng was the first regular opposition whip.

Such a task was Herculean. Opposition attempts to rally even those friends already in town suffered from two major disadvantages. Any organization had to be *ad hoc*, for there was no tradition or method of systematic opposition whipping, and members were not always prepared to take the trouble. The Duke of Newcastle, long familiar with administration practice, despaired of the Parliamentary situation when in opposition in 1765, writing of the House of Commons, 'I dont wonder that we miscarry there, as nobody takes care to apprise our friends, of what is to be done, or what we desire of them.'[5] In any case the leaders of opposition groups were unable to contact privately all their potential supporters, for fear of giving offence. They therefore resorted to publicity. The subjects opposition members proposed to raise in Parliament would be made known—by advance notice in the House,

---

[1] Debrett, *Parl. Reg.*, III, 224–5.
[2] Debrett, *Parl. Reg.*, III, 224–5. Wraxall, *Memoirs*, II, 420.
[3] See, for example, Debrett, *Parl. Reg.*, V, 203–5, 224, 248, 281–4.
[4] Wraxall, *Memoirs*, II, 420.   [5] B.M. Add. MSS. 32966, fo. 82.

private communication, and the deliberate release of information to the newspapers. But reliance on a considerable independent vote to make a respectable show remained an opposition weakness in any battle with ministers. No semblance of discipline was possible. If there were two or more divisions on the same day, the opposition vote dropped more rapidly than the ministerial vote. The effect of a longer delay was similar: George III observed to Lord North in 1772, 'Two days respite is always more favourable to Administration than to Opposition.'[1]

Private members used the same methods as political leaders to secure a good attendance of supporters for their own business. The support of individual members on particular occasions was solicited directly, or by approaches through relatives, friends and patrons. Sir Roger Newdigate made nearly forty visits on 6 February 1769 to obtain support for the Oxford Canal Bill he was then sponsoring.[2] Private members who introduced bills often also sent out circular letters to supplement such personal contacts. In 1771 John Dunning, answering a complaint about a card sent in his name, asserted, without contradiction, that the custom of sending out printed cards by the common messenger notifying members of the dates of private members' bills was a habit 'sanctified by practice'.[3]

Ministers, however, needed to exercise considerable discretion in bringing pressure on members over subjects where the King's government was not concerned. Many members made a clear distinction between questions of confidence in a ministry, and attempts by administration to control every decision of the House. In 1771 excessive use of ministerial circulars on a variety of occasions had already aroused comment before the matter was raised in the House on 25 March.[4] The practice was particularly liable to objection on that occasion, for the business was a question of Parliamentary privilege, the proceedings against the City of London for its protection of newspaper printers from the jurisdiction of the House. Lord Mayor Brass Crosby and Alderman Richard Oliver had been ordered to attend, and the Treasury, on the day before, issued the follow-

---

[1] Fortescue, *Corr. of George III*, II, pp. 331–2.
[2] Newdigate Diary, 6 Feb. 1769.   [3] B.M. Eg. MSS. 227, pp. 64–6.
[4] B.M. Eg. MSS. 226, p. 363. Wentworth Woodhouse MSS., R 1–1358.

ing letter to supporters of the ministry: 'You are most earnestly requested to attend early tomorrow, on an affair of the last importance to the constitution, and the rights and privileges of the people of England.' As soon as the business of the day began, Sir William Meredith drew attention to this circular: 'I am not going to take a very prudish language with regard to this letter. I am not going to arraign the propriety of issuing this kind of letter. They have of late got into a habit of issuing them out upon all occasions.' Meredith drew attention to the contrast between this practice and the procedure in courts of law, where the accused could object to members of the jury: 'I desire to know whether there is any other meaning in the letter than to signify the ministry takes a part in this business. I [call upon] gentlemen to recollect what the number of men are to whom these letters are sent. They are not sent to me. They are not sent to many persons who have not the honour of having their names printed in the Court Kalendar.' Paymaster Richard Rigby blandly replied that he had received many such letters, but did not obey them under any undue influence. 'I look upon this as only a memorandum to tell members there is a business of importance likely.' Meredith rejoined that such letters were not proper in cases of private property or criminal judicature. Sir Henry Hoghton, an independent member who usually voted with administration, also attacked the ministry's action. Hoghton declared that he had been 'extremely hurt' at receiving one of the letters. 'I am an independent country gentleman. I vote and speak *ex animo*, as much as any gentlemen. If I thought that the sense of the House was influenced by this letter, I would walk out and not give a vote at all.'[1]

No satisfactory evidence is available for actual attendance at the House of Commons. There was no official register of attendance, and voting-figures on divisions comprise the only regular and reliable source of information: but there are several disadvantages in their use. The evidence is very incomplete, because no divisions at all took place in the majority of debates, or even on most days that the House sat. Moreover only divisions in the House itself are recorded in the *Journals*:

[1] B.M. Eg. MSS. 227, pp. 61–6.

information on the many divisions in Committee depends on the chance survival of unofficial evidence. It is apparent, too, that the number voting at a division was lower than the total number of members present at some time during the same day. Boredom, fatigue and indecision meant that not all those who went stayed out even important debates. During the century, moreover, a further discrepancy between attendance and voting was introduced by the new custom of pairing.

Pairing began as an informal way for members present at a debate to go home early before the division. Evidence on the practice is scanty. Only a dozen references have been found throughout the period between 1714 and 1784, and a mere two of these occur before 1770, both in Lord Perceval's diary. In his report of the debate of 27 February 1730 on Dunkirk he stated that 'the lateness of the night obliged about thirty members to leave the House before the question was put, each taking away with him one of the contrary side.'[1] And on 8 March 1732 Lord Perceval noted that as a long debate was likely 'I agreed with cousin John Finch, who is against the salt duty, that we both come away.'[2] The paucity of information is misleading: that the new practice was becoming common and that it was regarded by some members as an evasion of Parliamentary duty was shown by a resolution proposed on 6 March 1744: 'That no Member of this House do presume to make any Agreement with another Member to absent themselves from any Service of this House, or any Committee thereof: and that this House will proceed with the utmost Severity against all such Members as shall offend therein.'

The motion was defeated by 171 votes to 139, and pairing gradually became an accepted part of Parliamentary life.[3] It was an obvious method for members to save themselves inconvenience on much routine or trivial business. George Grenville, in his speech of 28 February 1770 announcing the introduction of his Election Bill, mentioned as one of the abuses of the existing system the habit among members of pairing off for election cases.[4] That pairing had not become a widespread custom in important debates, however, is suggested both by the general absence of references to the practice and by the

---

[1] *H.M.C. Egmont Diary*, I, 75.   [2] *H.M.C. Egmont Diary*, I, 234.
[3] *Commons Journals*, XXIV, 602.   [4] Almon, *Debates*, VIII, 240.

explanation thought necessary by Matthew Brickdale when he paired with a friend on 27 February 1771.[1] The first contemporary use found of the actual word 'pairing' is in a report by Edmund Burke to Rockingham of the debate on 13 February 1771 over the Falkland Islands settlement: 'We divided 157, and Norton told William Burke that eighteen had paired off.'[2] This remark implies that members paired on their own initiative, and perhaps that they informed the Speaker when doing so. Pairing was most likely to occur when the same subject had been often debated. Reporter John Almon believed that one reason for the small attendance at a division on 7 February 1771 was that a number of members had paired to avoid yet another vote on the Middlesex Election case.[3] The scanty evidence suggests that the number of members pairing in major debates was rarely more than about twenty: and nothing has been found to indicate that systematic pairing took place beforehand.[4]

Calculations based on division-figures therefore tend to underestimate slightly the attendance of members at debates: but there is no doubt that attendance was erratic even on major political issues. This can be shown by an analysis of the voting on John Wilkes and the Middlesex Election case in 1769. Complete division-lists are available for the expulsion of Wilkes on 3 February, the seating of Henry Luttrell on 15 April, and the rejection of the Middlesex petition on 8 May: minority lists only have survived for a vote on a petition of grievances from Wilkes on 27 January, and that of 2 February concerning an alleged libel by Wilkes.[5] Altogether 269 different members voted in the majority on the three occasions, and 215 in the minority, according to the five known lists. Twenty-six members voted on various occasions on different sides, so only 458 members are known to have voted.

Of the 269 members in the majority in the three lists, 158,

---

[1] 'I did not vote having agreed with Laroche not to do so, who would have been for aye and I was for no.' Brickdale Diary, III, 58.

[2] Wentworth Woodhouse MSS., R 1–1361.

[3] Almon, *Debates*, VIII, 240.

[4] For some further instances of pairing see Debrett, *Parl. Reg.*, VI, 341, 486; XIII, 213–14.

[5] The location of these lists is given in Namier and Brooke, *The House of Commons 1754–1790* I, 527–8.

or about 60 per cent, voted in all three divisions. Over a hundred of these men held places or were army officers: many of the others had more indirect connections with administration, as contractors, through relatives, and so on. The consistent attendance of placemen gave them a voting-value quite disproportionate to their numbers in the House. Fifty-four members were in the majority on two occasions, and fifty-seven once. Twenty members voted only on 3 February, and a further thirty-five also on 15 April but not on 8 May. By that date the ministry had mustered thirty-six members who had not voted on either previous occasion. Since the administration suffered from desertions and abstentions over the seating of Luttrell, the organization of the majority stands in marked contrast to the irregular attendance of the opposition. Only ninety-two of the 202 members voting in the minority at the same three divisions were present at all three, roughly 45 per cent. In the five divisions for which there are minority lists, only fifty-seven members voted in all five, and forty voted only in one. Even more remarkable was the attendance at the first three divisions, which all occurred within a week of each other, on 27 January, 2 February, and 3 February. 190 members altogether then voted in the minority, yet no more than eighty-one were present on all three occasions, and the highest opposition vote was 137. Even though some of this fluctuation may be explained by differences in the issues involved, this was astoundingly casual attendance on a subject of great popular interest and on which the opposition leaders hoped to defeat the ministry. Apathy was one reason for the stability of eighteenth century administrations.

Even though about 500 members might be in London during a session, contemporaries regarded an attendance of over 400 as a very full House, and this is a useful rough criterion to adopt. Although at some time during the century this figure was passed in every month from October to June, it was rare for that number to attend any division before Christmas or after Easter. The peak attendance of a session would be reached between January and March. Of the forty-six days during the Parliament of 1768 to 1774 on which 300 or more members were present at divisions, only six were before Christmas and two after the end of March. All ten divisions attended by more than 400 members took place between late January and early March. This pattern reflected the reluctance of most members to spend the full Parliamentary session in London. When a session began before Christmas, many did not trouble to go up to town until after the recess. Even more marked was the drift of members back to their businesses and estates from March onwards. It was notoriously difficult to secure a full attendance after the Easter recess, for many members failed to return to town. These men were the independents whose votes were essential to any opposition success. In 1767 opposition leader Lord Rockingham was therefore anxious to secure a favourable decision on the question of the East India Company before the Easter recess, explaining to his wife on 9 April that 'it is thought to be right to press for some decision on this matter while the House is full, as Administration have always much advantage when the House is thin. Administration can easier keep their followers in town than we can keep the many individuals who if present would vote with us.'[1] In 1782 this point was of great political significance, for the opposition leaders knew that the beginning of the Easter recess on 28 March would make Lord North's ministry safe for the session. His resignation was forced only on 20 March.[2] By the last weeks of a long session it was often difficult and sometimes impossible for ministers to obtain the quorum of forty members necessary to carry on routine·business.[3]

During the century divisions involving over 400 members did not occur on average more than two or three times a session. Many sessions, especially in the political doldrums of mid-century, passed without any such attendance at all. Such crowded Houses tended to occur only at times of political crisis when the policy or existence of an administration was threatened, and there is no evidence of any trend towards greater attendance during the century. Indeed, the majority of very large divisions, with over 450 members present, occur towards the end of Sir Robert Walpole's ministry and just afterwards. The first high attendance of this long battle occurred

[1] Wentworth Woodhouse MSS., R 156–12.
[2] Wraxall, *Memoirs*, II, 557–8, 592–3.
[3] The absence of a quorum, when shown by a division or a count, is recorded in the *Journals*.

on 14 March 1733 for the introduction of Walpole's excise proposals: 473 members were present at the division in Committee that day, when Lord Perceval noted that 'the House was crowded to an insupportable degree'.[1] The renewed attack on Walpole over Anglo-Spanish relations produced an attendance of 495 over the Spanish Convention on 8 March 1739: and the same diarist, now Earl of Egmont, recorded that 'the House was fuller than has been known for many years. There never were so few absent in my memory.'[2] This peak was surpassed in the final assault on the ministry, 508 members being present when Walpole won a temporary reprieve by three votes, 253 to 250, on 21 January 1742. His son Horace wrote that this was 'the greatest number that ever was in the House'.[3] It remained a record until the admission of 100 more members after the union with Ireland in 1800. Indeed only two other divisions involving 500 members have been found: on 23 March 1742 a motion for a Committee to inquire into Walpole's conduct was carried, after his resignation, by 254 votes to 247: and there was an attendance of exactly 500 members at a division over the hire of Hanoverian troops on 18 January 1744.[4] Comparable totals were not attained on the famous questions of George III's reign. A mere 389 members were present on 9 December 1762 to vote on the Peace of Paris, 455 on 17 February 1764 over general warrants, and 447 on 21 February 1766 on the repeal of the Stamp Act. The largest division during 1769 over Wilkes was 414 members on 27 January. Nor did attendance at divisions rise much above 450 in the great Parliamentary battles of the years from 1780 to 1784, and on some important occasions it was less. 437 members took part in the vote of 17 February 1783 that decided the fate of the Shelburne ministry, and only 386 on 8 March 1784 when Charles James Fox's opposition majority over Pitt dwindled to one vote.[5]

Many debates even on matters of great political significance failed to attract Houses of 300 members unless there was popular interest. The attendance at the five divisions on

---

[1] *H.M.C. Egmont Diary*, I, 342–3. [2] *H.M.C. Egmont Diary*, III, 31–2.
[3] H. Walpole, *Letters*, I, 166. [4] *H.M.C. Egmont Diary*, III, 263, 283.
[5] *Commons Journals*, XXIX, 394, 846; XXXII, 156; XXXIX, 232, 978. *Parliamentary Diary of Nathaniel Ryder*, p. 310.

America in the period of the Coercive Acts of 1774 was respectively 215, 236, 132, 156 and 304 members.[1] For a great deal of other business voting attendance did not often rise above 150. This lack of enthusiasm embraced most debates on social, religious and economic problems, as well as much private business. The attitude of members towards business that held no appeal and involved no private interests was commented upon by General Henry Seymour Conway when on 23 April 1771 he complained of the poor attendance on the third reading of a bill to assist the East India Company to raise soldiers. He can be allowed the last word on the subject: 'I think it a reflection upon a British House of Parliament that in a matter so essential we can scarce muster the House to deliberate upon them. Let any little matter of faction or party, you shall see the House thronged. Let a river or a turnpike, the House thronged again. It is a bad picture of the times.'[2]

[1] *Commons Journals*, XXXIV, 595, 658, 690, 712, 785.
[2] B.M. Eg. MSS. 230, pp. 46–7.

7

THE SEATING OF THE HOUSE

T HE debating chamber of the House of Commons was too small to seat all the 558 members of the eighteenth century. Only one contemporary computation of the seating capacity of the House has been found, that announced by opposition member Temple Luttrell in a speech of 30 April 1777. He then said that there were nearly 800 feet of cushioned seating on the benches of the chamber and of the side galleries; and acceptance of his allowance of 18 or 20 inches for each member would give room for over 500 members. Luttrell's calculations, however, may have been optimistic, for he was arguing in favour of the admission of non-members to hear debates; hence his exclusion of those parts of the galleries 'below the bar'. In any case his speech implied that perhaps one-third of these members would be in the side galleries, and no more than some 350 in the chamber itself.[1] A less generous estimate was put forward by Joseph Hume in 1833, even though Wyatt's alterations had by then increased the capacity of the House. Hume said that less than 300 members could sit there in comfort, although about 350 might be crowded together on the benches.[2]

Sitting on these benches was the only correct mode of attendance in the House, for an order of 10 February 1698 forbade members to sit or stand in the passage, gangways, behind the Chair, or anywhere that was 'not a proper place'.[3] It is unlikely that the rule was strictly enforced; this entry in Sir Roger Newdigate's diary implies that he stood throughout the debate on the Address on 9 January 1770 after arriving at the House at eleven o'clock, too late to find a place. 'Could not sit, sick and faint but recovered and staid it out.'[4] There is ample evidence that members made use of the galleries, both

---

[1] Almon, *Parl. Reg.*, VII, 143–4.
[2] Hansard, *Parliamentary Debates*, 3rd Series, XVI, 370–9.
[3] Hatsell, *Precedents*, II, 92.   [4] Newdigate Diary, 9 Jan. 1770.

when the House was crowded, and on other occasions for writing, resting and sleeping while debates were in progress.[1]

Since there was not enough room for all members in the chamber, considerable competition occurred for seats, especially those in favoured positions, when business of great importance or controversy was expected. There was no formal priority in the matter of seating, and members could secure a right to a seat on a particular day only by occupying it at Prayers; it had been resolved as early as 26 November 1640 'that neither book nor glove may give any man title or interest to any place, if they themselves be not at Prayers'.[2] On 10 March 1735 a formal complaint was made that places were being kept for members not at Prayers; and a resolution was passed 'that no member is to keep any place in the House by book, glove, paper or otherwise, till after prayers, and then only for himself'. A mere three days later this prohibition on the securing of seats before Prayers was revoked by a declaration that the resolution was not to 'extend to a member who takes a place by and for himself only, before Prayers, and leaves a book, glove, paper, or other mark of the same, provided such member be at Prayers'.[3] The rule had obviously been too great an interference with prevailing practice. On several later occasions the resolutions of 1735 were read out and printed in the *Journals*:[4] but it is clear that members still continued the practice of reserving seats for their friends. Sir Roger Newdigate's diary entries often record that he took 'places', in the plural: and James Harris noted a complaint in the House on 4 December 1761 that 'one should not take for two or three'; but the Commons merely ordered another reading of the 1735 resolutions.[5]

---

[1] See, for example, N.L.W. MSS., 1352, fo. 87; Newdigate Diary, 25 Mar. 1771; H. Walpole, *George II*, I, 408; *General Evening Post*, 17 Feb. 1774; Almon, *Parl. Reg.*, XII, 23N; Wraxall, *Memoirs*, III, 262–3. There is a conflict of evidence as to whether members could take part in debates from the gallery. Hatsell stated 'a member may speak, and often does, from the gallery'. *Precedents*, II, 108. During a debate of 8 March 1739, however, a member in the gallery, Robert Willimott, was described by another member as 'sitting in a place from whence he cannot speak'; and Willimott took a seat in the House before speaking. Chandler, *Debates*, XI, 67.

[2] *Commons Journals*, II, 36.　　　[3] *Commons Journals*, XXII, 406, 414.

[4] *Commons Journals*, XXII, 97; XXIV, 67; XXVII, 332.

[5] Harris Diary, 4 Dec. 1761. *Commons Journals*, XXIX, 63.

The typical appearance of the House on occasions when important business was expected is shown by a newspaper description of the scene on 10 February 1773: at half past two o'clock few members were present, but 'the empty Benches [were] all covered with Tickets, on which were inscribed the names of such Members as had been in the House, and were determined to preserve their Places from Intruders'.[1] Before an anticipated debate over the Spanish Convention on 6 March 1739 'it was computed 400 had taken their seats by eight o'clock in the morning'.[2] M.P.s in diaries and correspondence often noted occasions when they had gone down to the House early in the morning, sometimes before breakfast, in order to 'take a place'. There are many such entries in the diary of Sir Roger Newdigate, like that for 10 December 1755: 'At 8 to the House to take a place. Stayed till 10. Prayers. Breakfasted at home. To House at 2. Debate till near 11.' John Campbell told his son on 18 December 1742 of a joke arising from this custom played on Lord Perceval: 'He has some parts, much industry and infinite Vanity. Some time ago he came early to the House and left a paper with his name writ upon it to keep his place, and then went away. Jack Pitt . . . took his paper and carry'd it across the House, and pin'd it to the place where Mr. Sandys usually sits, and then they whispered it about that there was a new Chancellor of the Exchequer.'[3] Sometimes the dignity of the House was impaired by quarrels between members who both claimed the same seat.[4] These incidents apparently arose when a member came in during Prayers and found another member in the place he had claimed beforehand: no decision as to the prior claim in such a dispute was made by the House.[5]

Any right to their seats, however, was lost by those members who attended the Speaker to the House of Lords. More important was the forfeiture at a division of the right to their seats by those members, except the tellers, who voted with the side

---

[1] *St. James' Chronicle*, 13 Feb. 1773.   [2] Chandler, *Debates*, XI, 1.

[3] N.L.W. MSS. 1352, fo. 90. Samuel Sandys was then Chancellor of the Exchequer.

[4] See, for example, the Harris Diary for 22 Mar. 1764, and the Newdigate Diary for 13 Mar. 1772. The *Journals* do not record such incidents even when appeals were made to the Chair for a decision.

[5] Hatsell, *Precedents*, II, 93.

that had to go out of the House into the lobby.[1] The indifferent
and the lazy would therefore vote with the side remaining in
the House. On private business early in the day members were
known to stay and vote contrary to their inclinations rather
than take the risk of losing their seats.[2] Voting on more important business might also be affected by this consideration. On
25 March 1774 a division took place early in the day over an
opposition motion to bring up a petition from William Bollan,
agent for Massachusetts. A debate on the Boston Port Bill was
expected afterwards, and although the attendance was only
215 diarist Henry Cavendish preferred to retain his seat
rather than vote according to his opinion: 'I voted against the
petition being brought up, although I thought it not absolutely
right; I wished to keep my place as much business was coming.'[3] Cavendish was a conscientious member, and a man of
strong political views: others may have been more easily
influenced in their voting by the factor of personal convenience.

Although no member could enforce a formal right to a seat
he had not claimed at Prayers the same day, 'the courtesy of
the House' did allow certain members the privilege of a
particular place. It was understood that a member who
received the Thanks of the House 'in his place' was entitled
to that seat for the duration of that Parliament. One member
who enjoyed the benefit of this courtesy for over a decade was
Thomas Harley: thanked in his place by the Speaker on 8
December 1763 for his action in suppressing Wilkite riots, he
was again thanked for similar measures early in the next
Parliament, on 16 May 1768, and would therefore have been
allowed to retain a place as his own until the dissolution of
1774.[4]

A more famous convention was the evolution of the front
bench on the right hand side of the Speaker's Chair as the
Treasury Bench. From at least the early eighteenth century
this bench was left for the Lords of the Treasury and other

[1] Hatsell, *Precedents*, II, 94. For the method of voting in the House see *infra*,
pp. 251–2.
[2] For a statement to this effect in 1833 see Hansard, *Parliamentary Debates*,
3rd Series, XVI, 372. It was also said then that members asleep in their seats
had been counted as voting for motions to which they were opposed.
[3] B.M. Eg. MSS. 255, p. 33 (shorthand). *Commons Journals*, XXXIV, 595.
[4] *Commons Journals*, XXIX, 698–9; XXXII, 12–13.

members who held important offices, such as the Secretaries of State and the Attorney and Solicitor Generals. On the opening day of every new Parliament, however, the four members for the City of London claimed the right, based on immemorial custom, to sit there.[1] On one such occasion, 31 October 1780, the evidence of the debate shows that both Lord North and opposition spokesman John Dunning were also sitting on the Treasury Bench.[2] At all other times office-holders were granted this privilege of the Treasury Bench, on the ground that their administration work prevented them from going to the House to take places. By the middle of the century an extension of this courtesy, based on recognition of their services to the state, gave to members who had held 'great offices' in the past the equivalent privilege of retaining particular seats without being obliged to go to the House to claim them: 'as in my memory', Hatsell recorded, 'Mr. Pitt, Mr. Fox, Mr. Grenville, and several others'.[3]

These developments were matters of courtesy and not of right. Hatsell himself was careful to qualify his account of the practice by mentioning a notable exception: 'I have heard that Mr. Pulteney, when in the height of opposition to Sir Robert Walpole, always sat on the Treasury Bench.'[4] William Pulteney had been an office-holder himself before assuming the leadership of the malcontent Whigs in 1725; and there is consistent evidence from debates of the period that he still continued to sit near Walpole on the Treasury Bench.[5] The well-known incident of his bet with Sir Robert Walpole over a Latin quotation on 11 February 1741 shows that even then he had not abandoned this habit. Walpole had ended a speech with this line of verse, 'Nil conscire tibi; nulla pullescere culpa'. But, according to John Campbell, 'instead of nulla he said nulli. Mr. Pulteney, who sat near him, told him his mistake but Sir Robert Walpole would have it that nulli was right, and laid his guinea upon it, which I saw him pay to Mr. Pulteney for he was soon convinced he had lost'.[6]

Pulteney was already the eccentric exception. Long before

---

[1] Hatsell, *Precedents*, II, 94.   [2] Debrett, *Parl. Reg.*, I, 5–6.
[3] Hatsell, *Precedents*, II, 94–5.   [4] Hatsell, *Precedents*, II, 94.
[5] Chandler, *Debates*, VII, 56, 98, 286; X, 284; XI, 23, 363.
[6] N.L.W. MSS. 1352, fo. 37. For a discussion of Pulteney's case see Foord, *His Majesty's Opposition*, pp. 156–7.

1714 it was becoming customary for opposition members to sit on the Speaker's left:[1] and the practice became firmly established during Sir Robert Walpole's ministry. Opposition speakers other than Pulteney who can be located were on the left side of the House.[2] After 1742 evidence to this effect is abundant and consistent.[3] The practice developed during the century for the most prominent members of the opposition to occupy the other front bench, and by 1770 the term 'Opposition bench' was in current political usage.[4] George Grenville apparently sat there from 1765 until his death in 1770, and William Dowdeswell from 1766 until his virtual retirement from Parliament in 1774.[5] But both were former Chancellors of the Exchequer, and that the custom was not adopted by all opposition leaders was shown by a curious distinction between the two main factions in opposition during the long ministry of Lord North. Isaac Barré and John Dunning, the chief spokesmen in the House of the group headed by Lords Chatham and Shelburne, both sat on the opposition front bench. Yet Charles James Fox, who succeeded Dowdeswell as leader of the Rockingham party in the Commons, never did so at this time: instead he sat with Edmund Burke and Lord John Cavendish, 'on the third row behind, close to a pillar supporting the gallery, and near to the Speaker's chair'.[6] Nearby, almost under the gallery, the young William Pitt also took his seat in 1781.[7]

From the beginning of George III's reign, and probably much earlier, changes of or within administrations were accompanied by changes of the seating within the chamber of the individual members concerned. Colonel Barré, who had held minor office under the Chatham ministry as a joint Vice-Treasurer of Ireland, remarked in 1772, 'I remember when I according to the usual form had the honour of sitting on that side of the House.'[8] In 1770 Charles Cornwall, the future

---

[1] For a reference in 1673 see Townsend, *House of Commons*, I, 291.

[2] Foord, *His Majesty's Opposition*, pp. 35–6, 155–6.

[3] Foord, *His Majesty's Opposition*, pp. 157–8.

[4] B.M. Eg. MSS. 220, pp. 68–9. There are many later examples in the printed reports of debates by Almon and Debrett, and in Wraxall's *Memoirs*.

[5] See, for example, B.M. Eg. MSS. 219, p. 111; 260, pp. 74–5.

[6] Wraxall, *Memoirs*, II, 229, 283.   [7] Wraxall, *Memoirs*, II, 336, 545.

[8] B.M. Eg. MSS. 232, pp. 46–7.

Speaker but then a member of the opposition, found cause to comment that 'whenever his Majesty dismisses a minister, the moment that minister is disgraced, he comes to this side of the House, and engages in the minority'.[1] Opposition politicians accepting office also crossed the floor of the House. A remark by Alexander Wedderburn during a speech of 6 May 1771 implied that he had done so on receiving the post of Solicitor-General a few months earlier.[2] Both Wedderburn and Cornwall himself, who became a Lord of the Treasury in March 1774, were sitting on the Treasury Bench in April 1774.[3]

There were notable exceptions to this practice. Richard Rigby sat on the opposition side of the House when Paymaster of the Forces under Lord North, but this was regarded as mere affectation. 'As if he had meant to show that he acted independently of Ministers, and was above their control, he never sat on the Government side of the House of Commons: but he did not on that account give the less unqualified support on all occasions to Administration.'[4] In contrast, General Henry Seymour Conway's genuine reluctance to profess avowed opposition to government was symbolized by his position under the gallery behind the Treasury Bench. He began to criticize Lord North's American measures from a seat there in 1774, and was still doing so from the same place in 1779 and 1780.[5]

Seating habits hardened during the period of the North ministry, when alignments were virtually unchanged for over a decade; and the kaleidoscopic effect of the frequent political changes of 1782 and 1783 on seating within the House of Commons aroused much contemporary interest and comment. Lord North himself must have been sitting on the Treasury Bench for at least his fifteen years as Chancellor of the Exchequer; but after his resignation in 1782 he crossed the floor and sat on the Opposition Bench.[6] Wraxall noted the scene when the House re-assembled on 8 April: 'The Treasury Bench, as well as the places behind it, had been during so many years occupied by Lord North and his friends, that it became difficult to recognize them again in their new seats

---

[1] B.M. Eg. MSS. 221, p. 356.   [2] B.M. Eg. MSS. 231, pp. 134–40.
[3] H. Walpole, *Letters*, VIII, 447.   [4] Wraxall, *Memoirs*, II, 212–3.
[5] B.M. Eg. MSS. 255, pp. 243, 248. Almon, *Parl. Reg.*, XVI, 160–1; XVII, 246–7, 620.
[6] Wraxall, *Memoirs*, III, 169, 260.

dispersed over the Opposition benches.'[1] The new occupants
of the Treasury Bench included Charles Fox and Richard
Sheridan, but not young William Pitt, who had refused office.[2]
The new political alignment lasted three months. Fox spoke
from the Treasury Bench for the last time on 2 July, before the
resignation of himself and his friends from the administration
being reconstructed under Lord Shelburne. The scene in the
House on 5 July was described in the contemporary press:[3]

> Yesterday, in consequence of the change of ministry, the House
> of Commons was uncommonly crowded, not less than three hundred
> and fifty members having taken their seats at three o'clock . . . a
> general commotion succeeded upon the appearance of Mr. Fox
> and Mr. Burke, who immediately took their Places on the Opposi-
> tion side of the House, in which they were followed by Mr. John
> Townshend, Mr. Sheridan, and many others of their friends. At
> this time, the Hon. Mr. William Pitt seated himself on the Treasury
> Bench, just where Mr. Fox used to sit.

Pitt took his seat on the Treasury Bench before accepting
office as Chancellor of the Exchequer. But Fox and his chief
supporters did not move to the front Opposition Bench: they
returned to their old seats on the third bench under the gallery.
Not until February 1783 did Fox sit on the Opposition Bench
proper; and he made the move then in order to signify his
coalition with Lord North. Their political success put Fox,
Lord North and Edmund Burke on the Treasury Bench in
April 1783, when Pitt took a seat on the Opposition Bench.
Finally, in December 1783 Fox and Lord North were back on
the Opposition Bench after their dismissal from office, while
the Treasury Bench was tenanted by spokesmen like Henry
Dundas until Pitt's re-election after taking office.[4]
By the later eighteenth century the physical division of the
House on political lines was not confined to the leading members of administrations and oppositions. A more general
significance is implied by the authentic Parliamentary language
recorded in the House by diarist Henry Cavendish between
1768 and 1774. By that time such phrases as 'the other side

---

[1] Wraxall, *Memoirs*, III, 27.
[2] Wraxall, *Memoirs*, III, 33, 150, 176. Debrett, *Parl. Reg.*, VII, 14.
[3] *Adams Weekly Courant*, 9 July 1782.
[4] Wraxall, *Memoirs*, III, 168–9, 176, 260–2, 389, 395; IV, 610, 623.

of the House' or 'the gentlemen over the way' were synonymous with the other accepted designations of political opponents.[1] It was to explain these references that Cavendish made the following statement in the draft preface to his diary: 'It is usual for every Ministry and their principal supporters, to sit on the right hand of the Chair, and for those in opposition on the left: so that when the Reader finds those words used, he will take notice who uses them; if he does not he will sometimes be at a loss to know what the Member means.'[2] In notes to his diary Cavendish himself refers to the opposition and ministry sides of the House,[3] and many contemporary statements would have been meaningless except in such a wider context. Professions of impartiality by the Chair, for example, were worded in terms of sides of the House.[4] That the designation 'side of the House' had become a convention of political terminology was shown by a complaint over the use of such a phrase by opposition member John Dunning during a debate of 19 March 1771 over the refuge given by the City of London to newspaper printers of debates. Attorney-General Edward Thurlow took exception to a reference by Dunning to a member on 'the other side of the House', expressing the hope that in a matter concerning the privilege of Parliament 'there would not be sides of the House'. Dunning at once rose to explain his remark. 'I alluded to an honourable gentleman on the other side of the House to distinguish him; but sides of the House never occurred to me. I concur that this is a question in which there ought not to be sides of the House.'[5]

Little evidence is available on the development and extent of this convention of 'sides' of the House. Members of political factions, whether in administration or opposition, would naturally tend to sit together, especially as such Parliamentary groups were often based on personal relationships. There was a trend for placemen to sit behind the Treasury Bench;[6] but the independence of the country gentlemen was reflected in their

---

[1] See, for example, B.M. Eg. MSS. 216, p. 109; 217, p. 99; 222, p. C 138; 224, pp. 21, 369; 258, p. 120.

[2] B.M. Eg. MSS. 263, fo. 3.

[3] B.M. Eg. MSS. 215, p. 267; 223, p. 525.

[4] B.M. Eg. MSS. 223, p. 391; 226, p. 76; 244, pp. 6–7; 3711, p. 86.

[5] B.M. Eg. MSS. 226, pp. 291–3.

[6] For references to this practice in 1734 see Chandler, *Debates*, VIII, 10, 84.

seating habits, and it would be unwise to regard their physical position in the House as anything but a very rough barometer of their allegiance. Information on the matter is scanty, as few spoke in debate: there may have been a corner of the House traditionally occupied by Tories or independents;[1] but known examples of the seating behaviour of independents suggest a frequent disregard of the convention of political sides of the House. Although then still in opposition to the ministry, Sir Edward Knatchbull was sitting very near to Walpole on 7 December 1724.[2] Sir Herbert Mackworth spoke in support of North's ministry from the opposition side of the House on 28 November 1777; and John Rolle supported Pitt when sitting 'opposite' him on 2 February 1784.[3] Truly independent members, and such a role was claimed for John Elwes by his contemporary biographer, sat indiscriminately on either side. But his behaviour is noted as being exceptional by the time he was a member, between 1772 and 1784: for it was then already 'the custom of members in general' to sit on a particular side of the House.[4]

The small size of the House undoubtedly inhibited the growth of any firm political convention in the matter of seating. On days when the chamber was crowded members would pay little heed to the situation of a seat if there was no alternative. Sir Roger Newdigate and William Burke, who quarrelled over a place on 13 March 1772, were opposed over every political issue.[5] On Budget Day in 1774 opposition member Thomas Townshend sat on the administration side of the House, while Sir Lawrence Dundas, a supporter of the ministry, was sitting next to Isaac Barré, the most vehement of opposition spokesmen.[6] But the House was rarely full, and its size did not prevent the development of the political practice imposed by its shape. It is an axiom of modern British history that the division of the seating of the House of Commons into two sides has been a significant factor in the evolution of a two-party political system. The admittedly unsatisfactory evidence of the eigh-

---

[1] Chandler, *Debates*, VIII, 171. B.M. Eg. MSS. 220, p. 244.
[2] *Knatchbull Diary*, p. 34.
[3] Almon, *Parl. Reg.*, VIII, 69. Debrett, *Parl. Reg.*, XIII, 48.
[4] Topham, *Life of John Elwes*, p. 52.
[5] Newdigate Diary, 13 Mar. 1772.
[6] B.M. Eg. MSS. 258, pp. 92, 120, 146, 149.

teenth century does confirm that seating conventions preceded the emergence of modern parties. Politicians and placemen could make appropriate decisions about their position in the House: and members wishing to demonstrate independence were faced with the dilemma that they had to sit on one side or the other.

8

STRANGERS IN THE HOUSE

'ORDERED, That the Serjeant of Arms, attending this House, do, from time to time, take into his custody any stranger or strangers, that he shall see, or be informed of to be, in the House, or gallery, while the House, or any Committee of the Whole House, is sitting.'[1] This order made by the House of Commons on 31 October 1705 was followed on 8 December 1711 by another, 'that no Member of this House do presume to bring any stranger or strangers into the House or gallery thereof, while the House is sitting.'[2] These orders were not the first regulations restricting the entry of strangers into the House: but they were renewed every session without significant modification until 1845, and were the prohibitions invoked during the eighteenth century.[3] Such orders were never made until the second day of a session, however, and there existed the anomaly that the House could not be cleared of strangers for the often important and crowded opening debate on the Address.[4]

The orders were not enforced until a member of the House formally drew attention to the presence of strangers: but if a member gave prior notice of his intention to do so on a future day strangers would not be admitted on that occasion. Any member could have the orders carried out, for on notice of strangers being taken by a member 'in his place' it was the Speaker's duty immediately to give instructions to the Serjeant. The order was not interpreted literally, strangers being merely

---

[1] *Commons Journals*, XV, 6. On 15 Nov. 1705 a similar rule concerning strangers during the sitting of any Committee in the House was made a standing order. See ibid., 26.

[2] *Commons Journals*, XVII, 3.

[3] See, for example, *Commons Journals*, XXXVI, 458. Hatsell, *Precedents*, II, 180, mentions only the orders of 1705. For some earlier actions against strangers see Redlich, *Procedure of the House of Commons*, II, 34–5.

[4] B.M. Eg. MSS. 3711, p. 44. This statement by Lord North on 9 Jan. 1770 is confirmed by the Clementson Diary, p. 21, and by the *Journals*.

ejected, and not arrested. The Speaker was, in form at least, merely the servant of the House in the matter: but on one occasion, in 1751, Speaker Onslow himself apparently took the initiative, asking for a member to spy strangers.[1] Attempts by members to initiate debates or divisions over the enforcement of the orders were overruled by the Chair, as was the case for all standing orders. When Colonel Barré demanded 'the sense of the House' on 14 March 1774 Charles Jenkinson replied that 'the member who gets up is in the nature of a witness'; and Speaker Norton declared, 'I trust and hope the House will do in this occasion as it always does.'[2]

The existence of the standing orders therefore did not mean the invariable exclusion of strangers from the House. For the vast majority of debates during the century there is no evidence as to whether or not strangers were present. Out of over 600 sitting days during the well-reported Parliament elected in 1768, definite information that strangers were excluded has been found only for some twenty occasions, and there is reference to their presence at debates on a mere dozen days. Throughout the earlier decades of the century the chronological distribution of the scanty information on both counts is random: strangers were both admitted and excluded in the same session, month, and week. The general paucity of information on the subject may reflect the lack of significance attached by contemporaries to the question of the admission of strangers during most of the century. The references of diarist James Harris to the presence of strangers in debates of the 1760s are casual and incidental; and he failed to note their ejection even when this occurred during debates which he reported in detail. The probability that strangers were usually present at debates is strengthened by some contemporary statements. On 1 December 1740 a discussion of the standing orders centred on the point as to whether strangers could be punished by the House for attendance at previous debates. The consensus of opinion was that the Serjeant could take action only against strangers actually present when the orders were enforced. The debate arose from a witness being asked whether he had been present on an earlier occasion; and various remarks by members confirm an overall impression that strangers frequently

[1] H. Walpole, *George II*, I, 27–8.   [2] B.M. Eg. MSS. 254, pp. 77–8.

attended debates in the House.[1] That they could and did attend unless the orders were specifically enforced is also the implication of a procedural explanation by Sir Edward Knatchbull in 1729.[2] There is, moreover, no validity in the assumption sometimes made that the opportunity for fuller and freer discussion in Committee was enhanced by the exclusion of strangers;[3] for the evidence of both general remarks and actual occasions shows that strangers could be present at Committees of the Whole House.[4] Prohibitions on the admission of strangers, too, were of varying severity. Despite the order of 1711 members could often introduce visitors on application to the Speaker even when entrance was denied to other strangers, but that order had to be obeyed if any member insisted: an objection by Rose Fuller prevented Sir Joseph Mawbey from introducing a friend on 18 May 1768.[5] Privileged categories of non-members were also often exempted from a general ban on admission.[6]

Although the galleries, one along each side, and one at the end of the House, had not been built for the purpose of accommodating visitors they soon came to be regarded as the usual place for strangers. This is stated or implied in various references to their presence in the early eighteenth century, and by 1733 the phrase 'clearing the galleries' meant the eviction of strangers.[7] For much of the century, however, the House did not restrict strangers to the galleries, and an extraordinary degree of latitude was depicted by Temple Luttrell on 30 April 1777. He then declared that under Speakers Onslow and Cust 'strangers were admitted even into the body of the House' when the elder William Pitt was speaking; and he claimed that 'strangers have been suffered to advance so far as beneath the rose which is in the centre of your roof.'[8] It was apparently in the early years of George III's reign that the custom evolved of the strict confinement of strangers to the galleries, apart

---

[1] Chandler, *Debates*, XII, 13–16.   [2] *Knatchbull Diary*, p. 1.

[3] For a statement to this effect see L. H. Gipson, *The British Empire before the American Revolution*, X, 386.

[4] See, for example, *H.M.C. Egmont Diary*, I, 12; II, 350; *Knatchbull Diary*, p. 1; Clementson Diary, pp. 24–5.

[5] B.M. Eg. MSS. 215, p. 75.   [6] See *infra*, pp. 149–52.

[7] Chandler, *Debates*, VII, 299. *H.M.C. Egmont Diary*, I, 12, 86, 268–9.

[8] Almon, *Parl. Reg.*, VII, 144.

from certain privileged exceptions; and it became the practice for the Speaker to order that the doors of the gallery should be locked when it was full.[1]

The motive behind the institution of the standing orders was stated by John Dunning on 13 December 1770 to have been the physical convenience of members, the avoidance of heat and other discomforts of overcrowding. 'This I do know, that the idea of standing orders of this House were never founded in so unconstitutional an opinion, that it was proper to exclude from the debate those who are so much interested in it. . . . The size of the House I take to be the ground of that standing order.'[2] This was sometimes the true reason for the exclusion of strangers, but not as often as it was professed.[3] Dunning in this very speech was protesting against the more usual reason for the exclusion of strangers, the maintenance of a veil of secrecy over Parliamentary proceedings. The two motives, of course, might coincide: it was the debates of major political significance that were crowded by members and strangers, and most known examples of the exclusion of strangers concern such debates.[4]

Even before 1770 it was therefore probable that strangers would be excluded from debates on subjects of great political controversy; but a more systematic application of such a ban is apparent from about that year. In 1777 Thomas Townshend blamed Sir Fletcher Norton for this development, asserting that the orders for the exclusion of strangers had never been 'vigorously put in force' before Norton's election in 1770.[5] This was an unfair imputation. The frequent exclusion of strangers under Speaker Norton was caused by the attempts of various members to prevent the publication of reports of debates in the press. Newspaper reporting of Parliamentary debates began tentatively in 1768, and became common by the end of 1770.[6] The deliberate retaliation of members to this

[1] See, for example, the *London Chronicle*, 16 Feb. 1773.

[2] B.M. Eg. MSS. 223, p. 453.

[3] For some genuine instances of this reason see *General Evening Post*, 6 April and 11 May 1773, 17 Feb. 1774; *London Chronicle*, 20 May 1773.

[4] See, for example, *Knatchbull Diary*, pp. 57N, 91. Chandler, *Debates*, VII, 299; VIII, 203. Harris Diary, 9 Dec. 1762, 24 Nov. 1763.

[5] Almon, *Parl. Reg.*, VII, 145.

[6] See my paper, 'The Beginning of Parliamentary Reporting in Newspapers 1768–1774', *Eng. Hist. Rev.*, 74 (1959), pp. 623–36.

development was heralded by the request of Sir John Turner for the House to be cleared of strangers on 7 February 1771. His ostensible motive was the heat and discomfort of the House, but Sir Joseph Mawbey tartly observed, 'Many gentlemen complain of cold. The honourable baronet who made the motion has got his greatcoat on.' Henry Seymour, who had entered the Commons in 1763, added the comment that 'since I have sat in this House, I do not recollect any motion of this sort, but on the right of election'. This statement was misleading, but served to remind members that their usual practice was to admit strangers. Colonel George Onslow, who had just started his campaign against newspaper printers for their reporting of debates, then revealed the true motive: 'Nobody wishes more to permit strangers to be in the House than myself; but there is one objection . . . No member would misrepresent the speeches made in this House. It must proceed from strangers.'[1] A comment on this incident by James Harris to the second Lord Hardwicke shows a secondary reason for enforcement of the standing orders: 'The House was cleared, which was supposed was the difference of an hour or two at least in the length of our orations.'[2]

The attempt in 1771 to stop newspaper reporting failed:[3] and the following years therefore saw the exclusion of strangers from debates of major political interest. This policy was adopted, for example, during the passage of the Royal Family Marriage Bill in 1772,[4] and also for the American legislation of 1774. In that year the House was invariably cleared and the gallery doors shut when the Orders of the Day were read for the American bills, although strangers were admitted to hear other business on the same days both before and after the debates on America.[5] The exclusion of strangers at this time, indeed, was selective, not total: remarks by members speaking

[1] B.M. Eg. MSS. 224, pp. 97–8.

[2] B.M. Add. MSS. 35609, fo. 315.

[3] For accounts of this episode see my paper, 'John Wilkes and the Freedom of the Press (1771)', *Bull. Inst. Hist. Res.*, 33 (1960), pp. 86–98; and R. L. Haig, *The Gazetteer 1735–1797*, pp. 102–18.

[4] The only statement found of such a ban concerns the debate of 9 Mar. 1772. Cobbett, *Parl. Hist.*, XVII, 399N. But it can be inferred from the almost complete failure of the newspapers to produce any reports.

[5] See the *General Evening Post*, 15, 17, 26, 29 Mar., 23, 26, 30 Apr., and 4 May 1774.

show that strangers were present at many debates.[1] The initiative to eject strangers always came from supporters of the administration. On 14 March 1774, when Timothy Caswall moved to have the orders enforced before the introduction of the Boston Port Bill, George Byng made this allegation: 'I did see people going about the House to get others to move the House to be cleared, when they dared not do it themselves ... When they could not prevail upon some, I am sorry to see they could upon my honourable friend.' Isaac Barré remarked from the Opposition Bench, 'Gentlemen on this side of the House do not move for strangers to withdraw.'[2]

The policy of excluding strangers continued after the beginning of the War of American Independence. Opposition members George Johnstone and Charles James Fox commented on 24 April 1776, Budget Day, that the gallery was then open after having been shut almost every other day of the session. Speaker Norton denied imputations of connivance between the Chair and ministers. He had no discretion if any members applied to have the standing order enforced.[3] The gallery was constantly kept shut in the next session as well;[4] and on 30 April 1777 Temple Luttrell opened a formal debate on the subject in a thin House:[5]

He thought it for the credit of all parties, that strangers should be admitted under proper restrictions; candour, policy, gratitude, and duty to the people, whose representatives they were, called upon them to open their doors—so far as the confined limits of the House would admit of. There was, he insisted upon it, a constitutional right in their constituents to satisfy themselves how far their delegates did, or did not, discharge the trust reposed in them with firmness and fidelity, and to form some judgement whether their principles and legislative suffrages might merit a renewal of that trust on a future occasion. The persons solicitous to be present during the debates of Parliament, are generally speaking, such as are more immediately interested in the question under debate; and he appealed to some of the ablest, and most diligent members of the

[1] See, for example, B.M. Eg. MSS. 241, p. 211; 243, pp. 302, 335; 245, pp. 109, 305; 246, p. 186; 252, pp. 74, 185; 257, p. 101; 260, p. 162; 262, p. 81.

[2] B.M. Eg. MSS. 254, pp. 76–84.

[3] Almon, *Parl. Reg.*, III, 484–6 (second numeration). For the gallery being shut in 1776 see also H. Walpole, *Last Journals*, I, 551.

[4] Almon, *Parl. Reg.*, VI, 298.

[5] The account of the debate is taken from Almon, *Parl. Reg.*, VII, 143–9.

House, whether in former times they had not often been put in possession of matters of fact happily decisive of the business in issue, by stepping for a minute into the gallery. To fabricate and enact laws ... with a clandestine privacy ... must, it stands to reason, in a free country like ours, be utterly repugnant to the vital principles of its constitution.

Luttrell's remarks on the special interest of many strangers in particular debates are confirmed by other observers. The gallery was often full of clergymen for debates on religion or the church:[1] and other groups of strangers like American merchants and agents, West Indies planters and merchants, or East India Company stockholders attended on business affecting their particular interests.[2]

Temple Luttrell concluded his speech by moving for 'a Committee of the Whole House, to consider the several orders relative to the exclusion of strangers from the galleries'. He had no particular proposals in mind, but envisaged some rule that would permit members to introduce one stranger each until four o'clock, suggesting that strangers could be assigned 'the entire gallery below the bar'. The end gallery held about 200 persons when full;[3] and this was the number of strangers Luttrell suggested in his speech. He was seconded by John Wilkes, and Charles Fox supported what he described as the moderate proposal for consideration, though not cancellation, of the standing orders. Thomas Townshend declared that only a sense of guilt could explain any ministerial objection to publicity. These remarks did not inhibit criticism. Lord North 'believed the House would be of his opinion, not to open the doors on any occasion'. Richard Rigby roundly opposed the motion. 'He thought it improper to let in strangers; they had no business in the House at all; and he had observed, that when they are thus indulged, scarce a day passes without some of the members being put to much inconvenience, and frequently they have been pushed about and insulted ... What good would result from strangers being in the gallery? Only to print speeches in newspapers of all sorts.' Another office-

---

[1] See, for example, B.M. Eg. MSS. 241, p. 211; *General Evening Post*, 23 Feb. 1773; Almon, *Parl. Reg.*, XII, 398.

[2] See, for example, B.M. Add. MSS. 35375 fo. 82; H. Walpole, *Last Journals*, I, 201.

[3] *Morning Chronicle*, 9 Mar. 1784.

holder, Sir William Meredith, also voiced the view that only members should be present at debates.

There were *Votes* published under the Speaker's authority, which sufficiently declared the sense and determination of the House of Commons on every important question. The arguments, the motives, the policy, and influence that might induce those decisions, were out of the pale of popular enquiry. The world at large, even our immediate constituents, had no just claim to be apprised of all the *minutiae* of debate.

Luttrell's motion was defeated by eighty-three votes to sixteen, but he had won his point. Speaker Norton ended the debate by asking the House how he should act, and the practice adopted was virtually the one suggested by Luttrell. The side galleries were reserved for members of the House of Commons;[1] but now members personally introduced individual strangers into the end gallery until it was full. That some such arrangement immediately followed the debate of 30 April 1777 is apparent from a discussion a fortnight later after the Budget debate on 14 May. Speaker Norton then reminded members, 'It was the sense of the House the other day, that strangers should be let in till the end gallery was full.' He had given instructions accordingly: but on that day several members had been offended because the doors to the gallery had been closed when the Serjeant mistakenly informed the Speaker that it was full. The brief ensuing debate produced the usual variety of opinions, but no change of policy.[2]

The restricted admission of strangers continued, and when on 29 January 1778 Colonel Henry Luttrell complained of misrepresentation in a newspaper he threatened to have the standing orders strictly enforced. Charles Fox replied that 'the public had a right to know what passed in Parliament'; Robert Vyner said that the ban on strangers should be imposed only when there was 'want of room' or 'secret business'; and Edmund Burke produced several reasons for the admission of strangers. The debates of the House, he said, were 'the channel of information to the constituents of the members . . . a school for the instruction of youth . . . the source of information and amusement to the ladies'. Speaker Norton twice inter-

---

[1] Wraxall, *Memoirs*, VI, 46.   [2] Almon, *Parl. Reg.*, VII, 193–4.

vened to request a decision, since it was 'with the acquiescence of the House' that he had relaxed the standing orders. Colonel Luttrell unexpectedly conceded the point, rising to announce that Burke's arguments had convinced him that there should not be an absolute prohibition on the admission of strangers.[1]

The only sustained attempt to exclude strangers was made by William Clayton in May 1780. On 3 May he had the gallery cleared, and on 10 May he gave notice that he would move for strangers to withdraw the next day as soon as he arrived at the House: accordingly none were admitted on 11 May. Only 150 members and thirty strangers were present when Clayton made this announcement, and his ostensible reason therefore met with disbelief from reporters. 'The plea on which this new and singular objection (for new and singular it is, considering the custom of late years) is grounded, is an opinion that strangers contribute to heat the House, to the inconvenience of the members.'[2] The sudden revival of a complete ban upon strangers led to a complaint on 18 May by David Hartley. Speaker Norton stated that one member, evidently Clayton, was responsible; and he explained that 'the reason why he had not ordered strangers to be excluded before was, because he conceived it to be the sense of the House that they should be admitted; that it was his duty to attend to the sense of the House, that they were masters of their own orders, but while they remained upon the book, he was bound to enforce them whenever he was called upon so to do.'[3]

This continued to be the duty of the Chair until 1875. In the eighteenth century all the discussions on the subject show unanimity on the need to retain the standing orders as a reserve power of the House. Hatsell thoroughly approved of this view, commenting that although members often 'winked at the breach of it . . . the order itself has notwithstanding existed, and, for the preservation of order and decency, must always necessarily exist, liable to be put into execution without delay or dispute'.[4] Nevertheless the decision of the House in 1777 to admit strangers was a permanent one. On 18 May 1780 the consensus of opinion was clearly in favour of this step, even Lord North now conceding that it should be a matter for

[1] Almon, *Parl. Reg.*, VIII, 323–6.
[2] Almon, *Parl. Reg.*, XVII, 637, 695.
[3] Almon, *Parl. Reg.*, XVII, 700–1.
[4] Hatsell, *Precedents*, II, 182.

members to consider.[1] For a few years after 1777 the ban on admission was sometimes enforced for a particular reason, usually of physical convenience rather than political censorship.[2] But between 1780 and the destruction of the old House by fire in 1834 the standing orders were invoked only on twenty-one occasions that are known.[3]

Reports of debates after 1777 contain many references, often casual or general, to the presence of strangers. By 1783 the newsworthy item was not whether strangers were admitted or excluded, but the time by which the gallery was full before important debates.[4] Strangers were not excluded even on the most crowded and significant occasions. One account of the proceedings on 20 March 1782, when Lord North announced his resignation, began with this remark: 'Since the beginning of the session, or perhaps during the present reign, there never were so many members in the House, as appeared there that day: and the crowds of spectators were in proportion greater than usual.'[5] And here is a newspaper report of the scene in the House of Commons on 17 February 1783, the occasion when the newly-formed coalition of Charles Fox and Lord North defeated the Shelburne ministry.[6]

The House was crowded with the greatest number of members that ever met there since the beginning of the present reign. The side galleries could scarcely contain all those who could not find room in the body of the House, either to sit or stand, and the front gallery was so full of strangers, and the footways leading into it were so completely choked up by those who could not get seats, that those who were within, and nearly overcome with heat, found it impossible to get out.

The stringent conditions of 1777 were soon relaxed. At first it was necessary for members to take the trouble of accompanying their friends to secure their admission to the gallery:

[1] Almon, *Parl. Reg.*, XVII, 702.

[2] For some instances see H. Walpole, *Last Journals*, II, 101, 105, 179. Almon, *Parl. Reg.*, VIII, 328, 359.

[3] A list is given by A. Aspinall, 'The Reporting and Publishing of the House of Commons' Debates 1771–1834', *Essays to Namier*, p. 230N. To it there should be added 21 Mar. 1781. Debrett, *Parl. Reg.*, II, 294.

[4] Almon, *Parl Reg.*, XII, 398. Debrett, *Parl. Reg.*, V, 46; IX, 108, 138, 411, 512, 688.

[5] Debrett, *Parl. Reg.*, VI, 491.

[6] *Morning Herald*, 18 Feb. 1783; quoted by Aspinall, op. cit., p. 235N.

within a few years, however, a written introduction from a member to the doorkeeper of the gallery was sufficient.[1] In 1782 the German traveller Carl Moritz was informed by his landlady that a small bribe of 2s. or 2s. 6d. to the doorkeeper would be an adequate substitute, and so it proved: indeed, once in the gallery, he found there some regular visitors, mostly newspaper reporters, who paid the doorkeeper a guinea beforehand for the whole session.[2] That strangers not introduced by members were present proved an early matter for complaint, and even an excuse for clearing the House: on 8 March 1784 Sir James Lowther, piqued that there was no room in the gallery that day for a friend of his, used this pretext to enforce the standing orders.[3] It soon became the custom for ordinary members of the public to obtain admission by the simple resort of queueing, often for several hours, until the gallery doors were opened when the House began business; but by that time much of the gallery space was often already taken by strangers with personal introductions from members.[4]

No distinction of nationality was observed in the admission of strangers. Foreigners were admitted along with other strangers, and foreign ministers were on occasions even allowed to stay when ordinary strangers were turned out.[5] For much of the century, too, ladies were admitted among the other strangers, although their attendance may at first have been a rarity. The indulgence of Speaker Onslow in permitting the attendance of ladies in the gallery on 5 May 1732 was evidently regarded as unusual, and thought to be explained by the particular business of that day.[6] That the admission of ladies continued without such special reasons is shown by the presumably unique incident on 25 January 1743, when some ladies urinated on members below. John Campbell sent this account to his son two days later: 'On Monday, some gentlewomen in our gallery not being able to hold their water, let it run on Mr. Dodington, and a Scots member who sat under. The first had a white duffel frock spoiled, the latter almost

[1] Aspinall, op. cit., p. 232N.   [2] Moritz, *Travels*, pp. 51–2, 59–60.
[3] Debrett, *Parl. Reg.*, XIII, 268.   [4] Aspinall, op. cit., pp. 232–4.
[5] See, for example, Harris Diary, 25 Nov., 9 and 11 Dec. 1761. H. Walpole, *George II*, II, 108N; *Letters*, VI, 14.
[6] *H.M.C. Egmont Diary*, I, 269.

blinded.'[1] In the early years of George III's reign references
to the presence of ladies at debates became less infrequent:[2]
but it is not always clear whether the designation 'lady'
denoted rank or merely sex. Certainly some accounts imply
that the privilege of attendance was being enjoyed only by
women of rank. James Harris referred in his diary to the
attendance of 'Members, Lords and Ladies' on 12 February
1762; and here is Horace Walpole's description of the feminine
attendance at two debates in February 1764: 'We had Patriot-
esses, too, who stayed out the whole. Lady Rockingham and
Lady Sondes the first day; both again the second day, with
Miss Mary Pelham, Mrs. Fitzroy, and the Duchess of Richmond.[3] Chivalry sometimes led members to excuse ladies
present from complying with the standing orders when they
were enforced. When Caswall moved to clear the House on 14
March 1774 he asked, 'I beg leave to have it understood that
the Ladies be excepted'; but other members and Speaker
Norton said that the orders must be enforced completely. All
strangers were ejected that day.[4] A similar incident on 2
February 1778 led to the more deliberate exclusion of ladies
from debates. When strangers were removed because of
disturbances, George Johnstone insisted on the eviction also
of the sixty ladies in the gallery, perhaps because they included
the Speaker's wife.[5] It is often stated that after this incident
ladies were never again admitted to the strangers's gallery of
the old House.[6] Any ban, however, was not absolute; for Carl
Moritz noted in 1782 that 'among these spectators are people
of all ranks; and even, not infrequently, ladies'.[7]

Certain categories of strangers had always been more
privileged than others in the matter of entry to the House,
although the right to exclude all strangers whatsoever was
sometimes exercised, as on 14 March 1774. Hatsell listed them

[1] N.L.W. MSS. 1352, fo. 112.
[2] See, for example, Harris Diary, 4 and 9 Dec. 1761, 9 May 1766; *Middlesex Journal*, 3 Mar. 1769.
[3] H. Walpole, *Letters*, VI, 3.   [4] B.M. Eg. MSS. 254, pp. 56–7.
[5] H. Walpole, *Last Journals*, II, 101.
[6] As by Aspinall, op. cit., p. 229N; Dasent, *Speakers*, p. 280; and Redlich, *Procedure of the House of Commons*, II, 35.
[7] Moritz, *Travels*, p. 59.

as 'Peers, Members of the Irish Parliament, Officers of the House of Lords . . . and other exceptions.'[1]

Members of the House of Lords were usually given admission on days when ordinary strangers were excluded, although they might be also turned out or refused entrance.[2] Quarrels between the two Houses of Parliament sometimes led to a more permanent exclusion of peers only, as when the Commons immediately retaliated in December 1770 after the Lords unceremoniously evicted all strangers.[3] A virtually complete ban lasted for some years. Not until December 1774, after the Lords had agreed to allow the entry of strangers again, did the Commons permit the admission of peers.[4]

Peers at first usually mixed with other strangers; even Frederick, Prince of Wales, sat in the gallery on his visits to the House in 1737 and 1739:[5] but they also claimed the special privilege of sitting under the gallery at the end of the House below the Bar. There is evidence of this habit under George II;[6] and in the early years of George III's reign peers usually sat under the gallery, but sometimes in it.[7] This privileged status aroused occasional resentment, for the peers offered no reciprocal arrangement to members of the Commons. On 16 December 1778 Sir Phillip Jennings Clerke reminded members of this grievance. A great number of peers came to their House for important debates and 'not only crowded the gallery, but filled the body of the House. This was extremely disagreeable . . . members of this House were obliged to stand for hours together below the bar of the Peers . . . indiscriminately mixed with a mob.' Clerke suggested that peers should be admitted only into the end gallery. Sir James Lowther favoured the side galleries as well; but nothing was decided.[8] The matter was again raised before the end of that session, by James Martin on 9 June 1779. He complained of the practice of peers sitting

---

[1] Hatsell, *Precedents*, II, 182.

[2] See, for example, Chandler, *Debates*, VI, 125; *Public Ledger*, 15 Mar. 1774.

[3] H. Walpole, *George III*, IV, 146, 152N. Clementson Diary, pp. 24–6.

[4] H. Walpole, *Last Journals*, I, 414. Almon, *Parl. Reg.*, I, 11–12. For a quarrel in 1721, with a similar result, see Redlich, *Procedure of the House of Commons*, II, 35.

[5] *H.M.C. Egmont Diary*, II, 350. Chandler, *Debates*, XI, 36N.

[6] N.L.W. MSS. 1352, fos. 189–90.

[7] Harris Diary, 25 Nov. 1761, 12 Feb. 1762, 23 Jan. and 28 Feb. 1765, 9 May 1766. H. Walpole, *George III*, I, 260; II, 35, 43.

[8] Almon, *Parl. Reg.*, XI, 174–5.

under the gallery when the House of Lords denied entrance altogether to their members, and suggested that if the Lords took no steps, the Serjeant-at-Arms should be given orders the next session not to distinguish between peers and other strangers.[1] Ill-feeling over the lack of reciprocity was widespread, even the moderate James Harris making this note in his diary for 13 November 1780: 'Lords turned out of the House. They turn us out, or blend us with the rabble.' Only James Martin took direct action. On 6 March 1783 he had Lord Walsingham removed from below the Bar to the gallery, and other peers ejected from the same place on 31 March.[2] Martin conducted an intermittent campaign against this privileged status of peers for some years,[3] but to no avail. In 1783 diarist Wraxall, commenting on the attendance of the Prince of Wales at debates of the House, referred to his presence 'among the peers, where he took his place under the gallery'[4]: and in 1786 he described the end of the House under the gallery as the customary place for peers to sit.[5] Perhaps by this time, and certainly by the early nineteenth century, there had come into existence for the benefit of successive Speakers a fixed list of the persons allowed to sit in this area 'below the Bar'. They included not only peers and their heirs, but also members of the royal family, and various judges and other office-holders.[6]

Contemporary references in the reign of George III confirm Hatsell's statement that members of the Irish House of Commons were usually exempted from any clearance of strangers from the House.[7] When they were evicted together with all other strangers on 14 March 1774 Henry Cavendish, himself an Irishman and a past and future member of the Dublin Parliament, at once started a discussion on the point: and he noted with satisfaction in his diary, 'it seemed to be understood that the Irish Members might be permitted to come in', naming one who was then admitted.[8] On the next day Speaker Norton told Cavendish that 'whenever any Member came to

---

[1] Almon, *Parl. Reg.*, XIII, 551–2.   [2] Debrett, *Parl. Reg.*, IX, 411, 552.
[3] Debrett, *Parl. Reg.*, XIII, 4; XV, 271.
[4] Wraxall, *Memoirs*, IV, 712. The Prince again attended in January 1784. Wraxall, *Memoirs*, IV, 717–18. Debrett, *Parl. Reg.*, XII, 582–3.
[5] Wraxall, *Memoirs*, VI, 46.   [6] Aspinall, op. cit., p. 233N.
[7] Harris Diary, 9 Dec. 1762. B.M. Eg. MSS. 224, p. 97.
[8] B.M. Eg. MSS. 254, pp. 82–5.

him, and assured . . . of such person being any Irish Member, he would admit him.'[1] Irish members apparently sat in the privileged position under the gallery, not with the general body of strangers.[2]

This same privilege was also given to important officials of government departments whenever there was business relevant to their work before the House.[3] Such civil servants were allowed to attend even when ordinary strangers had been excluded. The two secretaries of the Board of Trade were permitted to enter on 11 March 1774 when the gallery was shut, to listen to the reading of papers on America.[4] They accordingly stayed behind when the standing orders were invoked against all strangers before other American business three days later, but opposition members then demanded their arrest by the Serjeant and insisted on their eviction.[5]

Quite distinct from this privilege of a special position in the House was the lesser one of admission when other strangers were kept out. This was allowed by courtesy of the House to former members; to the eldest sons of members;[6] and to unsuccessful Parliamentary candidates who had submitted petitions, pending consideration of their election cases. The reason for this last concession was evidently the possibility that they might prove to be the rightful members: but on 16 December 1774 Bamber Gascoyne attacked the alleged abuse of this custom. 'Many persons, he believed, were petitioners for no other reason; he heard a petitioner once say, he was quite easy, for though he had not a *voice*, he had a *seat* for two years.' This view was challenged by other members, and was clearly an overstatement.[7] Nothing has been found on the origin and duration of these various courtesies. None of these categories of privileged persons appear in the list of those entitled to sit 'below the Bar', but they presumably obtained prior access to the gallery before other strangers.

---

[1] B.M. Eg. MSS. 254, p. 153.   [2] Almon, *Parl. Reg.*, XIII, 552.
[3] Aspinall, op. cit., p. 233N.
[4] *Lloyds Evening Post*, 14 Mar. 1774. *Commons Journals*, XXXIV, 552–5.
[5] B.M. Eg. MSS. 254, pp. 79–80.
[6] Harris Diary, 25 Nov. and 11 Dec. 1761. Almon, *Parl. Reg.*, VII, 147. Moritz, *Travels*, p. 60, made this note on the custom. 'I have now and then seen some of the members bring their sons, whilst quite little boys, and carry them to their seats along with themselves.'   [7] Almon, *Parl. Reg.*, I, 16.

9

THE DAY IN THE HOUSE

THE day in the House always began with Prayers. When the Speaker informed the Serjeant-at-Arms that he was ready to go to Prayers the doorkeeper was sent to call the Chaplain, while the Serjeant himself went round to all Committees, announcing to each Chairman, 'The Speaker, Sir, is going to Prayers.'[1] The House, however, did not usually commence business immediately after Prayers. The Speaker generally retired to his own Room or sat informally in the House at the Table. This delay was presumably to await a fuller attendance. If the requisite quorum of forty members was not present when the Speaker decided to take the Chair, the Serjeant again went to all Committees, to say that 'the Speaker wants to take the Chair', asking the members 'to walk in just to make a House'. If this step failed to produce a quorum the Speaker could adopt the formal expedient of sending round the Mace. Since the appearance of the Mace led to the dissolution of all Committees it was usual to give Committees prior warning of this step. As soon as the House was constituted the doorkeeper made public proclamation that 'the Speaker is in the Chair'.[2]

Private business was taken first, and almost invariably there was a considerable amount of it to be dispatched. Private business comprised petitions, reports of Committees appointed to examine petitions, reports of Committees appointed to draw up bills, and private bills in the various stages of legislation. Such was the volume of daily private business that by the middle of the century the Speaker would draw up an order paper, on which he entered petitions, reports, bills and other business of which he was informed. He then called upon the appropriate members in the order of the subjects on the paper.[3] The proceedings on private business were largely formal, and

[1] Clementson Diary, p. 3.   [2] Clementson Diary, pp. 4–5.
[3] Harris Diary, 17 Feb. 1762.

debates seldom arose in the House:[1] the Select Committees on the petitions and bills were doubtless the customary place for discussion and argument. Although the number of items to be dealt with was often considerable, sufficient to fill several pages of the *Journals* for most days, private business did not therefore usually take long to transact, perhaps between half an hour and two hours. The 'injustice' of Sir Fletcher Norton alleged by John Horne in a famous libel of 1774 was merely the Speaker's 'slovenly hurry' in doing private business.[2]

It was the custom that all the private business appointed for the day should be finished before the House began public business.[3] When Richard Sutton, under-secretary to Secretary of State Lord Rochford, presented official papers to the House on 4 February 1771, complaints were made that all the private business had not been concluded. Speaker Norton at once admitted, 'If there was any surprise, I was the occasion of it, as I told him the private business was over.'[4] This was the usual convention: but the Speaker had complete discretion as to when to start public business and sometimes exercised it, bowing to the temper of a crowded House even though all the private business had not been completed. On 19 March 1771 Speaker Norton reminded members that 'yesterday little or no private business was done' because members had been impatient for public business.[5] More common was the problem of waiting for a good attendance. Norton answered complaints on 3 June 1779 that an Order of the Day had been taken early in a thin House with this explanation: 'The report stood the first order of the day. The House, it is true, was very thin. I waited for a better attendance till within a quarter of four by that clock [pointing to the House clock]. The report was then offered to be brought up, it was received, and the question put upon it in the usual manner.'[6]

The Speaker signified the commencement of public business either by calling for the Orders of the Day in this way or by indicating a member who had given notice of his intention to

---

[1] From about 1774 newspapers contain many accounts of the transaction of private business.

[2] H. Walpole, *Last Journals*, I, 289–91.

[3] See, for example, Almon, *Parl. Reg.*, I, 415; VII, 143.

[4] B.M. Eg. MSS. 224, pp. 45–6.   [5] B.M. Eg. MSS. 226, p. 363.

[6] Almon, *Parl. Reg.*, XIII, 222–3.

make a motion. Public business also included many petitions, reports and bills, and most of them may have been arranged and dealt with in the same manner as similar items of private business. The decision on the priority of the various items of business arranged for any day lay with the House, the majority of members present at the time: but the Speaker probably gave guidance on the daily arrangement of public as well as private business. That this was the practice of Speaker Onslow is suggested by an incident in the House on 12 May 1738. William Pulteney's motion for the Order of the Day was opposed by Thomas Winnington, who wanted the House to proceed first on the report of a bill concerning the price of coal, and claimed that 'it has always been the method of this House to receive reports before any other business was engaged in'. The Speaker at once intervened: 'It is always my custom, gentlemen, before I take the Chair, to digest in my own mind the manner in which the affairs of the day may be best carried on, both for the ease of gentlemen, and the dispatch of business.' Onslow then suggested that the report should be taken first, and Pulteney agreed to this solution.[1] Much public business was a formality, and complaint was sometimes made by members that it was transacted so quietly that they did not know that items had been completed.[2] Often the whole of public business on a day might be routine or unopposed, and no debates would develop. Occasionally the disposal of business might be so rapid that the House had to sit idle until the time appointed for the next item, for it was contrary to order to begin early.[3] Even if there was no more business the House could not adjourn before four o'clock, being obliged to sit until that time because of the rule that members could take the oaths up to that hour.[4]

This remained the pattern of the Parliamentary day throughout the eighteenth century; but the period saw a significant change in its chronology—the final culmination of a long transition from the custom of sitting in the morning and afternoon, to the more modern practice of a daily session commencing in the afternoon and continuing in the evening.

[1] Chandler, *Debates*, X, 292–4.   [2] Almon, *Parl. Reg.*, XIII, 221–2.
[3] Harris Diary, 22 Jan. 1762.   [4] Hatsell, *Precedents*, II, 90, 175–6.

The result of later and longer proceedings in the House was that the customary time for Select Committees changed from the evening to the morning, since they were not allowed to meet while the House was sitting. The change is not reflected in the official record of the *Journals*: here the formal hour of meeting, to which the House adjourned, appears as 9 a.m. until 6 February 1770, when it was altered to 10 a.m.[1] Even early in the century the poor attendance of members made the appointment of this time rarely more than a pious hope and an archaic survival, for observance of the quorum rule nearly always prevented an early beginning to the Parliamentary day. Every Speaker from at least the reign of William III exhorted members to early attendance, or so it was said in 1769.[2] Certainly on 24 November 1691 complaint was made in the House that members came so late that the Speaker could not take the Chair until 'near eleven every morning':[3] and Burnet deplored the practice of the Commons at that time in general terms. 'They are seldom met till about twelve a-clock; and except on a day in which some great points are to be discussed, upon which the parties divide, they grow disposed to rise after two or three hours' sitting. The authority of the prince must be interposed to make them return to the old hours of eight and nine.'[4]

The evidence of the first Hanoverian decades is usually about when debates began rather than when the House met.[5] There was a great variety of practice, with important debates commencing at times between 10 a.m. and 5 p.m. From the beginning of the Hanoverian period the great majority of debates, however, began in the early afternoon, usually between midday and 2 p.m.; and this continued to be the custom until the second half of the century. Since the House would normally be sitting for at least an hour before the commencement of public business, the Speaker must often have taken the Chair in the morning during the first half of the century. On

[1] *Commons Journals*, XXXII, 645, 658.

[2] B.M. Eg. MSS. 219, pp. 323–4. Such exhortations regularly appear in the speech of thanks made by a Speaker after his election.

[3] Luttrell Diary, I, fo. 65.   [4] Burnet, *History*, VI, 214–5.

[5] Many instances of times when debates began and ended in the earlier eighteenth century may be found in Chandler's *Debates*, *H.M.C. Egmont Diary*, and the *Knatchbull Diary*.

days when important business was expected members often crowded the House early in the morning. On 1 March 1723 'the House was full by 8 o'clock in the morning and Speaker there at 9' for the report of the Secret Committee on the Atterbury Plot.[1] The same subject attracted full Houses by 9 or 10 a.m. on other days in March and April that year.[2] This was a matter of great interest to M.P.s, and it would be wrong to assume that the House of Commons in the earlier eighteenth century habitually or even frequently sat on public business in the morning, despite the misleading impression of such comments as that made by John Hatsell in 1818: 'The usual hour for commencing business has undergone consider-able retardation within the last hundred years . . . on the 8th of March 1738, Mr. Horace Walpole opened the Debate at half past Eleven o'clock.'[3] The example was an exception; for Lord Egmont remarked on this very occasion that 'the debate began very early, at an hour after eleven':[4] but it does appear to have been the custom in the first half of the century for important debates to start earlier rather than finish later. The debate ending in the rejection of the Peerage Bill of 1719 commenced about noon and concluded at 8 p.m.[5] The main debate over Walpole's tobacco excise, on 14 March 1733, began at 10 a.m. and ended at midnight.[6] The last important debate known to have started in the morning was that on 18 January 1744 over the employment of Hanoverian soldiers, which continued from 'eleven o'clock till past eleven at night'.[7]

The change from a morning to an afternoon start of the Parliamentary day was therefore gradual and erratic. In the early 1750s the House was often still meeting for Prayers before noon, but seldom for business. On 10 December 1755 the early attendance of members to claim seats for a debate on the Russian and Hessian subsidy treaties caused the Speaker to take Prayers at 10 a.m. Members then went home to breakfast,

---

[1] *Knatchbull Diary*, p. 14.   [2] *Knatchbull Diary*, pp. 15, 18, 21.
[3] Hatsell, *Precedents*, II, 184N. The date is Old Style.
[4] *H.M.C. Egmont Diary*, III, 31.   [5] Chandler, *Debates*, VI, 202, 213.
[6] *H.M.C. Egmont Diary*, I, 342. For other morning starts to important business see *H.M.C. Egmont Diary*, III, 43, 233, 247.
[7] *H.M.C. Egmont Diary*, III, 283.

and the debate did not begin until 2 p.m.[1] By mid-century the rare morning meetings of the House were usually concerned with formal proceedings, and the transaction then of controversial business could be a matter of complaint. On 19 March 1771 Alderman John Sawbridge drew attention to the Durham Yard Bill, which was being bitterly opposed by City members. The report of the bill, he said, had been 'smuggled in' that morning in a thin House. That was 'so unusual a Parliamentary proceeding', Sawbridge declared, 'I did think it necessary to make the report of it to the House.' The only reply of the sponsor of the bill, Robert Adam, was that he had given notice to another Alderman, James Townsend, that the report would be made that day.[2]

The official record of the *Journals* is thus misleading on both the hour of meeting and the times at which the House dealt with particular items of business. There could be no literal interpretation of the frequent orders appointing certain business for the morning or for particular hours varying from ten to two o'clock. Lord North reminded members of the usual practice of the House on 23 March 1772, when he was discussing an order for the third reading of the Royal Family Marriage Bill: 'The meaning of twelve o'clock is that it may be the first business. I hope that it will be early. At two o'clock is not impossible.' The House then ordered the third reading for 'tomorrow morning', but the order was not read until ten minutes past three o'clock.[3]

By the end of George II's reign an afternoon start was customary for all public business. Horace Walpole noted in 1755 that 'the lateness of hours was becoming a real grievance, few Debates of importance commencing before three in the afternoon'.[4] And here is the comment by Speaker Onslow in 1759 on Burnet's remark about the House's time of meeting over half a century earlier: 'This is shamefully grown of late, even to two of the clock. I have done all in my power to prevent it, and it has been one of the griefs and burdens of my life.

---

[1] Many times when the House met, and debates began and ended, are noted in the Newdigate Diary from 1751.

[2] B.M. Eg. MSS. 226, pp. 361–2.

[3] B.M. Eg. MSS. 239, pp. 120–1. *Commons Journals*, XXXIII, 609.

[4] H. Walpole, *George II*, II, 60.

It has innumerable inconveniences attending it. The prince of Wales that now is, has mentioned it to me several times with concern, and did it again this very day (7th of October 1759), and it gives me hopes, that by his means it may in time be corrected.'[1]

It may not have been coincidence that soon after the accession of the Prince as George III a formal proposal was made to check the long trend to later hours of meeting. On 18 November 1761 Sir John Philipps, an independent member now turned courtier, moved for a Committee to consider means of bringing members to the House earlier. He was seconded by Leader of the House George Grenville, and a Select Committee was appointed. Diarist James Harris added this sardonic note to his account of the debate: 'Question whether 10 Million would not be granted with more ease, than such a Regulation complied with?'[2] Philipps reported the resolutions of the Committee on 4 December, and the House made a new standing order 'that no private business be entered upon, any day in the House, after two of the clock'. This was qualified by another order that leave of the House must be obtained on the previous day if this rule was to be dispensed with: such permission was given as early as 21 December, and the regulation soon became a dead letter.[3] The order was repealed on 2 February 1769, after another Committee reported that it had been 'inconvenient and ineffectual'.[4]

It thus proved impossible to start public business at two o'clock in the 1760s. Three o'clock was the usual time when Sir Fletcher Norton was elected Speaker in 1770, and he rarely began the Parliamentary day at all before two o'clock. On 11 February 1774 he did not enter the House until nearly 3.15 p.m., and made a short apology for being late: this was an exceptional circumstance, arising from John Horne's libel on the Speaker published that day in the *Public Advertiser*.[5] Three days later members made no comment when Norton informed

[1] Burnet, *History*, VI, 214N. Hatsell believed that Onslow's aim was to establish two o'clock as the time for public business. *Precedents*, II, 184. While a praiseworthy aim by the end of the eighteenth century, this would have been a confession of defeat in the reign of George II.

[2] Harris Diary, 18 Nov. 1761.

[3] *Commons Journals*, XXIX, 20, 63. Hatsell, *Precedents*, II, 99.

[4] *Commons Journals*, XXXII, 174.   [5] *London Chronicle*, 12 Feb. 1774.

the House that printer H. S. Woodfall, who had been summoned to attend because of this libel, had sent a letter to the Clerk saying that he would be at the House by three o'clock, since he understood that was 'the usual hour of business'.[1] Four o'clock was already then the time when some debates began, and a decade later it was a common hour for the commencement of public business.[2]

The continuing change in Parliamentary habits was reflected in the difficulties arising out of George Grenville's Election Act of 1770. This specified that on receipt of any election petition a day and hour should be appointed for the choice of the Select Committee necessary under the act to examine the case; that if at this time a hundred members were not present the House should at once adjourn; and that the same procedure should be adopted on all subsequent days until the necessary quorum was found. The time for the appointment of Election Committees was always fixed at three o'clock, presumably because that was regarded as the normal hour for the start of public business: but this meant that a few days a session were lost for some years after a general election, and sometimes after by-elections. The quorum of 100 members was lacking on at least three days in 1775, four days in 1776, six days in 1777, two days in 1781 and three days in 1782. The *Journals* record the actual attendance at three o'clock on these days: in 1777, for example, only 49 and 83 members were present on 23 and 24 January, and 63, 68 and 86 respectively on 22, 23 and 24 April.[3] After this had happened on 26 January 1781, when only 91 members had been present at three o'clock, George III commented on 'the unwillingness of gentlemen to be members of the Committee of Elections, which as the law now stands is certainly an essential part of their duty'. The King was annoyed that the House of Commons had been unable to present an Address that day, and suggested two o'clock on 29 January so that Parliamentary business would be interrupted as little as

---

[1] B.M. Eg. MSS. 251, p. 169.

[2] The Parliamentary diaries of Henry Cavendish (1768–1774) and Matthew Brickdale (1770–1774) contain many references to the times at which debates began and ended. Times are also given sometimes in the reports written or compiled by Almon and Debrett, and in contemporary correspondence and memoirs.

[3] *Commons Journals*, XXXV, 255, 452, 496, 516, 563; XXXVI, 76–7, 436–7. Debrett, *Parl. Reg.*, III, 135; V, 248, 431.

possible. Lord North therefore reminded George III that the problem of securing the early attendance of members was permanent and not merely one that arose from the evasion of service on Election Committees. 'If it [be] equally convenient to his Majesty to receive the House of Commons at three o'clock, it will suit their business as well, and the House will not keep his Majesty waiting, which may happen, should an earlier hour be appointed, as it is very difficult to get a House much before three o'clock, but if his Majesty prefers two o'clock Lord North will endeavour to have forty members at the House by that time.' The King agreed on three o'clock.[1]

Even in the reign of George III, however, there still remained considerable variation in the times both of meetings and of the commencement of public business. Twice in 1770 the Speaker took the Chair at noon, and on three occasions in March 1771 Prayers took place at one o'clock.[2] Many members found such uncertainty annoying and inconvenient, and on 10 November 1780 Sir Philip Jennings Clerke asked the House to consider 'at what hour it was to be understood the Speaker was to take the chair, or at what hour public business was to be entered upon; let it be three o'clock, or half after three, or four, but let the hour be fixed.' He was supported by Sir Joseph Mawbey, who suggested that either the official time should be later, twelve or one o'clock instead of ten, or that some hour should be fixed for the Orders of the Day. Speaker Cornwall said 'that for his own part he had not a wish one way or the other; he would be directed by the House'. At the same time he observed that the necessity of meeting was not always the same; that, according to circumstances, there might be a latitude of meeting early or late. Sir Charles Bunbury commented that no particular hour could be fixed for reading the Orders of the Day, 'for that would depend on the time taken up by the private business'; but he agreed that the official hour of meeting should be changed to twelve or one o'clock. Sir George Yonge answered that any alteration in 'the nominal hour of meeting' was irrelevant, although he welcomed the idea of a fixed time

---

[1] Fortescue, *Corr. of George III*, V, p. 190.
[2] *London Evening Post*, 3 Feb. 1770. Newdigate Diary, 18, 19, 22 March 1771.

for the Orders of the Day. But the House, having discussed the problem, adjourned without any decision.[1]

The century after the Glorious Revolution therefore saw a gradual postponement of the beginning of the Parliamentary day by about four hours. The reason for this later start to the business of the House was pressure on ministerial time. Speaker Onslow told the Prince of Wales in 1759 that 'in King William's time, those of his ministers who had the care of the government business in the house of commons were dismissed by him to be there at eleven o'clock. But it is not the fault of the present king; his hours are early. It is the bad practice of the higher offices, and the members fall into it as suiting their late hours of pleasures, exercise, or other private avocations.'[2] Onslow might more accurately have emphasized the official work of administration rather than the need for attendance on the sovereign. Clerke's initiative on 10 November 1780 probably resulted from an incident on the previous day, when not a single Treasury office-holder had been present at three o'clock for an Order of the Day for a Committee of Supply: Secretary to the Treasury Sir Grey Cooper entered while Sir George Yonge was complaining of the insult to the House, and he promptly apologized for having been detained at the Treasury.[3] The next day Sir Charles Bunbury, when supporting Clerke's move, declared that the late start to Parliamentary business was caused by 'the necessity the servants of the crown were under of attending other business in the early part of the day'. Charles Jenkinson replied from the Treasury Bench that 'it was not a regard to the convenience of ministry only that delayed the meeting of the House; lawyers, merchants, and other men of business were employed in the forenoon in private business, and could not attend that of the public'.[4] This riposte was misleading. Many members undoubtedly found an afternoon start more convenient, for the various reasons ascribed by Onslow and Jenkinson: but the increasingly late attendance of members was due to the need for the House to await the arrival of relevant office-holders before proceeding to the numerous items of public business that concerned administration policy or expenditure. By the reign of George III it had

---

[1] Debrett, *Parl. Reg.*, I, 61–2.
[2] Burnet, *History*, VI, 214N.
[3] Debrett, *Parl. Reg.*, I, 57–8.
[4] Debrett, *Parl. Reg.*, I, 62.

become a matter of courtesy and expediency for public business to be delayed if the Leader of the House was late, even when the ministry was not directly concerned. Lord North was usually present in time for public business at about three o'clock, but even he kept members waiting on occasions. On 23 March 1775 he was not in the House when an Order of the Day was read for some administration business. 'It being late, and Lord North not come, Lord John Cavendish said, it was usual for the minister to come down at three, or a little after it; that he was the servant of the public, and ought to attend his duty; and that it was throwing an indignity on the House to thus keep them waiting, without even intimating what he meant to do.' Lord North soon appeared, and made an apology for his late arrival.[1] So astute a Parliamentarian was well aware of the danger of offending members, and the House usually made allowance for his official duties; on 13 February 1777 over 200 members waited for Lord North until four o'clock 'without the least murmur or discontent'.[2]

Debates not only started later during the eighteenth century: they also became longer on average; daily sittings of six or eight hours were common in the reign of George III, whereas they had been infrequent under his predecessors. Debates of exceptional length, however, occurred throughout the century, and the longest continuous sitting was not strictly or solely a debate; lasting nineteen hours, it took place on 22 December 1741, when 'the House of Commons sat from 10 in the morning till 5 next morning upon the Westminster Election.'[3] The precedent was often recalled by Horace Walpole. When the debate over the Address on 13 November 1755 continued until nearly five o'clock the next morning, he noted it as 'the longest debate on record, except on the Westminster election in 1741'.[4] After the House sat on 14 February 1764 from 1 p.m. until 7.30 a.m. the next day to consider evidence on general warrants, Walpole wrote to Lord Hertford, 'above seventeen

---

[1] Almon, *Parl. Reg.*, I, 369–70.

[2] Almon, *Parl. Reg.*, VI, 234. For other occasions when the House waited for Lord North's arrival see the *London Chronicle*, 20 May 1773 and 22 Jan. 1774; and Almon, *Parl. Reg.*, III, 80. The House did not always wait: pressure of Treasury work caused Lord North to arrive too late for routine business on two occasions in 1778. Almon, *Parl. Reg.*, XI, 94.

[3] *H.M.C. Egmont Diary*, III, 233.   [4] H. Walpole, *George II*, II, 49.

hours yesterday . . . in short yesterday was the longest day ever known in the House of Commons—why, in the Westminster election at the end of my father's reign, I was at home by six.'[1] Walpole was forgetting that the House had commenced business several hours earlier in 1741; and only three days later, after the actual debate on general warrants, James Harris noted that 'the House adjourned at 25 minutes past seven, a fine sunshine morning; and the longest day they have been known within memory to sit'.[2] The longest debate of the 1768 Parliament was that of 21 May 1773 on Lord Clive; it lasted for thirteen hours, until the question was put at 4.40 a.m. the next morning.[3] On 12 and 14 March 1771 the proceedings against the printers of newspapers for reporting debates were protracted by the obstructive tactics of some opposition members until about five o'clock.[4] Probably the longest single debate of the century was that of 17 February 1783 over the peace terms at the end of the American war, when defeat sealed the fate of the Shelburne ministry; the vote came after discussion and argument lasting from 4 p.m. until 7.30 a.m.[5]

Later and longer debates meant an increase in the number of occasions that the House sat after midnight; for by the reign of George III any debate lasting about eight hours or more was liable to encroach on the next day. When the House did sit after midnight, the proceedings and decisions were officially regarded as taking place on the same day.[6] No record of such occurrences was therefore made. For much of the century, however, it was customary for the House to adjourn over the next day when this happened, and late sittings were often noted in the *Journals* in connection with the arrangement of business or the next time of meeting. The *Journals Index* records only ten days between 1714 and 1761 when the House sat after midnight, but a further thirty-six days are listed for the period from 1761 to 1774. This comparison indicates the trend, but it is necessarily approximate: on many occasions there was no need to make special arrangements, since the House was

[1] H. Walpole, *Letters*, VI, 1.　　　　　[2] Harris Diary, 17 Feb. 1764.
[3] B.M. Eg. MSS. 248, pp. 1, 374.　　　[4] B.M. Eg. MSS. 226, pp. 84, 137.
[5] Debrett, *Parl. Reg.*, IX, 224–89.
[6] This is apparent from the *Journals*, and William Pitt reminded the House of the rule on 15 Nov. 1763. H. Walpole, *George III*, I, 249.

not going to sit on the next day; and the *Index* is defective in this as in other respects. During the 1768 Parliament the House actually sat after midnight on at least thirty-three occasions, but only twenty-one are listed in the *Journals Index*.[1] By 1775 sittings after midnight had become so common that the House abandoned the practice of automatically adjourning over the next day.

Lengthy proceedings were becoming more frequent, but always remained the exception. It usually happened that the House would complete all ordered and expected business within a few hours. Unless a member then made a motion the Speaker asked the House whether it was their 'pleasure to adjourn'. This motion would be proposed and seconded, and had precedence even if a member belatedly announced other business.[2] When a long debate or other proceeding occurred, the customary practice was for the House to postpone subsequent business arranged for that day. The *Journals* contain many instances of Orders of the Day being put off to future occasions. Sometimes the initiative may have come from the Chair: certainly protests by Speaker Norton brought proceedings to a close on at least two occasions. On 24 April 1771, after a long debate on one bill, the Order of the Day for the report of another bill was read. Norton promptly asked from the Chair, 'will you have no mercy on yourselves and me?' Although the report was read, other business appointed for that day was postponed.[3] On 19 May 1773 the Speaker brought to an abrupt end an examination into the affairs of the East India Company by this interruption: 'Does the House mean to sit through this business? For one I desire to be excused. I am not able to bear it.' The Commons at once adjourned.[4] There was always, indeed, a strong antipathy to the introduction of new business or the continuance of existing business in 'thin Houses' or

---

[1] Seven occasions noted in the *Journals* are omitted from the *Index*. *Commons Journals*, XXXII, 638; XXXIII, 251, 259, 275, 289, 584; XXXIV, 366. On five other occasions the House was not going to sit on the next day. B.M. Eg. MSS. 219, p. 283; 238, p. 165. B.M. Add. MSS. 35610, fo. 177; 35631, fo. 116. Fortescue, *Corr. of George III*, II, p. 70.

[2] See the *Journals* for the general practice, and the Harris Diary, 12 Feb. 1762, for such an incident.

[3] B.M. Eg. 230, p. 99. *Commons Journals*, XXXIII, 351.

[4] B.M. Eg. 247, pp. 116–17.

late in the day. On 29 March 1756 opposition members walked out in protest when a new item of business was introduced at 11 p.m., and there is abundant evidence of protests at other late sittings of the House.[1] No administration would risk annoying members by pushing official business too far and too fast in a single sitting, and ministers had to use particular discretion in the management of the great amount of Parliamentary business that had no natural point of termination in a question on a motion—such matters as the Committee stage of legislation and the conduct of inquiries either in the House or in Committee. Regard was therefore paid to the attendance of members and the lateness of the hour. During the examination of witnesses in the general warrants case on 13 February 1764 a motion to adjourn was defeated at eleven o'clock by 379 votes to 31; but 'so many members began to go out, that all sides by consent came into that which they had opposed and about twelve we adjourned.'[2] A decade later Lord North on several occasions agreed to adjourn the Committee stage of government bills when members started to leave.[3]

At any time the business of the House automatically came to a stop whenever it was discovered that there was no longer a quorum of forty members present. The House adjourned at once, unless the time was before four o'clock: then the Speaker would suspend proceedings, and the House had to wait until that hour or until sufficient members entered to make up a quorum. The lack of a quorum might be ascertained in two ways. Individual members could at any time take notice that forty members were not present. The Speaker would then count the House, and if a quorum was lacking he adjourned the House by his own authority: members could enter while the House was being counted.[4] The absence of a quorum might also be revealed on the report of the figures of a division. The Speaker thereupon adjourned the House immediately without declaring the result of the division.[5] The occasional discovery of this circumstance only on a division shows that the House did

[1] Newdigate Diary, 29 Mar. 1756. For other examples see *supra*, p. 93.
[2] Harris Diary, 13 Feb. 1764.
[3] See, for example, B.M. Eg. MSS. 259, pp. 240–1; H. Walpole, *Last Journals*, I, 57; *St. James' Chronicle*, 29 May 1773.
[4] Hatsell, *Precedents*, II, 176–7, 177N. [5] Hatsell, *Precedents*, II, 177–8.

sometimes sit without a quorum, despite a contemporary feeling that it was unconstitutional for the House to do business in this way. Lord Granville thought the Militia Bill in 1756 had been 'voted in not a legal House' because the attendance had been so low.[1]

Objections to the conduct of business in 'thin Houses' were frequent, but it was regarded as unparliamentary to take tactical advantage of the quorum rule. The *Journals* record many divisions where the attendance was so small that the decisions would have been voided if the members on the defeated side had walked out instead of voting, and examples of such behaviour are rare. After an adjournment motion on a private bill was defeated by thirty votes to twenty on 18 February 1725 the minority left the House so that there would not be a quorum to continue.[2] In 1774 opponents of the Copyright Bill resorted to systematic use of the same tactic. On 13 May an attempt to prevent a quorum on the bill failed.[3] Early on 19 May George Dempster, when opposing the report of the bill, asked for the House to be counted, and exactly forty members were found to be present. Diarist Henry Cavendish noted that soon afterwards 'some little disturbance was heard in the lobby, which arose from Mr. Charles Fox pressing Lord Beauchamp not to go into the House'. William Burke raised the matter in the House: 'I saw a member stopping a gentleman coming into the House. He not only does not do his own business, but prevents others.' Burke appealed to the Chair, but Speaker Norton refused to comment: 'I can have no opinion of this.' As the debate was about to resume Dempster again asked for the House to be counted. This time there was no quorum, and the House adjourned.[4] On government business there would be little chance for an opposition to have the House counted out, and only one instance has been found. On 18 May 1780 George Byng observed that only forty-three members were present when Lord North put forward a motion late in the evening. He therefore arranged for one opposition member to continue speaking while a dozen more left the

---

[1] H. Walpole, *George II*, II, 201.
[2] *Knatchbull Diary*, p. 40.
[3] Cobbett, *Parl. Hist.*, XVII, 1103–4.
[4] B.M. Eg. MSS. 259, pp. 142–3.

House. The result was the absence of a quorum when a division was forced.[1]

To modern eyes the striking characteristic of the Parliamentary day in the eighteenth century is the improvident and casual use of time. Not enough value had yet to be placed on Parliamentary time for it to require any organization or even any definition; the century never saw a fixed hour for the beginning or the end of proceedings. The convenience of members took precedence over any pressure of business. Most of this time, indeed, was taken up not with the conduct of business, but in debate. The House of Commons, however, did not debate without a purpose. The function of the House was to make decisions; and in accordance with this concept general discussions without a particular intention in mind were prohibited by the rule that members should not debate unless there was a question before the House. By the eighteenth century the basic modern practice in respect of motions had already evolved, but the age added its own refinements.

[1] Debrett, *Parl. Reg.*, XVII, 707–8. *Commons Journals*, XXXVII, 861.

10

MOTIONS

THE original debating custom of the House was recalled by John Hatsell in the reign of George III, when he noted that 'it was the ancient practice for the Speaker to collect the sense of the House from the debate, and from thence to form a question on which to take the opinion of the House; but this has been long discontinued'.[1] By 1714 it would seem that motions were always being made by ordinary members of the House, and not being framed from the Chair after the Speaker had heard the views of members: the *Journals* provide no help on the matter, but the various reports of debates suggest that this was now the invariable practice. Several later incidents, however, show that the old right of the Chair to state motions was remembered and sometimes asserted. It was still a debating-point to attack 'pocket motions', resolution prepared beforehand by members. When Samuel Sandys moved an instruction to the Committee of Ways and Means on 24 February 1729, Sir Robert Walpole's reply included 'reflections on pocket questions when it ought to be the business of the chair to collect questions on the debate and state them to the House'. This was an oddly old-fashioned remark by such an expert Parliamentarian, but Walpole may have meant no more than the claim put forward by Speaker Onslow. When his version of Walpole's amendment to the original motion was disputed Onslow asserted 'with some warmth . . . a right to state the question'. In the context of the debate this was merely a claim to say what words had been moved by a member.[2] Contemporaries, indeed, regarded this as a duty rather than a right. On 7 May 1723 William Clayton said that 'it was the duty of the Chair to state the question on the debate' even after a motion had already been made; and

[1] Hatsell, *Precedents*, II, 111–12. For a reminder of this practice by Barré in 1779 see Almon, *Parl. Reg.*, XIII, 421.
[2] *Knatchbull Diary*, p. 87.

Knatchbull afterwards made this note: 'I thought it pretty extraordinary because the question was stated before, since I took it the duty of the chair was to collect the sense of the House in a question when they were under difficulties as to the wording, but that was not the case here.'[1] Knatchbull's comment shows that the real nature of the Speaker's role in this respect was assistance, when needed, to members, in the formulation of suitable motions; and this help was still being given until late in the century.[2]

After 1729 the old right of the Chair 'to state the question' declined into the formal reading out of motions to the House, and if doubts arose members themselves could say precisely what they had proposed. Nothing more was heard of the subject, until on 15 February 1770 Sir Fletcher Norton, who had sat in the Chair less than a month, thought fit to revive the custom during a debate on a Sudbury election dispute.[3] No notice was taken of the matter at the time, but adverse comments probably led to the Speaker's remark on the following day: 'I do beg of the House that I may receive their commands in what manner I am to manage the debate, when there is no question.'[4] Three days later Thomas Townshend chose to criticize the Speaker's action in the House: 'You renewed the custom of framing a question from the Chair. It was dropped in the time of Mr. Onslow. It puts a dangerous power in the Chair. The Speaker may frame a very complicated question. A question has been formerly brought very different, by the assistance of Gentlemen who have happened to be on his right hand, from the question in debate. If a Speaker should have a collusion with men of power, and men of order, it is upon that ground dangerous.'[5] A year later, on 8 February 1771, during proceedings on a Shoreham election case, the Speaker again proposed a question. Henry Cavendish at once objected that it would be better for another member to make the motion, and Norton conceded, 'had any one done it, I should not'. The incident ended with a reminder from Cavendish of the danger of reverting to 'the old way of the Speaker's collecting and proposing the question'.[6] Sir Fletcher Norton was merely

---

[1] *Knatchbull Diary*, p. 23.
[2] See B.M. Eg. MSS. 215, p. 336.
[3] B.M. Eg. MSS. 220, p. 114.
[4] B.M. Eg. MSS. 220, p. 122.
[5] B.M. Eg. MSS. 220, p. 191.
[6] Brickdale Diary, II, 71.

seeking to expedite business: there is no evidence that after these criticisms he ever again tried to suggest a motion.

The danger mentioned by Townshend and Cavendish arose from the political independence, in varying degrees, of most members of the House. Great importance was often attached to the exact point over which a division was taken, and questions were so framed as to attract the support of as many members as possible. This strategy, in reverse form, was employed by opposition leader William Dowdeswell on 8 May 1769, when the House heard a petition from some Middlesex freeholders against the seating of Luttrell in place of John Wilkes. It was Dowdeswell who, with the declared intention of giving it a negative, made the motion 'that Henry Lawes Luttrell, esq., is duly elected a knight of the shire, to serve in the present parliament for the county of Middlesex'.[1] He thereby hoped to obtain the support of all members who could not agree to this resolution. Careless drafting of motions, on the other hand, might forfeit support. Some members who would otherwise have voted with the opposition on 9 January 1770 regarded as too extreme the description, in the amendment to the Address, of discontent 'in every part of his Majesty's Dominions': they felt that reference should have been made only to 'several parts'.[2]

Since the abandonment of what had become the anachronism of motions framed by the Chair, the custom was for the Speaker to intervene and ask for a motion on those occasions when several members had spoken and a general conversation seemed likely to develop. A Speaker had to use his discretion before interrupting a member, because it was the custom for a motion to come at the end of a speech.[3] The usual practice therefore appears to have been for a second or subsequent member to be stopped if one had previously spoken without proposing a motion.[4] There is insufficient evidence to assess the application of this rule before 1770, but frequent interventions by Speaker Norton suggest that it was usually enforced after that date.[5] Brief discussions might arise without a motion

---

[1] B.M. Eg. MSS. 219, pp. 357–8. [2] *Hope Letters*, p. 63.
[3] B.M. Eg. MSS. 246, p. 239. [4] Almon, *Parl. Reg.*, XIII, 420–1.
[5] See for example, B.M. Eg. MSS. 220, p. 32; 228, p. 27; 242, p. 302; 244, pp. 6–7; 251, p. 105; 260, p. 180.

being made, but such conversations were rare.[1] A formal motion was the almost invariable preliminary to any proceedings in the House.

Members were not free, however, to make any motions whenever they chose: and if the restrictions as to the time of motions were not enforced,[2] those concerning the content of motions were valid and important. No member could move to alter or repeal an act passed earlier in the same session. Speaker Cornwall explained the reason when called upon for his opinion on 21 November 1783: 'As the whole session was, in the eye of law, only as one day, the order would not suffer a bill to be brought in for the purpose of repealing an act passed the same session; the reason was, that it could not be supposed that any assembly would make and unmake a law in the same day.'[3] The same restriction applied to motions for resolutions, whether they had been previously passed or rejected. A motion put by General Conway on 27 February 1782, however, was avowedly the same in substance as one that had been defeated by one vote five days before: but he argued that the importance of the issue, an end to the American war, and the need for the opinion of a full House outweighed any formal objections; and none, indeed, were made in the debate.[4] The rule did not restrict motions in the various stages of legislation. Nor did it apply to reports from Committees: former Speaker Onslow privately confirmed to Hatsell a decision of 10 December 1762 to this effect after Sir John Philipps had objected to a renewal on report of the debate on the preliminaries of the Peace of Paris.[5]

A member making a motion had to give a written copy to the Speaker. This had been a rule since 1571, and Hatsell, who had been appointed Clerk Assistant in 1760, observed in 1818 that 'this custom has been uniformly adopted ever since I have been acquainted with proceedings of the House of Commons, now nearly 60 years'.[6] A motion had no standing, however, and

---

[1] For instances see B.M. Eg. MSS. 222, pp. B 87–90; 223, pp. 549–51.
[2] See *supra*, p. 97.
[3] Debrett, *Parl. Reg.*, XII, 94. For a similar statement by Robert Walpole on 2 June 1721 see Dashwood MSS., D. 1/2, fos. 1–8.
[4] Hatsell, *Precedents*, II, 134N.   [5] Hatsell, *Precedents*, II, 134–5.
[6] Hatsell, *Precedents*, II, 112 and N.

was ignored by the Speaker, unless it was seconded.[1] A motion not seconded could be superseded by a later question that was both moved and seconded, a procedural point exploited by Sir Robert Walpole's ministry during Onslow's first years in the Chair. On 27 February 1730 Sir William Wyndham moved a question on Dunkirk. To prevent Samuel Sandys seconding this Walpole arranged that Exton Sayer 'should instantly rise to oppose the motion and offer another': and, after a dispute, the Chair next called on the member who was to second him rather than on Sandys.[2] The same tactic was used to prevent discussion of a motion by Sandys on 27 February 1732, although several members rose to second him.[3] No later instance has been found of this manoeuvre, which involved the open co-operation of the Chair. When this was no longer possible or desirable, administration resorted to more frequent use of the various procedural devices for avoiding decisions on motions.

After a motion had been moved and seconded, the Speaker read it out to the House, which was thereupon said to be in possession of the question.[4] Not until then did the debate proper begin: on 13 May 1779 Speaker Norton reprimanded Lord Mulgrave for attacking a motion before he had even read it out.[5] No motion could be withdrawn if a single member objected. It was always customary, however, to allow a member to withdraw a motion if he wished to do so:[6] and the rule was so rarely enforced that Speaker Onslow had to remind the House of it on 8 March 1733 when Sir John Barnard asked leave to withdraw a motion. 'That being opposed, and some debate arising as to that point, Mr. Speaker acquainted the House of its being their constant rule, that when any motion is once made and seconded, the question, if insisted on, must be put upon that motion.'[7]

A celebrated incident arose from this technical point on

---

[1] Hatsell, *Precedents*, II, 120N. This treatment, described by Hatsell as frequent, was accorded to two motions by Lord George Gordon on 5 May 1779. Almon, *Parl. Reg.*, XII, 401.

[2] *H.M.C. Egmont Diary*, I, 72–3.　　　[3] Chandler, *Debates*, VII, 309.

[4] The Speaker had to read out a motion under debate for the information of any member whenever he was requested to do so. Hatsell, *Precedents*, II, 112.

[5] Almon *Parl. Reg.*, XIII, 7.　　　[6] Almon, *Parl. Reg.*, XVII, 612.

[7] Chandler, *Debates*, VII, 314.

14 February 1774, during the debate over the punishment of Henry Woodfall for printing John Horne's libel on the Speaker in the *Public Advertiser*. The original motion was that Woodfall should be committed to the custody of the Serjeant-at-Arms. Charles James Fox proposed an amendment substituting the more rigorous confinement of Newgate prison. Fox later consented to withdraw this on condition that a compromise amendment made by Lord North for commitment to another prison, the Gatehouse, was adopted. During an involved debate, however, North had offered to withdraw his amendment if a precedent could be found in such a case for commitment merely to the custody of the Serjeant. When Dowdeswell produced one, Charles Fox refused to allow the withdrawal of North's amendment. On the division North felt obliged to vote for his own motion, although he ensured its defeat by instructing his supporters to vote against it. This spectacle of a junior Lord of the Treasury coercing the head of the ministry aroused comment, and Fox's behaviour precipitated his dismissal from office a few days later.[1]

The general rule of the House was that the question first moved and seconded should be first put.[2] Several exceptions to this rule developed: by a standing order of 1668 motions for supply were not put, but referred to a Committee of the Whole House; and in 1772 standing orders of 9 April and 30 April respectively extended this practice to questions of trade and questions of religion.[3] Moreover, matters of privilege or order superseded consideration of the original question.[4] Otherwise, each motion had to be disposed of before another could be accepted by the Chair. A conspicuous feature of eighteenth century Parliamentary life, however, was the frequent reluctance of the House to put a direct negative upon a motion or bill. Members would vote on a subsidiary motion, and the main question was then usually passed or defeated without a division. This custom may have been based on a lingering survival of the old idea that decisions of the House ought to be unanimous, but there were also more practical reasons. A

[1] B.M. Eg. MSS. 251, pp. 245–52. Fortescue, *Corr. of George III*, III, pp. 68–9.
[2] Hatsell, *Precedents*, II, 111–12.
[3] *Commons Journals*, IX, 52; XXXIII, 678, 714.
[4] Hatsell, *Precedents*, II, 121.

common motive was the simple desire to avoid any decision on a particular question: opposition members occasionally put forward motions that the ministry could not negative, because their truth was evident, and yet did not want to accept because of underlying implications. The rule of the House that no resolution could be rescinded during the same session meant that there was sometimes a desire to avoid premature decisions. Another consideration was the tactical importance of the exact point over which a division took place; a number of members might be willing to postpone a motion when they would hesitate to reject it. Several devices had therefore been adopted or evolved for this purpose of evasion.

A motion that the Orders of the Day should be read took preference over an earlier question. This motion, to obtain priority, had to be 'for the orders generally, and not for any particular order'. Its use as a tactical weapon preceded the date of 1747 suggested by Hatsell.[1] When on 11 March 1729 Sir Robert Walpole followed an opposition motion with one for the Orders of the Day, Knatchbull noted this explanation: 'which question must be first put and is an artificial parliamentary way of getting rid of a popular question which the court have no mind to put a negative upon'.[2] Administration made frequent use of this device to counter opposition motions, for there were several advantages inherent in the method. If the motion was carried, the original question did not appear in the daily printed *Votes*, and so lost much of its propaganda effect outside the House.[3] The support was gained of any members who wished to proceed to the business appointed for the day, although it was a possible inconvenience that the orders then had to be read 'in the course in which they stand'.[4] Moreover, the discussion on the perhaps embarrassing subject of the debate was necessarily brought to an end as the House had to proceed to the Orders of the Day. No such motion, however, could be made if the House was already debating business arising from an Order of the Day,[5] nor when there were no

---

[1] Hatsell, *Precedents*, II, 110, 115.   [2] *Knatchbull Diary*, p. 90.
[3] Hatsell, *Precedents*, II, 115. It was printed in the *Journals*, for this was the record of the proceedings, as distinct from the decisions, of the House.
[4] Hatsell, *Precedents*, II, 115.   [5] Hatsell, *Precedents*, II, 121.

further orders. One alternative tactic in such circumstances was to move that the House should adjourn.

The motion 'that this House do now adjourn' was an easy counter to any awkward business, and it took precedence over any earlier question, even a motion for the Orders of the Day. If the motion was carried, the original question again did not appear in the *Votes*,[1] and the House at once adjourned to the next sitting day. Since this might be a Saturday or other inconvenient time, Speaker Onslow instituted the practice of permitting members before or between other business to move that the House when it rose would adjourn to a stated day and time—a custom that enabled simple adjournment motions to be made more freely in any subsequent debates, and also provided a safeguard against lapses of memory.[2] An adjournment motion that specified the time of the next meeting forfeited its technical priority.[3] Since successful adjournment motions put an end to the proceedings of the House for the day, the device could serve the double purpose of ending current business and also of avoiding further embarrassment on the same occasion: Lord North was accused on 25 May 1778 of deliberately preventing in this way any discussion of the opposition charges of maladministration expected after the motion then before the House.[4]

The adjournment motion had been used for this purpose of evasion since at least 1678,[5] but a procedural argument on 13 February 1735 shows that the tactic had hitherto been infrequent. An adjournment motion by Henry Pelham 'brought on a short debate about order, because it was said, that when a Question had been moved, and for some time debated, the House was so much in possession of it, that it could not be put off by Adjournment, without an unanimous consent: but Mr. Speaker declared, that, according to the general opinion, the rule mentioned was to be observed at all times before four o'clock in the afternoon: but after that hour, though a Question had been for some time debated, it was thought it might be put off by Adjournment, without any unanimous consent.'[6] Onslow made the qualification of four o'clock

[1] Hatsell, *Precedents*, II, 112–15. [2] Harris Diary, 31 Mar. 1763.
[3] Hatsell, *Precedents*, II, 113. [4] Almon, *Parl. Reg.*, IX, 214.
[5] Hatsell, *Precedents*, II, 109N. [6] Chandler, *Debates*, IX, i.

because the House could not adjourn before then:[1] this restriction was already of little significance, and tactical use of the adjournment motion became more common after this confirmation by the Speaker that it was in order. It could not be employed, however, if any further business was intended on the same day, and its use in the simple form was never extensive.

One variation that came into increasing use during the eighteenth century, and that retained procedural priority over an earlier motion, was the motion merely to adjourn the debate until a named day. Amendments could be made to such motions, however, even though simple adjournment motions could not be so altered. This was decided on 18 March 1771, when Speaker Norton overruled arguments against the practice by Jeremiah Dyson: 'As it is a question to adjourn the debate, I apprehend it may be amended. If the House thinks otherwise, I have no objection. I am very glad to be corrected. I confess I am not fortified with precedents. I am justified by common sense.' The *Journals* show that the House adopted this opinion from the Chair.[2] In similar fashion legislation often came to be opposed by a motion to adjourn a stage of a bill for a number of months. The period varied according to the time of year, and was always calculated to continue well beyond the end of the session: contemporaries understood the purpose to be 'the same thing as to put it off *sine die*'.[3] An alternative method was the motion to adjourn for a number of months a debate which had arisen at a particular stage of a bill. These tactics were usually confined to private legislation and to public bills of little importance, but an attempt was made to stop George Grenville's Election Bill of 1770 in this way. This popular measure, designed to remove the decision of election cases from the House to Select Committees, was opposed by Lord North's ministry: and, when on 30 March 1770 one of his supporters moved to adjourn further consideration of the bill for two months, North chose to interpret the motion literally, urging that such a postponement should not be treated as a rejection but only as making possible a summer's

[1] See *supra*, p. 155.
[2] B.M. Eg. MSS. 226, p. 271. *Commons Journals*, XXXIII, 264.
[3] *London Magazine*, 1774, p. 263.

reflection. Use of the tactic was an implicit admission of administration weakness on the subject, and the motion was defeated by 185 votes to 123.[1]

These refinements of the adjournment motion may have developed because occasions sometimes arose when members who wished to evade a decision on the original question did not find it desirable to use either a simple adjournment motion or a motion for the Orders of the Day. They might want further business that was not an Order of the Day. A procedure which had evidently been devised much earlier to meet such a contingency was the previous question, first used in 1604.[2] This device comprised the motion 'that the question be now put'. The side on whose behalf it was employed would then vote in the negative in order to prevent any decision on the original motion. The previous question was therefore merely a method of avoiding a Parliamentary decision on a subject.

Sometimes it was used precisely for that purpose, and the argument was put forward that the House should not take a particular decision. Sir George Savile adopted this view on 25 March 1771, after Welbore Ellis had moved that the action of some magistrates of the City of London in discharging a printer from custody was a breach of privilege. Savile put the previous question on this resolution, contending that since the magistrates had been refused counsel he was unable to form his opinion on the matter. After his motion had been defeated by 272 votes to 90, Savile and other members of the Rockingham group walked out before the main question was put.[3] In the same way the previous question could also be a method of avoiding a decision on a motion when either the proposer or his opponents prevented its withdrawal. Friends of the proposer who thought him unwise might themselves move the previous question to avoid embarrassment. On 19 February 1730 William Pulteney supported the idea of the previous question being put on a motion by another opposition leader Samuel Sandys, because most members regarded it as an unfair reflection on Sir Robert Walpole.[4] The acquiescence of the

---

[1] B.M. Add. MSS. 35609, fo. 169.
[2] Hatsell, *Precedents*, II, 111. *Commons Journals*, I, 226.
[3] B.M. Eg. MSS. 227, pp. 69–192. *Chatham Correspondence*, IV, 131.
[4] *H.M.C. Egmont Diary*, I, 54.

majority of members, however, was necessary for the success of any such manoeuvre, as Lord Folkestone discovered on 27 November 1775. Then, although sympathetic to a motion by Richard Oliver, he thought it 'one which ought never to have been made' and moved the previous question. Attorney-General Edward Thurlow opposed this, as he wanted to give the motion 'a flat negative'. Charles Fox attempted to avoid the procedural difficulty by moving the Order of the Day: but both this and the previous question failed, and Oliver's motion was then directly defeated.[1]

Although literal or subtle arguments were often advanced to obtain support for the previous question, it was generally regarded as the equivalent of a direct negative. Discussion of this point arose from its application on 22 November 1770. William Dowdeswell made a motion for papers relevant to the current Falkland Islands dispute. The ministry asserted that it was inexpedient to produce them when negotiations with Spain were in progress, but that there was no intention of preventing an inquiry later in the session. Charles Fox, then a junior Lord of Trade, accordingly moved the previous question. Immediate protest came from an independent member, Lord Belasyse: 'If we are to come into this House, and immediately a previous question is to be put on everything, I declare I shall not come into it; if my constituents ask me why, I shall say I can't do my duty in Parliament.' His views were echoed by other independents, but the administration carried the point by 225 votes to 101.[2] The strict interpretation of such a successful use of the previous question meant only that the same motion could not be made again on the same day:[3] and on 29 November Dowdeswell made a reference to 'the question which you have not condemned but only postponed'. Hans Stanley admitted that Dowdeswell would be in order to 'bring on the same matter again', but the usual practice of the House was described by Sir Gilbert Elliot when he forthrightly declared that the previous question was 'full as direct as an affirmative or negative'.[4]

The previous question was a favourite device of administra-

---

[1] Almon, *Parl. Reg.*, III, 215–30.   [2] B.M. Eg. MSS. 222, pp. C. 97–233.
[3] Hatsell, *Precedents*, II, 116. B.M. Eg. MSS. 226, p. 335.
[4] B.M. Eg. MSS. 223, pp. 2, 10, 26.

tion to avoid decisions on opposition motions, although a
minister who had a strong case scorned its use. When William
Adam moved the previous question on 8 March 1779 to kill
a motion by Charles Fox, he was not seconded; and Lord
North later explained to the House that he preferred a direct
negative on the motion as being more parliamentary, since
assertions were made without proof.[1] Every administration
found the previous question useful in countering resolutions,
bills and inquiries proposed by opposition when outright
rejection was undesirable. On 25 January 1734 Sir William
Yonge explained to indignant opponents, 'I did not intend
any trick when I moved for the previous question; it is what
has been always practised in this House, when any question
has been moved, which gentlemen have a mind to favour so
much as not to put a negative upon it.'[2] Ministers knew that
many members were reluctant to oppose popular motions:
it was avowedly for this reason that Sir Robert Walpole moved
the previous question on a motion for accounts on 24 March
1726.[3] It often happened, too, that members were willing to
defer motions or bills when they hesitated to reject them: on
16 February 1730 Sir Edward Knatchbull left the House rather
than vote against a Pension Bill, believing that the administration should have used the previous question rather than a
direct negative.[4] Sometimes a negative was inapplicable, as on
9 May 1770 when the previous question was put on a resolution
moved by Edmund Burke that simply stated that there had
been disturbances in North America.[5] Well might Burke
complain on 3 November 1775, 'I fear our liberty is nothing,
and that ere long, our rights, freedom and spirit, nay the House
itself, will vanish in a previous question.'[6]

The previous question was a clumsy method, involving
certain disadvantages. It might produce two divisions on the
same motion, although this seldom did happen. No amendments could thereafter be made to the original motion. The
correct procedure, if the House agreed, was to withdraw the
previous question so that the motion might be altered; one of

[1] Almon, *Parl. Reg.*, XII, 64–93.   [2] Chandler, *Debates*, VIII, 44.
[3] *Knatchbull Diary*, p. 56.   [4] *Knatchbull Diary*, p. 106.
[5] *Commons Journals*, XXXII, 969–70. B.M. Eg. MSS. 222, pp. B. 91–222.
[6] Almon, *Parl. Reg.*, III, 121–2.

the rare instances when this occurred was the improvement of
an opposition motion on 16 March 1778.[1] If the previous
question was carried in the affirmative, the main question had
to be put immediately, without any amendment or further
discussion. This was the opinion of Speaker Onslow, as recorded
by Hatsell,[2] and it was confirmed by Speaker Norton on
25 March 1771: 'There can be no debate. The question is
that the question be now put.'[3] Two further clarifications of the
rules about the previous question occurred under Norton.
From 27 March 1770, as the result of a decision during the
hearing of a Linlithgow election case, the previous question
could not be put on an amendment. Despite several precedents
to the contrary John Hatsell believed that this decision was
correct, for the sense of the House could be taken on the
question for the amendment itself.[4] The other change removed
an existing limitation on the use of the previous question. There
had long been an understanding that it could not be put in any
matter concerning the privileges of the House. On 14 November 1768, when John Calcraft tried to move the previous
question on a motion about a petition of John Wilkes, he was
called to order by Lord North, who declared that the previous
question was improper in a matter of privilege. Speaker Cust
gave the tacit approval of silence to this statement.[5] But on
12 March 1771, when Colonel Barré, in reference to a newspaper report of a debate, made the sarcastic motion that
'Jeremiah Weymouth, the D . . . n of this country, is not a
member of this House', Lord North himself moved the previous
question. Barré appealed to the Chair, and Speaker Norton
ruled that the previous question could be put in a matter of
privilege.[6]

The previous question was regarded as the characteristic
tactic of obstruction. Contemporaries used the term to embrace
the use of adjournment motions and motions for the Orders of
the Day: all might be loosely termed or explained as variations

---

[1] Hatsell, *Precedents*, II, 122–4. *Commons Journals*, XXXIII, 825.
[2] Hatsell, *Precedents*, II, 122. *Liverpool Tractate*, p. 69.
[3] B.M. Eg. MSS. 227, p. 191.
[4] *Commons Journals*, XXXIII, 834. Hatsell, *Precedents*, II, 116.
[5] B.M. Eg. MSS. 215, p. 143.
[6] B.M. Eg. MSS. 226, pp. 28–32.

of the previous question.[1] But the oldest, simplest and most frequent of all indirect methods of countering motions was the amendment. Opponents of motions, however, had to concert any strategy of amendments with care: for the order of any amendments had to be in accordance with the wording of the original motion, as Speaker Onslow explained when disallowing an amendment proposed by Sir Thomas Aston on 16 January 1733: 'That by the orders of the House, and the constant forms of their proceedings, the making of an amendment to any part of a motion was an approbation of every preceding part of that motion, and as that part of the motion which he proposed to amend, preceded that which the House had agreed to amend, therefore they could not now receive his motion.'[2]

Some amendments, of course, might be genuine attempts at compromise solutions: but there had developed the destructive amendment as a further method of avoiding a decision on a question. John Hatsell was of the opinion, 'This, perhaps, is not quite fair, but has often been done.'[3] Hatsell himself cited an instance from the *Journals* showing that when an objection was made on 17 April 1729 to a motion as being complicated it was altered by an amendment to omit certain words.[4] The House may then have taken the advice of Speaker Onslow, for he recommended another application of the same principle on 23 February 1731. A heated argument began when an administration amendment by Sir William Yonge transformed an opposition motion by Lord Limerick. William Pulteney contended that it was 'unparliamentary to leave words out of a question first proposed and to add others only to make it worse, and fling it out'. Sir Robert Walpole replied that 'he had frequently seen amendments made to questions in order afterwards to get rid of them'. Gilfred Lawson, who had first entered the House in 1701 and was described by Lord Perceval as 'an old member', later rose to attack the amendment. It was 'wholly unparliamentary to alter any question with intention declared to spoil it and throw it out. He said

---

[1] See, for example, Harris Diary, 1 Feb. 1763 and 2 Feb. 1764. H. Walpole, *George III*, I, 298–9.

[2] Chandler, *Debates*, VII, 259.   [3] Hatsell, *Precedents*, II, 117.

[4] Hatsell, *Precedents*, II, 110. *Commons Journals*, XXI, 326.

questions were to be amended to make them better, and to pass them, but to alter them only to spoil them was a Parliamentary artifice of late date to serve the turn of parties. He remembered when the House would not suffer such things, even when the design of altering a question to throw it out was concealed.' Yonge then announced that 'since his amendment was not agreeable to the House, he was willing to withdraw it, and let the question unamended be put'. Speaker Onslow 'hoped for the honour of the House . . . the amendment might be withdrawn'. It was, and the House voted on the original question.[1] That Onslow disapproved of destructive amendments was again shown in a Committee of 22 February 1749. After Henry Fox had moved that the Chairman should divide a complicated question, the Speaker gave his opinion that the Chairman ought to do so, and the question was divided by consent.[2]

None of these decisions constituted formal precedents. Withdrawal of any amendment, as of any motion, depended on the consent of the whole House; and after the retirement of Speaker Onslow in 1761 ministers used the device of destructive amendments against popular motions. The practice was sanctioned by the Chair on 29 January 1765, after George Hay had moved an amendment to render unacceptable Sir William Meredith's motion condemning general warrants as illegal. Opposition members protested in vain. Grenville's ministry held firm to the tactic of permitting no decision on the original motion. George Onslow, presumably aware of his father's views, claimed that the amendment was out of order. Speaker Cust, on being asked, ruled otherwise, and the House voted on the amendment.[3]

The device of the destructive amendment had taken its place in the armoury of the Parliamentary tactician: but there survived the feeling that it was reprehensible to alter a motion so that it bore a meaning entirely different from that intended by the proposer. William Dowdeswell brought this charge against Sir Fletcher Norton on 15 February 1769: 'The making

[1] *H.M.C. Egmont Diary*, I, 141–8.
[2] Harrowby MSS. Doct. 21, 22 Feb. 1749.
[3] *Commons Journals*, XXX, 70. Harris Diary, 29 Jan. 1765. H. Walpole, *George III*, II, 37–45. *Parliamentary Diary of Nathaniel Ryder*, pp. 239–53.

an amendment in order to oppose it, shows the ingenuity of the honourable gentleman.' Norton replied, 'I made the amendment to be explicit in what we were doing. While the motion stood doubtful or equivocal, nobody knew what he was to do.'[1] The next year saw an attempt to prevent the destructive use of amendments. In the Committee on the State of the Nation on 25 January 1770 Dowdeswell moved 'that it is the opinion of this Committee, that this House, in the exercise of its judicature in matters of election, is bound to judge according to the law of the land, and the known and established law and custom of Parliament, which is part thereof.' Such a proposition could not be openly negatived, yet it was avowedly intended as a foundation for resolutions criticizing the decision of the previous year on the Middlesex election. Since the debate was in Committee the question could not be evaded by any of the usual methods.[2] When Lord Clare announced that he would move to have the Chairman leave the Chair many members at once rose in indignation. After this indication of the feeling in the Committee confusion prevailed for a time on the Treasury Bench. Procedural expert Jeremiah Dyson, then nursing a grievance against administration, refused to appear despite three summonses from Lord North: but it was he who sent the minister these words to add as an amendment—'and that the judgement of this House, declared in the resolution of the 17th day of February last, "That John Wilkes, Esquire, having been in this session of Parliament expelled this House, was, and is, incapable of being elected a member to serve in this present Parliament", was agreeable to the said law of the land, and fully authorized by the law and custom of Parliament'. This amendment was carried on a division by 224 votes to 180.[3]

When the amended resolution was reported to the House on 16 February, Sir William Meredith at once claimed that it ought to be divided: 'I apprehend it is the right of every member of Parliament who does but think a question so complicated to have it separated, so that he may be able to give a free opinion upon each part of it.' Thomas Pitt said that

---

[1] B.M. Eg. MSS. 217, p. 334.   [2] See *infra*, pp. 275–6.
[3] B.M. Eg. MSS. 3711, pp. 106–73. Chatham MSS. 30/8/25, fos. 33–4. *Chatham Correspondence*, III, 410.

it might become impossible for members to vote on any question. Jeremiah Dyson replied that there was neither an order nor any precedents to uphold such a claim. An altercation between Dyson and George Grenville ended with an appeal to the Chair. The Speaker, now Sir Fletcher Norton himself, then gave his opinion: 'This I understand is the proposition, that by the rule of the House, whenever a complicated question is put, it is in the power of any single member, as a matter of course, a matter of common right, to have that question separated.' This idea had arisen in former times when it was the duty of the Speaker 'before business was done with precision . . . to collect a motion from the debate: the person who made the motion then had a right to say this was not my motion.' Norton therefore had no hesitation in ruling, 'I think no single member has a power of right to separate a complicated question . . . I know but one universal rule that is universally true without exception, with regard to large assemblies, composed of great numbers of people, that the majority shall bind the minority, that the act of the majority is the act of the whole.'[1]

The matter did not end there. Sir William Meredith reaffirmed his view that it was 'the fundamental right of every member of Parliament to have a question put in that state, to which he could give a negative or an affirmative', and announced his intention of taking the sense of the House on the subject.[2] On 19 February he accordingly moved 'that it is the rule of this House, that a complicated question, which prevents any member from giving his free assent or dissent to any part thereof, ought, if required, to be divided.' After a long debate the motion was defeated by 243 votes to 174, in a division based on the alignment between government and opposition.[3] John Hatsell, in his commentary on the incident, approved this decision, for he thought the practice advocated in the motion would produce confusion. He held it to be an absurd doctrine, moreover, that any member could insist on any point, apart from the execution of standing orders, for another member might insist on the contrary. The only

---

[1] B.M. Eg. MSS. 220, pp. 114–28.   [2] B.M. Eg. MSS. 220, pp. 128–30.
[3] B.M. Eg. MSS. 220, pp. 148–210.

method of decision was to take the sense of the House on a motion.[1] Questions could still be separated by general consent. On 19 February 1770, after this decision of the House, the controversial motion was divided on Lord North's suggestion and put in two parts.[2] But the attempt to nullify the use of destructive amendments had failed.

This was the tactical framework within which the Parliamentary battle was waged. All business had to be introduced by a motion, and on this foundation an apparatus of devices had been constructed. The previous question, the adjournment, the motion for the Orders of the Day, the amendment— all had a special purpose. A method had been evolved for a majority to meet every question that might arise.

---

[1] Hatsell, *Precedents*, II, 119–21.
[2] B.M. Eg. MSS. 220, p. 211. For some later instances of motions being divided by consent of the House, see *Commons Journals*, XXXIII, 89, 681; XXXIV, 330.

THE HOUSE IN DEBATE

No debate could take place unless there was a question before the House.[1] The Speaker would therefore begin a debate by pointing to a member who had given notice of a motion or who was responsible for an item of business for which there was an Order of the Day. On free days, when no particular business was arranged, any members might rise and initiate a debate without prior intimation: and such debates also took place before and between items of planned business. Unless circumstances had predetermined the proposer and seconder of a motion, there was no prior arrangement of the order of speaking. That would have been an infringement of the privilege of individual members, for during debate the right of speaking lay in the member who was pointed to by the Chair. It seems, however, that courtesy and curiosity were already creating the convention that priority should be given to maiden speeches. On 25 January 1781 Nathaniel Wraxall and Lord John Cavendish rose at the same time, 'but the eagerness of the House to hear a new member, and Lord John's natural politeness, obtained Mr. Wraxall a hearing first.'[2]

The only official limitation of this power of the Speaker was a rule of 1604 that whenever two members stood up to speak on a bill, the one against the bill 'being known by demand or otherwise' was to speak first.[3] Although this rule was recorded by Hatsell it had probably lapsed by the eighteenth century, for no instance of its application has been found. Priority was always accorded, however, to any member who had just previously moved to clear the House or Committee of strangers, or for counsel to withdraw: but this was simply 'because it is

---

[1] See *supra*, pp. 171–2.
[2] Debrett, *Parl. Reg.*, I, 357. Wraxall does not mention the incident in his own memoirs.
[3] Hatsell, *Precedents*, II, 102.

presumed he had something to offer when he first proposed it'.[1]
Various other claims to priority did exist. They were made by
any member raising a point of privilege, and also by any
member with an official message from the sovereign. A clash
between these two priorities on 15 November 1763, with both
claims arising out of the *North Briton* case and being put forward by John Wilkes and George Grenville respectively,
was decided by the administration's majority in favour of the
latter.[2] Such priority depended on a minister's control of the
House. On 12 January 1784, with William Pitt and Charles
James Fox both on their feet to speak, Speaker Cornwall ruled,
against Pitt's claim for a message from the King, that Fox
was in possession of the House, 'having begun his speech, . . .
and was entitled to go on'.[3] This assertion that a member's
speech could not be interrupted for a royal message was
thought by Wraxall to be 'in subversion of all usage'.[4]

Apart from such privileged circumstances, the decision as
to which member should speak lay at all times in the Chair:
but the basis of the Speaker's decision was his opinion that the
member indicated had been the first one up, and it was an
old right of the House to overrule the Speaker by a question.
In the later eighteenth century Hatsell clearly regarded this as
obsolete,[5] and no instance has been found of the actual exercise
of this power by the House;[6] but its use was sometimes
threatened when disputes arose. On 3 February 1769, with the
motion for the expulsion of John Wilkes before the House, two
members rose to speak together, office-holder Sir Gilbert Elliot
and radical William Beckford. When Speaker Cust pointed to
Elliot, Beckford threatened to appeal to the House, and Lord
North called him to order: 'I do believe the ultimate decision
is in the House, but they have delegated it to the Chair.'
Cust himself then made a statement that implied the Speaker's
absolute freedom of choice. 'It is a painful thing to me, when I
see five or six gentlemen up. I can point but to one. I have
endeavoured to point to the gentleman that is first in my eye
except when gentlemen have been up five or six times.'[7]

[1] *Knatchbull Diary*, p. 1.					[2] Harris Diary, 15 Nov. 1763.
[3] Debrett, *Parl. Reg.*, XII, 492.				[4] Wraxall, *Memoirs*, IV, 695.
[5] Hatsell, *Precedents*, II, 102, 106.
[6] For one occasion in Committee see *infra.*, p. 275.
[7] B.M. Eg. MSS. 217, pp. 144–5.

Complaints were few because the point was seldom a matter of consequence, and because members knew that repeated challenges would merely produce disorder. Realization of the practical inconveniences of any exercise by the House of its formal power was reinforced by increasing respect for the Chair, and by the discretion of successive Speakers in the application of their choice. In cases of disputes Speakers often endeavoured to make their choice according to the majority opinion of the House, and they were willing to accept correction if they had misjudged the situation. When on 25 March 1771 Speaker Norton indicated Charles Jenkinson as the next member to speak, George Dempster declared, 'I stand upon my right.' Norton conceded, 'If he was up first he has a right to speak . . . Though I heard his name I did not see him.' Jenkinson protested that 'the rule is that whoever you permit [is] to speak first; it is not asserting that he was up first': but Norton permitted Dempster to speak.[1] Norton again changed his decision on 10 May 1773, when Lord Clive and Robert Henley Ongley rose together to speak during a debate on the affairs of the East India Company: 'The Speaker called to Mr. Ongley, but the House calling out Lord Clive! Lord Clive!, the Speaker said that he had called to the honourable gentleman, but from the particular situation of the noble lord the House seemed desirous to hear the noble lord.' Lord Clive, favoured because members knew that he faced charges over his conduct in India, then spoke.[2] Sometimes the decision of the Chair was postponed until the opinion of the House was clear. On 2 December 1778 'Lord North and Admiral Keppel both stood up for upwards of half a minute: but the cry for Admiral Keppel at length prevailing, he was pointed to by the Chair.'[3] Speaker Cornwall followed this example of Norton on 19 December 1783 just after the formation of the minority Pitt administration. 'Mr. Baker and Mr. Henry Dundas rose together, or at least nearly together; there was for some time great noise and confusion in the House . . . but if the cry from the Treasury Bench side of the House was strong, that from the new Opposition side was still stronger. The Speaker at length declared that Mr. Baker had met his eye first, and after some

[1] B.M. Eg. MSS. 227, p. 137.   [2] B.M. Eg. MSS. 246, pp. 147–8.
[3] Almon, *Parl. Reg.*, XI, 89.

altercation on the point of order, Mr. Dundas gave up the point.'[1]

Such incidents show that the compliance of the Chair with the wishes of the majority was not necessarily subservience to ministers; and motives of fairness to those members who had been first up or who faced personal accusations obviously influenced the opinion of the House: but it was inevitable that opposition members should sometimes allege that the decisions of the Chair on the point gave unfair advantages to administration. Ministers were usually able to frame the motion on any important matter, in the form of an Address of Thanks; and this was often a factor in determining the particular course of the debate on the subject. In 1771, after the consideration of the Falkland Islands agreement with Spain had been fixed for 13 February, the leading opposition politicians arranged among themselves that William Dowdeswell should move some resolutions criticizing the terms: and the Duke of Richmond reported the plan to Lord Rockingham on 12 February:[2]

We expect the ministers will start first and move an address of thanks. We shall endeavour to get the lead, but in the Lords they may do as they please, as the House determines who shall speak first, but in the Commons it is the Speaker (who is at present out of humour) and may call to Dowdeswell first. The debate and division may perhaps be as strong against a fulsome address, as upon the resolutions, but we must have the resolutions stand on the *Journals*.

On the next day, however, Speaker Norton pointed to the ministerial spokesman Lord Beauchamp, who opened the debate by moving an Address of Thanks. As soon as this had been seconded by Lord Palmerston, Dowdeswell rose to complain that when a member engaged himself to introduce a question, as he had done, 'according to the common practice of Parliamentary proceedings that gentleman, whoever he might be, would have been permitted to take the lead . . . I was apprehensive of some management.'[3] Opposition complaints about the partisan conduct of the Chair usually arose

---

[1] Debrett, *Parl. Reg.*, XII, 451–2. See ibid., XIII, 209, for a similar incident on 20 Feb. 1784 involving William Pitt and Charles Fox.

[2] Wentworth Woodhouse MSS. R 1–1358.

[3] B.M. Eg. MSS. 224, pp. 303–62.

from some such denial of the opportunity to put forward motions; and attacks being pressed by means of a series of motions on the same subject were sometimes frustrated by the refusal of the Chair to accept the contention that a member was entitled to move a second question as soon as his first motion had been decided. Speaker Compton declined to allow the claim of Sir John Rushout on 7 March 1727 when he said 'he thought he had a right to speak first, being to the last business.'[1] It was the same point that gave rise to a long discussion of the rule on 12 March 1771, an occasion later cited by Hatsell to show that the choice lay entirely in the Chair, and that no right existed in the claim of any member to have been up first.[2]

Early in the day Colonel Isaac Barré had announced his intention of making two frivolous motions to ridicule the measures being taken against the newspaper printers of debates; but after the division on the first one Speaker Norton pointed to George Onslow, a Lord of the Treasury. William Baker claimed that Barré was in possession of the House, and Barré himself said that 'it is, I believe, the usual custom'. Sir Fletcher Norton declared, 'I give the honourable member my word, and honour, too, that he was not so much in my eye.' When William Burke threatened to divide the House, the Speaker replied, 'I wish my actions may be under the control of the House. If I do not see gentlemen I ought to have seen I hope the House will give their sense upon it.' Charles Jenkinson supported the Chair: 'The rule of the House is, whoever the Speaker first points to is to speak.' William Burke then moved, 'That Mr. Onslow, not being first up, do now speak.' Jeremiah Dyson promptly made an amendment to insert after Onslow the alternative wording 'to whom the Speaker has pointed, and whom the Speaker has declared to have been the first in his eye'. Opposition members differed among themselves. John Sawbridge maintained that the decision should not rest with the House, for 'gentlemen in the minority will not be allowed to speak'; but Edmund Burke replied, 'The Speaker may have his eye upon one side of the House rather than the other.' When some later speakers also cast doubts on the

[1] *Knatchbull Diary*, p. 66.   [2] Hatsell, *Precedents*, II, 105.

impartiality of the Chair, Lord North denied that the Speaker favoured the administration. A few members raised the practical point that they were not in a position to judge who was up first, and they urged that the Speaker was better able to decide than the House. After an adjournment motion made by John Dunning had been negatived, the original question was withdrawn. The minority thus gave up the point, and Onslow made his motion.[1] The debate showed the perennial dilemma of opposition in this matter; an appeal over a partisan decision from the Chair to a vote of the House could serve no useful purpose: but the rarity of complaints does suggest that the instances of bias in the Speaker must have been infrequent.

If all members were equal in the eyes of the Speaker, some were more equal than others. One reason why the leading men of administration and opposition sat on the front benches was to have the best chance of attracting the attention of the Chair. Personal status was more important than position in the House. A Speaker would be well aware that members were eager to hear ministers like Walpole and Lord North and their chief adversaries in preference to less eminent and able orators. Accounts of important debates show that not only ministers but also their principal supporters and opponents were usually able to speak at the times they chose to do so. At the other end of the scale, there were members unable to speak at all on particular occasions. Contemporary reports occasionally noted that members had risen several times in a debate without catching the Speaker's eye;[2] and the diaries of Sir Roger Newdigate and James Harris show that sometimes they were not able to make speeches they had intended. Such frustrations were rare. Newdigate made over fifty speeches in the Parliament of 1768 to 1774, but only once in his diary for that period did he note that he 'could not get to speak'.[3] Only one member has been found making open complaints to the Chair that he was unable to speak, James Martin under Speaker Cornwall. On 10 May 1782 he began a speech by saying 'that he had

[1] B.M. Eg. MSS. 226, pp. 33–55. *Commons Journals*, XXXIII, 249–50. For a similar incident on 9 April 1772 see B.M. Eg. MSS. 240, pp. 96–100.

[2] See, for example, N.L.W. MSS. 1352, fo. 87. H. Walpole, *Last Journals*, II, 103.

[3] Newdigate Diary, 17 Feb. 1772.

several times offered himself to the Speaker's attention, but without success: that he was well aware that he had neither high rank, great abilities, or mean servility to any party whatever to recommend him to the attention of the House'.[1] On 19 June 1782 Martin complained that he had not been able to attract the Speaker's attention in previous debates:[2] and on 21 February 1783, after he had vainly risen several times to speak in a debate dominated by Pitt, Fox and Lord North, 'he insisted that he had as much right to speak as any man, though his abilities might not be so great. The Speaker acquainted the honourable member, that he always endeavoured to call on the gentlemen who first caught his eye, that from the vast noise and uproar in the House, he sometimes was deceived; but then he generally suffered himself to be guided by the House.'[3]

No member was allowed to speak more than once to the same question, although any new motion, such as an amendment or an adjournment, did entitle every member to speak again. The ingenuity of members and the weakness of the Chair led to growing disregard of this rule. This development was blamed by John Hatsell as the chief cause of the increasing length of debates after 1760. 'It is to this, more than to any other cause, that the House is kept sitting in debate so much later than it formerly used to be; since, even in my memory, Mr. Onslow kept this order tolerably strict.'[4] The same trend had soon been noted by George III, who observed to George Grenville on 24 November 1763 that 'the breaking the Orders of the House, which allow each Member to speak but once, and to make an explanation, is grown to be a constant evil, which if not put a stop to, will cause long debate on matters that formerly an hour would have determined.'[5]

The general acceptance of the rule under Speaker Onslow mentioned by Hatsell is implied by the absence of information on the subject in the reign of George II, for that is usually derived from disputes over its abuse; by the failure of contemporary commentators to distinguish, as they often do later, between the number of speakers and the number of speeches

---

[1] Debrett, *Parl. Reg.*, VII, 155.
[2] Debrett, *Parl. Reg.*, VII, 248.
[3] Debrett, *Parl. Reg.*, IX, 361.
[4] Hatsell, *Precedents*, II, 105-6.
[5] *Grenville Papers*, II, 165.

in debates; and by such incidents as the declaration of Hume
Campbell on 12 December 1755 that he would have answered
William Pitt in the previous debate on the Russian subsidy
treaty, 'but he had inquired, and found it was contrary to the
order of the House'.[1] Only one complaint by members of an
abuse of this rule has been found for the period of Onslow's
tenure of the Chair, and that provides evidence of its enforcement. On 13 March 1741 Henry Fox and Sir William Yonge
objected to an attempt by Sir John Barnard to speak a second
time, and Speaker Onslow confirmed the rule: 'It cannot be
denied, Sir, that you have already spoken on this question,
and that the rules of the House do not allow you to speak a
second time.'[2]

Relaxation of the rule was part of the general decline of the
authority of the Chair under Sir John Cust, and his successors
failed to recover the lost ground. Sir Fletcher Norton began
with the intention of doing so; on 24 January 1770, during the
first debate after his election to the Chair, he made this declaration: 'I take it to be clear order, that no member shall speak
twice on the same question.'[3] Norton did make some early
attempts to enforce the rule, even against Lord North,[4] but he
found the task beyond him: the detailed reports by Henry
Cavendish of the debates between 1770 and 1774 show that
members often spoke more than once during the same debate.
If greeted with cries of 'spoke, spoke' they were able to advance
a variety of excuses to justify infringements of the rule.

One old and accepted right of members was that 'to explain',
after alleged misrepresentation or misunderstanding of a first
speech. Alexander Wedderburn correctly described the practice
of the House when on 9 May 1770 he began a second speech
with the remark, 'I presume the House will have the usual
indulgence for me, called upon as I am either to retract or
justify what I have said.'[5] This right was acknowledged by the
Chair, and sometimes even enforced by Speakers in the face
of protests from the House. When Alderman Beckford was met

---

[1] H. Walpole, *George II*, II, 125.   [2] Chandler, *Debates*, XII, 304–5.
[3] B.M. Eg. MSS. 3711, p. 98.
[4] See, for example, B.M. Eg. MSS. 222, p. C 211; 226, p. 116; 228, p. 29;
230, p. 190.
[5] B.M. Eg. MSS. 222, p. B. 198.

by shouts of 'spoke, spoke' on rising a second time during the debate of 15 March 1770 on the City Remonstrance Colonel Barré spoke to order: 'Is that rule invariably to be adhered to. Whether there are not circumstances upon that bench that make men rise up five or six times?' Speaker Norton then ruled that Beckford should be allowed to speak again: 'There should certainly be an equal indulgence to all members. I think there was an indulgence due to the honourable gentleman. He was accused.'[1] As Barré implied, the right 'to explain' was exploited above all by administration spokesmen. Hence the exchange between Speaker Norton and opposition member John Dunning in the House on 2 December 1777:[2]

Mr. Speaker said . . . It was the custom of that House, to adhere to one certain rule. The rule was, that no person should twice rise to speak to the same question unless to explain; that rule was departed from, in the present instance, by his learned friend having been up before. He therefore hoped, while he acted fair and impartial in the discharge of his duty, he would have the support of the House. If not, they must take the consequences.

Mr. Dunning exculpated the chair from any designed partiality. He could not, however, avoid taking notice, that the same irregularity was permitted to be practised by gentlemen on the other side of the House. Nevertheless, if the rule was strictly observed, he would be content; if not, he looked upon himself equally entitled to indulgence with any other member.

Other exceptions became established by custom. One was the right to reply to the debate sometimes claimed by the member who had made the original motion. This practice was endorsed by Speaker Norton on 11 March 1779 when he permitted proposer Sir Joseph Mawbey to speak again despite noisy protests, declaring that 'it was usual to indulge with a reply, those who had introduced a motion to the House.'[3] On 12 June 1781 Speaker Cornwall ignored a clamour for the division to allow Charles James Fox to reply at the end of a debate; and Fox, who had proposed the motion, said that 'he was the more obliged to the House for this indulgence, because, according to the strict rules of Parliamentary order, he was not

---

[1] B.M. Eg. MSS. 221, p. 243. For other instances see B.M. Eg. MSS. 230, p. 93; and Debrett, *Parl. Reg.*, XIII, 153.
[2] Almon, *Parl. Reg.*, VIII, 82–3.   [3] Almon, *Parl. Reg.*, XII, 127.

entitled to rise a second time to speak to the same question.'[1]
On 27 November 1781 this privilege of a reply was even
extended to a member who had moved an amendment to the
original question, 'after some debate on the point of order,
respecting the right of reply, claimed by those who had made a
motion'.[2] Another excuse for second speeches, long established
but not always accepted, was to rise to a point of order. This
had been permitted even by Speaker Onslow,[3] but it remained
in the discretion of the Chair. On 13 May 1779 Speaker Norton
obliged Lord North to sit down when he rose to speak to order:
he had already spoken three times out of five attempts during
the debate, and Charles Turner complained of 'such improper
indulgence to any minister'.[4] A further pretext for rising again
was the claim to be giving necessary information to the House.
On 16 March 1779 Temple Luttrell made a motion on 'the
rapid decay' of the navy, altered it after an objection by Lord
North, and was making a third speech when 'the Speaker
objected to Mr. Luttrell's rising so often to speak. Mr. Luttrell
contended he was within the rules of usage, justified by daily
precedent, and by the chair itself, in so far as the Speaker had on
a former occasion declared, that in professional questions,
gentlemen might rise to give information more than once.'[5]

A variety of excuses for breaking the rule had evolved, and
the validity of some claims is impossible to assess: on 26 May
1774, for instance, no other member commented on an assertion by George Dempster that there was no restriction on the
number of speeches that might be made on points of privilege.[6]
On 6 December 1782, however, an overall definition of the
practice of the House in the matter was made by Speaker
Cornwall.[7]

The Speaker said, it was his duty, with great humility and
deference to the House, to state the point of order. He then with
infinite precision laid down the rule, that no gentleman was to
speak more than once in a debate: to which there were only two
exceptions, which custom and convenience had introduced. The
one, where a Minister, or Member in office rises to give the House

[1] Debrett, *Parl. Reg.*, III, 575.   [2] Debrett, *Parl. Reg.*, V, 46.
[3] H. Walpole, *George II*, II, 74.   [4] Almon, *Parl. Reg.*, XIII, 86–7.
[5] Almon, *Parl. Reg.*, XII, 169–70.   [6] B.M. Eg. MSS. 260, p. 136.
[7] Debrett, *Parl. Reg.*, IX, 65.

necessary information; the other, where a gentleman rises to explain, in order to prevent his facts or his reasoning from being misconceived and misrepresented.

A Speaker might assert the rule, but he needed the co-operation of the House to enforce it, as Hatsell knew from his long experience as Clerk. 'The strict observance of this rule, so highly necessary to the despatch of business, must, after all, very much depend upon the good sense and modesty of the members themselves.'[1] Self-restraint was lacking on 13 May 1774, when Charles Fox spoke four times, Edmund Burke five times, and George Dempster three times during the course of a brief debate: Speaker Norton intervened to say, 'I wish gentlemen for their own sakes would content themselves with speaking once.'[2] The authority of the Chair did not extend beyond such appeals: if individual members persisted in speaking repeatedly, a Speaker needed the general co-operation of the House. Cornwall himself ended his definition of the rule on 6 December 1782 with this qualification: 'The Speaker begged it to be understood, that whenever he attempted to enforce the order, and the House overruled him, as they undoubtedly had the power to do, whenever they pleased, it was not to be imputed to him as a neglect of duty.'[3] Whether the rule against second speeches was strictly enforced on particular occasions depended on the feeling of the House at the time, and this did not necessarily reflect political allegiance: on 3 May 1779 members eager for the end of the debate would not permit Lord North to reply to opposition speakers, even though the administration motion was then carried without a division; but on 5 December 1777, when opposition member Edmund Burke was called to order for beginning a second speech, 'the House almost unanimously called upon Mr. Burke to go on.'[4] The practice under George III was expounded on 4 February 1771 by Colonel Barré, who had entered the House ten years before, a few months after the retirement of Speaker Onslow: 'I know the custom is not to speak twice upon the same subject, but in the time I have been in

[1] Hatsell, *Precedents*, II, 106. [2] B.M. Eg. MSS. 259, p. 47.
[3] Debrett, *Parl. Reg.*, IX, 65.
[4] Almon, *Parl. Reg.*, VIII, 129; XII, 398.

Parliament I remember the Speaker seldom interrupts anybody unless the House was tired of hearing him.'[1]

A notable feature of contemporary debates was the constant emphasis on their genuine character. To some extent this arose from concern with mere convention. When on 13 May 1779 Lord Mulgrave attempted to reply to a motion by Charles James Fox as soon as he entered the House, Speaker Norton condemned his behaviour as irregular, and successfully 'pressed the propriety of his waiting a while, till he heard some of the arguments urged in favour of the motion'.[2] The decencies of debate had to be observed, even though Lord Mulgrave must have known Fox's motion beforehand. There was also the element of courtesy, in heeding and answering the views of opponents: William Pitt gave offence on 7 February 1766 when he left the House after an attack on George Grenville's American policy without waiting to hear Grenville's reply.[3]

It was therefore the usual custom for a Speaker to call alternately on members for and against the question. This was obviously the natural pattern of a debate, and most debates retained this general character of a constant exchange of arguments, although sometimes one side would lack an adequate supply of spokesmen: on 10 June 1774 during a debate on the Quebec Bill Edmund Burke pointedly remarked that he had waited before speaking to allow 'some gentlemen on the other side' to answer the two previous speeches.[4] So much was this the custom that during the debate of 21 May 1773 on Lord Clive the right to reply to the previous speaker was openly asserted by a member. When Sir Richard Sutton sat down, a number of members rose together, among them Robert Henley Ongley, who called out to Speaker Norton, 'Sir, I speak against the gentleman who spoke last.' Norton, however, declared that the member first in his eye was Henry Seymour, who then spoke. Immediately afterwards Ongley complained of this decision: 'It is the order of this House when a person is to speak against the opinion of the person who spoke last, he is to speak.' Speaker Norton replied, 'I do not

---

[1] B.M. Eg. MSS. 224, pp. 72–3.   [2] Almon, *Parl. Reg.*, XIII, 77–86.
[3] Harris Diary, 7 Feb. 1766. *Cust Family Records*, III, 96.
[4] B.M. Eg. MSS. 262, p. 210.

know perfectly whether a gentleman will be for, or against. I endeavour to guess as well as I can.' Henry Cavendish at once suggested a way out of this difficulty:

> It would save you a deal of trouble if this matter could be settled upon some permanent footing, so that you could never mistake the side upon which a member means to speak. To be sure, you have a pretty good guess how almost every member means to speak, but then a gentleman may now and then change sides and take you in that way. To make it quite clear to you, suppose every gentleman when he gets up were to say Mr. Speaker *for*, Mr. Speaker *against*, that would prevent all dispute and you would know at once, according to the honourable gentleman's notion of order, whom to call to.

No notice was taken of this idea, and the debate was resumed without further discussion of the point.[1]

The precise order of speaking formed part of debating tactics. Leading spokesmen would manoeuvre to avoid rising first, preferring to wait until late in a debate in order to deal with opposing arguments. In the great debate of 17 February 1764 on general warrants 'Pitt and George Grenville ran a match of silence, striving who should reply to the other', until Pitt at last rose first.[2] Pitt usually scorned to seek this tactical advantage, as Horace Walpole noted in 1755: 'His greatest failure was in argument, which made him, contrary to the rule of great speakers, almost always commence the debate.'[3] This failing doubtless explains Pitt's notorious habit of speaking more than once in the same debate.[4] Edmund Burke, a man less likely to be so indulged by the House, soon learned to speak near the end of debates as a matter of policy.[5] The very last speech before the division was often deemed of especial importance; the German observer Carl Moritz noted in 1782 that 'the contending members are both anxious to have the last word.'[6] James Harris recorded that at the end of a debate on 24 November 1763 'opposition did not like to leave off with such an impression' as an administration spokesman had given, and Henry Legge therefore made a reply: 'His

[1] B.M. Eg. MSS. 248, pp. 105–7.
[2] H. Walpole, *Letters*, VI, 10.
[3] H. Walpole, *George II*, II, 149.
[4] H. Walpole, *George III*, II, 187.
[5] *Burke Correspondence*, II, 259.
[6] Moritz, *Travels*, p. 59.

14—H.O.C.

impressions were not to be left: so the Chancellor of the Exchequer rose.'[1]

All this concern arose from the practical motive of votes to be won in the House itself. The care taken to phrase motions and to manoeuvre divisions on favourable questions had to be backed by oratory and argument. Spontaneous political conversion was rare. The great majority of members voted steadily for each administration and opposition at divisions of political significance: and most of those whose votes did fluctuate between the two sides had probably made up their minds before entering the House. The long-term effect was more significant than any single debate: undoubtedly it was the cumulative impact of opposition attacks that helped to swing an increasing proportion of independent members against the ministries of Walpole and Lord North, until both eventually lost control of the House. But votes were also often influenced by particular debates. The evidence of personal correspondence, memoirs and diaries shows that individual members did change their opinions as a result of the debates they had just heard; and that some went to the House with an open mind, prepared to support either side, and perhaps being convinced by neither.[2] One notable triumph of personal argument occurred in the Committee on the Royal Family Marriage Bill of 1772: Speaker Norton was thought to have won over more than thirty members who had previously been inclined to support the bill.[3] Argument was most likely to be effective on subjects of sectional interest, when many of the members might be guided by the merits of the case as presented in debate. During the Committee of 18 April 1774 on a Hops Bill George Dempster was reproached by brewer Samuel Whitbread for changing his mind: and in a classic exposition of the duty of a member in debate Dempster replied that that was an unusual ground for reproof: 'I sit here to change my mind just as often as my reason is convinced.'[4] It was during such a minor debate, one on Georgia, that John Howe said on 21 January 1741 that 'he had observed gentlemen

[1] Harris Diary, 24 Nov. 1763.

[2] See, for example, B.M. Add. MSS. 35375, fos. 81–2; 35609, fo. 282. B.M. Eg. MSS. 259, p. 239.

[3] B.M. Add. MSS. 29133, fo. 94.   [4] B.M. Eg. 255, pp. 160–1 (shorthand).

frequently changed their minds and opinions in the House, and sometimes suddenly':[1] and his remark should not be regarded as a comment on the general political behaviour of members. Argument was important, but the reward was seldom immediate.

The real danger that votes might be lost combined with respect for the feeling of the House to compel every administration to take part in virtually every debate. Ministerial failure to do so, whether apparent or real, usually provoked immediate criticism from opponents. When no official spokesmen had risen after some hours in the debate of 31 October 1776 on the Address, Thomas Townshend complained of the slight on the House: 'I never saw such a scene on the first day of a session, in a most important hour, as I have seen today. Ministers do not think themselves bound to attend, or to give answers to the questions that have been put to them by many respectable gentlemen today: nay, they do not even preserve the least appearance of attention.' Such a charge was too damaging to remain unanswered. Lord North at once rose to reply in a speech that fully accepted the need for debates in the House.[2] But even North did not agree that administration had to reply to every repetition of every argument. On 30 May 1781 he gave this answer to an attack by Sir George Savile on the evident inclination of ministers to meet a motion on the American war with a silent vote: 'He understood it to be a tolerable general maxim, that when a subject has been repeatedly discussed, and the sense of the House taken and known on it, it was not common to debate it again, but to proceed to a vote.'[3] This certainly happened sometimes during the North ministry over such annual motions as those by John Sawbridge for Shorter Parliaments or by John Wilkes for the rescinding of the Middlesex Election resolution of 17 February 1769.[4] It had also been the occasional practice of ministers throughout the century to reject opposition motions without debate, either because they concerned the royal prerogative or because the subjects had already been discussed.[5] Any such action,

---

[1] *H.M.C. Egmont Diary*, III, 181.   [2] Almon, *Parl. Reg.*, VI, 27–33.
[3] Debrett, *Parl. Reg.*, III, 432.
[4] Almon, *Parl. Reg.*, VII, 136, 151; XI, 249; XIII, 369.
[5] For some examples see Chandler, *Debates*, VIII, 120–2; H. Walpole, *George II*, II, 174; B.M. Add. MSS. 32863, fo. 107.

however, involved the risk of giving offence by apparent disregard for the views of members. When there was no defence by the Rockingham ministry of the window tax bill on 12 May 1766 the independent member Velters Cornewall, although a supporter of the measure, blamed the ministry for taking no notice of country gentlemen:[1] and the administration failure to answer a motion by Charles James Fox on 2 February 1778 was thought to have lost the North ministry some votes at the division.[2]

Despite the importance of argument and oratory as a factor in the contemporary Parliamentary scene, the number of members who took part in any one debate tended to be small. In most debates on public business there were fewer than a dozen speakers, and even for debates of major political significance the number was usually between twenty and thirty. No trend towards an increase during the century has been discerned in the several hundred instances of debates for which the number of speakers is known. That debates tended to last longer was due to the greater length of individual speeches and to the growing exploitation of excuses for further speeches by members who had already spoken. When forty-three members spoke on 7 December 1743, on a motion to disband the Hanoverian troops in British pay, Lord Egmont noted in his diary that this was 'a greater number than was ever known',[3] and no larger total has been found for any subsequent single debate. 25 March 1771, however, saw the unprecedented circumstance of sixty-five different members speaking at some time during the protracted proceedings against officials of the City of London for sheltering newspaper printers of Parliamentary reports.[4] Eighty-two speeches were made on 15 November 1763 over the issue of John Wilkes and the *North Briton*, fifteen of them by William Pitt.[5] Sixty speeches were made in one debate by forty different members in the Committee on the State of the Nation on 25 January 1770.[6] These occasions were exceptional: it was less than once a session on average that more than thirty members spoke in the same debate.

[1] Harris Diary, 12 May 1766.   [2] H. Walpole, *Last Journals*, II, 99.
[3] *H.M.C. Egmont Diary*, III, 278.
[4] B.M. Eg. MSS. 227, pp. 61–226. Brickdale Diary, V, 13–44.
[5] Harris Diary, 15 Nov. 1763.   [6] B.M. Eg. MSS. 3711, pp. 106–73.

The German traveller, Carl Moritz, noted the informality with which members could speak in the House of Commons. 'All that is necessary, is to stand up in your place, take off your hat, turn to the Speaker, to whom all the speeches are addressed, to hold your hat and stick in one hand, and with the other hand to make any such motions as you fancy necessary to accompany your speech.'[1] A member speaking had to remain standing until he had finished his speech. Only two occasions have been found when members were given leave by the House to speak sitting down, on account of indisposition: this concession was made to the elder William Pitt for his long speech of 9 December 1762 against the proposals for the later Peace of Paris, and to Lord Mayor Brass Crosby on 25 March 1771.[2] In both cases circumstances made it desirable that the two members should speak, the peculiar eminence of Pitt as the successful war minister, and the impending charge against City magistrates for protecting newspaper printers. Members had to have a seat, and were not permitted to speak from the passage-ways.[3]

Members were not allowed simply to read out speeches. Orations completely prepared beforehand had to be committed to memory, and the eighteenth century saw the decline of such 'set speeches'. The trend was noted by Horace Walpole in 1755: 'As set speeches were no longer in vogue, except on introductory or very solemn measures, the pomp and artful resources of oratory were in great manner banished.'[4] Members selected to propose and second measures on formal occasions, however, were often men inexperienced in Parliamentary speaking, and they usually prepared themselves for the ordeal by writing out the complete text of their speeches. James Harris made this comment on the proposal of the Address on 17 December 1765: 'Lord George Cavendish moved ... Lord Palmerston seconded: both speeches were set, and delivered rather with tremor and incoherence.'[5] Lapse of memory led to embarrassment. Knatchbull recorded that when Sir George Oxenden moved the Address on 21 January 1729 'he was out

[1] Moritz, *Travels*, pp. 53–4.
[2] Hatsell, *Precedents*, II, 107. Harris Diary, 9 Dec. 1762.
[3] Hatsell, *Precedents*, II, 108.   [4] H. Walpole, *George II*, II, 144.
[5] Harris Diary, 17 Dec. 1765.

once or twice and would have been more but that Tomson had his speech wrote out in his hat and sat next him and prompted him.'[1] Set speeches were also sometimes used by individual members during the ordinary course of debate, their motives varying from nervous inexperience to the desire to have an accurate text published in the contemporary press: and occasionally they were a device employed by members eager to create an impression. Horace Walpole recorded that on 15 April 1769 Ralph Payne made 'another pompous oration ... protesting on his honour that his speech was not premeditated; but forgetting part, he inadvertently pulled it out of his pocket in writing.'[2] By the reign of George II 'set speeches' were rare enough to be noted by diarists.[3] Contemporary opinion frowned on the device, and even on the frequent resort of members to the use of notes.

Members intending to speak in debates often prepared notes beforehand, and many sketches of proposed speeches can be found among the political papers of the century. But a widespread feeling that the use of such prepared notes was undesirable was reflected in a boast by Charles Turner on 3 March 1774: 'I never came into this House before with a note in my hand.'[4] During the course of debates, too, members took notes of what was being said in order to frame their own subsequent speeches, and this was especially the practice of ministers. That Sir Robert Walpole used to take notes for the purpose of replying to the debate is shown by this story told by his son Horace about the eloquence of Sir William Yonge: 'Sir Robert Walpole has often, when he did not care to enter early into the debate himself, given Yonge his notes, as the latter has come late into the House, from which he could speak admirably and fluently, though he had missed all the preceding discussion.'[5] Lord North frequently used notes when he was minister, and they were apparently taken down for him by Secretary of the Treasury Sir Grey Cooper.[6] By the reign of George III, however, the use of notes incurred criticism and evoked apology, and Lord North preferred

---

[1] *Knatchbull Diary*, p. 80.　　　[2] H. Walpole, *George III*, III, 238.
[3] *H.M.C. Egmont Diary*, I, 140; III, 337, 342.
[4] B.M. Eg. MSS. 253, p. 139.　　　[5] H. Walpole, *George II*, I, 23N.
[6] H. Walpole, *Letters*, VIII, 34N. Wraxall, *Memoirs*, II, 129.

whenever possible to trust his memory.[1] Most speeches were then extempore in both form and content: diarist Henry Cavendish gives this as the reason for the lack of clarity and frequent lapses of grammar to be found in many of them.[2]

One concession allowed to members at the discretion of the House, however, was that papers could be included as part of speeches. On 7 April 1741 Lord Gage asked permission to read out a letter, and after an objection he appealed to Speaker Onslow, 'who seemed to think it was regular':[3] but on 20 March 1771 Speaker Norton refused to allow Sir Joseph Mawbey to read out a provocative letter from John Wilkes.[4] On 24 January 1780 there occurred an extraordinary defiance of the House by Lord George Gordon, who read out a pamphlet as part of his speech, despite frequent and vociferous protests from other members.

After he had proceeded about half-way, a member rose, and asked the Speaker, if any gentleman had the right to introduce a pamphlet, and read the whole as a part of his speech, whether the House liked it or not? Because if he had, he said, there would be an end to business, as another member might take up a folio volume and insist on reading it through. The Speaker said it lay altogether with the House, who were masters of their own orders, and could either give permission or not in the present case, or any other. . . . the Speaker more than once gave it as his opinion that the pamphlet had no analogy or reference whatever to the motion then before the House: Lord George, however, in a manner altogether unexampled in Parliament, contrived to begin again and again, and at length so tired the House, which was by this time reduced to a bare forty members, that they even consented to let him finish it, finding him deaf to all attempts to prevent it, whether founded on order or not.

Lord George Gordon attempted a repeat performance the next day. He read out reports of Irish debates from a newspaper, two letters of Lord Hillsborough, extracts from Irish newspapers, and was proceeding to read again the pamphlet he had read out the previous day when 'a general murmur took place', and he then agreed to desist.[5] The context of the debates

---

[1] B.M. Eg. MSS. 220, p. 92; 222, pp. C 187, C 203; 224, p. 269; 228, pp. 239, 246; 229, p. 3. Debrett, *Parl. Reg.*, III, 263. Wraxall, *Memoirs*, II, 129.
[2] B.M. Eg. MSS. 263, fo. 5.   [3] *H.M.C. Egmont Diary*, III, 209.
[4] B.M. Eg. MSS. 226, pp. 497–9, 510.   [5] Almon, *Parl. Reg.*, XVII, 62–4.

shows that his motive was not a filibuster, and his behaviour may be regarded as a symptom of his notorious eccentricity. The episode serves as a reminder of the extent to which the efficiency of the House depended on the decorum of members rather than the constraint of rules.

The rule of standing, the need often to shout rather than talk, the reliance on memory—all meant that speaking in the House involved physical and mental strain. Even such an experienced speaker as Robert Walpole found in 1717 that a speech of nearly two hours 'strained his voice to that degree, that he was taken with a violent bleeding at the nose, which obliged him to go out of the House'.[1] A country squire like Sir Roger Newdigate was 'much fatigued' after a speech of about an hour.[2] Most speeches were therefore very brief. The majority of the members who spoke were rarely up for more than five or ten minutes, even for set speeches on formal occasions: James Harris noted that he took only nine minutes on 9 December 1762 to move the Address on the terms for the Peace of Paris. Few speeches lasted more than half an hour, and those of an hour or more were often thought worthy of mention by contemporaries in memoirs and correspondence. The eighteenth century, however, witnessed a trend towards longer speeches. One of two and a half hours by Horatio Walpole on 8 March 1739 when he moved an Address on an agreement with Spain was evidently regarded as a herculean effort,[3] but almost every session after 1760 saw at least one speech of comparable length. The famous orators of the day set the fashion. The length of the speeches made by the elder William Pitt was already attracting attention by the middle of the century;[4] and his great attack of 9 December 1762 on the peace terms was timed by several diarists at exactly three hours twenty-five minutes, a record in contemporary memory.[5] John Hatsell, who as Clerk was to hear even longer speeches, later commented that this was 'then thought very long'.[6] During the next two decades an hour soon became the usual

---

[1] Chandler, *Debates*, VI, 138.   [2] Newdigate Diary, 17 Mar. 1773.
[3] Hatsell, *Precedents*, II, 107.   [4] H. Walpole, *George II*, II, 60, 138.
[5] H. Walpole, *George III*, I, 95. Harris Diary, 9 Dec. 1762. Newdigate Diary, 9 Dec. 1762.
[6] Hatsell, *Precedents*, II, 107N.

length of speeches by leading politicians in important debates, and two hours not uncommon.[1] Horace Walpole noted of a debate on 29 January 1765 that 'Grenville spoke his usual hour';[2] and on 21 February 1766, for example, Attorney-General Charles Yorke, William Pitt and George Grenville each spoke for about an hour on the motion to repeal the Stamp Act.[3] By the ministry of Lord North an hour tended to be the minimum length for chief spokesmen in major debates, and Edmund Burke occasionally spoke for two or three hours or even longer.[4] The major speeches of Charles James Fox, at first rarely more than an hour, expanded to about the same length after a decade in the House, and young William Pitt was nearly matching him within a few years of taking his seat.[5] Here is Wraxall's comparison of these two debating giants at the end of the century.[6]

He [Fox] assumed that one-third of his Audience was always either absent, or at Dinner, or asleep; and he therefore usually made a short Resumption or Epitome of his Arguments, for the Benefit of this Part of the Members. So that, after speaking at great Length, and sometimes apparently summing up, as if about to conclude; whenever he saw a considerable Influx of Attendance, he began anew: regardless of the Impatience manifested on the Part of those, whose Attention was already exhausted by long Exertion. Pitt never condescended to avail himself of such a Practice; neither lengthening his Speeches, nor abbreviating them, for any Consideration except the Necessity of fully developing his Idea. Indeed, so well was the relative Proportion of Time generally taken up by the two Speakers, on great Occasions, known to the old Members, that they calculated, whenever Fox was three hours on his Legs, Pitt replied within two.

It was an old rule of the House that members had to address their speeches to the Speaker. Carl Moritz observed in 1782 that 'all the members always preface their speeches with, *sir*; and he, on being thus addressed, generally moves his hat a

---

[1] For some speeches of two hours or longer see Harris Diary, 24 Nov. 1763; B.M. Add. MSS. 35608 fo. 354; 35609, fos. 353–4: *Parliamentary Diary of Nathaniel Ryder*, p. 235: H. Walpole, *George III*, I, 263: *Malmesbury Letters*, I, 215.

[2] H. Walpole, *George III*, II, 44.   [3] Harris Diary, 21 Feb. 1766.

[4] *Malmesbury Letters*, I, 174. Almon, *Parl. Reg.*, I, 365; VIII, 8. H. Walpole, *Last Journals*, I, 450, 494. Wraxall, *Memoirs*, IV, 566.

[5] H. Walpole, *Last Journals*, II, 99. Debrett, *Parl. Reg.*, XII, 285–313.

[6] Wraxall, *Memoirs*, IV, 647–8.

little, but immediately puts it on again. This *sir* is often introduced in the course of their speeches, and serves to connect what is said: it seems also to stand the speaker in some stead, when any one's memory fails him, or he is otherwise at a loss for matter. For while he is saying, *sir*, and has thus obtained a little pause, he recollects what is to follow.'[1] The rule meant that members had to face the Speaker as well as formally direct their language to him, and speakers who offended in this respect sometimes found themselves interrupted by shouts of 'Chair! Chair!'[2] Invariable observance of this rule was not practised: Henry Cavendish, soon after his entry into the House, recorded 'the very disorderly custom of one member upon his legs, and another upon his seat holding a sort of conversation together'.[3]

Strict attention was paid to the rule that members were not allowed to refer to each other by name.[4] Lord Perceval noted in his account of a debate of 27 February 1730 that 'it is unparliamentary to name persons.' Since he was explaining why not only Sir Robert Walpole but also Lord Bolingbroke had not been directly mentioned, the diarist evidently thought that the prohibition applied to use of proper names.[5] Here he was mistaken. The rule was intended to prevent personal altercations, and concerned only reference to other members present.[6] In 1774, however, the interpretation was put forward that the rule covered any reference whatever to a member. During the Committee on the Quebec Bill on 8 June, George Johnstone mentioned that a report of the Board of Trade had been signed by, among others, one Soame Jenyns. 'I dont know whether he is a member of the House.' The Chairman, Sir Charles Whitworth, immediately intervened: 'I have always understood it as disorderly to mention the name of a member, present or not present.'[7] This view was not in accordance with the purpose of the rule, and was not sustained by later practice: on 26 November 1778, for instance, Colonel

---

[1] Moritz, *Travels*, p. 55.

[2] See, for example, B.M. Eg. MSS. 220, p. 161; 226, p. 265.

[3] B.M. Eg. MSS. 215, p. 29.

[4] Some diarists, including Matthew Brickdale and Nathaniel Ryder, did write the names of members as if they had been used by speakers in debate, but this was a matter of their own personal convenience.

[5] *H.M.C. Egmont Diary*, I, 74.   [6] *Liverpool Tractate*, p. 70.

[7] B.M. Eg. MSS. 262, p. 96.

Barré referred to 'a member of that House, whom he did not now see in his place; he should therefore take the liberty to mention his name. It was Mr. Oliver.'[1]

The only exception to the rule was the Speaker when in the Chair. Various incidents show that he called upon members to speak by name. On 16 February 1774, when Speaker Norton beckoned to Alderman Sawbridge, he called him Alderman Oliver by mistake and then begged his pardon.[2] Another mistake by the Chair was when Speaker Cust on 14 February 1764, pointing to Isaac Barré, called him Colonel. Barré, recently deprived of his army commission on political grounds, remarked, 'I beg your pardon, Sir, you have pointed to me by a title I have no right to.'[3]

Other members had to use circumlocutory terms. The modern practice of referring to members by their constituencies had not yet been adopted. Since most constituencies had two representatives there was a certain awkwardness in this method, and only two instances have been found. On 13 December 1770 Barré referred to James Harris as 'the member for Christchurch, who lives at Salisbury'; and on 2 April 1781 Thomas Townshend indicated Philip Yorke as 'the representative for Cambridgeshire'.[4] It must have been the increasing frequency of the practice, however, that led to a general condemnation of it by Speaker Cornwall on 28 November 1781. 'The Speaker blamed the gentlemen for making use of the names of the respective places for which they served.'[5]

Reference by constituency was not only clumsy: it also served as a reminder of the representative function of the House; and it was a reflection of implicit political and social attitudes that the common designation was not 'member' at all, but 'gentleman'. Such terms were used, when appropriate, as 'the noble lord', the worthy baronet', 'the right honourable gentleman', 'the learned gentleman', 'the worthy alderman', and so on. Since these vague references often led to confusion, the member's place in the House was often appended: allusion would be made to 'the gentleman over the way', the gentleman behind me', or

---

[1] Almon, *Parl. Reg.*, XI, 59.　　[2] B.M. Eg. MSS. 251, p. 295.
[3] H. Walpole, *Letters*, VI, 5.
[4] B.M. Eg. MSS. 223, p. 473. Debrett, *Parl. Reg.*, III, 197–8.
[5] Debrett, *Parl. Reg.*, V, 57.

'the gentleman below'. Such acknowledged heads of an administration as Sir Robert Walpole and Lord North would be styled 'the minister'; and reference was also often made to Lord North as 'the noble lord on the floor' and, after his acceptance of the Garter in 1772, 'the noble lord in the blue ribband'. A point of political significance was the occasional use of the term 'friend' to denote a political ally: it was used not merely by members of the same faction, but also with reference to the wider political alignment of administration and opposition; on 26 February 1733 opposition Whig William Pulteney designated Jacobite William Shippen as 'my honourable friend'.[1] A deliberate refusal to employ this mode of reference implied a recognition of hostility. Lord North on 14 December 1778 referred to George Johnstone as 'the honourable gentleman, for he could not call him his honourable friend'.[2] On 23 January 1756 Chancellor of the Exchequer Sir George Lyttelton called his former ally William Pitt 'his *friend . . .* correcting himself to say *the gentleman*, and the House laughing, Sir George said, "If he is not my friend, it is not *my* fault."'[3]

Collective references or designations of political alignments were usually made in one of three ways—in terms of the respective 'sides' of the House, of 'administration' and 'opposition', and of 'the majority' and 'the minority'. Little use was made of the party terms Whig and Tory, and then almost always in reference to individual members. Sometimes a member might assert that he was expounding Whig doctrines; rarely did any claim to be a Tory, and that term was often used as a reproach.[4] Although collective references to members were permitted, the fiction of the independence of individual members was maintained. No allusion to collective action was allowed. On 12 May 1774 Lord Advocate James Montgomery complained of attempts to postpone a Committee on the linen trade. 'I do say a party was formed against this bill.' He was interrupted by shouts of 'Order! Order!', and Speaker Norton ruled that 'it is not orderly to say a party is formed in the House against a bill.'[5]

---

[1] Chandler, *Debates*, VII, 302.　　　　[2] Almon, *Parl. Reg.*, XI, 165.
[3] H. Walpole, *George II*, II, 153.
[4] See, for example, *Cavendish Debates*, I, 370, 457.
[5] B.M. Eg. MSS. 257, p. 285.

Another fiction to be observed in debate was that all members of the House were equal. Thomas Powys aroused a storm of protest on 15 March 1782 by his observation that he would say nothing to support the motion of Sir John Rous until some member as independent as the proposer opposed it; and the altercation was ended by this pronouncement from Speaker Cornwall: 'The Speaker stated the point of order to be, that as by the rules of that House, all the members were equal, whether they represented counties or boroughs, so no distinction whatever ought to be made on account of fortune, situation, or any thing else, which might have a tendency to make a distinction, which the rules of the House did not allow.' Powys was indignant: if this declaration was correct, he said, what was the meaning of place bills? 'He could not suppose that he had rightly understood the right honourable gentleman, for such a doctrine was highly deterimental, as there would be an end to all freedom of debate.' He was silenced by the reminder that members should not debate a decision of the Chair. 'His way was not to argue upon it, but to take the sense of the House by a question.'[1]

The manner of reference to members of the House was a matter for the discretion of the Chair: but if the Speaker took no action, other members could do so. On 9 April 1725 Speaker Compton stretched this rule, which was intended to prevent members using 'unmannerly or indecent language' about other members, by stopping a member, Sir William Thomson, who was making a speech in praise of himself. 'The Speaker took him down, by saying gentlemen should neither make personal reflections nor personal commendations in the course of their debates.'[2] John Hatsell thought that it was impossible to formulate any precise definition of the rule: so much depended on the tone of voice, the manner and intention of the person speaking, the degree of provocation, and other considerations.[3] A later commentator believed that 'the sliding-scale, by which offensive phrases and indiscretions of speech appear to have been weighed, was the prevailing opinion of the majority.'[4] A practical definition was put forward by Lord North on 24

---

[1] Debrett, *Parl. Reg.*, VI, 464.
[2] *Knatchbull Diary*, p. 44.
[3] Hatsell, *Precedents*, II, 233–5.
[4] Townsend, *House of Commons*, II, 306.

April 1780, in criticism of some remarks by Charles James Fox: 'It was disorderly, because no words or expressions used there ought to be permitted, but what would pass current among any other society of gentlemen; that, he presumed, was one of the fixed principles of order in that House, and in every other popular assembly.'[1] But two years later Carl Moritz formed the impression that only a formal standard of decorum was being maintained.[2]

> The little less than downright open abuse, and the many really rude things, which the members said to each other, struck me much. For example, when one has finished, another rises, and immediately taxes with absurdity all that the right honourable gentleman . . . had just advanced. It would indeed be contrary to the rules of the house, flatly to tell each other, that what they have spoken, is *false*, or even *foolish*: instead of this, they turn themselves, as usual, to the Speaker, and so, whilst their address is directed to him, they fancy they violate neither the rules of parliament, nor those of good breeding and decorum, whilst they utter the most cutting personal sarcasms against the member, or the measure they oppose.

Abundant evidence survives as to the latitude of behaviour permitted to speakers in debate. In the heat of the moment language often became intemperate, as when Edmund Burke denounced the North ministry on 27 November 1781: 'The British Nation, as an animal, is dead; but, the Vermin that feed on the Carcase, are still alive.'[3] Most abuse came from the opposition side of the House. Violence of expression by opposition speakers may even have been thought to be in some sense justified by the historic role of the House as a check on the executive: for on 22 February 1782 the opposition right to attack administration with complete freedom of language was advanced by Colonel Barré, after Lord North had apologized for calling previous abuse from Barré 'insolent and brutal'. Diarist Wraxall recalled how Barré 'then proceeded to demonstrate that every Member possessed a Right to use with Impunity, the most severe Epithets towards a public Functionary, the Servant of the State, though that Right was not reciprocal'.[4] Barré's attitude and behaviour were not typical. Most members observed verbal decencies in debate, and those who began

[1] Almon, *Parl. Reg.*, XVII, 563. [2] Moritz, *Travels*, pp. 57–8.
[3] Wraxall, *Memoirs*, II, 441–2. [4] Wraxall, *Memoirs*, II, 134–5.

to forget them usually had friends to restrain them, even forcibly, as happened to Sir John Cope on 20 April 1725. During a personal attack on Lord Bolingbroke Cope 'was going on to say something that he might have been called to the Bar for, but somebody pulled him down and so he left off in great confusion'.[1]

That was the traditional procedure threatened on such occasions—for offending words to be taken down by the Clerk, and then for the member concerned to be called before the Bar and ask pardon of the House on his knees.[2] This had to be done immediately or at the end of the speech, so that the precise words could be written down, and an opportunity for explanation given.[3] No instance has been found after 1715 of members being treated in this way for words spoken in debate. Members who had given offence always made a withdrawal and apology, as on 18 November 1766 after George Grenville had asked for the Clerk to take down an assertion by William Beckford that the King had a dispensing power, in times of absolute necessity. Such a statement was contrary to the Bill of Rights, and Beckford withdrew it on Grenville's insistence that otherwise he would take the sense of the House on the words.[4] Interventions to enforce the rule nearly always came from other members, not from the Chair; and no occasion has been found when a Speaker condemned any expression as unparliamentary unless the member concerned had already admitted his fault. Not until William Pulteney had asked pardon of the House on 7 May 1728 did Speaker Onslow declare that Pulteney should not have equated supporters of a government motion with pickpockets and highwaymen.[5] Sometimes offending words were retracted by the member himself without subsequent condemnation from the Chair, as when Lord George Gordon conceded on 13 April 1778 that his epithet 'villainous' was unparliamentary.[6] Often there was no observation from the Chair when members were called to order on this ground: Speaker Cust remained silent on 23 November 1768 when James Townsend protested that Lord Barrington should not have called John Wilkes a criminal,

---

[1] *Knatchbull Diary*, p. 47.   [2] *Knatchbull Diary*, p. 76. See *infra*, p. 348.
[3] Townsend, *House of Commons*, I, 297–8.   [4] *Grenville Papers*, III, 386–7.
[5] *Knatchbull Diary*, p. 126.   [6] Almon, *Parl. Reg.*, IX, 158–9.

as Wilkes was then a member of the House;[1] and Speaker Norton merely restored order on 27 January 1778 after Charles Turner had deliberately replied with the assertion that 'the ministry were combined to betray this country' to a reference by Henry Luttrell to opposition members as 'abettors of treason and rebellion'.[2] The difficulties involved in the enforcement of the rule led the Chair to deem discretion a better course of action than detailed definitions of unparliamentary language.

Apart from the rules concerning references to members, there were a number of formal restrictions on the content of speeches. Like those against abuse, these rules were enforced by the potential threat that any members might move to have offending words taken down by the Clerk, and then move to put a question to the House on the matter. Members were not allowed to argue against any decision of the House made during the same session, or any decision in force through the whole Parliament: on 15 April 1769 George Onslow therefore called William Beckford to order for criticizing previous resolutions on the Middlesex election case, threatening to have Beckford's words taken down if he repeated the offence; and Speaker Norton called George Johnstone to order on 6 December 1770 for declaring that the Cumberland election case had not been decided on its merits in 1768.[3] These rules were evidently intended to avoid waste of time as well as to maintain formal respect for the House; for such decisions could not be rescinded while they remained in force.

No reference could even be made to anything that had been said in a previous debate; when this restriction was debated on 29 January 1730 the practice was said to be one long regarded as unparliamentary.[4] This rule was usually enforced, as when Lord George Germain criticized opposition members for a breach of it on 14 December 1778. 'He was sorry that the House should have indulged gentlemen with this licentiousness in debate, and permit them to deviate from the old Parliamentary rules, never to mention what passed on a former occasion.' The reason for that rule, Germain declared, was that members

---

[1] B.M. Eg. MSS. 215, p. 213.   [2] Almon, *Parl. Reg.*, VIII, 318.
[3] B.M. Eg. MSS. 219, p. 232; 223, p. 49.
[4] *H.M.C. Egmont Diary*, I, 12–13. *Knatchbull Diary*, p. 102.

could never remember exactly what had been said.[1] The rule, however, imposed a formal restraint on the free play of political argument, and met growing resistance from members. On 28 November 1781 Thomas Townshend unsuccessfully tried to assert the right on the report of the Address to refer to what had been said in the debate of the previous day; 'he was regular, for the present was in the nature of an adjourned debate.'[2] The next year, when the Address was reported on 6 December 1782, no attempt was made to check the claim of Humphrey Minchin to refer to 'last night's debate, of which the present was, in a parliamentary sense, a continuation'.[3] The growing practice of adjourning debates had accustomed members to break this old rule in principle; and the establishment of Parliamentary reporting in the press had destroyed the original reason for the rule stated by Germain.

Further rules were connected with the other parts of the legislature. The name of the King could not be used either irreverently or to influence a debate.[4] Direct attacks on the sovereign, being impolitic, were rare; but a famous incident occurred on 4 December 1717. Jacobite William Shippen then made some offensive statements about George I, among them the comment that it was 'the only infelicity of his Majesty's reign, that he is unacquainted with our language and constitution'. After his refusal to withdraw his remarks his words were voted by the House as 'highly dishonourable to, and unjustly reflecting on, His Majesty's Person and Government', and Shippen was committed to the Tower. Each decision was opposed, and no later attacks on a sovereign received such severe punishment.[5] The rule concerning reference to the sovereign was primarily intended, of course, to prevent knowledge of royal opinions influencing decisions of the House. This principle was accepted by administration as well as opposition,[6] but government supporters sometimes broke the rule. George Grenville protested on 2 March 1769 that accusations were being made against opposition members of personal disrespect to the

---

[1] Almon, *Parl. Reg.*, XI, 160. For some examples of the enforcement of the rule see B.M. Eg. MSS. 219, p. 103; 221, p. 327; 227, p. 33.

[2] Debrett, *Parl. Reg.*, V, 57.   [3] Debrett, *Parl. Reg.*, IX, 43.

[4] Hatsell, *Precedents*, II, 235.   [5] Chandler, *Debates*, VI, 154–61.

[6] See, for example, B.M. Eg. MSS. 219, pp. 45–6; 221, p. 269: Harris Diary, 11 Dec. 1761: *H.M.C. Egmont Diary*, II, 359; III, 283.

Crown: 'It is not a fair, nor a candid, it is not a parliamentary reflection. It is the first principle of the House, that naming the Crown is a most dangerous language.'[1] During a similar incident on 24 January 1770 Lord North agreed that 'it is undoubtedly a great breach of the rules of Parliament to attribute anything said in this House to an opposition to the King.'[2] Speaker Norton intervened on 15 June 1779 to stop persistent defiance of the rule by Advocate-General Henry Dundas, ruling that 'no member has any right to use the King's name in a debate of what his Majesty did or wished etc., and the reason of that principal order was, lest the introduction of his Majesty's name might have the appearance of influencing the decision from improper motives.' Lord John Cavendish then added that 'the true Parliamentary language' was to say 'the Crown'.[3] Members were even sensitive to announcements by ministers of the King's leave for the House to debate or legislate on matters affecting the royal prerogative; Sir Robert Walpole had to explain on 24 February 1730 that he had meant the King's permission not his command after Wortley Montagu had raised the point of order.[4] In the annual debates on the Address in reply to the King's Speech difficulties were avoided by the convention adopted throughout the century of treating the speech as the words of the minister.

No reference might be made to proceedings in the House of Lords, apart from an inspection of the Lords' *Journals*.[5] A general observance of this rule was practised, but members sometimes sought political advantage from infringements of the prohibition. Lord North said in a debate of 18 May 1775 on a motion by Sir George Savile to repeal the Quebec Act that no such bill could pass the House of Lords that session, for a similar motion had been rejected there the previous day. Thomas Townshend called him to order, a call 'instantly echoed from almost every part of the House'.[6] On 2 December 1777, during a debate on an opposition motion for papers, news came that the House of Lords had agreed to a similar motion. It was Lord North's turn to object that reference to

---

[1] B.M. Eg. MSS. 218, pp. 296–7. [2] B.M. Eg. MSS. 3711, pp. 93–4.
[3] Almon, *Parl. Reg.*, XIII, 414. [4] Chandler, *Debates*, VII, 63–4.
[5] Harris Diary, 9 May 1765. B.M. Eg. MSS. 215, p. 201; 220, p. 67.
[6] Almon, *Parl. Reg.*, I, 483.

events in the other House was disorderly, and Thomas Townshend who denied this contention: 'That nothing was more usual, than to take notice of what passed in the other House; that a knowledge of each other's deliberations and general sentiments was the prime motive for relaxing the respective standing orders of each House' about the admission of strangers.[1] On 20 March 1780, however, when William Fullarton complained of an attack on him by the Earl of Shelburne in the House of Lords, Charles James Fox declared that it was contrary to Parliamentary rules both to state what had been said in another House, and to mention peers by name. Richard Rigby agreed that this was correct, to prevent ill-humour and to preserve the freedom of debate.[2]

More important than all these specific restrictions on the content of speeches was the general rule of relevance, which had existed since at least a standing order of 1604 and was noted by Hatsell in this form: 'If a Member speak besides the question, it is the duty of the Speaker to interrupt him; and the House ought for their own sake to support the Speaker in such interposition.'[3] There is little evidence of the direct enforcement of this rule, which depended essentially on the good sense of the members speaking as well as on the support of the Chair by the House. Interventions by Speakers were so rare that members sometimes resented such interruptions when they took place. When Speaker Cust refused to allow Charles Townshend to answer an admittedly irrelevant statement by Lord North on 16 December 1763, 'Townshend was angry with the Speaker, and harsh. Why may he not transgress order as well as another?'[4] The Chair was doubtless deterred from intervention by the frequent difficulty of judging whether or not remarks did have a direct or indirect connection with the ostensible subject of debate: and the point also led to arguments when the rule was invoked. After Charles Cornwall was called to order by Speaker Norton on 24 January 1770 William

---

[1] Almon, *Parl. Reg.*, VIII, 77–81. On the admission of strangers see *supra.*, p. 145.

[2] Almon, *Parl. Reg.*, XVII, 372–4. A duel later took place between Fullarton and Lord Shelburne: see Fullarton's biography in Namier and Brooke, *The House of Commons 1754–1790*, II, 475–6.

[3] *Commons Journals*, I, 975. Hatsell, *Precedents*, II, 107.

[4] Harris Diary, 11 Dec. 1763.

Dowdeswell rose to protest: 'My honourable friend was stopped by you, Sir. I am sorry to differ, but it did not strike me, that he was going beyond order . . . I know nothing that can be done, but to take the words down, and take the sense of the House', a threat not carried out.[1] Even Speaker Onslow failed to enforce the rule by his own authority. On 12 February 1730 Sir Edmund Bacon complained of a digression by Charles Caesar: 'the Speaker then got up and said with great resentment it was not to be borne, that he sat there to keep the House to orderly debating, and he never saw such liberties taken in flying from the point before us. He desired gentlemen would confine themselves as they ought to do.' A few minutes later Onslow rose to rebuke Shippen on the same point, 'saying he would by the grace of God oblige every gentleman to be orderly'. Sir Joseph Jekyll commended this firmness, and noise silenced further irrelevance by Shippen: yet even such resolute action had only a temporary effect. Later in the same debate Edward Vernon 'brought in the Pope, the Devil, the Jesuits, the seamen, etc., so that the House had not patience to attend to him, though he was not taken down'.[2] Another attempt to enforce the rule the next month met with open disrespect towards the Chair: after calling for relevance on 25 March 1730 Onslow 'ended with saying he would die in the chair rather than suffer such things: whereupon Will. Pulteney said he believed he would die in the chair if he could, meaning, I suppose, that he liked the honour and profit of being Speaker.'[3] Onslow may have become discouraged after his early experience: the only other occasion found when he invoked the rule was much later, on 28 February 1757. He then interrupted an altercation between the two leading debaters of that period, Henry Fox and William Pitt. 'The Speaker observed, that two-thirds of what both had said, was nothing to the question. Pitt replied, that he was surprised at being coupled with Mr. Fox, who had spoken five times, he but once: Yet Fox had not been suppressed . . . The Speaker vindicated himself, talked of his unbiassed impartiality and integrity.'[4] Pitt's apparent misunderstanding of the reason for Onslow's intervention may

[1] B.M. Eg. MSS. 3711, pp. 84–6.   [2] *H.M.C. Egmont Diary*, I, 43–4.
[3] *H.M.C. Egmont Diary*, I, 86.   [4] H. Walpole, *George II*, II, 350.

have been due to the rarity of the enforcement of the rule of relevance. If Onslow failed, lesser Speakers were unlikely to succeed. When John Sawbridge complained of irrelevance on 16 May 1774 Speaker Norton admitted his inability to enforce the rule;[1] and no more than a dozen attempts by the Chair to do so have been found under Onslow's three immediate successors.[2] The difficulty experienced in the task is shown by the debate of 12 December 1770 on a motion to postpone the land tax until after Christmas. This soon resolved into a discussion of the need for an increase in the tax. It covered general financial policy, and was developing into an argument between Sir Edward Hawke and Colonel Barré on the state of the navy when Speaker Norton rose to order: 'If we are to beat every point of the compass for all kinds of subjects we shall never close the present debate.' Hawke started to resume his previous theme, but was stopped by Norton: 'I must break in upon the honourable gentleman's argument going on. That has nothing to do with the present question.' Barré then took up the same subject. He was called to order by George Rice, and Sir Fletcher Norton stated, 'It is, as it ought to be, to me perfectly indifferent, whoever are disorderly, let it come from one side of the House or the other. I hope we shall come back now to the question.' The debate then returned to its proper course.[3]

Such firmness in a Speaker over this point was rare. Indeed, quite apart from the difficulties of definition and enforcement, it appears to have been the usual practice of the Chair not to check the first member guilty of irrelevance, in the hope that he or the next speaker would return to the proper subject of the debate: and, on grounds of fairness, this lenity might then be deliberately extended to the second speaker, and even subsequent ones.[4] But the enforcement of rules was not solely at the discretion of the Chair; and if the Speaker took no action any other member could do so. One method was to ask the Speaker to read the question, as the way of bringing the

[1] B.M. Eg. MSS. 259, p. 81.
[2] Apart from instances cited in the text see B.M. Eg. MSS. 222, pp. C 211, C 356; 223, p. 311; 226, pp. 109, 513; 245, p. 167; 3711, p. 90: Almon, *Parl. Reg.*, XI, 130; XVII, 56–7; Debrett, *Parl. Reg.*, XII, 85.
[3] B.M. Eg. MSS. 223, pp. 390–1.
[4] See, for example, Debrett, *Parl. Reg.*, VII, 154; Wraxall, *Memoirs*, III, 171–2.

debate back to the subject.[1] More common was the direct interruption of speeches of opponents with shouts of 'Order! Order!' whenever the situation warranted or excused such interference. A flow of eloquence could be cut short by such means. On 15 April 1769 William Beckford, waxing biblical on the Middlesex election, had just uttered the words 'to your tents, O Israel' when Lord Clare rose to order: 'If he cant apply what he has said, he is out of order.' Thrown out of his stride, Beckford soon stopped and sat down.[2] The excessive number of times that members were called to order itself led to complaints, and Thomas Pownall had ample ground for his assertion on 4 March 1774 that 'by this method of calling to order freedom of debate is interrupted.'[3]

Custom led the House to relax the rule of relevance in certain respects. Debates on formal motions, such as those to adjourn or for the Orders of the Day, were never restricted to the merits of the question: if that had not been so, any motion for the previous question, for example, might automatically prevent further debate on the original motion; for if it was decided in the affirmative, that motion then had to be put immediately.[4] Debates on the Address ranged widely over government policy, and were not restricted to the desirability of the motion of thanks. Debates on motions for papers were not usually limited to a discussion of the need to examine the particular papers. Such relaxations of the standing order were sanctioned by convention only, and members were at liberty to object. On 4 February 1771 Charles Jenkinson and Sir Gilbert Elliot claimed that Edmund Burke should confine himself strictly to the motion that papers relative to the Falkland Islands convention with Spain should lie on the Table. During the argument on this point Burke's ally William Dowdeswell therefore drew up a motion for more papers and gave it to Henry Seymour, who proposed it as soon as the current debate had finished.[5] Too strict an interpretation of the rules of procedure often led to easy evasion or circumvention.

The dignity of the House required that each speaker should

---

[1] See, for example, B.M. Eg. MSS. 223, p. 386; 226, p. 507; 249, p. 2.
[2] B.M. Eg. MSS. 219, pp. 236–8. [3] B.M. Eg. MSS. 253, p. 167.
[4] See *supra.*, p. 181. [5] B.M. Eg. MSS. 224, pp. 45–55.

receive due respect. Other members had to sit down. They were not allowed to walk up and down the chamber, nor could they stand about on the floor, in the gangways or in the gallery. When in their seats they were not permitted to read letters or printed books, or to smoke.[1] These rules appear to have been more or less strictly observed, but attention and silence did not always ensue. No rule could guarantee a speaker that his audience would stay, and members of the House, then as now, left the chamber when speakers notorious for dullness or prolixity were on their feet. Here is a story told by Wraxall about one of them, David Hartley.[2]

His rising always operated like a Dinner Bell. One day, that he had thus wearied out the Patience of his Audience, having nearly cleared a very full House which was reduced from three hundred to about eighty persons, half asleep; just at a time when he was expected to close, he unexpectedly moved that the Riot Act should be read, as a document necessary to elucidate, or to prove some of his foregoing assertions. Burke, who sat close by him . . . laid hold of Hartley by the coat, "The Riot Act! my dear friend, the Riot Act! To what purpose! Dont you see that the mob is already completely dispersed?"

Even if the members present were quiet many often paid little attention to the debate, and late at night some doubtless dozed off when waiting for the question to be put. On 18 March 1772 Henry Cavendish noted government supporters sitting with their eyes shut during a midnight debate on the Royal Family Marriage Bill.[3] The most sleepy member of the century was probably Lord North, whose position as Leader of the House from 1768 to 1782 made necessary his regular attendance in the chamber. He soon began his famous habit of sleeping on the Treasury Bench, for Barré complained as early as 22 November 1770, 'Is there a minister that ever slept so much in Parliament? He has taken his doze and his nap, whilst notes have been taken for him'.[4] Wraxall recorded the

[1] Hatsell, *Precedents*, II, 235–6. During debates the Serjeant-at-Arms, and presumably other officials of the House, had to go up to the Table or the Speaker's Chair on the opposite side of the chamber from that from which a member was speaking. Clementson Diary, p. 14.

[2] Wraxall, *Memoirs*, IV, 490–1.   [3] B.M. Eg. MSS. 238, pp. 156, 169.

[4] B.M. Eg. MSS. 222, p. C 203. For another reference, on 10 Dec. 1770 ; see B.M. Eg. MSS. 223, p. 286.

same phenomenon towards the end of North's administration:
'In addition to his defection of sight, Lord North was subject
likewise to a constitutional somnolency, which neither the
animated declamations of Fox, nor the pathetic invocations of
Burke, nor the hoarse menaces of Barré, could always prevent.
It attacked him even on the Treasury Bench, sometimes with
irresistible force.'[1] That Lord North was merely resting his weak
eyes and not actually asleep, however, is suggested by this
story appended by Wraxall to his description: 'His odd revenge
on Burke should have been mentioned. The orator was
inveighing against him while he slept, or seemed to sleep, till
our language being insufficient for his abuse of such a Minister,
Burke quoting Latin against him, pronounced the word
Vēctigăl, here accentuated. "*Vĕctīgal!*" said Lord North, and
slept again.'[2]

Both speakers and sleepers had to contend with a background of noise. When debates were in progress there was a
fairly constant hum of private conversation in the chamber,
and members sometimes moved to chat to friends in other
parts of the House: on 7 April 1772 Horace Walpole saw
Charles Fox 'running about the House talking to different
persons and scarce listening' to Burke's speech on his own
motion.[3] Henry Cavendish laid part of the blame for the
imperfections of his reports on 'the disorder that, now and
then, used to prevail in the House: where sometimes members
from an eagerness to hear others, or themselves, made so much
noise as to drown the voice of the person speaking'.[4] One
such occasion was a debate of 19 May 1773 on East India
Company affairs. Cavendish noted in his diary that 'the House
were got into very great disorder, a circumstance that now and
then happens', and then rose himself to complain: 'Such a
hubbub, Sir, as has been in the House for some time past was
never heard even in the Senate of Pandemonium.'[5]

Noise might arise from inattention, or from attention: for
speeches were punctuated not only by interruptions from
members alleging breaches of rules but also by sounds of
approval and dissent. Carl Moritz observed in 1782 that

[1] Wraxall, *Memoirs*, II, 128.   [2] Wraxall, *Memoirs*, II, 128N.
[3] H. Walpole, *Last Journals*, I, 81.   [4] B.M. Eg. MSS. 263, fo. 2.
[5] B.M. Eg. MSS. 247, p. 97.

when a favourite member, and one who speaks well and to the purpose, rises, the most perfect silence reigns: and his friends and admirers, one after another, make their approbation known by calling out *hear him*; which is often repeated by the whole house at once; and in this way so much noise is often made that the speaker is frequently interrupted by this same emphatic *hear him*. Notwithstanding which, this calling out is always regarded as a great encouragement; and I have often observed, that one who began with some diffidence, and even somewhat inauspiciously, has in the end been so animated, that he has spoken with a torrent of eloquence.[1]

Charles Fox did not need the stimulus of encouragement, but often received it, and this reaction to his speech on 22 May 1777 was described as 'unprecedented' by a reporter: 'Several of the members, in a transport of approbation, forgot themselves so far, as to testify it in accents of bravo! hear him! which they accompanied with a clapping of hands.'[2]

Spontaneous or organized support of speeches might inadvertently disrupt a debate or drown the speech itself: in the preface to his diary Cavendish complained that 'sometimes premature applause for a former part of a sentence prevented the House from hearing the latter; and sometimes those favourite words "Hear! Hear!" so frequently echoed through the House, forbad all hearing.' This expression, Cavendish said, might signify 'approbation, disapprobation, irony, sarcasm':[3] and the real problem of disorder came from deliberate attempts to interrupt and stop speeches. Carl Moritz reported this as a frequent occurrence.[4]

If that happens, that a member rises, who is but a bad speaker, or if what he says is generally deemed not sufficiently interesting, so much noise is made, and such bursts of laughter are raised, that the member who is speaking can scarcely distinguish his own words. This must needs be a distressing situation, and it seems then to be particularly laughable, when the Speaker in his chair, like a tutor in a school, again and again endeavours to restore order, which he does by calling out *to order, to order*; apparently often without much attention being paid to it.

---

[1] Moritz, *Travels*, pp. 54–5. [2] Almon, *Parl. Reg.*, VII, 228.
[3] B.M. Eg. MSS. 263, fo. 2. [4] Moritz, *Travels*, p. 54.

The maintenance of silence and decorum in the House was the most difficult task facing occupants of the Chair: it is probable that even Arthur Onslow was not always successful, and other Speakers often found the task beyond them.[1] Other members might speak to order if there was noise, as when Thomas Hampden on 28 February 1770 declared that he would point to any man 'who interrupted gentlemen in their speaking'.[2] Such individual protests usually had little effect: that the temper of the House was the dominant factor is apparent even from Clerk John Hatsell's tactful survey of contemporary practice.[3]

> Every member is entitled to be heard quietly, and without interruption, but if he finds that it is not the inclination of the House to hear him, and that by conversation, or any other noise, they endeavour to drown his voice, it is his most prudent way to submit to the pleasure of the House, and sit down, for it hardly ever happens that they are guilty of this piece of ill-manners without reasonable cause ... It is the Speaker's duty to keep members quiet, but that is very difficult when love of talking gets the better of modesty and good sense; and, indeed, the House are very seldom inattentive to a Member who says anything worth their hearing.

Moritz and Hatsell both fail to mention the two main reasons for noise, dislike of the speakers or the views they expressed, and impatience if the hour was late. How the House showed its displeasure to those who had offended it can be seen from this treatment of Isaac Barré on 12 May 1762: 'Colonel Barré set out in a flaming scurrilous speech as usual, but was discountenanced by the House. Many Gentlemen as soon as he rose went out of the House; many of those who stayed shuffled about from their places, talked with one another, coughed and would not hear him.'[4] Antipathy to opinions was usually political: the minister of the day was heard with respect, but prominent opposition speakers were not always so fortunate. In 1773 a writer in the *London Magazine* asserted that deliberate attempts were made to silence William Dowdeswell, then the leading spokesman in the House of the Rockingham group.[5]

---

[1] For assessments of the individual Speakers in this respect see *infra.*, pp. 349–63.
[2] B.M. Eg. MSS. 220, p. 241. [3] Hatsell, *Precedents*, II, 107–8.
[4] B.M. Add. MSS. 6839, fos. 268–9. [5] *London Magazine*, 1773, p. 272.

This inflexible patriot, who, as he was Chancellor of the Exchequer, and is therefore deemed by the courtiers the antagonist of Lord North, is heard with impatience by the ministerial side of the House. Accordingly, when he rises, they begin to murmur and chatter like magpies, that his severe sarcasms and poignant observations may not be heard. The same manoeuvre they attempted several times against Edmund Burke, but the thunder and lightning of his eloquence has at last laid that venal crew prostrate at his feet.

That Burke was a natural target for interruptions can be seen from Wraxall's pen-portrait of him in action: 'Burke constantly wore spectacles. His enunciation was vehement, rapid, and never checked by any Embarrassment: for his Ideas outran his Powers of Utterance, and he drew from an exhaustless Source. But his Irish Accent, which was as strong as if he had never quitted the Banks of the Shannon, diminished to the Ear, the enchanting Effect of his Eloquence on the Mind.'[1] The dazzling oratory of Edmund Burke, adorned with metaphors and similes, makes magnificent prose: but it must often have been incomprehensible to a large part of his audience. He spoke too long as well as too fast, and it was his practice to speak late in debates. He lacked the personal or social stature to command respect. His views were often predictable, and usually unpopular with the majority of members present.[2] Attempts to stop him were therefore frequent, and sometimes mentioned by Burke himself. On 10 December 1770 he made this comment during his speech: 'I must address myself to some gentlemen, and I will do it with humility, that they have a disposition, when any gentleman gets up, they don't choose to hear speak, to endeavour the best they can, to drown him with noise, and clamour. I never knew it was formed into a regular system till today.'[3] Later in the same session Burke reported to Rockingham that on 13 February 1771 he had waited 'for the general reply, until after twelve; a detachment of Macaronies endeavoured to prevent me from speaking, but they did not succeed.'[4] During his speech Burke remarked,

---

[1] Wraxall, *Memoirs*, II, 277. Parliamentary diarists and reporters had conspicuous difficulty in recording Burke's speeches.

[2] These comments are based on the reports of some 600 speeches by Burke between 1766 and 1784.

[3] B.M. Eg. MSS. 223, p. 287.   [4] Wentworth Woodhouse MSS., R 1–1361.

'I am very glad that the House is full; but there is another point not so easy to gain—a patient attendance, a very full and a very patient House.'[1] Even age and experience did not give Burke immunity from such treatment. Carl Moritz noted this incident during a speech by him on 9 July 1782 in praise of the recently deceased Lord Rockingham: 'As he did not meet with sufficient attention, and heard much talking and many murmurs, he said, with much vehemence and a sense of injured merit, "this is not treatment for so old a Member of Parliament as I am, and I will be heard!" On which there was immediately a most profound silence.'[2]

Other opposition members often suffered from interruptions intended to make them sit down, and usually responded with predictable defiance.[3] Such noise was especially liable to occur towards the end of long debates of political importance. Few members sat through them. Many administration supporters only returned to or entered the House when a division was expected, 'full of dinner . . . without hearing one word of debate'.[4] Thomas Townshend, alluding on 8 June 1774 to a division on the previous evening in the Committee on the Quebec Bill, declared, 'I will venture to say two-thirds of that majority never heard it debated. It consisted of those gentlemen who took their meals regularly and are now taking their dinners.'[5] These members had no wish to be detained by orations from opposition speakers. Late in many debates there were constant interruptions by shouts of 'Question! Question!' Henry Seymour became so exasperated during a debate of 28 February 1770 that he declared 'he would make use of a synonymous term to question, question, question, and call out majority, majority, majority'.[6] The debates on the Royal Family Marriage Bill of 1772 were found especially tedious by the ministerial supporters pressed into attendance. On 9 March Constantine Phipps complained of 'the gentlemen who have called for the question so repeatedly . . . a midnight impatience to drown every argument'.[7] On 23 March there was such a

---

[1] B.M. Eg. MSS. 224, p. 315.   [2] Moritz, *Travels*, p. 219.

[3] See, for example, B.M. Eg. MSS. 224, p. 61; 226, p. 265; 228, p. 109.

[4] B.M. Eg. MSS. 225, p. 471. For similar remarks see B.M. Eg. MSS. 222, p. A 198; 226, pp. 84, 507; 237, p. 162; 254, p. 145; 262, pp. 210–11.

[5] B.M. Eg. MSS. 262, p. 71.   [6] B.M. Eg. MSS. 220, p. 241.

[7] B.M. Eg. MSS. 235, p. 210.

noise during a speech by Sir George Savile that Speaker Norton reproved the House: 'Gentlemen will be afraid to get up if this is to be the consequence.' That was the intention, however, and his intervention had no effect. The next speaker was soon forced by the noise to sit down, and the division was then taken.[1]

Reporter John Almon, an opposition partisan, professed to regard such behaviour as a deliberate part of ministerial tactics in the House:[2] but this interpretation failed to take account of a normal reaction to long and often wearisome discussions. Administration supporters were not the only members who objected to being detained in the House by long debates. The scene described by James Harris in the Committee on the Nullum Tempus Bill on 24 February 1769 must have been typical of the end of many debates: 'The debate was informing, and full of legal history, but to many of the hearers I should imagine dry and fatiguing, so that when Grenville had done speaking they seemed resolved to hear no more; opposition talked so loud, they silenced Dyson, and administration talked so loud they silenced Burke, and about ten we came to a division.'[3] Such a mass defiance of order was beyond the control of any Speaker or Chairman, although Cornwall did make a general denunciation of the practice on 26 March 1781:[4]

A number of Members, who through the greatest part of the debate had been in the coffee rooms now crowded in, and called with loud and continued uproar for the question. The Speaker thought fit to rise, and call them to order. In a sensible and pointed speech, he severely reprehended the custom. There were, he said, a regular and uniform set of gentlemen of a particular description, who did not think it at all necessary to attend to any part of the debate, in order to receive information or judge where the merits of a question lay, that they might decide with decency, or vote with conviction; but they went to the coffee-houses and there spent the whole day, and came in towards the conclusion of the debate, and with the utmost disorder and incivility called for the question, and put a hasty stop to the calm deliberations of such members as acted up to their duty, in attending seriously to the business of the House.

[1] B.M. Eg. MSS. 239, pp. 102–3. [2] Almon, *Debates*, VIII, 47; IX, 25.
[3] B.M. Add. MSS. 35608, fos. 340–1. [4] Debrett, *Parl. Reg.*, II, 370.

He hoped, that as it was a practice so derogatory of the honour and the dignity of Parliament, and so inconsistent with the gravity of a House of Representatives, he would not have occasion again to take notice and complain of the indecency.

It was already then after midnight, and the reproof won only a temporary respite from noise even in that same debate.[1] Two years later, however, in the stormy debate of 8 December 1783 on the third reading of Fox's East India Bill, Cornwall not only attacked such deliberate disorder but even declared that it did not achieve the obvious purpose of ending debates.[2]

The House growing extremely clamourous, and calling for the question so vociferously, that Sir Watkin Lewes, who was upon his legs, could scarcely be heard. Mr Alderman Townshend rose, and spoke to order. He called upon the Speaker to enforce regularity, and declared, if he had not authority enough to keep the assembly in order, so that every member might be heard, that House would be a mob, and not a Parliament. The Speaker rose to desire the House would be orderly, and declared, that if gentlemen imagined, by creating a confusion and clamouring for the question, they would shorten the debate, his long experience in Parliament, and his acquaintance with the effect such endeavours generally produced, enabled him to assure them, that they took the most unlikely way in the world to attain their ends.

Speaker Cornwall spoke with more assurance than accuracy. In theory debates could continue until every member who wished to speak had done so. In practice they were often brought to an end by the refusal of members to hear any more speeches.

[1] Debrett, *Parl. Reg.*, II, 370–1.　　　[2] Debrett ,*Parl. Reg.*, XII, 395–6.

12

SPEAKERS IN DEBATE

'YOU must first make a figure there if you would make a figure in your country.' Sir Lewis Namier began his most famous book *The Structure of Politics at the accession of George III* with this quotation from the advice of Lord Chesterfield to his son in 1749 on his entry to the House of Commons:[1] but he then proceeded to demonstrate the variety of other motives for election to the House in the eighteenth century. Few members entered Parliament with the desire to shine in debate: and the inadequacy of the sources for debates during the century makes impossible any precise assessment of the proportion of members who did speak at all. Reporters, correspondents and diarists alike tended to concentrate their attention on the leading speakers in important debates. Contemporary attempts even to list all the members who spoke in major debates are rare, and seldom successful. Tentative conclusions, however, may be derived from a sample estimate made possible for the Parliament of 1768 to 1774 by the detailed and accurate diary of Henry Cavendish.[2]

692 members sat in the House of Commons at some time during that Parliament, and 303 are known to have spoken on public business in the House or in Committee of the Whole House, a proportion of just under 44 per cent. Other members, of course, may have spoken whose speeches have not been traced or recorded: and a few members silent in this Parliament spoke during other periods that they sat in the House. But even when allowance has been made for these factors, it would seem that more than half the members returned to the House of Commons in the later eighteenth century never spoke at all on public business.

[1] Sir Lewis Namier, *Structure of Politics*, p. 1.

[2] B.M. Eg. MSS. 215–63, 3711. For the problems of using the diary for this purpose, and a list of members known to have spoken in the Parliament, see my note, 'Check List of M.P.s Speaking in the House of Commons, 1768 to 1774', *Bull. Inst. Hist. Res.*, 35 (1962), pp. 220–6.

The number may have been slightly smaller in the first half of the century, when debates were fewer and shorter: but only rough estimates are possible. As many as 196 different members are named in Chandler's *Debates* as speaking in the two Parliaments of the reign of George I, even though the reports of debates are so incomplete as to occupy only one volume.[1] Moreover, for the period from 1722 to 1730, when Chandler's compilation and other printed reports name only 100 members as speaking, diarist Knatchbull gives the names of 157 members, 73 of whom are different.[2] It is therefore likely that between 200 and 300 members spoke during the lifetime of each early Hanoverian Parliament. Any rise in the proportion of speaking members during the Georgian period must have been very slow. There were said to be 400 out of a House of 658 members by 1832: but nearly all the increase above the number for the middle of the previous century was thought to be the result of the admission of 100 Irish members after 1800, only four of whom were reputed to stay silent.[3]

The over-all figure of speaking members is misleading, for the proportion that took any regular part in debate was markedly smaller. In the 1768 Parliament 62 of the 303 speakers spoke only on one occasion, and then almost always on some matter of local or personal interest. Not more than 132 members made over a dozen speeches, an average of two or more each session. Only forty members spoke over a hundred times during the six years of the Parliament. That debates were usually dominated by a small number of members is implied by the remark made by Horace Walpole with reference to a reshuffle of Newcastle's ministry at the end of 1755, after a decade of political lassitude had followed the lively debates of his father's administration: 'It called forth a display of abilities that revived the lustre of the House of Commons, and in the point of eloquence carried it to a height it perhaps had never known. After so long a dose of genius, there at once appeared near thirty men, of whom one was undoubtedly a real orator, a few were most masterly, many very able, not one a despicable speaker.'[4] Such Parliamentary prominence was frequently

[1] Chandler, *Debates*, VI.   [2] *Knatchbull Diary*, p. xi.
[3] Townsend, *House of Commons*, II, 390–1.
[4] H. Walpole, *George II*, II, 143–4.

fleeting. Twelve of the twenty-eight members named by Walpole in 1755 still sat in the House of Commons between 1768 and 1774, but only six were among the forty who then made over a century of speeches—Lord Barrington, William Beckford, Henry Seymour Conway, Sir Gilbert Elliot, Welbore Ellis and George Grenville.

The reasons why the great majority of members spoke seldom or not at all are not difficult to trace. They lacked the modern incentives of political convictions and constituency pressures. Apart from lawyers and professional politicians, most members needed the positive spur of specialist knowledge, vested interests or personal prejudice before rising to speak. This lack of motive was reinforced by the deterrent to many of the ordeal of speech-making in such a confined space; for members who rose when the House was full found themselves surrounded by a sea of faces. John Craufurd described to Stephen Fox his embarrassment on one occasion, probably 18 December 1772: 'I had the misfortune to speak a few days ago in the House of Commons . . . It was a prepared speech, ill-timed, ill-received, ill-delivered, languid, plaintive, and everything as bad as possible. Add to all this, that it was very long, because being prepared, and pompously begun, I did not know how the devil to get out of it . . . Certainly it was not the intention of nature that I should be a public speaker and I shall never attempt it any more.'[1] The poise of a member unaccustomed to speaking might be upset by any slight embarrassment. John Roberts was speaking on 8 May 1781 when he remarked that so far from assertions about crown influence being true, 'the reverse was the contrary. This trifling error occasioned a hearty laugh. Mr. Roberts felt himself somewhat confused, and not easily recovering his self-possession, he apologized by saying, that whenever he spoke in that assembly, he felt himself greatly awed.'[2] The same reason undoubtedly inhibited many from speaking at all, among them the historian Edward Gibbon. He entered the House in 1774 with the intention of speaking, but soon found that he lacked the nerve. He told John Baker Holroyd on 25 February 1775, 'I am still a Mute, it is more tremendous than I imagined, the great speakers fill me with despair, the bad ones with terror';

[1] *Memorials of Charles James Fox*, I, 81–2. [2] Debrett, *Parl. Reg.*, III, 220.
16—H.O.C.

and again on 8 April, 'I have remained silent and notwithstanding all my efforts chained down to my place by some
invisible unknown invisible power.' Even in 1780 he remained
ashamedly 'a dumb dog'.[1]

The eighteenth century saw the establishment of the practice
that the head of the ministry should sit in the Commons as
Leader of the House. From mid-century opposition members
were likely to make complaint, or at least a debating-point,
if the First Lord of the Treasury was a peer. After the long
ministries of Sir Robert Walpole and Henry Pelham the Duke
of Newcastle's attempt in 1754 to head an administration from
the Lords aroused immediate comment. Lord Chancellor
Hardwicke informed Newcastle on 14 November 1754 'that
Mr. Potter threw out that *they had been used to see a Minister
sitting in that House*, or something to that effect; but that it was
not attended with one *Hear Him*, nor with the least symptom
of being taken or tasted by the House'.[2] Thomas Potter's
remark may have fallen on deaf ears, but the practical problem of managing the House of Commons in this way soon
caused Newcastle to abandon the experiment, and when the
Duke of Grafton tendered his resignation as First Lord of the
Treasury to George III on 22 January 1770 a contemporary
newspaper reported that he had given this reason to the King:[3]
'As he found the great strength of the increasing minority was
in the Lower House, he thought it most natural as well as
advisable, to nominate a Premier there, in the scene of action,
as he found, by daily experience, that that was the fittest place
for a Prime Minister, and that there was no doing any thing
without it, as in the cases of Walpole, Pelham and Pitt; and
that he saw it was impracticable to stem the tide of opposition
from above.'

His successor was Lord North, already Leader of the House:
and Horace Walpole noted of the first important debate after
North's appointment, 'It was obvious how much weight the
personal presence of a First Minister in the House of Commons carried with it.'[4] It is from the Parliamentary activities

---

[1] *Letters of Edward Gibbon*, II, 51, 59, 61–4, 241.
[2] B.M. Add. MSS. 32737, fo. 344. [3] *London Evening Post*, 27 Jan. 1770.
[4] H. Walpole, *George III*, IV, 51.

of Lord North between 1770 and 1774, as revealed by Henry Cavendish's diary, that the role of a First Minister in the House can best be illustrated. He had a dual function—specific duties as the King's Minister in the Commons, and the general task of defending government policy in debate.

Any first minister was the official administration spokesman, announcing decisions and arranging the timetable of government business. If Chancellor of the Exchequer, and the First Lord of the Treasury invariably was when a commoner, he conducted all necessary financial measures through the House.[1] It fell to the Leader of the House to announce, as required, the King's assent to bills 'so far as his interest is concerned'. It was also 'the Minister' who brought messages from the sovereign: but in 1737 the former Speaker Sir Thomas Hanmer, who by then had retired from the House for a decade, thought that 'it was wholly un-parliamentary for Sir Robert Walpole to read messages from the King, which when sent in writing were used to be sent to the Speaker.'[2] It is not clear whether the novelty was the delivery or the reading of the message by the minister. On 16 April 1717 a message was brought by the Comptroller of the Household:[3] and it may have been the custom for any convenient official to do so until Walpole incorporated the function in his general role of King's Minister. By the middle of the century the leading minister in the House always brought royal messages,[4] and George Grenville's practice was doubtless typical. He stood at the Bar of the House to present any message from the Crown: it was delivered to the Speaker, who then read it out, with all members having removed their hats 'according to order'.[5]

These duties were routine. The real Parliamentary significance of the King's Minister as Leader of the House was his role in debate. Lord North when minister often proposed the motions on important subjects himself, and he was usually the leading administration speaker in other major debates. He

---

[1] Lord North did not regard the two offices as inseparable. In 1778 he suggested to George III that he could lessen his burden by making Charles Jenkinson Chancellor of the Exchequer, while remaining himself in the Commons as First Lord of the Treasury. Fortescue, *Corr. of George III*, IV, pp. 216–7.

[2] *H.M.C. Egmont Diary*, II, 359. [3] Chandler, *Debates*, VI, 125.

[4] See, for example, Newdigate Diary, 23 Feb. 1756 and 17 Feb. 1757.

[5] See Harris Diary, 15 and 29 Nov. 1763, 15 Jan. 1765.

frequently rose several times a day, and no other member made so many long speeches. Altogether during the six years of the 1768 Parliament North made at least 904 speeches and interventions in debate, more than twice as many as any other member except the Speaker. He was especially concerned to defend both the principles and the details of official legislation. In 1772 he spoke sixty-five times on the Royal Family Marriage Bill. In 1773 he made eighty-one speeches on the East India Regulating Bill, and a further fifteen speeches on the East India Company Loan Bill. In 1774 North made seventeen speeches on the Boston Port Bill, fifteen on the two Massachusetts Bills, and seventy-two speeches on the Quebec Bill.

This onerous task of continual argument reflected a less obvious obligation of a Leader of the House, the necessity of his presence in the chamber on almost every occasion of public business. Members awaited his daily arrival before it began,[1] and his unexpected absence often led to its postponement.[2] A rare failure by Lord North to attend a debate aroused newspaper comment,[3] and such notice in the House as that by Edmund Burke on 3 April 1772 during a debate on a Protestant Dissenters' Relief Bill: James Harris told Lord Hardwicke that Burke had 'pleasantly remarked on seeing Lord North was absent, that twas plain no danger from the measure was apprehended to the state'.[4] The eternal vigilance of 'the Minister' was the price of his administration's safety: and to this motive were added others of lesser importance. His attendance was often a matter of practical necessity, for his approval was vital to many decisions of the House. On 11 May 1778 a motion that Lord Chatham should be given a state funeral was made after Lord North had left the House; he was sent for, and returned to give his consent.[5] The mere non-attendance of the Leader of the House, moreover, could be politically damaging to administration when portrayed by opposition speakers as a slight to members. Hence the sharpened edge to North's sense of injustice when he was criticized by Thomas Townshend for leaving the House during a debate

---

[1] See *supra*, p. 162–3.
[2] See, for example, Harris Diary, 25 and 26 Feb. 1765.
[3] *General Evening Post*, 1 Apr. 1773.   [4] B.M. Add. MSS. 35610, fo. 185.
[5] H. Walpole, *Last Journals*, II, 173–4.

of 31 October 1776. 'I really thought', said Townshend, 'some time ago, that the minister in the blue ribbon had left the House entirely, and meant to depute the care of the division to his clerks and secretaries, who might afterwards report the numbers to him at his own House.' North replied that he had been absent ten minutes on a matter of urgent business from a debate that would probably last fourteen hours:[1]

> I may, Sir, be deficient in many respects, but of all wants I never imagined that a want of respect, diligence as a member, or attention to this House, would have swelled the long catalogue. I trust, however, that I shall have the justice done me, to allow that there is no member in this House longer keeps his place, I mean my place in Parliament, or attends with greater patience and resignation, the whole length of tedious debate, than I do.

The Parliamentary burden fell on Lord North because of the absence of adequate support.[2] During the six years of the 1768 Parliament only six other members on the administration side made any speeches of major importance at all, Henry Seymour Conway, Charles Jenkinson, Hans Stanley, Welbore Ellis, and the two leading government lawyers in the House, Attorney-General Thurlow and Solicitor-General Wedderburn. Lord North, moreover, was the only member of the Cabinet in the Commons from 1771 to 1775, a common situation for 'the Minister' throughout the century. Thirteen other members on the government side made over a hundred speeches during the 1768 Parliament, but they were not men who could speak with the weight of high office: Conway was Lieutenant-General of the Ordnance, Jenkinson a junior Lord of the Treasury, Stanley Cofferer of the Household and Ellis a Joint Vice-Treasurer of Ireland. Amid such company, holders of minor offices and junior members of the three Boards of Treasury, Admiralty and Trade, Lord North stood out as 'the Minister', at once the main target for opposition attacks and the respected spokesman of the King's government.

It was nevertheless the political function of many such

---

[1] Almon, *Parl. Reg.*, VI, 27–34.

[2] The general remarks in the rest of this chapter are based primarily on an analysis of the debates of the 1768 Parliament. For further details and documentation see my 'The Debates of the House of Commons 1768–1774', (Ph.D. thesis. Univ. of London. 1958), pp. 180–9, and my 'Sources for Debates of the House of Commons 1768–1774', *Bull. Inst. Hist. Res., Special Supplement No. 4* (Nov. 1959).

posts to reward administration speakers in the House. Contemporary attitudes and assumptions are illustrated by this
story about Sir Robert Walpole, recorded by James Harris
after a meeting at George Grenville's house in 1765: 'A friend,
who had deserted Sir Robert, hearing a person speak for
Administration, remarked that he dared say that fellow had
£6 or 700 a year for talking so—Sir Robert, who sat just before
him, hearing this, turned round and said "Tom, you and I
remember the time when half that money would have done."'[1]
Of the many offices and incomes earned by Parliamentary
service rather than administrative competence, places at the
Treasury Board appear to have been especially reserved for
spokesmen in the House: when in 1780 John Buller was
promoted to this Board after fifteen diligent years at the Board
of Admiralty, Lord North told George III that he was 'much
concerned that he can not have a more useful speaker than
Mr. Buller'.[2] Of the nine Commoners at the five Boards
constituted during the 1768 Parliament all but Pryse Campbell,
who died in December 1768, spoke in debate in that Parliament; and they included five who made over a hundred
speeches, North himself, George Onslow, Charles Jenkinson,
Jeremiah Dyson and Charles James Fox. If an active part in
debate enhanced a member's chances of office and advance-
ment, the converse was also true. In April 1770 George III
refused a request from Secretary of State Lord Weymouth for
the promotion of his brother Henry Thynne, who never spoke in
debate, on the ground that such a step would 'hurt those that
stand forward in the House of Commons'.[3]

Many office-holders, however, did not consider that their
duties extended to participation in the debates of the House.
Of the sixteen members who sat at the Board of Trade during
the 1768 Parliament, eight never spoke at all and two once
each. The only two who made more than a dozen speeches
during the six years were George Rice and Bamber Gascoyne,
both ambitious for the further promotion that they were to
obtain. A high proportion of the office-holders who did speak
confined their speeches mainly to subjects concerning their

---

[1] Malmesbury MSS., Memo. of 5 Jan. 1765.
[2] Fortescue, *Corr. of George III*, V, p. 115.
[3] Fortescue *Corr. of George III*, II, p. 63.

departments. Of the twelve members who were Lords of the Admiralty during the 1768 Parliament, five spoke on naval matters when they were in office. Sir Edward Hawke, First Lord until January 1771, spoke a dozen times in that capacity: he moved for the annual naval supplies, deprecated the value of Corsica as a naval base at the time of the French annexation in 1768, and defended the management of the navy during the Falkland Islands crisis of 1770. All but three of the twenty speeches by John Buller were made as a Lord of the Admiralty; after Lord Sandwich had succeeded Hawke, he was the senior Admiralty spokesman in the House. Lord Palmerston and Augustus Hervey spoke in Committee of Supply on the naval estimates, and Charles Townshend on the behaviour of seamen in the riots of May 1768. The contrast with the politician pure and simple is shown by the failure of young Charles James Fox, a frequent speaker on other subjects, to speak on anything to do with the navy or maritime affairs during his two years as a Lord of the Admiralty.

Characteristic of the attitude of those who regarded themselves as administrators rather than politicians was Lord Barrington, Secretary at War from 1765 to 1778. Between 1768 and 1774 he took little part in general politics, and confined himself almost entirely to the military aspects of political questions. In February 1773 he rose eight times to defend the St. Vincents' expedition from the charge of mismanagement, and in the debates on the East India Company later that year his main concern was to defend the behaviour of army officers. His only speech on the American legislation of 1774 was on a quartering bill. Officials with this attitude were of limited value in Parliamentary debate.

Legal posts given to members of the House, however, were usually for services in debate, past or future. Any administration expected the legal profession to provide a formidable battery of hired speakers: appointments were often in the nature of political retaining fees, divorced from personal connections and opinions; and failure to honour this implicit obligation of office incurred criticism. Henry Fox, Leader of the House during the Bute ministry of 1762–3, justifiably complained to James Harris about his Attorney-General Charles Yorke; for he had 'appeared in the House not above once or twice this session, and then had spoken against the measures of government'.[1] During the 1768 Parliament fourteen speakers on the side of administration held legal office, and North's ministry also enjoyed a significant degree of support from other lawyers presumably ambitious for appointments. The holders of the great legal offices, Attorney-General Thurlow and Solicitor-General Wedderburn, were among the main administration speakers in many political debates, and they contributed long and learned speeches on subjects where legal issues were important. Thurlow made twenty-nine speeches and Wedderburn nineteen speeches on the Royal Family Marriage Bill of 1772. Both also gave frequent support on other official legislation. Wedderburn alone made nine speeches on the East India Regulating Bill of 1773, fourteen speeches on the American legislation of 1774, and fifteen speeches on the Quebec Bill of the same year. Argument inside the House of Commons was as an essential part of the function of government lawyers as their legal duties outside it; and this service, as in the case of both Thurlow and Wedderburn, usually formed their chief claim for further promotion.

A final advantage to government in debate during the earlier years of George III's reign was the formidable grasp of procedure possessed by Jeremiah Dyson. This knowledge, acquired when Clerk of the House from 1748 to 1762, he placed at the disposal of each successive administration from his entry into the Commons in 1762 until his death in 1776, enjoying office throughout the period as his reward. No evidence has been found of the existence of any comparable expert earlier in the century. Debating tactics were then less refined and intricate, and Sir Robert Walpole may not have needed such assistance; for he appears to have been as well-informed a Parliamentarian as any member in the House. A man with such a role as Dyson was not popular: his Parliamentary tactics were 'vexatious to his enemies', while the rapid change of ministers during his first years in the House made him appear 'slippery to his friends as fast as they fell'.[2] Many members must have relished Edmund Burke's pointed reference to Dyson on 25 February 1774: 'There are persons in the world, whose whole soul is a

---

[1] Malmesbury MSS., Memo. of 11 Apr. 1763.
[2] H. Walpole, *George III*, I, 317.

previous question, and whose whole life is the question of the adjournment.'[1]

More than an encyclopaedic knowledge of precedents was needed to be an expert on procedure: Dyson's predecessor as Clerk, Nicholas Hardinge, was a failure as a Parliamentarian.[2] But, as Horace Walpole conceded in an unflattering portrait, Dyson was a man of ability: he was, Walpole wrote, 'excellently useful, from his parts and great knowledge of parliamentary business, to all who employed him'.[3] Even before Dyson had entered the House, apprehension about his role as 'the master of order' was the reason given by Henry Legge for refusing to lead the opposition in the Commons in 1762: the Duke of Newcastle reported his reply to the Duke of Devonshire: 'He says he is not qualified to be the sole Leader in the House of Commons. That he shall have nobody with him; that, if he had Mr. Dyson, who is perfectly acquainted with the rules of business, and forms of the House of Commons, he could do something; to supply which last defect, I assured him, that the Old Speaker Mr. Onslow would be ready at any time to give him his advice.'[4] Dyson soon won notoriety among opposition members by never deciding points of order against administration:[5] and he was adept at all forms of Parliamentary obstruction. The detailed evidence available for the 1768 Parliament shows the value of such a procedural expert. Many of his 327 'speeches' in that Parliament were interventions on points of order. Dyson was often able to suggest suitable amendments to motions, and other counters to opposition tactics. He frequently called opposition members to order for transgressing the rules of debate, a tactic successful in annoying speakers and disrupting speeches. Inside the House Dyson sometimes based arguments on purely technical grounds, and he was always profuse in his citation of precedents: and outside the House he was able to advise ministers beforehand on motions and tactics. Dyson was thus an invaluable aide to ministers in the cut and thrust of the Parliamentary battle.[6]

[1] B.M. Eg. MSS. 252, p. 212.   [2] H. Walpole, *George II*, I, 134.
[3] H. Walpole, *George III*, I, 317.   [4] B.M. Add. MSS. 32945, fos. 280–1.
[5] B.M. Add. MSS. 32966, fos. 55–7.
[6] Instances of Dyson's role as procedural expert are scattered throughout this study.

It was a common feature of the political scene in the eighteenth century that opposition should overmatch administration in both the eloquence and the number of its spokesmen: William Pulteney, William Pitt, Edmund Burke and Charles James Fox are famous names in the annals of Parliamentary oratory. An unbalance of argument existed during the 1768 Parliament, when twenty opposition members made over a hundred speeches, as against fourteen for government. Seven were connected with the Rockingham group, among them the brilliant Burke and the duller William Dowdeswell: both spoke over 400 times in the six years of the Parliament. The leading spokesman in the House for the Chatham group, Isaac Barré, made over 350 speeches. George Grenville and radical William Beckford were speaking just as frequently, making over fifty speeches a session, until their deaths in 1770.

Little part in the political battles between administration and opposition was taken by independent members: indeed, they never made their voice heard in proportion to their numbers. No archetypal country gentleman, unconnected with trade or a political group, made a century of speeches in the 1768 Parliament. The county representation may be taken as a rough sample of the independents who were country gentlemen. 39 of the 101 members who sat for English counties during the Parliament are known to have spoken, but ten spoke only in one debate. The political subjects that roused the country gentlemen to speech were not government measures or even votes of confidence in ministers, but popular measures like the Nullum Tempus Bill of 1769 or Grenville's Election Bill of 1770, allegations of corruption, and matters of privilege. On social and economic matters—Corn Bills, Cattle Bills, Game Bills, and Canal Bills—many spoke as local magistrates or from other personal experience: James Harris noted that several squires who had never spoken before took part in a debate of 29 March 1762 on a Game Bill.[1]

On such topics the gentry were often speaking as representatives of the largest economic interest in Parliament, land. Other interests were also well represented in the House elected in

---

[1] Harris Diary, 29 Mar. 1762.

1768. About forty members were connected with the East India Company, and at least nineteen of them spoke during the debates of 1773 on the Company's affairs. The House also contained at least another forty merchants, a score of bankers, and a few industrialists. The proportion of these members that spoke in debate was markedly above the average, about three in five, for subjects of particular concern to many of them came before the House. A notable performance by a member otherwise unaccustomed to speaking was achieved on 18 April 1774 by Samuel Whitbread, founder of the brewery: in one day he made sixteen speeches during a Committee on a bill about the packing of hops.[1]

Some of these members were undoubtedly taking advantage of their representative status to further their own economic interests: but others were following the tradition of the House that members should make available the benefit of their professional knowledge and experience. This custom is apparent in the contribution of many lawyers and members of the armed forces. Lawyers always played a conspicuous role in Parliament, for much business was of legal character in content and form. Forty-two members in the 1768 Parliament were barristers in active practice, and no fewer than thirty-one of them spoke in debate. Members of the military professions were less forward in speaking. Only twenty-one of the seventy-four serving army officers who sat in the Commons during that Parliament spoke at all in debate, and eight of them did not speak on military affairs. Six officers confined themselves to descriptions of conditions in North America and India from their service experience there. Only seven serving officers therefore made any technical contributions to debates. Naval members were more helpful. The House contained twenty-five past or present officers of the navy: nine of the twelve who spoke in debate did so on some matters affecting the service.

Examination of Henry Cavendish's diary and other sources therefore reveals what might have been expected: that, for instance, the political leaders made the most speeches, and that country squires and army officers were less active in debate than lawyers and merchants. A number of members

---

[1] B.M. Eg. MSS. 255, pp. 148–63.

spoke only on subjects that directly concerned them: all the twenty-two speeches made during the 1768 Parliament by Henry Crabb Boulton, a Director of the East India Company, were on matters connected with that Company, and the doubt must arise as to whether he would otherwise have spoken at all. If the total proportion of members who took part in debate did not vary much during the century, the chance of current affairs determined to a certain extent which individuals or groups of members spoke at any particular period.

13

THE METHOD OF DECISION: DIVISIONS

IF every debate had to begin with a motion, it had to end with a decision, when the Speaker would put the question to the House: he would signify this by rising from the Chair.[1] He could not do so if any member still wished to speak, and members could even speak between the affirmative and the negative.[2] After hearing the shouts from the Ayes and from the Noes, he would then declare the result. On rare occasions, often on formal business, a motion passed unanimously and it was recorded in the *Journals* as having been carried '*Nem Con*'. Contemporaries made a clear distinction between such a decision and one merely by 'voices': at the end of the debate on the Address on 17 January 1734 'four or five gave a loud No to agreeing, that it might appear the Address was not voted unanimously, thus shewing their teeth where they could not bite.'[3] Sometimes a solitary member would say 'No' with the deliberate intention of preventing such unanimity. On 28 February 1760 Speaker Onslow refused to accept a claim by Lord Barrington that a motion of his had passed *nem con*, as Bubb Dodington had faintly said 'no'.[4] And here is the account by James Harris of the passage of a motion on 18 April 1764 for an address of thanks to the King: 'The address went without a division, and would have been nem contradicente, had not Onslow very conspicuously placed himself at the bottom of the House, and given a single and audible No.'[5]

The comparative volume of noise on each side as the Speaker

[1] *H.M.C. Egmont Diary*, III, 104. The procedure in Committee is discussed *infra*, pp. 278–9.
[2] Hatsell, *Precedents*, II, 102–3. On 14 Feb. 1783, Thomas Townshend informed George III, a debate took place 'in an extraordinary manner' after the Chair's decision on a question: Speaker Cornwall had been too hasty, not expecting any discussion. Fortescue, *Corr. of George III*, VI, p. 241.
[3] *H.M.C. Egmont Diary*, II, 8.   [4] H. Walpole, *George II*, III, 265.
[5] Harris Diary, 18 Apr. 1764. This was George Onslow.

put the question was the sole procedural basis for his decision as to whether the Ayes or the Noes were the majority. When he was doubtful, it was a frequent practice for him to put the question a second time, before he gave his opinion.[1] This decision was sometimes peremptory, as 'the Noes have it', and sometimes doubtful, as 'I think the Ayes have it'.[2] In either case any member could force the House to divide, by saying 'the contrary voice has the question.'[3] Once a division had been requested it had to proceed, unless all members agreed to waive it.[4] Divisions were sometimes abandoned at this point by general consent, when the members who had demanded them perceived how little support they would get.[5] A division was still an infrequent step. The basic procedure was the decision by 'voices', and this usually sufficed. The purpose of a division, in strict theory, was merely to clarify uncertainty. This interpretation was favoured by Onslow, and it was recorded nostalgically by John Hatsell in the later eighteenth century: 'The old rule, and practice, too, were, that the House should be divided only when the Speaker's determination upon the voice was wrong, or doubtful.'[6] In practice it was political calculation rather than respect for the House that explained the low proportion of divisions.

It was a rule that the doors into the chamber were to be closed before the Speaker put any question, and that they were to remain shut until he had announced the decision of the House.[7] Contemporary evidence shows that this procedure was not adopted for every question. Serjeant-at-Arms John Clementson noted that the doors were not shut on the first and second readings of private bills that were not contested, although this was always done on the third reading and the title. On public business the doors were always shut before every question. When a division was expected or requested the Serjeant-at-Arms shut the doors as usual himself, and instructed the doorkeeper and messengers to have the lobby and galleries cleared of strangers. When the House and lobby had been cleared the lobby doors were locked, and the House

---

[1] Hatsell, *Precedents*, II, 187N.   [2] *Liverpool Tractate*, p. 67.
[3] Hatsell, *Precedents*, II, 199N.   [4] Hatsell, *Precedents*, II, 194N.
[5] See, for example, *H.M.C. Egmont Diary*, II, 163; and the *London Chronicle*, 28 Apr. 1774.
[6] Hatsell, *Precedents*, II, 199N.   [7] Hatsell, *Precedents*, II, 202.

doors opened again.[1] A description of this procedure was given by Carl Moritz from his observation of proceedings in 1782. He noted that when the Speaker's decision was challenged, 'all the spectators must then retire from the gallery: for then, and not till then, the voting really commences. And now the members call aloud to the gallery, withdraw! withdraw! On this the strangers withdraw; and are shut up in a small room, at the foot of the stairs, till the voting is over, when they are again permitted to take their places in the gallery . . . In this manner we, the strangers, have sometimes been sent away two or three times, in the course of one day, or rather evening; afterwards again permitted to return.'[2] If, as must often have been the case, it was known before the end of a debate that a division would occur, the Chair might issue appropriate orders in advance. On 5 June 1773 Speaker Norton sent a message to ask William Dowdeswell whether he was going to force a division over a motion he had made. Dowdeswell made a public complaint, and Norton explained that his reason was obvious, 'clearing the House':[3] but the usual practice appears to have been for the Chair to wait until a division began before enforcing the withdrawal of strangers.

The House and lobby were therefore completely sealed off from the outside world during the whole procedure of a division. The reason for this step was the relationship of the division to the previous decision by 'voices'; but there was also the practical motive that the lobby was used in the method of voting. Since the purpose of the division was merely to remove the doubt over the decision, every member's vote had to be in accordance with his 'voice' when the question was put. All members present in the House when the question was put were obliged to vote, and no members then absent were allowed to do so. The House for the purpose of this rule was understood to embrace the gallery and the passages, including the passage between the gallery and the House behind the clock that disappeared in 1801 when the gallery was enlarged after the Union with Ireland brought 100 more members into the Commons; Charles Baldwyn tried to conceal himself there during a division on 21 February 1780, but was discovered by

[1] Clementson Diary, pp. 9–11. [2] Moritz, *Travels*, p. 59.
[3] B.M. Eg. MSS. 245, p. 246.

the tellers. The 'Old Committee Room' was not considered part of the House, and the door into it was closed when a division took place: but two places included in the definition were the Speaker's Room and 'Solomon's Porch'. Any member who had been in these two places at the time of the question was deemed not to have heard it; he had the right to have the question stated to him, and could then vote as he wished.[1] Members often did withdraw behind the Chair or into the Speaker's Room to avoid voting; and it was to Solomon's Porch that Jacobite William Shippen withdrew on 13 February 1741 to signify his disapproval of the personal attack on Sir Robert Walpole.[2] If any other member insisted, however, the tellers had to fetch such members and compel them to vote.[3] On 28 May 1773, when the House divided over the first reading of the controversial Adelphi Lottery Bill, Rose Fuller requested that the tellers should look for members in the Speaker's Room. They went, and brought down several members, including the head of the ministry Lord North, to take part in the division.[4] Any member who wished to make sure of abstaining from a division therefore had to go into the Committee Room or out of the House before the end of the debate; on 2 March 1762 about a dozen members went to the Committee Room and others left the House, all anxious to avoid voting on an election case.[5]

If any bill or other business affected a particular member he was expected to leave before the question was put. Hatsell recorded a number of examples of this practice, such as the case of Lord Clive during the examination into his conduct in India on 21 May 1773; he spoke before any motion had been made, and then withdrew: but Hatsell also made this comment: 'The rule ... is not, in many cases, sufficiently observed: it was always attended to in questions relative to the seat of the member ... and has been strictly observed in cases of very great moment: but in matters of lesser importance, yet where

[1] Hatsell, *Precedents*, II, 187N, 195–8. H. Walpole, *Letters*, I, 142.
[2] *H.M.C. Egmont Diary*, III, 192.
[3] Hatsell, *Precedents*, II, 196.
[4] B.M. Eg. MSS. 249, pp. 55–6.
[5] Harris Diary, 2 Mar. 1762. For some other examples see *H.M.C. Egmont Diary*, I, 270: B.M. Add. MSS. 35375, fos. 81–2; 35609, fo. 282.

the private interest of the Member has been essentially concerned, it has been entirely neglected.'[1] Even this is a flattering picture of contemporary practice. When Lord North's ministry was being pressed so hard over Edmund Burke's Establishment Bill of 1780 that the difference of a few votes might have been decisive, office-holders threatened with the abolition of their posts stayed to vote on the particular clauses concerning their own offices. After Lord George Germain had previously stayed to vote against the abolition of his post as the third Secretary of State, Sir Joseph Mawbey complained on 13 March that those members who were on the Board of Trade were obviously intending to stay and vote on the relevant clauses that day. His protest was vain. All the Lords of Trade present except Soame Jenyns stayed for the division.[2]

The rule that only members present when the Speaker put the question could vote meant that the House began to fill in anticipation of the end of a debate; but it happened frequently that latecomers found themselves locked out of divisions, perhaps as many as a dozen or more on the same side. Sometimes the result of a division would otherwise have been much closer: on 23 March 1772, when the administration obtained a majority of eighteen over one clause in the Royal Family Marriage Bill, fourteen members, twelve on the opposition side, were shut out; and on 23 March 1742, when a motion for a Committee to inquire into Sir Robert Walpole's conduct as minister was carried by 252 votes to 245, John Campbell bitterly remarked, 'About four of our friends like fools were shut out.'[3] Only one instance has been found when the result might otherwise have been different: on 10 April 1780 an opposition motion was carried by two votes at a time when four members found themselves on the wrong side of the door; three of them were ministerial supporters.[4]

Apart from the procedural reasons for the shutting of the doors before a division, there was also the motive of preserving an official veil of secrecy over the voting of individual members.

---

[1] Hatsell, *Precedents*, II, 167–72. For confirmation that sitting members left in election cases see Clementson Diary, pp. 13–4.

[2] Almon, *Parl. Reg.*, XVII, 316–17. H. Walpole, *Last Journals*, II, 282.

[3] H. Walpole, *Last Journals*, I, 67. B.M. Add. MSS. 29133, fo. 94. N.L.W. MSS. 1352, fo. 47.

[4] H. Walpole, *Last Journals*, II, 298.

17—H.O.C.

This veil was sometimes penetrated, however, by design or accident. On 14 December 1770, during a debate on a dispute with the House of Lords, Henry Seymour complained that the orders had not always been strictly enforced, at least with regard to members of the Upper House:

> I have seen peers, perhaps of a higher description than the generality of peers, concealing themselves during the time of a division. I will tell the House what I did myself. I saw this custom practised, I saw it repeated. I was appointed to tell the House. I have seen peers of a very high description, concealed behind the benches, to see what men voted in the question of Mr Wilkes . . . I applied to the Speaker, that I would not tell the House, until he assisted me to clear it.[1]

If peers sought to claim unofficial exemption from the rule, other non-members were also sometimes present at divisions; a remarkable incident on 27 February 1771 was subsequently reported in an opposition newspaper:[2]

> When the House divided, a stranger, one Mr. Hunt, a Bermudan merchant, and whose son is Collector at Bermudas, having very much the appearance of a Scotch Member, was told in the majority, for the Ministry. George Byng, Esq., one of the tellers, suspected that he was not a member, as he did not recollect to have seen him; and when the counting was finished, Mr. Byng asked him if he was a Member? He said he was not. Upon which Mr. Byng and Mr. Buller seized him by the collar, and brought him up to the table. A great confusion arose, concerning the manner in which the House should proceed with him. At length he was set at the Bar; and being asked, how he came to be among the Members in the Lobby? he said that when the Lobby was cleared, he went into the Vote Office, instead of going out at the great door towards the Court of Requests; and soon after, hearing a cry 'that the doors were opened', he went into the Lobby, and mixed with the Members, in hopes of getting with them into the House; and that he was totally ignorant of the division, and of the nature of it.

It so happened that the circumstances were such as to foster suspicion of ministerial malpractice. The division was on a

---

[1] B.M. Eg. MSS. 233, p. 521. The only division relative to Wilkes in which Seymour had acted as a teller was that of 14 Apr. 1769, on a motion to take the Middlesex poll in the fourth election into consideration on the following day. *Commons Journals*, XXXII, 385.

[2] *London Evening Post*, 2 Mar. 1771.

motion to go into Committee on the bill to repeal a clause in
the Nullum Tempus Act, an opposition measure strongly
resisted by the North ministry, and now at a third division
apparently defeated by ten votes, 165 to 155. Diarist Henry
Cavendish recorded that when the stranger was questioned by
the Speaker and other members, he stated that some of his
friends might also have voted, and that he himself had been
counted in divisions before! All members were agreed, however,
that there had not been any sinister purpose behind his
behaviour, and the man escaped with a reprimand. On a new
division the ministry again triumphed by ten votes, 164 to
154.[1] No record of any similar occurrence has been found.

When a division began, it was the duty of the Speaker to
appoint two tellers for each side. It happened on very rare
occasions that there were not even two members on one side,
and the division would then be abandoned; on 12 May 1772
George Dempster found himself the only member wishing to
oppose an amendment to a Gunpowder Bill.[2] After the tellers
had been nominated, the division would proceed even if it was
found that no members were voting on one side: on 13 May
1774 Attorney-General Thurlow and Charles James Fox acted
as tellers for a minority of 'none' against the Copyright Bill.[3]

The selection of tellers lay completely within the discretion
of the Chair, but there were apparently members unable to
perform the task: on 12 March 1771 William Burke remarked,
presumably in reply to an observation that he was being chosen
often, 'if gentlemen dont know how to tell I cant help it.'[4] It
was necessary for the Speaker to know the alignment of members chosen; and it is clear that on this ground of convenience
he usually made his choice from among the members who had
spoken in the preceding debate. Often the member who had
moved the question was appointed a teller: the various radical
members who proposed and seconded the motion for a Bill for
Shorter Parliaments made every session for over a decade from
1771 always acted as tellers for the Ayes. Sometimes a member
speaking would ask to be selected. During the debate of

[1] B.M. Eg. MSS. 225, pp. 267–75. *Commons Journals*, XXXIII, 385.
[2] *Commons Journals*, XXXIII, 752.   [3] *Commons Journals*, XXXIV, 752.
[4] B.M. Eg. MSS. 226, p. 82. William Burke was a teller 5 times that day.
Commons Journals, XXXIII, 250–1.

10 December 1770 on a dispute with the House of Lords this request was made by Lord George Cavendish, who as the son of a peer was clearly anxious to show that his sympathies lay with his own House: 'I beg the favour of you, when this comes to the question, that you will appoint me one of your tellers, an office I never exercised since I have sat in Parliament. . . . I am only anxious that my name should be on your Journals, having been in question where the dignity of the Commons of England is concerned.'[1]

Tellers were frequently chosen from among the speakers in the preceding debate, but it is apparent that certain other conventions in the choice of tellers had developed. There was a tendency for the Speaker to make his selection from among those members who were actively concerned on both sides with securing the attendance of supporters; and also one for the choice not to fall on the political leaders on either side of the House, even though they were usually present and often spoke. These trends are evident from an examination of the names of the tellers in 230 divisions on subjects of major political importance during the period from 1768 to 1780. On the administration side the members appointed most frequently to act were the two Secretaries to the Treasury: Grey Cooper performed the duty in sixty-seven of the divisions, John Robinson in forty-one. Many of the other regular tellers for the ministry were men in office, such as George Onslow, a Lord of the Treasury, who acted in twenty-six divisions until he lost his seat in 1774. No other members acted as tellers for the ministry in as many as twenty of these divisions of political significance. Many of those whose names appear frequently held minor office, like Charles Townshend and Lord Lisburne of the Admiralty Board. Lord North and other such leading office-holders as the Attorney-General and Solicitor-General were never called on to undertake the task in important debates. For the opposition George Byng's role as 'political muster-master' embraced the duty of teller, and he acted in forty-nine of these divisions. Often to be found among the names of opposition tellers are those of men destined for future office: the task of counting heads was performed on forty-six occasions by

---

[1] B.M. Eg. MSS. 223, pp. 297–8. Lord George Cavendish, who had been a member since 1754, was appointed. *Commons Journals*, XXXIII, 58.

Thomas Townshend, later to be Pitt's Home Secretary as Lord Sydney; on fifteen occasions by Sir George Yonge, a future Secretary at War under Shelburne and Pitt; and on fourteen occasions by Frederick Montagu, a Lord of the Treasury under Rockingham and the Fox-North ministry. Convention also excused opposition leaders. Not once did the Chair choose Isaac Barré, chief spokesman for the followers of Chatham and Shelburne; or William Dowdeswell, leader of the Rockingham group in the House until 1774; or George Grenville before his death in 1770. This exemption did not apply to Charles James Fox, perhaps through his own choice: three times a ministerial teller by 1774, he was to be twenty-four times an opposition teller on important occasions in the next six years, even though he was then the effective leader of the opposition in the House.

After the tellers had been appointed the division took place by the process of one side going out into the lobby while the other stayed in the House. This method had apparently begun when the Commons took the chapel of St. Stephen as their meeting-place in the reign of Edward VI. Since the lobby was previously the ante-chapel, out of which the House itself opened, there was only a single outer door to the whole area.[1] The decision as to which side was to go out lay with the Speaker,[2] but he was guided by an elaborate series of precedents. They were based on the general rule, established in 1640, 'that those that give their votes for the preservation of the orders of the House, should stay in; and those that give their votes otherwise, to the introducing of any new matter, or any alteration, should go out.' During the stages of a bill, for example, the Ayes always had to go out.[3] When motions were superseded by amendments, adjournments, and other devices, individual members were sometimes confused as to the correct way to vote. On 12 March 1771 even such an informed Parliamentarian as Henry Cavendish by mistake voted in the lobby with the majority in a division on an adjournment motion that had been put on the second amendment to the original motion.[4]

[1] Sir Goronwy Edwards, 'The Emergence of Majority Rule in the Procedure of the House of Commons', *T.R.H.S.*, 5th Series, Vol. 15 (1965), pp. 171–84.
[2] Luttrell Diary, II, fo. 407.
[3] For a list of precedents see Hatsell, *Precedents*, II, 186–94, 203–11.
[4] B.M. Eg. MSS. 226, p. 81. *Commons Journals*, XXXIII, 250.

The point was more than a matter of convenience. The side remaining in the House might gain the votes of the lazy, the indifferent, and those who did not want to lose their seats: indeed, a division early on a day when an important debate was expected might be used as a tactical weapon to deprive opponents of their seats. In a crowded House there might also occur such absurd incidents as that on 13 February 1764. After a long debate on general warrants an adjournment was moved at midnight: Horace Walpole told Lord Hertford what happened next. 'On a division, in which though many said *Ay* to adjourning, nobody would go out for fear of losing their seats, it was carried by 379 to thirty-one for proceeding—and then half the House went away.'[1]

The doors into the lobby were shut after one side had gone out. The order to shut them was left to the discretion of the tellers, so that no unfair advantage could be taken, or blame thrown on the Serjeant-at-Arms, if the doors were shut too soon or left open longer than necessary.[2] All members then present were regarded as voting with the side remaining in the House, even if they had failed to go out merely through inattention or negligence: members might therefore be made to vote 'entirely contrary to their known and avowed inclination'. Any members, however, who had been in Solomon's Porch or in the Speaker's Room, and so had not heard the question, were permitted to go out even after the doors were shut.[3] The tellers first counted the members in the House. The members had to sit on the benches, and were not allowed to move once the telling had begun. Silence was necessary so that the tellers should not be interrupted.[4] The members on the other side were then counted as they came back from the lobby.[5] The tellers concerned themselves only with the numbers, not the names, for no official division-lists were compiled. When all the tellers had agreed on the totals, they reported the result to the Speaker, who immediately announced the decision of the House. It was already the practice for the tellers for the majority

---

[1] H. Walpole, *Letters*, VI, 2.
[2] Hatsell, *Precedents*, II, 196N. Clementson Diary, p. 11.
[3] Hatsell, *Precedents*, II, 196.
[4] Hatsell, *Precedents*, II, 198.
[5] *London Magazine*, 1770, p. 624. Clementson Diary, pp. 11–12.

to take the right hand side in approaching the Chair; if the result was a tie, they were mixed alternately.[1]

If the numbers on a division were equal, it was the duty of the Speaker, or Chairman if the House was in Committee, to give a casting vote. The *Journals* appear to record only nine casting votes by Speakers between 1714 and 1790. Seven of these decisions were on procedural or comparatively minor issues, usually in very thin Houses, and only two on matters of political importance: one was the famous occasion on 29 March 1742 when Speaker Onslow incurred criticism by deciding in favour of administration the last two places on the Committee of inquiry into Sir Robert Walpole's conduct as minister; the other was on 27 February 1786, when Speaker Cornwall gave a casting vote against Pitt's ministry over the question of the Duke of Richmond's plan for the fortification of naval dockyards.[2] The modern convention is that a Speaker in a tie should vote in such a way as to avoid a final verdict by the House. In the eighteenth century his decision was given according to his personal opinions, but the *Journals* do not always record the Speaker's reasons for his vote even when these were stated to the House. Sometimes the Speaker's decision was avowedly based on his own assessment of the merits of the question. On 23 April 1771 a division on the third reading of the Bill to raise a military force for the East India Company resulted in forty-five votes on each side. In his only casting vote Speaker Norton thereupon announced this decision: 'In a case so circumstanced the Chair is called upon to give a vote, and this is a case in which I have no doubt . . . I know so much of the shameful methods to which the India Company is driven to get recruits . . . I am therefore for reading the bill a third time.'[3] Speaker Onslow gave particular reasons for two casting votes, on 2 March 1749 and 15 May 1759.[4] No examples of the modern practice are clearly established; but the two decisions by Speaker Compton, both about excusing members absent from a Call of the House, were intended to give them another chance to attend before action

[1] Hatsell, *Precedents*, II, 224.
[2] *Commons Journals*, XXIV, 153–4; XLI, 263. For the former occasion see *infra*, p. 288.
[3] B.M. Eg. MSS. 230, p. 52.   [4] *Commons Journals*, XXV, 761; XXVIII, 585.

was taken against them.[1] The two decisions by Sir John Cust
were also based on the principle of postponing a decision. On
17 March 1766, after a motion to pass a bill concerning the
East India Company had resulted in a division of forty-three
votes on each side, Cust said that 'he was not properly informed
as to the merits of the bill, so should vote against it; if bad, he
would not confirm; if good, it might be brought in another
year.'[2] On 25 March 1766 Cust gave his casting vote in favour
of referring a petition for a bill to a Committee.[3] The modern
convention was also foreshadowed in the only instance found
of a casting vote by a Chairman of a Committee. On 22 April
1771, in a Committee on a bill to prevent the export of live
cattle, a division on a clause resulted in twenty-three votes on
each side. Sir Charles Whitworth from the Chair then
announced that it was his opinion that the decision ought to be
taken in a fuller House, and he would accordingly give his
vote for the clause.[4]

The clumsy and slow procedure of voting meant that a
division was responsible for a considerable waste of time,
varying with the number of members present. Contemporary
reports suggest that a division in a fairly full House, involving
about 350 or 400 members, lasted about half an hour; but that
if the number was significantly smaller the division could be
conducted more expeditiously. The inconvenience caused to
members by the trouble and delay involved in voting helps to
explain why divisions were infrequent; and why a majority
sometimes chose not to humiliate opponents who had demanded
a division and then changed their minds.

Any decision, whether by 'voices' or voting, was in form and
law the verdict of the whole House; and in 1730 Lord Wilmington, the former Sir Spencer Compton, who had first entered the
Commons in 1698, recalled a custom formerly used after a
division to signify this, but which had fallen into abeyance. 'He
said it was quite wrong to mention majorities and minorities at
all, for what is once carried is the Act of the House, and that
anciently when a question had been carried upon a division,
the minority were obliged to go out by themselves to show their

[1] *Commons Journals*, XVIII, 658, 686.   [2] Harris Diary, 17 Mar. 1766.
[3] *Commons Journals*, XXX, 693.   [4] B.M. Eg. MSS. 229, p. 253.

assent to what the majority had carried against them, but this was not in use since he was in Parliament.'[1]

The procedure of putting the question and the Speaker's consequent decision was usually a formality. On political issues his opinion would normally favour the ministry, and opposition members would then judge whether a division should be forced. Usually these decisions lay with the foremost spokesmen on the opposition side, those members who proposed the motions or were otherwise either the acknowledged leaders or the 'whips' of the various factions: but sometimes the decision was taken from them, unwisely by their own supporters, unfairly by adherents of the administration, and extraordinarily on one occasion by the Speaker himself. This happened at the end of the debate on the Address on 13 November 1755, with Arthur Onslow in the Chair, the question being whether some words relating to Hanover and attacked by the opposition should stand. This is how Horace Walpole recorded the episode: 'Pitt and those who were for leaving them out, but did not intend to divide on that, as the least unpopular question, said *no*, faintly. The Speaker, who was strongly for leaving out the Hanoverian words, gave it for the *noes*; so they were forced to divide, and were but 105 to 311.'[2]

The common reason for decisions of opposition leaders to avoid divisions was simple reluctance to disclose numerical weakness: but they were at the mercy of enthusiastic followers. 'Thus one hot-headed fellow can spoil a fair game', commented Knatchbull after describing how Sir Christopher Musgrave on 23 January 1725 had forced a division resulting in an administration victory by 245 votes to 139.[3] John Huske was thought to have been unwise to divide the House over a motion by Edmund Burke on 8 March 1769, for the question was defeated by 245 votes to a mere 39.[4] John Campbell wrote gleefully to his son about this end to the debate of 21 January 1743, on a report from Committee of a resolution for the employment of Hanoverian soldiers: 'I think the Heads of the

---

[1] *H.M.C. Egmont Diary*, I, 44.
[2] H. Walpole, *George II*, II, 61. For a biased decision by the Chairman of the Committee of Supply on 27 Jan. 1741 see *H.M.C. Egmont Diary*, III, 185.
[3] *Knatchbull Diary*, p. 37. [4] *Malmesbury Letters*, I, 174–5.

Opposition had no inclination to divide, but when the Question was put to agree with the Committee and the Speaker gave it for the Ays, Carew divided the House, and we were not willing to let them yield, so we divided Ays 245, Nos 156.'[1] It was reckoned a fair tactic for a ministry to take advantage of such blunders, but most unfair for the majority or any members of it to force a division themselves. Such incidents were rare, but one occurred on 2 April 1770, when the question was put on a motion to put an end to the Committee on the State of the Nation: the only surviving account is one by opposition reporter John Almon.[2]

Lord North said 'the Ayes have it', but Mr. A. Bacon, a majority man, either out of fun or spite, said 'the Noes have it', upon which the majority insisted upon a division . . . The minority did not chuse to divide, and on the contrary, the majority exulting in their numbers insisted on the division, to which, at last, the minority were obliged to comply, and the numbers were 208 to 75. (Any person, on a question, may divide the House, but it is looked upon as a mean trick to divide it against your own opinion, and Mr. Bacon was a good deal abused for it, though he divided with the minority; yet when the question was resumed the next day, he voted with the majority.)

Despite these hazards of challenges from friends and foes, it is apparent that leaders of Parliamentary oppositions in the eighteenth century were usually able to enforce their decisions as to whether or not votes should take place on subjects of political importance. The decision whether to divide on a particular occasion was nearly always taken beforehand, and seldom resulted from the volume of noise support on the day. At times of extreme weakness leaders of the organized groups in opposition would adopt a strategy of not dividing on any questions at all. Such a confession of impotence was quite different from the genuine unanimity that existed in the later 1750s, recalled by Lord John Cavendish when he wrote to Lord Rockingham after the opposition had decided to force no divisions early in 1774: 'In Parliament we are as unanimous as in the days of Mr. Pitt . . . It is a comical state we are in,

---

[1] N.L.W. MSS. 1352, fo. 110.
[2] Almon, *Debates*, VIII, 315–16. Clementson Diary, p. 2. A division was also forced by the majority on 27 Nov. 1775. H. Walpole, *Last Journals*, I, 496.

but though I think our inaction much better than a frivolous bustle, yet I think we make a very silly figure.'[1]

There were times when the political balance in the House was close, and many occasions when the subjects of debates cut across or were not related to political alignments at all. The Speaker would then attempt to give his opinion in favour of the louder noise. The *Journals* do not record what decision a Speaker made before a division, but discrepancies between his judgement of the opinion of the House and the final verdict of a division were clearly very uncommon, and usually a matter for contemporary comment. The most famous instance was on 17 February 1764, over Sir William Meredith's motion that general warrants were illegal, an issue on which the Grenville ministry was threatened with defeat by the opposition. Here is the account of the decision by diarist James Harris, then a Lord of the Treasury: 'At near six in the morning the House divided, whether to adjourn the resolution for four months or no—on giving the Ayes and Noes, the Speaker declared for the Noes, which so invigorated the opposition, that they were so indecent as to clap. When we went out twas quite dubious where the majority lay.'[2] Horace Walpole's description came from the viewpoint of opposition: 'The Noes were so loud, as it admits a deeper sound than Aye, that the Speaker who has got a bit of nose since the opposition got numbers, gave it for us. They went forth; and when I heard our side counted to the amount of 218, I did conclude we were victorious; but they returned 232 . . . the floor of the House looked like the pool of Bethesda.'[3] On a close issue in a crowded House the Speaker could do no more than guess, and in any case his opinion then was merely the prelude to a division.[4]

The noise at the putting of the question was important on subjects of little or no political significance, when it might indicate the relative strength of the two sides. On many matters of business the Speaker was obliged to rely on the noise as a guide to the House's decision. Speaker Norton was faced with this problem on 25 May 1773 on a motion for leave to

---

[1] Wentworth Woodhouse MSS., R 1–1478.
[2] Harris Diary, 17 Feb. 1764.   [3] H. Walpole, *Letters*, VI, 10–11.
[4] For two wrong decisions by Speaker Onslow before close divisions see *H.M.C. Egmont Diary*, III, 261; and B.M. Add. MSS. 32863, fo. 332.

introduce a petition for the Adelphi Lottery Bill. 'The voices sounding pretty equal, the Speaker called them again, and then Mr. Ongley divided the House.' The motion was carried by 109 votes to 64.[1] Members could be influenced in their decision about forcing a division by the comparative volume of the two shouts. Sir William Meredith on 5 May 1774 proposed a motion for a Committee to review the Thirty-Nine Articles; but when the question was put, 'there did not appear to be above twenty Ayes, and the Noes made so strong a sound, that Sir W. Meredith declined dividing the House.'[2] The noise, however, was not always a true guide to opinion within the chamber. On 29 March 1723 Arthur Onslow, when Chairman of a Committee, was mistaken over an issue where the alignment of ministry and opposition had become blurred: 'the question was put and though the ayes were vastly superior in the noise and so given yet Cholmley divided the House and the question lost by 290 against 91.'[3]

If the volume of noise was encouraging to the prospective minority, the outcome might be a planned division at a future debate on the same subject rather than an unplanned division at the time. It was with reference to such a decision that Horace Walpole commented on the misleading deception of a verbal response from safe anonymity, when he learnt that George Onslow was determined to force a division at the report stage of the Regency Bill of 1765 against the clause inserting the name of the Princess Dowager of Wales as a possible regent, 'encouraged by the many negatives on the Princess's question. This was judging weakly, for many would cry 'No!' who would not have voted, when they would have been personally distinguished by a division.' Walpole's comment is in his *Memoirs*: he already knew that when Onslow forced the vote, on 10 May, the clause had been carried by 167 votes to 37.[4]

Members were restrained from forcing numerous divisions by conventions as well as political expediency. It was widely held to be unparliamentary to call on members to vote unless this was necessary in cases of genuine doubt. After the rout of

---

[1] *London Chronicle*, 27 May 1773. *Commons Journals*, XXXIV, 335.
[2] *London Chronicle*, 7 May 1774.   [3] *Knatchbull Diary*, p. 18.
[4] H. Walpole, *George III*, II, 105. *Commons Journals*, XXX, 418.

the opposition groups in December 1762 over the prospective terms of the Peace of Paris, James West told the Duke of Newcastle that he did not think there should be 'an opposition to the measures of the public, in trifling divisions, which become contemptible, by violence being added to weakness'.[1] Lord John Cavendish on 23 March 1773 could claim credit by asserting, 'I do not much love making divisions in this House';[2] and another opposition member, Richard Hopkins, declared on 27 April 1780 'his great dislike of dividing the House on every trifling occasion. It only bred animosity, and extended division.'[3] Divisions did not usually take place when the opinion of the House was already manifest, and most debates, even many of great length, ended without a vote. 'A strong Aye, a faint Noe—no division': this conclusion to a debate of 17 March 1758, noted by Sir Roger Newdigate, was typical of the end of many Parliamentary discussions of the century. Members would avowedly begin debates with no intention of forcing a vote. When George Byng rose on 23 March 1774 to oppose the Boston Port Bill, he said that he did so 'not with a view to dividing the House'.[4]

'The first division is generally understood as the sense of the House', Horace Walpole observed in 1755.[5] Apart from the danger of causing annoyance to members, a minority had practical reasons for not forcing subsequent votes. Opposition supporters were more likely to leave through fatigue and despair. 'Usually they who lose the first division on the same points lose it the second time by a greater majority than the first', noted Lord Perceval in 1732.[6] It was therefore the custom that the sense of the House should be taken only once during the course of each debate, even when the main question had been superseded by another motion. On 5 March 1770, after an opposition amendment had been proposed to include tea among the articles on which Charles Townshend's colonial duties were to be repealed, Thomas Townshend uttered a mock warning: 'I could almost have the malice to divide the House upon the second question, after the division upon the

---

[1] B.M. Add. MSS. 32945, fo. 278. [2] B.M. Eg. MSS. 245, p. 77.
[3] Almon, *Parl. Reg.*, XVII, 587.
[4] B.M. Eg. MSS. 254, p. 253 (shorthand).
[5] H. Walpole, *George II*, II, 61. [6] *H.M.C. Egmont Diary*, I, 220.

amendment.' He did not carry out this threat; after the amendment had been defeated by 204 votes to 142, the main question was carried without division.[1]

The most conspicuous breach of this convention during the century was the obstruction of a small group of opposition members during the proceedings of March 1771 over the printing of debates in newspapers. Sir Roger Newdigate had good reason to note 'the perverseness and ill-manners of a few of the opposition' in his diary for 12 March. These members forced the House to divide twenty-three times, in order to show their dislike of the measures against six printers. Despite an early protest from George Onslow that it was improper to divide upon every point after the sense of the House had once been taken, they took systematic advantage of the forms of procedure, resorting to adjournment motions, amendments, and other devices.[2] When the House met again, on 14 March, Lord North precipitated an argument on this conduct by remarking that 'there has been an attempt in a very unusual way to avoid coming to a decision.' Sir William Meredith promptly defended the right of every member to put a negative on any question, and professed alarm at such dangerous language from a minister. Lord North mildly replied that since the behaviour had been without precedent it might be called unusual, but he ended with the comment that the authority of Parliament would be at an end if small minorities resorted to frequent divisions. Constantine Phipps and Thomas Townshend chose to detect a threat in this remark, and the view of the obstructive minority was put by Edmund Burke, who declared that the business had been made as troublesome as possible to allow time for feeling to subside: 'Posterity will bless the pertinacity of that day.' Burke nevertheless emphasized that he was not defending the indiscriminate use of such tactics. He would not forsake arguments for adjournment motions when the navy, army, finance or other important business was before the House. In reply Sir Gilbert Elliot conceded that 'something of the same kind' had happened once or twice before in the heat of the moment, but he attacked any doctrine of obstruction: 'The man may properly be called

[1] B.M. Eg. MSS. 221, pp. 86, 94.
[2] Brickdale Diary, IV, 1–13. *Commons Journals*, XXXIII, 246–52.

an advocate for disorder, who asserts that he does so divide barely and solely with a view to stop and disappoint all business.' Even William Burke, who had taken a leading role in the tactics of 12 March, agreed that there should not be 'a system of opposition to stop all business'.[1] Twelve more divisions were forced over the same issue on that day, 14 March;[2] but no attempt was made to delay the later proceedings in the case. Henry Cavendish gave a clear if ungrammatical statement of contemporary opinion in a diary note to explain why the punitive resolutions against Lord Mayor Brass Crosby were carried on 27 March after only one division: 'The doctrine delivered when the minority had tried their strength upon one division, rather unparliamentary, or some such language, to divide the House again. That was the reason why they did not divide the House.'[3]

The same convention applied to the passage of legislative measures through the House. On bills that appeared certain to pass, there might be one division to test the feeling of the House, or as a token gesture. Bills could seldom be defeated by sustained opposition, although the North ministry did achieve at least two notable victories by this tactic: February 1771 saw the defeat at a third division of an opposition bill to repeal a loophole clause in the Nullum Tempus Act; and in 1780 Edmund Burke's Establishment Bill was defeated clause by clause in Committee. Growing opposition to Sir Robert Walpole's Excise Bill in 1733 forced the withdrawal of that measure without a formal defeat in the House. But little purpose was served by obdurate resistance to a bill unless opinion in the Commons was evenly divided, and this seldom occurred. Opposition would therefore be concentrated at the point thought tactically most suitable. Divisions were often forced on the initial motions for leave to introduce bills. Statistically this was the most formidable hurdle; during the sample period from 1768 to 1780 thirty-six bills were defeated in fifty-eight divisions at this stage. The other main threat came at the second reading, when divisions might occur on that motion or on the succeeding one to commit the bill; in the same period sixteen bills failed here in fifty-eight divisions. That bills were

---

[1] B.M. Eg. MSS. 226, pp. 91–104, 123–5.
[2] *Commons Journals*, XXXIII, 258–9.　　[3] B.M. Eg. MSS. 228, p. 108.

thereafter usually safe is shown by the incidence of divisions on legislation, both public and private, in the twelve years from 1768. The table also reveals that the Commons voted over legislation only on 205 occasions altogether, in a period when well over 2,000 bills came before the House.[1]

Incidence of Divisions on Bills in the House of Commons 1768–1780.

STAGE	PASS	FAIL
Leave to introduce	22	36
First Reading	2	2
Second Reading	27	7
Motion to commit	15	9
Motion to leave Chair	10	6
Motion to report bill	18	3
Motion to ingross	4	1
Third Reading	16	1
Passage	23	3

The contemporary feeling that it was unparliamentary to force many or unnecessary divisions; consideration of the trouble to which members were put by divisions, and a consequent desire to avoid causing annoyance; the reluctance of oppositions either to parade their weakness, or to dissipate the goodwill of friends and independent members by repeated demands: all these were factors tending to reduce the number of divisions. The average number each session during the first decades of the reign of George III was about fifty. 301 occurred in the six full sessions between 1768 and 1774, and 298 in the six sessions of the next Parliament from 1774 to 1780. These are the totals only for divisions in the House itself, but the average is not likely to be significantly higher if all divisions in Committees of the Whole House were known; an exhaustive search of sources for the Parliament of 1768 to 1774 produced evidence of only fifty-two divisions in such Committees, an average of under nine a session.[2] The number of divisions may

---

[1] The figures given are occasions, not the total number of divisions. Only votes on a whole bill are included, not motions for amendments. No account is taken of divisions in Committee, nor on subsidiary motions, such as motions to print bills.

[2] Divisions also occurred in Select Committees, but information is too scanty for any numerical assessment.

have been slowly rising throughout the century, as a reflection of the increase in the amount of Parliamentary business. It certainly did so afterwards; by the middle of the nineteenth century the average was 200 a session, and by the year 1900 nearly 400.[1] A division was then becoming an automatic procedure to end a debate. In the eighteenth century it was a calculated step, and motions and bills on every variety of subject were usually passed or negatived without any voting by members. In no aspect of its business, public or private, political or otherwise, had the House developed the convention of a preference for a division on every occasion.

[1] Redlich, *Procedure of the House of Commons*, II, 395N.

14

COMMITTEES OF THE HOUSE

COMMITTEES were an integral part of Parliamentary life. Committees of inquiry were a frequent precursor of action by the Commons: a preliminary Committee before important legislation became such an established procedure that Constantine Phipps rose on 31 May 1774 to make the complaint about the Quebec Bill that since it had originated in the House of Lords, the Commons had not held a Committee of inquiry on the subject; this was, he declared, a most unusual proceeding before such an important bill.[1] Committees had to make reports the same session, or not at all: nor could the House make any decisions or take any action based on inquiries undertaken by a Committee in an earlier session.[2] There was always a Committee stage on legislation, Committees of the Whole House on public bills and Select Committees on private bills.[3] In finance, all proposals for income and expenditure were first considered in Committees of the Whole House.[4] Contemporary terminology is inconsistent and misleading, and tends to conceal the fact that there were only two forms of Committee as regards composition. 'Private Committees' were the same as Select Committees, comprising a limited and nominated number of members: so were Committees 'above stairs', for such Committees met in one of the Committee rooms adjoining the House. 'Grand Committees' was an early name for Committees of the Whole House, which all members could attend: identical in composition were those Committees, such as the Committee of Privileges and Elections, whose appointment began with the nomination of various members, but ended with the order that 'all who attend have voices'. These Committees, however, unlike the Committees of

[1] B.M. Eg. MSS. 260, p. 173.
[2] Harrowby MSS., doc. 21, no date. Sir Dudley Ryder added, 'so said but query'.
[3] See *supra*, Chapter 3.   [4] See *supra*, Chapter 4.

the Whole House, enjoyed a separate existence, meeting at times when the House was not sitting: Sir Roger Newdigate's diary for 1755 shows that the Committee of Privileges and Elections was then regularly meeting at 7 p.m., after the House had risen.

Select Committees were the instrument of the House for detailed inquiry into and consideration of particular topics and subjects. They examined witnesses and papers, and then made a report to the House of this evidence and usually also of the opinion of the Committee on it. Such reports were intended to serve as a basis for legislative or other action, but many suffered the customary fate of most Committee reports, oblivion. The growing importance of the House of Commons in the practical government of the country was reflected by the increasing frequency of Select Committees during the eighteenth century. In 1725 Robert Walpole, opposing a motion by William Pulteney for a Select Committee, said that it would be 'a round about way and create delay', claiming that there were only four precedents for such a step, the first on the Popish Plot and the others on such important matters as the South Sea Bubble.[1] This assertion merits doubt and qualification even by that date, and there was soon no lack of precedents. Select Committees, and motions for them, became a regular feature of opposition attacks on Walpole and later ministers: in 1742 the phrase 'committee of accusation' was a political synonym for such a Committee.[2] From the middle of the century Select Committees were a regular part also of constructive Parliamentary action. Many Select Committees were Committees of Secrecy, a more effective variant. In 1773 it was the small Secret Committee instituted by the North ministry that provided the basis for the legislation of that year concerning the East India Company: the larger and much publicized open Select Committee investigating alleged malpractices by Company servants produced only disappointment for its sponsors.

Select Committees could meet on any normal sitting day of the House itself, any weekday of the session.[3] When a short

---

[1] *Knatchbull Diary*, p. 38.

[2] Foord, *His Majesty's Opposition*, pp. 194, 211.

[3] *Knatchbull Diary*, p. 39. For a detailed contemporary account of the different kinds of Select Committees, see the *Liverpool Tractate*, pp. 40–50.

adjournment took place it was the usual although not the invariable custom for the House to order that all Committees 'have leave to sit'. Such Committees could not meet, however, when the House itself was sitting: and in the earlier part of the century Select Committees sat either in the early morning or in the evening after the House had risen. On 5 May 1721 an order that all Committees be adjourned was explained by Speaker Compton to apply only to Committees on that day, not to any arranged for the next morning: this was, he said, according to an order of 1699.[1] As the House abandoned morning sittings altogether and sat late on many evenings, it became increasingly the practice for Select Committees to meet only in the mornings, and the time appointed for such meetings might be as late as noon. By mid-century this was the regular custom. The personal diary of Sir Roger Newdigate, covering several decades from 1751, shows that Select Committees usually met at a fixed hour in the morning and sat for several hours. It appears to have been the duty of the member sponsoring the relevant business to claim a Committee room beforehand. Certainly Newdigate's diary for 1769 shows that he did so on several occasions for the Oxford Canal Bill: a typical entry is that for 6 March: 'At 9 took the Committee room. Breakfast. Dressed. Walked to Committee at 11, till $\frac{1}{2}$ past 3.'

Select Committees varied in size from eight to over thirty members. They rarely included leading ministers, who found the time and duration of meetings inconvenient: Lord North announced on 30 March 1778 that he would not be able to attend a proposed Select Committee 'on account of public business'.[2] The Committees were either chosen informally and openly in the House, or by secret ballot at an appointed time. Members could be nominated by the former method even if they were not present. Most of them usually were, and they were selected because of their known interest in the subject; it is clear that members who had spoken in a preceding debate in support of the motion were almost always chosen. But there appears to have been no invariable custom: and on 15 January 1723 it was thought desirable that a Select Committee should

[1] Dashwood MSS. D 1/2, fos. 1–8.   [2] Almon, *Parl. Reg.*, IX, 91–5.

comprise the nine members, including the Speaker, who were Privy Councillors.[1]

This casual procedure of immediate nomination was not appropriate for matters of great moment. It became increasingly the custom for Select Committees on 'important subjects, and all Secret Committees, to be chosen by ballot, a development that opened the way to political guidance from ministers and their opponents. An administration often sent round lists of the proposed membership of a Committee beforehand, and rival lists were sometimes circulated by opposition or independent members. Not until the middle of the century did the procedure of a ballot become standardized. On 23 March 1742 Lord Limerick suggested that the ballot for his Secret Committee to inquire into the last ten years of Walpole's ministry 'might be by two Members going to each Member who was to put in his list open'. The House rejected this method, and agreed that 'it should be by calling over every Member as in a Call, and each Member to come to the table with his list and these put into a glass.'[2] This was the procedure that became formalized, for here is the detailed description of a ballot noted by James Harris in 1763:[3]

> The ceremony of balloting was thus. Two large glass receivers were placed on the table before the Speaker. Then the Members were called over according to the alphabetical order of the counties, those for cities and boroughs immediately following their proper county—the English counties finished, the Welsh followed, then the Cinque Ports, then Scotland. Every Member got up from his place when his name was called, went on the floor, bowed to the Chair, then, lifting up his hand to show his list between his fingers, put it into one of the two glasses. Defaulters were called over again, and the whole being finished, which might last perhaps 3 hours, the glasses were covered with paper, tied down, and a Committee appointed for the scrutiny, on whom fell the majority.

The result of a ballot would be reported to the House the next day and recorded in the *Journals*: the Speaker had the casting vote in any tie. When the membership of a Select Committee had been decided, by nomination or ballot, the Committee was given powers and instructions appropriate to

---

[1] Chandler, *Debates*, VI, 297. [2] Harrowby MSS., doc. 21, 23 Mar. 1742.
[3] Harris Diary, 1 Mar. 1763.

its task. Power to send for persons, papers and records was a routine formality; when Speaker Cust reminded members of the need for such a resolution on 5 March 1763, a debate arose as to whether such a motion was superfluous.[1] The papers before a Select Committee were not open to inspection by other members of the House without the prior permission of the Chairman.[2] Select Committees were usually empowered to report opinions, but sometimes instructed merely to examine the evidence. This limitation, however, could be removed at any time by the House, as happened in 1723 after the order to report was accidentally omitted from the instructions to the Secret Committee on the Atterbury Plot.[3] Decisions within Select Committees were taken on a vote in the absence of unanimity.[4] Reports from Select Committees were often printed by order of the House, but never any reports concerning either revenue or the privileges of the House.[5]

A Committee of the Whole House was simply the House meeting in Committee. Such Committees were either *ad hoc* bodies appointed with reference to particular subjects, or standing Committees permanently in existence: this second category may be stretched to include the two Committees of Supply and of Ways and Means, although they were not ordered at the beginning of each session and always closed before its end. Only the Committee of Privileges and Elections was in existence for the whole duration of a session: this had been a Committee open to all members since 1673.[6] Throughout the century the *Journals* also record the appointment at the beginning of each session of four other 'Grand Committees' that were to meet weekly on specified afternoons in the House—for religion on Tuesdays, grievances on Thursdays, trade on Fridays and courts of justice on Saturdays. This was an archaic formality. No contemporary evidence has been found of the actual existence of such Committees, and there are several indications that their creation had been overlooked: the standing orders of 1772 that all matters of trade and religion

---

[1] Harris Diary, 5 Mar. 1763.　　　　[2] Debrett, *Parl. Reg.*, IX, 587.

[3] *Knatchbull Diary*, p. 14.

[4] For an example see Harris Diary, 8 Mar. 1762.

[5] Harris Diary, 28 Mar. 1764. This was stated by Speaker Cust.

[6] *Commons Journals*, IX, 284. *Parliamentary Diary of Sir Edward Deering*, pp. 110, 157.

should be referred to Committees of the Whole House show that the nominal 'Grand Committees' on these subjects had been forgotten;[1] while in popular regard the 'Committee of grievances' was the quite different Committee on the State of the Nation.

The Committee on the State of the Nation was an *ad hoc* institution periodically created by the initiative of opposition members on the pretext that government policy had produced exceptional discontent or disaster; in 1775 the Committee was said to have originated in the Convention Parliament of 1689.[2] Proceedings in this Committee were not confined to any single subject, and opposition members might announce a list of grievances intended for examination by the Committee. The Committee on the State of the Nation in 1730 was established 'in respect to our alliances on the continent': two of the three meetings were concerned with the fortifications of Dunkirk, the other with the French claim to the West Indies island of St. Lucia.[3] Meetings of the Committee were infrequent. The Committee of 1730 was the first since the Hanoverian Succession,[4] and other meetings have been found only in 1770, 1778 and 1783–1784: that of 1770 arose from the Middlesex Elections case, and that of 1778 from the American war; the Committee of December 1783 and January 1784 was the forum for Foxite motions against the Pitt ministry. This rarity was not due to any administration veto. Only once during the century was an opposition request for such a Committee refused; on 17 November 1742 a motion made by John Philipps was defeated by an adjournment motion.[5] Ministers, indeed, usually deemed it policy to welcome the Committee. In 1727 opposition members were challenged to move for a Committee; and when in the debate on the Address in 1729 William Pulteney reserved the right to debate the particulars of the King's Speech in a Committee on the State of the Nation, Sir Robert Walpole called his bluff. The minister not only accepted

---

[1] *Commons Journals*, XXXIII, 678, 714. Although appointed until 1831, these Grand Committees were described as 'obsolete' in 1762 in the *Liverpool Tractate*, pp. 38–40.

[2] Almon, *Parl. Reg.*, III, 33.

[3] *Knatchbull Diary*, pp. 99, 104–5, 109–10, 112–13. For an account of proceedings n this Committee see Foord, *His Majesty's Opposition*, pp. 187–93.

[4] *Knatchbull Diary*, pp. 104–5.   [5] N.L.W. MSS. 1352, fo. 128.

the idea, but also promised to second Pulteney and remind him of his intention: no such Committee took place that session.[1] On 8 December 1741 Walpole did second Pulteney's motion for this Committee, but although ordered the Committee was postponed and never met.[2] On the occasions when the Committee met, administration permitted an opposition Chairman to be chosen and opposition motions to be made. Such resolutions were defeated in normal circumstances, and even when the minority Pitt administration failed to prevent the passage of hostile motions in 1783–1784 they had no practical effect. The Committee on the State of the Nation always attracted a good attendance from members, and to outside observers its very creation might appear an indictment of government by the House: but the Committee was an empty threat to administration; the fall of ministers like Walpole and North resulted from attacks in the House itself.

Committees of the Whole House could meet only when the House was sitting, for they came into existence when the House resolved itself into a Committee.[3] A Committee might meet almost every day and occupy virtually all the time of the House for some weeks, as did the Committee on the American colonies in 1766.[4] Committees of the Whole House made no report of evidence, only of resolutions; for all members were presumed to have been present to learn the facts for themselves. This rule did not apply to Committees that members might attend as a privilege rather than a duty; the Committee of Privileges and Elections, for example, therefore reported evidence. The competence of a Committee was also limited by its instructions, and freedom to report even opinions might be deliberately restricted: in 1764 a Committee on the Cider Tax was specifically empowered to consider only amendments to the tax and not its repeal.[5] Nor could a Committee of the Whole House

---

[1] *Knatchbull Diary*, pp. 59, 80.

[2] Foord, *His Majesty's Opposition*, p. 208. *Commons Journals*, XXIV, 12, 53.

[3] This restriction did not apply to the Committee of Privileges and Elections or the other Committees for which some members were nominated and the attendance of all others permitted by the order that 'all who attend have voices.'

[4] For an account of the working of this Committee see L. H. Gipson, 'The Great Debate in the Committee of the Whole House of Commons on the Stamp Act, 1766, as Reported by Nathaniel Ryder', *Pennsylvania Magazine of History and Biography*, 86 (1962), pp. 10–41.

[5] Harris Diary, 24 Jan. 1764. H. Walpole, *George III*, I, 281–2.

send for papers or witnesses. The House beforehand had to
order named witnesses to attend the Committee, and to refer
particular papers that members wished to consider there. On
10 February 1730 Speaker Onslow reminded the House of the
need to make such arrangements before the Committee on
the State of the Nation: 'The Speaker acquainted us with the
Rule of Parliament, that before the House resolved itself into a
Committee, gentlemen should call for the papers they judged
necessary for a foundation of their proceedings, that they
might be referred to the Committee for that whatever was not
so referred could not be made use of.' After members had
discussed the point Onslow modified his statement: 'The
Speaker then desired to explain himself, and said that by not
using papers uncalled for, he did not mean they might not be
used as part of gentlemen's speech, and if he was of another
opinion formerly he was not ashamed to own his mistake; but
they could not be made a foundation of their debates.'[1] The
rule was strictly interpreted.[2] Resolutions could therefore only
be based on evidence specifically referred to the Committee:[3]
but this limitation was not a serious disadvantage, for the House
could at any time order further papers or witnesses to a
Committee.

After the Speaker had put the question that he should leave
the Chair and the motion had been carried, he did so. The
Mace was taken off the Table and placed under it instead,
remaining there throughout the Committee.[4] The intended
Chairman then left his place in the House and went down to the
Bar, proceeding with three bows to take his seat at the Table.[5]
The Speaker's Chair remained empty in Committee, although
diarist Knatchbull recorded an impudent action by a member
on 14 November 1722: in a crowded Committee of Privileges
and Elections James Brudenell 'for want of a seat got into the
Speaker's Chair, and though all the House took notice of it
as well as the Chairman, yet he continued there the whole
committee with great confidence, a thing never done before'.[6]

In any newly constituted Committee the first step was the

---

[1] *H.M.C. Egmont Diary*, I, 34–5.
[2] See, for example, Debrett, *Parl. Reg.*, IX, 466–7.
[3] *Knatchbull Diary*, p. 104.   [4] Hatsell, *Precedents*, II, 141N.
[5] Harris Diary, 15 Mar. 1763.   [6] *Knatchbull Diary*, p. 6.

appointment of a Chairman. Usually the choice was obvious or pre-arranged. In Committees on legislation the custom was for the Chair to be taken by the member who had introduced the bill or by one closely connected with it. On other business the common practice was for the Chair of a Committee to be 'the usual compliment to anybody that first moved a thing in the House'.[1] This might be inconvenient, since a Chairman could not take part in debate or propose motions, and a friend would then act instead, as Velters Cornewall did for William Dowdeswell in the 1764 Committee on the Cider Tax. These were conventions, and the choice of a Chairman lay in the majority of members present. If there was a dispute, the decision was made not by the Committee but by the House itself after the Speaker had resumed the Chair. The Speaker himself might put the question on one of the candidates, or a motion would be made by another member in the usual way. In the eighteen known instances of such disputes between 1714 and 1790 only twice did a division take place.[2] The one occasion when a minister overruled convention from political motives occurred in 1729, when Sir Robert Walpole did not want John Barnard to chair a Committee to examine complaints about Spanish attacks on British commerce, even though Barnard had presented the original petition on which the inquiry was founded. Despite the cry for Barnard when the Committee first met on 6 March, Walpole therefore arranged for his supporter Thomas Winnington to be proposed as well. When the matter was referred to the House, administration carried the point by 252 votes to 133.[3] Later meetings of the Committee showed that the purpose of Walpole's manoeuvre was to prevent the discussion of embarrassing resolutions.[4]

Committees that met regularly had permanent Chairmen who often served for a number of years. At the election of Speaker Compton in 1715 the Chair of the Committee of Privileges and Elections, which Compton had held, was described by his proposer Lord Hertford as that 'which next

---

[1] *Knatchbull Diary*, p. 89.

[2] *Commons Journals*, XVIII, 124, 430, 444, 580, 695, 739; XIX, 50, 112; XX, 420, 822; XXI, 165, 255; XXVI, 446; XXX, 147, 812; XXXV, 83; XL, 47, 1126.

[3] *Knatchbull Diary*, p. 89. *Commons Journals*, XXI, 255.

[4] *Knatchbull Diary*, pp. 91–2.

to that of the Speaker is the highest we have': and his seconder Lord Finch referred to it as 'the second Chair . . . entrusted with the Rights and Liberties of the Commons'.[1] The eighteenth century saw a decline in the relative importance of this Chair, as members became less concerned with the overriding importance of their privileges, and as the decision of controverted elections gradually ceased to be a significant part of the political clash between administration and opposition, until in 1770 the Committee lost this function altogether. The 'second Chair' from mid-century, and one carrying an unofficial salary, was that of the twin Committees of Supply and Ways and Means.

Rules for proceedings in Committees of the Whole House were very much the same as those for the House itself. It was necessary for a quorum of forty members, including the Chairman, to be present, practice having extended this rule of the House to Committees.[2] Although members had formerly had the option of sitting in a Committee when making a speech, they now had to rise to speak.[3] Even in Committee, too, members had to speak to a motion. On 8 June 1774 Sir Charles Whitworth reminded members of this rule when he was Chairman of the Committee on the Quebec Bill: 'I have always understood when gentlemen have a mind to debate they must make a question.' A few minutes later, finding that his reproof had been ignored, he announced, 'the only way I can confine gentlemen is to go on with the bill.'[4] Chairmen of Committees on legislation could indulge in this arbitrary use of their authority: on 12 December 1724 Knatchbull noted that Chairman Sir Charles Turner 'huddled over' a clause in a bill and then declared that it had passed when a member stood up to speak.[5] Chairmen of other Committees lacked this recourse, and could do no more than make repeated requests for a motion. Arthur Onslow when a Chairman on 29 March 1723 did state a motion himself, but the Committee gave preference to an earlier motion by another member.[6]

---

[1] *Commons Journals*, XVIII, 16–17.　　[2] Hatsell, *Precedents*, II, 178.
[3] Hatsell, *Precedents*, II, 107N. *Knatchbull Diary*, pp. 111–12. B.M. Eg. MSS. 246, p. 290.
[4] B.M. Eg. MSS. 262, pp. 87–8.　　[5] *Knatchbull Diary*, p. 35.
[6] *Knatchbull Diary*, p. 18.

Motions in the Committee, as in the House, had to be given in writing to the Chairman.[1]

Declaratory motions, merely expressing an opinion, formed the distinctive feature of Committees, and their main purpose. Lord North, objecting on 5 December 1777 to a list of resolutions announced by David Hartley, even claimed that 'he never heard such motions made in a House; they were proper for a Committee.'[2] There was no such procedural distinction, however, between House and Committee, and many instances occur of similar motions in the House throughout the century. Many contemporaries wrongly thought that there was another procedural difference about motions in Committee. By the reign of George III there had arisen the common misconception that they need not be seconded; and Chairman Frederick Montagu actually gave a ruling to that effect on 29 April 1779.[3] This was contrary to earlier practice,[4] and did not prove a precedent; for Hatsell was apparently unaware of it when he observed that there was no basis for the contention.[5]

The chief characteristic of Committees was their greater freedom of debate, arising from the fact that there was no limit to the number of speeches.[6] This was regarded by Hatsell as their purpose. 'It is to allow more ample and frequent discussion ... that a Committee is instituted where every Member may speak as often as he pleases.'[7] Carl Moritz recorded his opinion in 1782 that 'a Committee means nothing more than that the House puts itself into a situation freely to discuss and debate any point of difficulty and moment.'[8] Members themselves sometimes expounded this great advantage of Committees.[9] The distinctive character of debates in Committee can be seen from a study of Henry Cavendish's diary.[10] Cavendish's reports show that there were many more speeches in Committee than in debates of comparable length in the House: that a greater number of members spoke, and

---

[1] *Knatchbull Diary*, p. 18. [2] Almon, *Debates*, VIII, 128.
[3] Almon, *Parl. Reg.*, XII, 359.
[4] See, for example, *Knatchbull Diary*, p. 18; *H.M.C. Egmont Diary*, I, 72–3.
[5] Hatsell, *Precedents*, II, 112N.
[6] Burnet, *History*, IV, 538N. A note by Speaker Onslow.
[7] Hatsell, *Precedents*, II, 105–6. [8] Moritz, *Travels*, pp. 52–3.
[9] B.M. Eg. MSS. 246, p. 290. Almon, *Parl. Reg.*, VIII, 370–3.
[10] B.M. Eg. MSS. 215–63, 3711.

that many freely rose several times in a single discussion. Nor was a Committee the place for long studied orations. The ring of genuine argument comes through more strongly from Committees of the Whole House than from the more formal debates in the House itself.

The choice of speakers lay with the Chairman, whose duty, like that of the Speaker in the House, was to indicate the member 'first in his eye'. A controversy on 13 March 1729 reminded members that the ultimate decision lay in the Committee itself. Argument raged for two hours on the rival claims of John Hedges, pointed to by the Chairman, and Sir John Barnard, who was said by several members to have risen first. It was ended by a formal motion that Barnard should speak: this was, Knatchbull observed, 'the first time ever such a question was put in a Committee, and is now a rule laid down that, if the Committee cannot agree who first was up to speak, it must be determined by a question.' The motion was defeated by 180 votes to 145. Most opposition members then walked out, as Barnard had been prevented from proposing a motion about Spanish depradations on British commerce.[1] Such a rule was obviously inconvenient in practice, and within a year the same diarist noted, after another dispute, 'acquiesced that who the Chairman pointed to was first to speak'.[2] It became the custom in Committee, as in the House, to accept the decision of the Chair in the matter.

Committee debates were also freer in the more technical sense that none of the three devices of procedural obstruction to motions was applicable when the House was in Committee. Motions for the House to adjourn and for the Orders of the Day were alike impossible: nor could the previous question be moved, although Hatsell was unable to suggest a reason for this rule. The usual method of avoiding a decision on a question, therefore, was to move that 'the Chairman do leave the Chair'. This had the same effect as an adjournment, and took precedence over every other motion.[3] Use of this motion was frequent, but it was sometimes deemed reprehensibly evasive. On 6 April 1780 it was withdrawn after having been put on

[1] *Knatchbull Diary*, pp. 91–2.
[2] *Knatchbull Diary*, p. 109. For this incident see *H.M.C. Egmont Diary*, I, 72–3.
[3] Hatsell, *Precedents*, II, 116–17.

Dunning's famous motion about the influence of the Crown, the voting being directly on the main question, as members clearly preferred.[1] The device was also clumsy, for if successful it put an end to the Committee altogether. It was always interpreted as dropping the business of the Committee for that session if a Chairman left the Chair without asking leave to sit again, so Walpole reminded Speaker Compton on 16 March 1726.[2] His ministry brought the Committee on the State of the Nation in 1730 to an end by this tactic on 10 March.[3] It was Lord North's reluctance to employ this weapon at the first meeting on 25 January 1770 of a new Committee on the State of the Nation that explained his resort to the only alternative tactic of a destructive amendment.[4]

Protests at this move caused him to fall back on a motion to leave the Chair at the next meeting of that Committee on 31 January. Opposition leader William Dowdeswell then made the motion 'That by the law of the land, and the law and usage of Parliament, no person eligible of common right can be incapacitated by a resolution of the House, but by an Act of Parliament alone.' Several administration supporters, foremost among them the eminent constitutional lawyer William Blackstone, announced that they could not vote against such a motion, even though the allusion to the Middlesex Election was obvious. Lord North accordingly moved to leave the Chair, emphasizing, however, that he did not intend to stop the Committee altogether: 'I dont mean to put an end to the Committee but that you do report a further progress and desire leave to sit again . . . I shall put that as soon as you have left the Chair, if the question should be carried.'[5] North's ministry secured a majority of only forty, 226 votes to 186, and the opposition reporter John Almon attributed the loss of the original motion to this tactic.[6]

The motion to leave the Chair was usually employed as a simple equivalent to a direct negative. In a Committee of the Whole House on the corn trade on 1 March 1771, a motion to permit importation from the American colonies was defeated

[1] Almon, *Parl. Reg.*, XVII, 467–73.
[2] *Knatchbull Diary*, p. 56. For the rule see also *Liverpool Tractate*, p. 37.
[3] *Knatchbull Diary*, p. 112.   [4] See *supra*, p. 184.
[5] B.M. Eg. MSS. 3711, pp. 173–246.   [6] Almon, *Debates*, VIII, 223–4.

by this method.[1] So was a bill in 1774 designed to prevent abuses in the packing of hops. In the Committee of 18 April on this bill Samuel Whitbread, after the defeat of a clause which he regarded as vital, moved to leave the Chair. Despite protests from other members that the bill had not been finished, Whitbread maintained that he was in order. The result was recorded by Henry Cavendish: 'the question was carried for leaving the Chair and so ended this bill.'[2]

The Speaker had to be in attendance throughout every Committee of the Whole House. He could speak and vote like any other member, and Speakers did so until well into the nineteenth century.[3] The Speaker did not have to be present at the Committee itself, but it was necessary for him otherwise to be in his private room, since he might be required at any time in the House to resume the Chair. Committees could end unexpectedly. Occasional emergencies occurred, as on 2 December 1724, when a Chairman became 'very ill', and Speaker Compton temporarily took the Chair in the confusion so that members could choose a new Chairman.[4] Whenever there was found to be no quorum in a Committee, the Speaker had to adjourn the House. The official reason given by Hatsell for the Speaker's constant attendance, however, was simply that it might be necessary for him to resume the Chair if disorder arose in a Committee.[5] No instance of this step has been found, but Speaker Onslow did restore order in a Committee of Supply on 28 January 1744. Here is John Campbell's account:[6]

One would have thought that all would have gone into confusion till the Speaker . . . got up to speak, and with difficulty procured attention, which I believe nobody else could have done . . . Before the Speaker spoke I saw him take some pains to clear the way to the Chair which he thought he must have resumed to prevent the last degree of Disorder and Confusion. For I believe at first he scarce hoped to be heard from his place in the Committee.

It was to be expected that Chairmen of Committees would

---

[1] B.M. Eg. MSS. 225, pp. 75–88.
[2] B.M. Eg. MSS. 255, pp. 162–5 (shorthand).
[3] For a discussion of this practice see *infra*, pp. 283–4.
[4] *Knatchbull Diary*, p. 32. *Commons Journals*, XX, 353.
[5] Hatsell, *Precedents*, II, 243N.   [6] N.L.W. MSS. 1352, fos. 177–8.

often encounter difficulty in maintaining order. They lacked the experience and the prestige of a Speaker. Debates in Committee were less formal, and therefore harder to control; and they often concerned highly controversial matters. Nor were Chairmen always innocent of bias. Horace Walpole made this note on the debate of 21 February 1766 in the Committee on the American colonies: 'Many speakers had not been attended to; others forced to sit down without being heard. Something of this was imputed to the partiality of Rose Fuller, the Chairman; and, before he could make his report, Mr. Shifner ironically proposed to thank him for his great impartiality.'[1] A significantly high proportion of the more notorious scenes of disorder in the House during the century occurred in Committees. Among the most turbulent of all occasions must have been the behaviour of members in the Committee on the Cider Tax on 31 January 1764, when James Harris wrote at the end of his report, 'there was more indecent riot and noise, than I had even seen in the House before.'[2] When the Committee resumed on 7 February 1764 Chairman Velters Cornewall 'complained of the riots of the last Committee, said he had not yet recovered his hearing, begged the Committee's assistance as to order'.[3]

At the end of each debate the Chairman put the question in the same way as the Speaker did in the House itself, giving his opinion, in theory at least, according to the respective volumes of sound from the Ayes and the Noes. Few were as openly partisan as Velters Cornewall on 31 January 1764, when 'he said he could not say, but that in his own inclinations he wished it might be the Ayes.'[4] The rules for divisions in the House—that all members present when the question was put were obliged to vote and that none then absent could do so, also operated in Committees, but an exception was made for the Speaker; since his attendance was compulsory, he was not compelled to come out of his Room with any other members who happened to be there.[5]

The procedure for the divisions that took place in Committee when a Chairman's decision was challenged differed from that

[1] H. Walpole, *George III*, II, 212–13.
[2] Harris Diary, 31 Jan. 1764.
[3] Harris Diary, 7 Feb. 1764.
[4] Harris Diary, 31 Jan. 1764.
[5] Hatsell, *Precedents*, II, 243N.

for divisions in the House. The whole process took place within the chamber of the House, one side going to the right of the Chair, the other to the left. The door of the House therefore had to be shut when a question was put: and if it was opened again too soon, so that members entered or left, a division was prevented even when it had been demanded, and the Chairman's decision remained valid.[1] A Chairman who took deliberate advantage of this rule was Phillips Gybbon, when Chairman of the Committee of Privileges and Election on 22 January 1723. He gave his opinion for the Ayes on an adjournment motion, and when a division was demanded 'he leaped out of the Chair and ran away, his pretence was that a member had gone out of the House, and so the committee could not divide after the question, but everyone said it was a partial proceeding, for he as Chairman should have taken care the doors had been shut after the question.'[2]

For divisions in Committee the same rules determining which side should go out into the lobby in a division in the House also applied, the side that would have gone out dividing to the left of the Chair. Supporters of any declaratory resolutions propounded divided to the right, however, presumably because it was the purpose of Committees to formulate such opinions.[3] Only one teller on each side was deemed necessary, and they were appointed by the Chairman. The members were then counted bench by bench on each side in turn.

Errors easily arose from such informality. Sir George Colebrooke told Lord Rockingham that he believed that in the Committee on the State of the Nation on 12 February 1770 'the tellers told a bench for the majority twice over. The side of the House below stairs occupied by a majority last night was occupied before by the minority in the two former divisions —and when quite filled, it held one time 154, and another time 155. Sir George Colebrooke cannot conceive, without a mistake, how it could now hold near 180. Sir G. Colebrooke believes this the more possible, because in a former division, they made a similar mistake in the favour of the minority of

---

[1] Clementson Diary, pp. 1–2. Harris Diary, 31 Jan. 1764.

[2] *Knatchbull Diary*, p. 11. For an occasion in 1693 when a Chairman left the Chair 'contrary to the general sense of the House' see Luttrell Diary, II, fo. 268.

[3] Harris Diary, 31 Jan. 1764.

19—H.O.C.

telling a bench twice over, till called upon and set right.'[1] Colebrooke was probably correct in his surmise, for Lord North's majority had jumped from the crisis level of forty-four and forty on the two previous days in the Committee to a safer seventy-five. The initial stability of his administration was undoubtedly assisted by this error!

Confusion also sometimes occurred at the moment of dividing in a small, crowded and noisy chamber. In the Committee of 18 March 1772 on the Royal Family Marriage Bill, a motion to adjourn and report progress was made by Sir William Meredith and opposed by Lord North. Later in the debate the motion was attacked as unfair even by leading opposition spokesmen like Isaac Barré and Edmund Burke. The Committee divided shortly before one o'clock in the morning. Bewildered by the various arguments, the point of procedure, and the disturbance at the division, the majority of the administration's supporters, many of whom had been dozing with their eyes shut, did not know which side to choose and stood on the floor in the middle of the House. Eventually most of them failed to follow Lord North and voted for the motion, since they had heard it attacked by Barré and Burke; and it was carried by 222 votes to 56. The ministry was able to retrieve the situation, however, by defeating the ensuing motion to leave the Chair, by 182 votes to 113, and the debate continued.[2]

A Committee always ended by this formal question that the Chairman should leave the Chair, either to make his report to the House or to ask leave to sit again. If this last instruction was omitted by the Committee, by accident or design, the Committee terminated altogether. When a Committee ended its sitting the Mace was placed on the Table again, and the Speaker resumed his duties.[3] The first business then was to receive the report of the Committee. All Chairmen of Committees stood at the Bar, either to report 'progress' and request permission to meet again, or to present the findings and views

---

[1] Wentworth Woodhouse MSS. R 1–1273. For a similar but smaller error on 28 Feb. 1755 see H. Walpole, *George II*, II, p. 11: and for one on 31 Jan. 1764, denied by both tellers, see Harris Diary, 31 Jan. 1764.

[2] B.M. Eg. MSS. 238, pp. 149–69. Almon, *Debates*, X, 355–6.

[3] Harris Diary, 15 Mar. 1763. For some general rules about Committees see the *Liverpool Tractate*, pp. 50–8.

of the Committee.[1] This last step was usually postponed until a future day. The House had the right to debate a Committee report, but only to accept or reject it. During the century three Speakers declared their opinion that alterations to a Committee report were unparliamentary and out of order, Onslow in 1756, Norton in 1777, and Cornwall in 1782: since amendments were not allowed, they intervened to prevent detailed criticism.[2]

This rule was in accordance with the acknowledged purpose of Committees—to digest evidence and present conclusions. Select Committees were usually better suited to this task than Committees of the Whole House, where proceedings were often marked by political bias or marred by disorder. If Select Committees were an effective method of conducting business, Committees of the Whole House often served merely as a safety-valve for the temporary and public indignation of members.

[1] Debrett, *Parl. Reg.*, VII, 272.

[2] B.M. Add. MSS. 32861, fo. 202. Almon, *Parl. Reg.*, VII, 125. Debrett, *Parl. Reg.*, VII, 272–3. This rule did not apply to reports of bills or to reports from the Committees of Supply and Ways and Means.

15

MR. SPEAKER:
POLITICAL ASPECTS

EVER since Sir Lewis Namier's analysis of the political structure of Hanoverian Britain, it has been evident that the question of the political bias or allegiance of the Speakers of the eighteenth century could no longer be seen in relation to any traditional party distinction between Whig and Tory. Since the political battle in the Commons was simply between the supporters of each administration and its opponents, any attempt to examine the evolution of the impartiality of the Chair during the century must therefore be a study of the decline of the control of the King's ministers over the Parliamentary behaviour of the Speaker.[1] This development had clearly started long before 1714, and was certainly not completed until well after 1800: yet the Parliamentary tradition, centring on Speaker Arthur Onslow, that the earlier Hanoverian period saw a significant advance in this respect is soundly based on contemporary evidence. The cause was a voluntary cession of power by ministers at least as much as a struggle for freedom by the incumbents of the Chair.

There were two main advantages an administration might derive from the support of a Speaker, the importance attached by members to his views and his co-operation in the management of the House. Political pronouncements by a Speaker carried more weight than those of ordinary members, especially on any matters concerning the House, and even speeches by former Speakers met with particular attention. The Speaker could not, of course, take part in debates in the House; and he was debarred from voting by a decision of 1601, except in the case of a tie:[2] but there still remained opportunities for a

[1] J. Steven Watson has reviewed some political aspects of Speaker Arthur Onslow's career in this context in 'Arthur Onslow and Party Politics', *Essays in British History*, pp. 139–71.

[2] Dasent, *Speakers*, p. 160.

Speaker to express his personal opinions on political matters. Advantage could be taken of such formal occasions as speeches to the throne on the presentation of money bills at the close of a session: both Onslow and Norton certainly voiced their political views in this way. In any case, a Speaker could still speak and vote as freely as any other member in Committees. It was on this ground that Constantine Phipps objected on 12 March 1771 when Richard Rigby asked Speaker Norton for his opinion on the proposed proceedings against newspaper reporting of debates. It was against the order of the House for the Chair to enter into debates, Phipps declared; the proper way to obtain Norton's opinion was to move for a Committee so that the Speaker could there give his views. Norton agreed that 'the honourable gentleman is certainly right in point of order.'[1] This may have been correct constitutional theory: but the House did not either then or at any other time during the eighteenth century resolve itself into a Committee merely to obtain the benefit of the Speaker's opinions. Indeed, it is clear that already some impropriety was felt in the participation of the Chair in Committee debates. Speakers rarely exercised their right to speak then: and, instead of attending Committees, they usually sat in the gallery or withdrew into the Speaker's Room until the time came to resume the Chair. In 1755 there was apparently even an attempt by Onslow to restrict the complete freedom of the Speaker to speak in Committee. The occasion was the Committee of Supply on 12 December 1755 to consider the Russian subsidy treaties. The whole subject had been discussed in the House at great length two days before, and a comment made by Andrew Stone in his report to the Duke of Newcastle is significant in the context of Onslow's subsequent contention: 'The question of the legality or illegality of the Treaties, having been so fully debated, cannot be resumed in the Committee, when the debate must regularly be confined to the expediency of them.'[2] Here is Charles Yorke's report to Lord Hardwicke of Onslow's behaviour in the Committee:[3]

The Speaker in the minority, but did not open his mouth; and, it seems, he had propagated a distinction of some use in the debate

[1] B.M. Eg. MSS. 226, pp. 19–21. [2] B.M. Add. MSS. 32861, fo. 275.
[3] B.M. Add. MSS. 35353, fo. 183.

and had given it as his reason, why he should say nothing, that upon the former debate, for referring the treaties to the Committee of Supply, the sense of the House on the question of legality had been taken; and it was improper, to resume it in the Committee, tho' it may be revived upon the Report. This is a distinction only made for himself, to avoid speaking in the Committee; when it comes again into the House, he will be stuck in the Chair.

The rule Onslow had put forward was that since Speakers could speak only in Committee, they were permitted to comment only on the details of Parliamentary decisions, and not on the principles involved. This was an application of the general practice of the House to the particular circumstances of the Chair. Onslow's motive was thought to be entirely personal, the dilemma posed by his known antipathy to foreign subsidies and his reluctance to engage in open criticism of the ministry. There is insufficient evidence to determine whether his immediate successors adopted his interpretation: in any case it could apply only to the finance Committees and to the Committee stage of legislation, and not to other Committees of the House.

The practical advantages an administration might derive from the support of the Chair in the daily business of the House were negative rather than positive: it was not in the general interests of government for any suspicion of bias to jeopardize a Speaker's control over the House. When ministers had legislation to pass or other business to lay before the House it was at least convenient, and often a tactical advantage, if the Speaker pointed to the appropriate official spokesman to open the debate. Every first minister was apparently allowed to speak at the moment he chose to do so during a debate. At the end of almost every debate the Speaker would give the decision on the question in favour of administration, throwing the responsibility for forcing any division on the opposition. It is true that in all matters, such as the order of business or the choice of members to speak in debate, a majority of the members present could overrule the Speaker in any dispute by means of a resolution: but this step could not be used as a daily weapon to coerce the Chair, and any rumours that a Speaker might cause difficulties for administration raised opposition morale. Apart from his co-operation in the avoidance of unnecessary obstruction and delay, a Speaker might also help ministers by his knowledge of procedure, of forthcoming business, and even of political opinion in the House: certainly there is abundant evidence of consultations by ministers with the Speaker, and of his attendance at meetings of leading administration supporters.

A minister had two direct methods of influence over the Chair, the threat of removal at the end of the Parliament, and the inducement that the inadequate official income of the Speaker might be supplemented by a post given him by the administration. By the end of the eighteenth century the former means had markedly lost its efficacy, and the latter had altogether ceased to exist.

Since the appointment of a Speaker was the choice of the majority of the House of Commons, his initial election was the decision of the minister then in power. No attempt was made to disguise this circumstance. The nomination to the Chair at the beginning of each Parliament was usually made and seconded by office-holders, and in the reign of George III there even began to develop a convention that a new Speaker should be proposed by the Leader of the House. This had not earlier been the case. Compton was proposed in 1715 by Lord Hertford, Onslow in 1728 by Lord Hartington, both minor figures in the House: but in 1761 the motion for Cust was made by George Grenville, that for Norton in 1770 by Lord North, and in 1780 Charles James Fox criticized Lord North, still Leader of the House, for not proposing Cornwall himself. William Pitt was apparently intending to propose Addington in 1789 until John Hatsell advised against the step, on the ground that the Speaker should appear the choice of the House, not the administration, and the practice of open ministerial nomination ceased.[1]

During his tenure of office the threat of dismissal at the end of a Parliament served to remind a Speaker that he had been appointed by government, whether or not there occurred any change of ministry; and that sanction was rendered a very real one by the political practice prior to 1714. The reign of Queen Anne saw different Speakers in all five Parliaments.

[1] Debrett, *Parl. Reg.*, I, 10–12. Laundy, *The Office of Speaker*, p. 15.

There was a sharp contrast afterwards. Spencer Compton sat in the Chair for both Parliaments of George I's reign, and quitted it for a seat in the Lords. Arthur Onslow was Speaker throughout the reign of George II, for thirty-three years and five Parliaments, and then retired with a pension. His successor, Sir John Cust, was re-elected to the Chair, but died two years afterwards, in 1770. Sir Fletcher Norton filled the vacancy, but ten years later, since his behaviour had given offence to George III and Lord North, the administration replaced him after the general election of 1780 by Charles Cornwall. The climate of opinion had by then so changed that an opposition protest was made on the ground that the Chair was not vacant.[1] 1780, indeed, proved to be the only occasion in the era of non-party politics between the reign of Queen Anne and that of William IV when a ministry removed a Speaker from office against his will. The King's government might have a final sanction of dismissal, but it could be used only as a last resort.

The other circumstance affording a lever to ministers was the insufficiency of the Speaker's income. Information on the revenues of the Chair may be found in the report made by Speaker Arthur Onslow on 2 February 1732 of his income for the previous four sessions, and in the debates of 10 and 15 March 1790 in the House of Commons on the Speaker's emoluments.[2] The only fixed income received by Onslow was for the expenses of the Speaker's table £5 a day throughout the year, paid out of His Majesty's Exchequer without any deduction but the common fees. This allowance was estimated in 1790 at 'about £1,680'. Speaker Onslow also enjoyed the residual profit on the sale of the daily *Votes*, after the Clerk of the House and the Serjeant-at-Arms had taken their fees and the printer his profit at a fixed rate. Speaker Onslow in 1732 certified that his income from this source in the four sessions of 1728 to 1731 had varied between £456 and £493. By the middle of the century the Speaker's profit fluctuated a great deal, according to the length of the session and the cost of production. It was only £127 in 1761 and £161 in 1768, but

---

[1] Debrett, *Parl. Reg.*, I, 5–6.
[2] See respectively O. C. Williams, *The Clerical Organisation of the House of Commons 1661–1850*, pp. 307–9; and Cobbett, *Parl. Hist.*, XXVIII, 506–18.

rose to £376 in 1769.[1] Then the beginning of Parliamentary reporting in the newspapers caused a catastrophic fall in the public demand for the *Votes*. Speaker Norton complained in 1774 that this practice had cost him £500 a year.[2] Certainly the Speaker's profit had then fallen to a mere £64. From the session of 1776–1777 the *Votes* made a loss. In 1780 Speaker Cornwall found a total deficit of over £400, and handed the account over to the Treasury.[3] The third main source of income for the Chair came from fees. Each Speaker obtained a fee of five guineas for every private bill or enacting clause, and one of ten guineas for every bill which concerned a county or a corporation. This perquisite provided a steadily increasing revenue, despite frequent attempts by sponsors of legislation to evade fees through a definition of their proposed bills as public. From 1728 to 1731 Onslow received between £400 and £545 a year in such fees. By 1790 the Speaker's fees from this source were computed at averaging between £1,200 and £1,300 a year.

The total income of the Speaker therefore compared unfavourably with the official salaries or customary perquisites of many members of the House.[4] During Onslow's first years in the Chair it was about £2,700, and in 1790 was estimated to be under £3,000. In 1780 the Marquess of Rockingham thought the net income was £2,600 a year.[5] The total might have been higher in the middle of the century before the loss of profits from sale of the *Votes*: but little credence can be given to a hostile newspaper estimate of January 1770 that the income of the Chair under new Speaker Sir Fletcher Norton amounted to nearly £6,000.[6]

[1] Sheila Lambert, 'Printing for the House of Commons in the Eighteenth Century', *The Library* (1968), pp. 27–8.

[2] *The Middlesex Journal*, 25 Jan. 1774.   [3] Lambert, op. cit., pp. 28–9.

[4] There were also some non-recurring payments, money given specifically for expenses, and such minor perquisites as some game from the royal parks and an annual two hogsheads of claret. Each Speaker was given £1,000 for his equipment, on his appointment, according to Onslow: but in the debate of 1790 this was stated to be at the commencement of a new Parliament. Onslow also reported annual 'stores' to the value of just over £100: this might correspond to the £100 for stationery mentioned in 1790.

[5] J. E. Tyler, 'Lord North and the Speakership in 1780', *Parliamentary Affairs*, 8 (1954—5), p. 366.

[6] *London Evening Post*, 23 Jan. 1770. This newspaper gives his total income as nearly £9,000, but Norton held a legal office worth £3,000. The income from fees

The position of Speaker, moreover, involved the holder in considerable expenses for entertainment and other obligations of maintaining the dignity of the office. It was therefore reasonable that administration should supplement this income by the bestowal of a Crown appointment. This was the practice for much of the century: but any such office involved an apparent or real hold by ministers on the Speaker's political allegiance. There was also a legal snag: since by the Place Act of 1706, acceptance of any office of profit under the Crown automatically vacated a member's seat, it was only possible for a Speaker to receive any such recompense during the interval between the dissolution of one Parliament and the election of the next. It was therefore in 1722 that Compton accepted the post of Paymaster of the Forces. Although his re-election as Speaker on 9 October of that year was unanimous, a personal attack on him by Sir John Pakington included 'notice of his great places'.[1] It was during the interval between his first and second Parliaments in the Chair that Arthur Onslow was given office as Treasurer of the Navy in 1734. No adverse comments on this appointment were made at the time of his subsequent re-elections to the Chair, but his possession of the post led to a famous incident in 1742. After the resignation of Sir Robert Walpole a ballot for a Committee of inquiry into the last ten years of his administration ended with four members having received an equal number of votes for the last two places. Two were hostile to Walpole, two were his friends. Onslow, knowing that the fallen minister had only three supporters among the other nineteen members of the Committee, and disapproving in principle of such a Parliamentary persecution, gave his casting vote in favour of Walpole's two friends, and not to one member on each side. His decision was criticized as being the consequence of the additional salary given him by Walpole, and Onslow resigned the post of Treasurer of the Navy within a few days.[2]

It has long been recognized that by this action Onslow

---

may, however, have been higher at that date than a decade later. See the table for 1776–1788 printed in O. C. Williams, op. cit., p. 319.

[1] *Knatchbull Diary*, p. 2.

[2] H. Walpole, *Letters*, I, 206–8. Cobbett, *Parl Hist.*, XXVIII, 515. See also J. Steven Watson, op. cit., pp. 153–4.

established the principle that for a Speaker to hold an office of profit at pleasure under the Crown was incompatible with the dignity and independence of his position. But the financial problem remained. Onslow was obliged to spend heavily from his own pocket on the social duties expected of him: his son George recalled in 1771 that 'he spent his whole income in keeping up the necessary dignity of his office.'[1] Sir John Cust's mother gave him an estate specifically to meet the expenses of the Chair.[2] An accidental and temporary solution was then found in the bestowal of life sinecures on the next two Speakers. In 1769 Sir Fletcher Norton was appointed Chief Justice in Eyre South of Trent. He obtained the post, worth £3,000 a year, before any question of the vacancy of the Chair arose: but such a post, virtually a legal sinecure, was seen to give an opportunity of supplementing the Speaker's income without the stigma of political office. Before his election to the Chair in 1780 Charles Cornwall therefore accepted the post of Chief Justice in Eyre North of Trent. These appointments were made for life, and so avoided the objection that they would be a means of influence over the Speaker: but such rewards still involved the implication of ministerial choice, or at least the need of administration approval. Nor could such offices be given during a Parliament, and Cornwall died while still Speaker, on 2 January 1789. This vacancy occurred during the Regency crisis over George III's illness when the political future was in doubt. The Chair was filled as a temporary measure by William Wyndham Grenville, who remained Paymaster of the Forces and a member of the Board of Trade.[3] He resigned in June to become Home Secretary, being succeeded by Henry Addington. These circumstances must have reminded members of the close connection between the Chair and the King's government, and it may not have been coincidence that the question of the Speaker's income was resolved during Addington's first year in the Chair, before a dissolution would enable the ministry to give him a sinecure.

The obvious solution was a large and fixed salary. This had been suggested by Speaker Arthur Onslow on 28 April 1758, during a debate in the Committee of Ways and Means over a

---

[1] *H.M.C. Onslow*, p. 521.   [2] *Erthig Chronicles*, II, 98.
[3] Stanhope, *Pitt*, II, 35.

tax on places and pensions. Onslow intervened to oppose an exemption for the Speaker, and then commented on the financial position of the Chair: 'That he was many thousand pounds the poorer for being Speaker, would accept of nothing and wished he was able to serve without receiving a shilling. It would be right to give a salary to his successor, but then not to suffer him to accept of any place or employment.'[1] This report of Onslow's speech was sent to the Duke of Newcastle, but, although First Lord of the Treasury, he took no action then or on Onslow's retirement in 1761. Over twenty years later, in 1780, the idea of a salary bestowed on the Speaker by the House was suggested by opposition leader the Marquess of Rockingham, when discussing with his friend Frederick Montagu an offer of the Chair made to Montagu by Lord North.[2]

The point which I shall now consider, is relative to your embarking in an office, the Emoluments of which are not adequate to the extra Expences which the support of the honour of the Office may require. I understand the actual neat Receipt of the Emolument accruing from the Chair amount to about 2600 per annum. It has long been acknowledged too small, and the practice has been for the Crown and its Ministers to add a lucrative office to be held in commendam with the Chair. There is a little savour of Impurity in this, tho' customary and expedient, for as the Speaker of the House of Commons is or ought to be the Free and uninfluenced choice of the House, it seems awkward that so honourable an election should become an onerous Burthen inflicted on the person chosen, unless his Majesty or his Ministers should be graciously pleased to dole him out an additional stipend, the Quantum of which may depend upon their Liking or Disliking. The Speaker is considered as the servant of the House. They are his Masters and should be the appointers of his Pay. I could much wish that this amendment could be made on your being chosen Speaker. I think the House would relish it . . . The annual Emolument of 4000 per annum would prevent the Expences of the office from being hurtful to your private Fortune.

Frederick Montagu refused the offer of the Chair: but it was he who, as a veteran opposition member, finally raised the

[1] B.M. Add. MSS. 32879, fo. 331.
[2] Wentworth Woodhouse MSS., R 162, printed by J. E. Tyler, 'Lord North and the Speakership in 1780', *Parliamentary Affairs*, 8 (1954–5), p. 366.

subject in the House of Commons on 10 March 1790. Montagu announced his intention of proposing a fixed salary of £5,000 as 'the price paid for the purchase of the Speaker's independence'; his plan was to include all existing fees and allowances and to supplement them to guarantee the desired income. He accordingly moved for a Committee of the Whole House to consider the subject on 15 March. The motion met with the general approval of the House, only one member dissenting on the illogical ground that Crown influence would thereby increase. William Pitt declared, as minister, that George III recommended that a provision be made for the Speaker, a statement that revealed prior government knowledge of the motion. When Montagu made his proposal in the Committee five days later, the only question argued in the debate was whether the sum was adequate. An amendment was moved for another £1,000: and despite Pitt's support for the lesser sum, a resolution for an annual salary of £6,000 was carried by 154 votes to 28.[1]

The close connection of the Speakership with each administration throughout Anne's reign had been highlighted by Robert Harley's acceptance of the post of Secretary of State in 1704 while he was still in the Chair: and contemporary assumptions about the political role of the Speaker are reflected in this letter of congratulation sent to Sir Thomas Hanmer in 1713:[2] 'The world is well pleased with the Speaker who is designed for the next Parliament. I shall make many vows for his good success. But I fear he must lay aside sometimes those sentiments of honour and truth which are natural to him and in order to govern by the power of a party, he must suffer himself to be ruled by the directions of a ministry.'

Although Hanmer was a Hanoverian Tory, few in 1715 can have doubted that after the Whig triumph there would be a Whig Speaker. A wide spectrum of Whig opinion could approve the political pedigree of the man chosen, Spencer Compton. An M.P. since 1698, apart from the Parliament of 1710, Compton had been a close friend of Robert Walpole by 1704:[3]

---

[1] Cobbett, *Parl. Hist.*, XXVIII, 506–18.   [2] Bettisfield MSS., no. 77.
[3] Cholmondeley Houghton MSS., nos. 358–9, 362. I owe these references to Dr. E. L. Ellis.

and his subsequent voting record left no doubt of his Whiggism. His election to the Chair on 17 March 1715 was unanimous, no debate arising after he had been proposed by Lord Hertford and seconded by Lord Finch.[1]

Under George I Compton's personal political allegiance was to the Prince of Wales: both sponsors at his election were Gentlemen of the Bedchamber to the Prince, and Compton himself acted as the Prince's Treasurer from 1715 until his accession as George II in 1727. After the quarrel between King and Prince in 1717, this circumstance led to the fortuitous situation of a Speaker in opposition to the King's ministers for the next three years. Contemporary lists name Compton as voting against administration in 1719 on the two most important issues of that year, the Peerage Bill and the repeal of the Occasional Conformity and Schism Acts:[2] this was clearly an assumption of his general attitude; the Peerage Bill never reached the Committee stage, but he may have voted in Committee on the other measure. It was during the same period that Compton made his only known speech as Speaker in Committee. The occasion was the debate in the Committee of Supply on 8 April 1717 on a motion for a vote of credit to the Crown to provide for an expected war with Sweden. Compton recalled the incident in 1730 when talking with Lord Perceval:[3] 'That being a novelty, and a very ill precedent, it was his duty as Speaker to oppose it, and that it was remarkable all the members who had in their times been Speakers opposed it, as John Smith and Mr. Bromley, who both spoke against it, and Sir Thomas Hanmer, who though he spoke not, which he was blamed for, yet voted against it.'

Compton had added his voice to the protests of opposition members that it was unparliamentary to vote a supply in principle before any estimate of the cost had been laid before the House. He presided as Speaker on the report to the House next day of the resolution for a supply, and heard Richard Hampden declare that Compton himself had made a similar motion in the previous reign without laying any estimate before the Commons. The indignant Speaker replied from the Chair to this attack: 'He wondered that gentlemen would

---

[1] Chandler, *Debates*, VI, 9.   [2] Chandler, *Debates*, VIII, Appendix.
[3] *H.M.C. Egmont Diary*, I, 88.

bring in as a precedent, a business that was transacted so many years ago, and which was not parallel to the present case.' John Smith again opposed the supply at this report stage, and also in the Committee of Supply on 12 April when the ensuing motion was made for £250,000. Both William Bromley and Sir Thomas Hanmer spoke when that motion was reported to the House on 13 April.[1] Speakers past and present clearly accepted some obligation to defend the accustomed practices of the House against dangerous innovations.

By the dissolution of the Parliament in 1722 both the Whig split and the quarrel in the royal family had ended, and no question arose of replacing Compton on political or other grounds. Samuel Sandys has left a record of his re-election. On 7 October 1722, the Sunday before the new Parliament was due to assemble, Walpole as chief minister in the Commons held a private meeting of prominent members at his house: there he proposed Compton as Speaker, and named the members who were to move and second him. The same decision was announced to a more general meeting of ministerial supporters at the Cockpit the next day. On 9 October 1722 Compton was proposed by Lord Stanhope, another Gentleman of the Bedchamber to the Prince, and seconded by Charles Talbot.[2] No opposition was made, but Knatchbull noted a personal attack on Compton by Sir John Pakington.[3]

No evidence on Compton's political conduct in the House during this Parliament has been found; but an incidental reference in 1725 does show that he voted as an ordinary member in Committee.[4] The accession crisis of 1727, however, serves as a reminder that contemporaries did not regard the Chair as above the political arena. For several days it was generally believed in London that the new King George II would replace Walpole by Compton as his first minister. Instead, the anticipated royal favourite contented himself with a peerage as Earl of Wilmington, and the retention of his post as Paymaster of the Forces.[5] His successor in the Chair was

---

[1] Chandler, *Debates*, VI, 117–25.   [2] *Knatchbull Diary*, p. 115.
[3] *Knatchbull Diary*, p. 2.   [4] *Knatchbull Diary*, p. 41.
[5] Plumb, *Walpole*, II, 162–70. During the ministerial crisis of 1722 there had also been a rumour that Compton would replace Walpole at the Treasury. *H.M.C. Portland*, VII, 313. Even in July 1727 gossip said that Compton would continue as Speaker and 'share the power' with Walpole. Ibid., 399.

perhaps the most famous Speaker to preside over the House of Commons, Arthur Onslow.

The Onslows were a Surrey family with a long Parliamentary tradition: two of them had already been Speakers. Such a background gave Arthur Onslow pride, ambition and advantage. In his autobiographical memoir he recalled his aim on entry into the Commons at a by-election for Guildford on 16 February 1720: 'I will not disown that I was very intent to succeed in this new situation, and found an ambition about me which I had never perceived before, not for profitable employments or riches which I have ever perhaps too much contemned but for fame and respect, which perhaps I have too much courted.'[1]

Onslow soon made his mark in the House. He spoke in debate within a few weeks of his election, and the favourable impression he created was enhanced by several speeches on the South Sea Bubble in the next session.[2] Before the new Parliament of 1722 Walpole summoned him to a private meeting of prominent members of the House on 14 October, to consider both the draft Address and a proposed bill to suspend the Habeas Corpus Act because of the Jacobite conspiracy known as the Atterbury Plot. Onslow was one of those who raised Whiggish objections to the length of the suspension, from fear of the precedent, but all finally agreed on the measure.[3] Onslow accordingly supported the bill in debate, but he showed his independence the next month by opposing on 23 November a tax on Catholics, as suspected Jacobites, declaring it was a religious persecution.[4] At another private meeting called by Walpole Onslow agreed to second the Bill of Pains and Penalties against John Plunket, the conspirator most obviously guilty on the evidence. He did so on 8 March 1723, and subsequently took the Chair when the bill was in Committee.[5] Two years later he again assisted Walpole's ministry by acting as one of the managers for the House of Commons in their

---

[1] *H.M.C. Onslow*, p. 503.   [2] *H.M.C. Onslow*, pp. 505, 512.

[3] *Knatchbull Diary*, p. 115.

[4] *H.M.C. Onslow*, p. 513. Chandler, *Debates*, VI, 295.

[5] *H.M.C. Onslow*, p. 514. *Knatchbull Diary*, pp. 15, 18. Chandler, *Debates*, VI, 300.

impeachment before the Lords of Lord Chancellor Maccles-
field.¹ But his stout Whiggism was demonstrated by his opposition in that same session of 1725 to the restoration of the former
Jacobite Lord Bolingbroke to his estates. It was Onslow who on
20 April vainly moved the rejection of Bolingbroke's petition.
He continued to oppose the consequent bill despite a personal
request to him by Walpole in the House that 'the old Whigs'
would not do so: and such was Onslow's personal stature in the
House that Lord Bolingbroke's father came to press him on the
same subject.²

For the remainder of the Parliament independence over
popular issues continued to qualify his general support of
government. In a debate of 21 February 1726 on supply he
seconded a motion to cancel proposed salary increases for some
legal officials, 'giving the reason for it that, though it was but a
trifle of 2 or £300 per annum, yet it would shew the world
that the House another year intended to pare off all unnecessary charges in the estimates both sea and land'.³ Onslow spoke
for administration on 25 March over a proposed increase in the
navy: yet two days later he supported an opposition bill to
prevent bribery in Parliamentary elections.⁴ At the beginning
of the next session, on 17 January 1727, Onslow publicly
signified support of Walpole's ministry by moving the Address.⁵
On 1 February he spoke for administration in the Committee
of Supply on the Ordnance; and on 26 April he supported
government on a controversial measure of finance.⁶ But his
hostility to the hire of foreign mercenary soldiers, a characteristic of Onslow throughout his career, caused him to side with
opposition on 13 February over a demand for explanation of a
deficiency of £125,000 in the payment of Hessian troops: and
it may have been the attitude of men like Onslow that caused
the administration to concede the point next day. The reason
given to the House on 21 February, however, proved to be
vague and general; and Onslow reinforced the opposition
criticism by a direct attack on Walpole. 'Mr. Onslow chiefly

¹ *H.M.C. Onslow*, pp. 514–15. Chandler, *Debates*, VI, 345.
² *Knatchbull Diary*, p. 47. Chandler, *Debates*, VI, 343. *H.M.C. Onslow*, p. 515.
³ *Knatchbull Diary*, p. 52.   ⁴ Chandler, *Debates*, VI, 370–1.
⁵ *Knatchbull Diary*, p. 59. Chandler, *Debates*, VI, 376.
⁶ *Knatchbull Diary*, p. 61. Chandler, *Debates*, VI, 396.

insisted on the promise made to the House the last session, by a great man in the administration, that they should have a particular account of all the Money that should be expended upon that vote of credit, which promise induced the House to come so readily into it.'[1]

Onslow's early career makes it hard to recognize him as the tame and obscure member depicted by Lord Hervey as Walpole's choice of Speaker in 1727:[2] 'As he had no great pretensions to it from his age, his character, his weight in the House, or his particular knowledge of the business, Sir Robert Walpole imagined that he must look upon his promotion entirely as an act of his favour, and consequently think himself obliged, in honour, interest and gratitude, to show all the complaisance in his power to his patron and benefactor.'

Hervey's comments reveal a courtier's ignorance of the status and attitude of independent members. The man Walpole invited to be Speaker in the new reign was already a leading personality of the Commons: Onslow was important enough to be one of two absentees from a division on 12 April 1727 noted by diarist Knatchbull, and he was one of the representative group of prominent members, both administration and opposition, who on 13 March 1727 rose in the House to express unanimous resentment of recent behaviour by the Imperial ambassador.[3] Yet Hervey may well have been correct in his assumption that one motive behind Walpole's decision was a desire to avoid advancing a possible rival. Hitherto the Chair had been an office from which most incumbents had stepped down to resume their seats in the House, and from which several had afterwards advanced to high posts in administration. Walpole himself had just survived a crisis in which he had feared replacement by the retiring Speaker. Indeed, Compton was returned again for Sussex in 1727, and may have accepted a peerage only when Walpole made clear his refusal to tolerate such a rival in the Commons. Onslow had the attraction for Walpole of genuine independence and lack of ambition for executive office. Contemporaries at first did not perceive Onslow's new conception of his office as the ultimate ambition of a career, and assumed that the occupant of the Chair was

---

[1] Chandler, *Debates*, VI, 385–8. [2] Hervey, *Memoirs*, I, 74.
[3] *Knatchbull Diary*, p. 68. Chandler, *Debates*, VI, 391.

still a contender for ministerial appointment. Lord Perceval made this entry in his diary for February 1730: 'I have not been in the wrong in thinking a long time past that the Speaker is forming a party in the House of reasonable Tories and discontented Whigs, to rise upon the ruins of Sir Robert Walpole.'[1] This was to misunderstand both Onslow's aim and the nature of his influence. In 1750 this diarist's son, then second Earl of Egmont, listed the Speaker among seven members to be excluded from the Commons in the anticipated event of a new administration to be formed after the accession of the then Prince of Wales. But he gave as his reason Onslow's procedural knowledge, not his leadership of any faction: 'Will be a very inconvenient man to stay in the House of Commons if not continued Speaker which can hardly be—For he is of an overbearing temper and has acquired great authority.—His bias will draw him towards the routed faction—and his vanity will make him constantly puzzling our Speaker and our Chairman of Committees, in points of order, which in reality he will know better than they ... in such circumstances it is incredible how much trouble he will give.'[2] Addington's move in 1801 from the Chair to the head of the ministry has given rise to the idea that an eighteenth century Speaker could use his position to create his own political group.[3] Speakers, like other members, were concerned to maintain family interests, and to give electoral support to friends and relatives: but no evidence has been found to suggest the existence of any 'Speaker's party' under Onslow, Cust, Norton or Cornwall.

Independence was a luxury Onslow especially valued because he had not always enjoyed it. A failure at the Bar, he was at first dependent on his uncle Sir Richard Onslow, and gratefully accepted through his patronage minor posts of little income: £600 as secretary to his uncle when he was Chancellor of the Exchequer in 1714–1715, and then £400 from a place in the Post Office until he was obliged to resign the office on his entry into the Commons.[4] His financial circumstances were transformed by his marriage to Anne

---

[1] *H.M.C. Egmont Diary*, I, 31.

[2] A. N. Newman, ed., 'Leicester House Politics 1750–1760', *Camden Miscellany XXIII*, p. 170.

[3] J. Steven Watson, op. cit., p. 142.   [4] *H.M.C. Onslow*, p. 503.

Bridges in October 1720, for he then acquired possession of the estate of Imber Court in his native Surrey. Onslow recorded in his memoirs the delight he felt in his new situation: 'Being thus settled in a very creditable place and as it were the heir of it, in my own country, it much increased my consideration there, and the certain expectancy of a tolerable estate strengthened my own wishes and resolution to keep myself independent in Parliament.'[1] Onslow's personal standing as a member of an old county family and as the owner of a respectable landed estate was an asset to him during his tenure of the Chair. But his Parliamentary role as a responsible independent member prepared to support the King's government unless it offended his own Whig or 'country' views had made him a man respected in the Commons, and had been, Onslow later thought, the main reason for his elevation to the Chair at the early age of thirty-six.[2]

I had not been a frequent speaker in debates, and never long, always diffident of my performances there, and endeavoured to found my character, rather upon the rectitude of my actings, than upon any other fame, and therefore often voted with both parties as I thought them to be in the right. I loved independency, and pursued it. I kept firm to my original Whig principles, upon conscience, and never deviated from them to serve any party cause whatsoever; and all this I hope, and am persuaded, was what chiefly laid the foundation of my rise to the Chair of the House of Commons without any the least opposition, although Sir Robert Walpole sometimes said to me, that the road to that station lay through the gates of St. James.

Certainly the choice of Speaker lay with the King's minister. The first discussion between Walpole and Onslow concerning the Chair occurred during the political crisis at George II's accession. Onslow visited Sir Robert at the very time when it was generally believed that Compton would be the new minister, a gesture much appreciated by Walpole. Among the possible changes that might result from such a new administration, Onslow later recollected, 'I found he would not dislike my being the next Speaker; but of that nothing was ever said by him to me till he was in the full return of his

[1] *H.M.C. Onslow*, p. 506.   [2] *H.M.C. Onslow*, p. 516.

former power.' Onslow may have hinted to Walpole at this meeting that he would like the Chair, for it is clear that Walpole had developed the firm intention to offer Onslow the post by the time of the general election of 1727. This was his comment on learning that Onslow was standing a contest for Surrey in order to preserve the family interest there: 'What! Will you take a county upon you? Consider what that is with regard to re-election; and should any accident happen to prevent your being chosen Speaker, you will, I suppose, be not unwilling to come into other offices and trusts, perhaps frequent elections may not be so practicable in a county as in a borough.' Onslow retained his Guildford seat as a precaution against defeat, but his triumph in the county was so overwhelming that he never again met with opposition there.[1]

Arthur Onslow was unanimously chosen Speaker when the new Parliament met on 23 January 1728,[2] and he drew encouragement from his previous career: 'I had never made myself personally obnoxious to any party, and had, by my manner of acting in Parliament, some regard shewn to me from many of every denomination and they had reason to believe, I should be respectful and impartial to all.'[3] Although anxious to maintain this reputation, Onslow made no attempt to avoid political commitment: he apparently voted, for example, in six out of the seven divisions in Committee for which lists survive during the next twenty years. Information on his political views during the period is nevertheless difficult to obtain: reports of debates are scanty, and Onslow's opportunities for expressing his opinions were now limited. His general attitude continued to be the same as before, support for Walpole's ministry tempered by criticism or opposition on matters about which he held strong prejudice: and one such subject, the army, came up every year in the Committee of Supply. He supported the army estimates in Committee on 28 January 1730 in a balanced speech. 'He said he would sacrifice his life before he would concur in keeping up a formidable army by way of rule and maxim as necessary to our govern-

---

[1] *H.M.C. Onslow*, pp. 517–19.
[2] Coxe, *Walpole*, II, 545–6. *Commons Journals*, XXI, 19–20.
[3] *H.M.C. Onslow*, p. 520.

ment, but thought, considering how affairs stand at present in Europe, that the question proposed ought to pass.'[1] Onslow's known dislike of large armies gave his opinion more weight; and an attempt to prevent the Speaker showing his approval of the hire of Hessian soldiers was understood to be the motive behind the curious tactic adopted a few days later by opposition member Daniel Pulteney. On 4 February he unsuccessfully opposed a motion to refer the relevant supply to Committee, asserting that the matter should be debated in the House itself.[2] Two years later, when the army had not been reduced despite a renewed prospect of peace, Onslow voted against the ministry on the subject. By 1734 there was again the threat of war; and Onslow then spoke in favour of the administration proposal for an increase.[3]

Walpole's attitude to the Speaker depended on his political behaviour. Late in 1731 Onslow was reputed to be out of favour with the minister, and consequently he found himself snubbed by the Queen at court.[4] But before the end of the following year Onslow attended 'a meeting of the great men' summoned by Walpole to consider the request of the Dissenters for repeal of the Test Act: he advised strongly against the measure, saying that 'if it came into the House of Commons, not five members would be for it'.[5] In 1733 Onslow gave open support to administration on Walpole's controversial Excise Bill: for on 14 March 1733 he voted in support of the proposals which formed the basis of the bill, when they were under consideration by a Committee of the Whole House.[6] After the withdrawal of the measure Onslow attended among 263 members at a special Cockpit meeting called by Walpole on 23 April to counter an opposition attempt to follow up this success by the appointment of a Committee to inquire into the customs service: and he spoke in support of Walpole's plan that an administration list of names should be voted in the ballot for the Committee members next day.[7]

Onslow, voting and speaking when he might well have been

[1] *H.M.C. Egmont Diary*, I, 12.　　　　　　[2] *Knatchbull Diary*, pp. 102–3.
[3] *H.M.C. Egmont Diary*, I, 217; II, 24.　　[4] *H.M.C. Egmont Diary*, I, 205–6.
[5] *H.M.C. Egmont Diary*, I, 301.
[6] Chandler, *Debates*, VII, 317–53; VIII, Appendix.
[7] *H.M.C ·Egmont Diary*, I, 365–6.

inactive, could not have demonstrated his allegiance more clearly. After the general election of 1734 there was a rumour that Samuel Sandys, a prominent opposition member, would also be proposed as Speaker.[1] This challenge did not materialize, Onslow being elected unanimously on 14 January 1735.[2] But that the Chair was still regarded as one of the political offices at the disposal of administration is shown by Lord Egmont's account of some unsuccessful negotiations between Walpole and a few opposition Whigs for a ministerial reconstruction in 1737: he noted a report that Sandys had declined to replace the Duke of Newcastle as Secretary of State because of a preference to be Speaker in the next Parliament.[3]

Reports of only two speeches by Onslow in Committee have survived for the Parliament of 1734. On 11 February 1740 he expressed his concern at a speech implying that the House of Commons did not have the sole right to grant money; and on 4 March 1741 he spoke avowedly as Treasurer of the Navy in defence of the method of paying seamen's wages.[4] The Speaker also gave expression to his political views in several speeches on formal occasions; Onslow's general refrain was sympathy with opposition demands for strong action against Spain, but he combined this view with support for Walpole as minister.[5] In 1739 Lord Egmont noted that his speeches were 'understood to be the sense of the ministry', and his end-of-session speech on 14 June, attacking Spain, was widely and correctly believed to herald a more vigorous administration policy.[6] Onslow remained close to Walpole until his fall in 1742. The minister consulted the Speaker over an abortive plan to recover his popularity by a proposal to sever the connection between Britain and Hanover after George II's death; and confided in him the hope of a majority of forty-seven in the new Parliament after the general election of 1741.[7]

Onslow's general conduct in the Chair nevertheless saved him from a contest over his re-election as Speaker in that year.

---

[1] *H.M.C. 15 Report Pt. VI, Carlisle MSS.*, p. 143.
[2] *H.M.C. Egmont Diary*, II, 142. Chandler, *Debates*, IX, 1.
[3] *H.M.C. Egmont Diary*, II, 366.
[4] Chandler, *Debates*, XI, 294–5; XII, 216–17.
[5] J. Steven Watson, op. cit., pp. 151–3.   [6] *H.M.C. Egmont Diary*, III, 70.
[7] Burnet, *History*, IV, 490N. *H.M.C. Egmont Diary*, III, 257.

Opposition leaders considered a challenge to him, but deemed it unwise to have the first trial of strength on the point, Lord Chesterfield writing to Bubb Dodington on 8 September, 'As for opposition to their Speaker, if it be Onslow we shall be but weak, he having by a certain decency of behaviour made himself many personal friends in the minority.'[1] Onslow was elected unanimously after being proposed and seconded by two office-holders, Paymaster-General Henry Pelham and Lord of the Treasury Thomas Clutterbuck: but Sir Robert Walpole's son Horace tartly commented that 'the Opposition, to flatter his pretence to popularity and impartiality, call him their own Speaker'.[2] Horace Walpole later recalled that his father 'always thought the Speaker not enough attached to him, and treated him very roughly, especially on his first visit after his disgrace'.[3] This was unfair: Onslow's resignation from his post as Treasurer of the Navy soon afterwards was caused by his desire to see justice done to the fallen minister, and the Speaker continued to give broad support to the other 'old Whig' administrations after 1742. His name appears among the majority in two of the three surviving division-lists for this Parliament, over the employment of Hanoverian troops in 1742 and 1744; and he was marked as absent on the third occasion, in 1746. The only political speech by him of which a report has been found was made in support of the army estimates in the Committee of Supply on 7 December 1742. Here is John Campbell's report of a characteristic performance by Onslow: 'The Speaker spoke, though not so well as he used to do; he was for the question, yet blamed the Ministry for having undertaken the measures that occasioned it, without as he thought the advice of Parliament. I thought he blamed them more than they deserved, and more than was proper for one who voted for the question.'[4]

By the end of the Parliament in 1747 Onslow's prestige and success as Speaker enabled him to express public disapproval of the dissolution without any fear that his re-election to the Chair would be anything but a formality: his objection was that the Parliament had another year to run.[5] After he had

---

[1] Coxe, *Walpole*, III, 579.   [2] H. Walpole, *Letters*, I, 134.
[3] H. Walpole, *George II*, I, 129N. [4] N.L.W. MSS. 1352, fos. 78–9.
[5] H. Walpole, *Letters*, II, 277.

been proposed and seconded when the new Parliament met on 10 November 1747, further speeches were made in his praise, John Willes declaring that 'the great difficulty in this Question is not, Whether Mr. Onslow shall be chosen Speaker? But whether he will do this House the Honour to accept of it?'[1] Consciousness of the strength of his position as Speaker undoubtedly made it possible for Onslow to attack administration measures when during the next few years issues arose on which his opinions differed from those of ministers. Hitherto the Speaker had been content with the policies of Walpole and Pelham despite criticisms stemming from his own prejudices, a dislike of hired foreign soldiers and a preference for the navy and the militia:[2] but this new Parliament saw the introduction of two legislative measures he disliked, the Regency Bill of 1751 and Lord Chancellor Hardwicke's Marriage Bill of 1753.

The Regency Bill became necessary when the death of Frederick Prince of Wales left his young son George heir to the throne. The solution devised by the Pelham administration was to name the Dowager Princess of Wales as prospective regent, but to limit her authority by a council including the Duke of Cumberland, her brother-in-law and chief rival in the royal family. Onslow attended the meetings called by ministers to approve this decision, and openly attacked the measure.[3] It should have been no surprise to administration when he rose in Committee on 16 May 1751 to criticize the bill with the full weight of his authority. 'He professed that he would not have begun an opposition to the Bill, but could not avoid, when once it was opened, to declare that he thought the regulations dangerous; and that having so much studied the constitution, as it was his duty to do, he was obliged to speak his opinion. It was, that the Royal Power must not be divided.' Onslow's interpretation of the constitution was not accepted by the Committee, and he found that for the Speaker to debate a controversial subject diminished the respect for his office. When the Committee was resumed the next day the elder Horace Walpole 'ridiculed the Speaker, and was glad that with

---

[1] Almon, *Debates*, III, 61-74. [2] J. S. Watson, op. cit., pp. 155-7.
[3] J. S. Watson, op cit., p. 160. Onslow told Attorney-General Ryder that he thought 'the disposition of House of Commons' was to give the Regent 'as much power as possible'. Harrowby MSS., doc. 21, 29 Apr. 1751.

all his pomp and protestations he had no more influence'. Onslow nevertheless returned to this subject the next month in his speech at the end of the session. 'The Speaker touched but gently and artfully on the Regency Bill, enough to show his disapprobation, and not enough to reflect on the decision of the House; praying for the King's life, because of the difficulties in which the Princess would be involved in a Regency without Sovereignty.'[1]

In the next session Onslow's only known political gestures were also critical of government policy. He voted with opposition for a reduction of the army in the Committee of Supply on 27 November 1751; and in his end-of-session speech on 26 March 1752 'the Speaker ... launched out in invectives against the management in Scotland.'[2] A more significant political intervention was his attack on the Marriage Bill of 1753. This was a hotly contested measure, involving at least 18 divisions in the Commons during its passage. In the Committee stage Onslow joined Henry Fox in vehement criticism of the bill, and on 28 May made a formidable speech against the clause to annul any marriage contrary to it: he was answered and, Horace Walpole said, misrepresented by Attorney-General Sir Dudley Ryder.[3] In the eyes of Henry Pelham, however, the convenience of a strong and able Speaker outweighed the embarrassment of his occasional hostility. When, before the general election of 1754, the minister heard that Onslow was intending to retire from the Chair, he made a personal visit to the Speaker to urge Onslow to reconsider his decision. Onslow recorded the conversation that persuaded him to change his mind.[4]

> That upon my observing to him, that if I was to be Speaker again, he must not expect that I would act otherwise than I had always done, and which he knew was not always pleasing to Ministers, his answer was, 'Sir, I shall as little like, as any one else in my station, to have a Speaker in a *set* opposition to me and the measures I carry on; but I shall as little like to have a Speaker over-complaisant, either to me or to them.' I thought it nobly said, and mention it to his honor, and the rather as he and I had often differed.

---

[1] H. Walpole, *George II*, I, 126–8, 139, 200.
[2] H. Walpole, *George II*, I, 216, 275.
[3] H. Walpole, *George II*, I, 342; *Letters*, III, 162, 168. *Erthig Chronicles*, I, 327.
[4] *H.M.C. Onslow*, p. 517.

Onslow's re-election to the Chair on 31 May 1754 was again a matter for self-congratulation by members.¹ Henry Pelham had died before the Parliament met, and his brother and successor the Duke of Newcastle was characteristically worried about Onslow's attitude: it is difficult to understand why Hardwicke had to assure him on 14 November 1754 that 'the Speaker, in his conversations in the House was very full of praise of the King's speech and the Address'; for the Address had been voted unanimously that day by the Commons.² In the next year, however, the impending war with France raised again the question of subsidies for foreign soldiers on which Onslow held such strong views. In private conversations during September 1755 he criticized the proposed Hessian and Russian subsidy treaties as being unconstitutional.³ He voted against them in Committee on 12 December 1755.⁴ And in his end-of-session speech on 27 May 1756 he showed his dislike of foreign subsidies and foreign troops.⁵ Even hostile Horace Walpole conceded that, in contrast to politicians like Pulteney and Pitt, on this subject 'Mr. Onslow has preserved his chastity'.⁶

In his last Parliament Onslow also gave further evidence of his role as a interpreter of the constitution. In March 1755 he criticized in Committee a bill strengthening the control of the administration over Scottish sheriffs—depute, evidently scenting a threat to a free judiciary. 'He was against the principle, as it was against the Revolution.'⁷ At the pre-session meeting of office-holders in November 1755 on the King's Speech Onslow objected to the phrase 'my Kingdom and dominions' as contrary to the Act of Settlement, since that had established the need for the prior consent of Parliament for the defence of any foreign possessions of the sovereign. He threatened he would speak to this effect when the matter came before the Committee of Supply, and Lord Hillsborough, who was due to move the Address, promptly announced he would make an alteration to meet the objection.⁸ Onslow

¹ Almon, *Debates*, V, 141–9.
² B.M. Add. MSS. 32737, fo. 344. Almon, *Debates*, V, 149–52.
³ H. Walpole, *Letters*, III, 349–50.   ⁴ B.M. Add. MSS. 35353, fo. 183.
⁵ Cobbett, *Parl. Hist.*, XV, 770.   ⁶ H. Walpole, *Letters*, III, 409.
⁷ H. Walpole, *George II*, II, 15–16.   ⁸ J. S. Watson, op. cit., pp. 163–4.

conceived it to be one of his functions as Speaker to defend the constitution from the executive.

Onslow's career shows that it would be mistaken to assume that his political achievement as Speaker was in any sense to establish the impartiality of the Chair. It had already been acknowledged in the seventeenth century that the Speaker, in his capacity as Chairman, should act fairly between members with conflicting opinions: and Onslow made no attempt to embark on the next step of elevating the Chair altogether above the political arena. Throughout his period of office he made known his opinions on many controversial issues both inside and outside the Commons.[1] During debates members must have been aware that the Speaker himself had given his views on many of the subjects under discussion before him in the House. What was significant to contemporaries was that Onslow retained the Chair despite the fact that many of his opinions had been critical of ministers and their policies. Onslow, indeed, made political capital out of his success as Chairman of the House: for at least his last two Parliaments it would have been very difficult for a minister to remove him from the Chair against his own wishes. This establishment of the practical independence of the Chair from government was, however, a personal achievement only. The example had been given, but the constitutional advance was not to be finally consolidated for nearly a century.

The political significance of Onslow's career in the Chair needs further qualification on two points. It is probable that the surviving evidence exaggerates Onslow's hostility to ministers. His criticisms were likely to attract contemporary notice, for the Speaker was regarded as virtually a member of the administration. There may well have been many silent votes and unrecorded speeches by Onslow in support of government. The second consideration is that no important change occurred in the political background throughout his tenure of the Chair. The two ministers, Walpole and Pelham, in power at the times of his successive nominations to the Chair, were 'old Whigs', like Onslow himself. No serious clash ever occurred between the Speaker and administration.

---

[1] For further instances see J. S. Watson, op. cit., pp. 145–65.

In his preparations of about 1750 for the accession of Prince Frederick, Lord Egmont assumed that Onslow would support the Pelham group in opposition to the new administration he was planning,[1] and in 1760 Lord Hardwicke made a comment to Newcastle that summarized Onslow's political behaviour in one sentence: 'The present Speaker, our good friend, will sometimes take up Patriotic Notions, and bounce in the Chair; but these vanish in him and give no real wounds':[2] Onslow's tenure of the Chair during a time of political stability did not provide a suitable precedent for periods of controversy.

The Duke of Newcastle, as First Lord of the Treasury, began to consider the appointment of a successor to Onslow by 1760. In August of that year, indeed, he was still hoping that Onslow would continue in the Chair: for the Speaker visited him to say 'that if I wished . . . he should continue another Parliament, *that* would have more weight with him than anything else'.[3] Onslow, however, decided not to seek re-election to the Chair at the age of sixty-nine, and accepted a pension of £3,000 for two lives, his own and that of his son. Even before his formal retirement in March 1761 Horace Walpole regarded the choice of his successor as firm news. 'George Grenville is to be Speaker.'[4] Grenville, then Treasurer of the Navy, was a prominent figure in the Commons but had never held high office. A man keenly interested in both the procedure and the prestige of the House, he might well have proved an excellent choice for the Chair. When Newcastle offered him the post, Grenville insisted on consulting the new king George III personally, and his recollection of the interview was recorded two years later by James Harris:[5] 'The King approved the measure, said he should keep his office of Treasurer of the Navy; that he would make Cabinet Counsellor and that if his health did not permit it, he should resign his Speakership.'

This plan was abandoned after the resignation of William Pitt as Secretary of State on 2 October 1761. Grenville refused an offer of this post from the King's favourite, Lord Bute; but, at the request of George III, agreed to assume the leadership of

[1] *Camden Miscellany XXIII*, p. 170.   [2] B.M. Add. MSS. 32910, fo. 168.
[3] B.M. Add. MSS. 35419, fo. 253.   [4] H. Walpole, *Letters*, V, 37.
[5] Malmesbury MSS. Memo. of 14 Apr. 1763.

the Commons. Part of the price was the reversion of the Teller-ship of the Exchequer, an office that his eldest son obtained for life in 1764.[1] Horace Walpole, writing later with the advantage of hindsight, considered Grenville's decision to have been a mistake.

Grenville had been destined for Speaker; an office to which his drudgery was suited; and which, being properly the most neutral place in government, would have excused him from entering into the contest between Mr. Pitt and the Favourite. But Grenville's temper, though plodding and laborious, had not the usual con-comitant prudence. He lent himself to the views of Lord Bute to promote his own ... Grenville, who would have filled the chair with spirit and knowledge, had been taken off to a province for which he was far less qualified.[2]

Grenville himself expressed regret when in his new role he began to offer the Chair to other candidates.[3]

The King having been pleased to signify to me his earnest wishes that I should decline going into the Chair of the House of Com-mons ... it becomes me from every motive both of gratitude and duty to obey, though I will freely own to you, for many reasons, that I do it in this particular and at this time with the greatest reluctancy, as I should have looked upon the Chair as the highest honour that could have befallen me, and as a safe retreat from those storms and that uneasiness to which all other public situations, and more especially at this juncture, are unavoidably exposed.

After Grenville's withdrawal, Newcastle fought an un-successful battle with Lord Bute for another candidate with an 'old Whig' tradition. He considered Edward Bacon, M.P. for Norwich, 'who had more Whiggism than abilities', accord-ing to Horace Walpole.[4] Bacon was then at the Board of Trade, and also Chairman of the Committee of Privileges and Elections. But Newcastle found that he was unpopular, and did not press his candidature. The Duke also suggested Sir George Savile, who had been M.P. for Yorkshire only since 1759, informing Gren-ville on 7 October that 'I find a Tory will not go down well.' This was a riposte to Lord Bute's nomination of Thomas Prowse, who had sat for Somerset since 1740 with a record of

---

[1] Fortescue, *Corr. of George III*, IV, p. 146.
[2] H. Walpole, *George III*, I, 65–7.
[3] *Grenville Papers*, I, 398.   [4] H. Walpole, *George III*, I, 68.

'country party' opposition. But within a week Newcastle told Grenville that he had changed his mind. 'Since I saw you I have received some letters from some of my principal Whig friends (not Courtiers) in the country, and I am very happy to find that Mr. Prowse will go down very well with them, and, indeed, better than anybody. This eases me of the only difficulty which I would ever have, and I hope you may make good use of it, as it shows how unanimously and honourably Mr. Prowse will be chose.'[1] Prowse, however, refused the offer of the Chair now formally made to him by Grenville, on grounds of ill-health.[2]

The post eventually fell to Sir John Cust, M.P. for Grantham since 1743. A pleasant man who had given offence to nobody by either his character or his politics, Cust was to prove an unfortunate choice; and Newcastle displayed sagacity as well as pique in his complete disclaimer of any responsibility for this final selection. 'He is not of my recommendation; and consequently I am not answerable for his fitness for his office.'[3] Nor was Cust a nominee of Lord Bute. He had been Clerk of the Household to Frederick, Prince of Wales, from 1747 to his death in 1751, and thereafter to the Dowager Princess: but he had resigned this post in 1756 through dislike of the growing influence of Lord Bute at the court of the young Prince. This action was found to be an obstacle in 1761 by Sir John's brothers when they initiated negotiations on his behalf over the Chair; but his nomination soon obtained the approval of both Grenville and Lord Bute.[4] On 3 October 1761 Cust was proposed by Grenville himself, the Leader of the House, and seconded by Lord Barrington, then Chancellor of the Exchequer: after a third flattering speech from his friend Lord Egmont he was placed in the Chair without any opposition or further debate.[5]

A Lincolnshire squire of respectable family rather than substantial estate, Sir John Cust became a man of significant wealth only at his election to the Chair, when his mother made over to him an estate at Belton in his own county that she had inherited in 1754 from her brother Lord Tyrconnel.[6] Cust

[1] *Grenville Papers*, I, 393–7. [2] *Grenville Papers*, I, 398–403.
[3] B.M. Add. MSS. 32929, fo. 409. [4] *Cust Family Records*, III, 205–8.
[5] Harris Diary, 3 Oct. 1761. [6] *Erthig Chronicles*, II, 98.

neither needed nor received an office from government while
he was Speaker; but he regarded it as part of his duty to give
advice and assistance to ministers. He attended their pre-
Cockpit meetings of leading members of the House, at least
during the Grenville and Rockingham administrations.[1] He
was also present at other meetings on matters of policy particularly concerned with either the House of Commons or the
constitution: only illness prevented him from attending one
on 5 November 1763 at George Grenville's house on the *North
Briton* case; and he was among some thirty members who met
there on 23 April 1765 on the proposed Regency Bill.[2] The
caveat should be added, however, that many known instances
of Cust's co-operation with government occurred during
Grenville's ministry, and may have reflected to some extent
his personal predilections.

The political aspect of the Speaker's functions exposed Cust
to the charge of pro-administration bias, although only one
direct attack on him in the House has been found: in the debate
of 16 November 1763, three days after Cust had attended a
ministerial meeting, opposition member William Beckford
blamed 'the communication which the Speaker seemed to
have with the Crown'.[3] The background to Cust's re-election
as Speaker in 1768 emphasized the continuing contemporary
view of the Chair as an adjunct of the administration. By that
time none of the politicians concerned with the original choice
of Cust in 1761 were in office: yet the Rockingham group then
in opposition considered the nomination of a rival candidate
in William Dowdeswell, who had been Chancellor of the
Exchequer in the first Rockingham ministry of 1765–1766 and
was their leading spokesman in the House. Two years earlier,
just after the dismissal of the Rockingham administration, there
had been a rumour that Cust would receive a peerage and
Dowdeswell take the Chair: but Grenville was informed, or
perhaps misinformed, that Dowdeswell had been so offended
at being replaced as Chancellor of the Exchequer by Charles
Townshend that he had refused to be Speaker or accept any
other office.[4] Cust's applications for a peerage in 1766 and

---

[1] Harris Diary, 13 Nov. 1763 and 8 Jan. 1765. *Grenville Papers*, III, 111.
[2] Harris Diary, 5 Nov. 1763 and 23 Apr. 1765.
[3] Newdegate MSS., B2543.   [4] *Grenville Papers*, III, 281, 289.

1767 were unsuccessful;[1] but administration accepted the already implicit obligation to retain a Speaker willing to serve. The opposition plan to challenge ministers by the rival candidature of Dowdeswell was dropped:[2] and on 10 May 1768 Sir John Cust was unanimously chosen after being proposed by Lord Charles Spencer and seconded by Lord Palmerston, both members of the Admiralty Board.[3]

An ambivalent attitude to the Chair was bound to exist so long as the Speaker remained as an active politician. Cust followed Onslow's practice, and made known his opinion on major political controversies during his period of office. His approval of the decision to end the Seven Years' War was signified in a speech presenting bills to the King on 12 April 1763: he then 'praised the Peace, which had put an end to a bloody, and expensive war'.[4] In the Stamp Act debates Cust took the opportunity to express his views in Committee: he spoke on 5 and 7 February 1766, supporting Grenville's policy of strong measures against the American colonies in criticism of the current Rockingham ministry.[5] The issues arising from the Middlesex Election case were never discussed in Committee while Cust was Speaker, but he left contemporaries in no doubt of his opinion, even taking political advantage of his office. When during the summer of 1769 the opposition leaders were organizing a campaign of petitions on the subject from the constituencies, Sir John personally intervened to frustrate the attempt to send one from Lincoln: Rockingham was informed by Frederick Montagu in July that 'the Speaker came to explain the resolution of the House of Commons.'[6] Cust was strongly critical of the opposition tactics, for here is a comment on the petitioning movement from a letter of 5 November: 'I wish . . . that gentlemen of Property and real well-wishers to this Country would set their faces against the Creations and Factions.'[7]

Only once, however, was Sir John Cust accused of conduct in the Chair biased by his own personal opinions: the incident

[1] *Cust Family Records*, III, 266–7.
[2] B.M. Add. MSS. 32989, fos. 396–400. *Grenville Papers*, III, 288.
[3] B.M. Eg. MSS. 215, pp. 1–9.   [4] Harris Diary, 12 Apr. 1763.
[5] Newdegate MSS. B 2546/16. *Parliamentary Diary of Nathaniel Ryder*, p. 291.
[6] Wentworth Woodhouse MSS. R1–1212.
[7] *Erthig Chronicles*, II, 105–6.

arose not from an important issue, but over the Cumberland Election of 1768. On 9 March 1769 Cust spoke three times when arguing with George Grenville over the proceedings against the sheriff. Edmund Burke rose to complain of the Speaker's behaviour: 'My eyes are dim. Some people have thought the Chair was in the debate. Sir, they were wrong: if all their senses interposed, they were wrong. The Chair was not in debate.' Hans Stanley rose to defend the Speaker: 'I have always understood that however unusual for the Chair in matters of a political nature to give his opinion, yet in matters relative to the Order it was usual.' The matter ended with this excuse.[1]

The resignation and death of Sir John Cust in January 1770 produced a sudden vacancy in the Chair. The stormy debates of the previous decade had made it clear that the first requisite in a new Speaker must be strength of character, and the choice of the Duke of Grafton, First Lord of the Treasury, fell on Sir Fletcher Norton. Although a lawyer of considerable ability, Norton was not regarded by contemporaries as a man of integrity. The common opinion was not merely that Norton concerned himself more with profits than principles in his practice at the Bar, but that he asked exorbitant fees and sometimes even acted for both sides in the same case: a contemporary nickname for him was 'Sir Bull Face Double Fee'.[2] Norton's political connections also made him suspect in the eyes of many professed 'Whigs'. It had been during Lord Bute's ministry that he became Solicitor-General, in June 1762: and from December 1763 until July 1765 he was Attorney-General under Grenville, taking a foremost part in the debates arising from the *North Briton* case. It was on 17 February 1764, in criticism of the famous opposition motion to declare general warrants illegal, that Norton made this long-remembered remark when arguing that Parliament sat to make laws and not to expound them: 'If I was a Judge I should pay no more

---

[1] B.M. Eg. MSS. 219, pp. 99–100.

[2] For adverse contemporary comments on his character see H. Walpole, *George III*, I, 189; Wraxall, *Memoirs*, I, 373; and Dasent, *Speakers*, pp. 276–7. See *Erthig Chronicles*, II, 36, for a remark in 1768 by Brownlow Cust, M.P., that 'he never goes into the country though it should even be upon the Home Circuit for less than £300'.

regard to this resolution than to that of a drunken porter.' However sound the legal doctrine, such a blunt statement, as Horace Walpole commented, was 'a sentence that would have made Old Onslow thunder forth indignation'.[1] Able but unpopular and distrusted, Norton was in the political wilderness from 1765 until the Duke of Grafton secured his support in 1769 by a legal sinecure of £3,000 a year.

The negotiations for his acceptance of the Chair the next year were conducted through an intermediary, Richard Rigby, Paymaster-General of the Forces. Norton accepted the offer only with reluctance, and on condition both that he could keep his sinecure and that he might resign the Chair to take the first vacant place as Lord Chief Justice.[2] Cust's resignation coincided with the disintegration of the Grafton ministry during the same month: and Horace Walpole regarded the offer of the Chair as compensation to Norton for the simultaneous elevation of his great rival Charles Yorke to the post of Lord Chancellor. 'Another great thorn is drawn out of its side, Sir Fletcher Norton, who vomited fire and flame on Yorke's promotion, having consented to be Speaker of the House of Commons. I do not yet hear whether the opposition will set up a candidate for the chair against him. Nothing can exceed the badness of his character even in this bad age; yet I think he can do less hurt in the Speaker's chair than anywhere else.'[3] When Yorke's sudden death upset the ministerial reorganization, however, Walpole paid a reluctant tribute to Norton on 22 January 1770, the day fixed for the election of the new Speaker: 'Even Sir Fletcher Norton acts moderation. He was destined for Speaker of the House of Commons. On Yorke's death it was expected that he would again push to be Chancellor. No such thing: he says he will not avail himself of the distresses of Government; but, having consented to be Speaker, will remain so . . . there is Cassius as self-denying as Brutus.'[4]

During the week before the election circular letters went out to administration supporters, requesting support for Norton.[5]

---

[1] H. Walpole, *George III*, I, 298.

[2] This is the account Norton gave to the House on 13 Mar. 1780, and it was confirmed by Rigby. Almon, *Parl. Reg.*, XVII, 330–3.

[3] H. Walpole, *Letters*, VII, 354.   [4] H. Walpole, *Letters*, VII, 357.

[5] *London Evening Post*, 23 Jan. 1770.

Ministers must have been aware that he would not be a popular choice: there was widespread detestation of his personal character; members jealous for the honour of the Commons might dislike the prospect of having as the symbol and guardian of their prestige a man who had publicly compared a resolution of the House with 'the opinion of a drunken porter'; and there was the fear of opposition members that Norton was a bully chosen to coerce them during debates. There resulted the first contest for the Chair since 1714. This resistance to Norton was spontaneous, not the concerted strategy of the opposition leaders: for Horace Walpole informed Sir Horace Mann next day that 'two or three of the opposition, only to mark their disgust to him, proposed the younger Thomas Townshend, one as little qualified for the office as you are, and whose consent they had not asked.' The tactic was known the day before to Solicitor-General John Dunning, who thought the candidature instead of William Dowdeswell or George Grenville against Norton would be successful.[1]

Sir Fletcher Norton was proposed by Lord North, Leader of the House and Chancellor of the Exchequer; he urged, among other arguments, the advantage of having lawyers as Speakers. 'They acquire an early knowledge of business, and by that early knowledge, a facility and dispatch in business . . . they also learn a much more important science, a thorough knowledge, and with it a hearty and zealous love of our excellent constitution.' A second point in Norton's favour was his previous administrative experience. 'We should naturally look for some person whose fidelity and abilities have been tried in offices of great trust, nicety and importance.' Rigby seconded the motion, but there followed a speech by a leading member of the Rockingham group, Lord John Cavendish. He questioned the need of the Speaker having held offices of trust or of his being a lawyer. 'I have heard it said by Mr. Onslow, that it was a point got to the constitution, when the Chair was taken from the long robe.' In proposing the younger Thomas Townshend, avowedly without his permission, Lord John stressed the personal qualities popularly supposed to be lacking in Norton: 'The first qualification is temper, a sense

---

[1] H. Walpole, *Letters*, VII, 358. P. Brown, *The Chathamites*, p. 289.

of honour, integrity.' Lord George Sackville seconded him, and the House then heard the two candidates. Norton accepted nomination and Townshend declined. His claims were nevertheless urged by Frederick Montagu and Edmund Burke; and opposition members forced a division over the election of Norton, who was chosen by 237 votes to 121, receiving the votes of Townshend and his personal friends.[1]

Many contemporaries expected that Norton would be not only a formidable but also a partisan Speaker. At first, opposition fears of unfair conduct seemed to be justified by his quarrel on 16 February 1770 with an old enemy, Sir William Meredith, whom he accused of 'uncandid' behaviour by raising a point of order without previous notice to the Chair. An unsuccessful vote of censure on the Speaker was then moved, and during the debate thinly veiled attacks were made on Norton. Constantine Phipps asserted, 'Two pillars support that Chair, experience and impartiality. Experience you have told us you have not.' Isaac Barré declared, 'We may see pensioners lifted there to preside over us.'[2] The incident aroused comment outside the House. Former M.P. Thomas Lewis thought that 'Norton, being so long accustomed by his audacious insolent temper to bear down all before him, is, I hope, made sensible it will not do there.'[3] Less optimistic was this observation in the hostile *London Evening Post* six days later:

> Freedom of speech, and other essential orders of a House, are very likely to be endangered by one who knows no order but a majority, and if he ventured to speak so plainly whilst he was aiming at that honour, which has since been conferred upon him, how will he, on all occasions, tyranise with a majority that he is sure of finding, now he is possessed of the Chair.

Norton, although he often made the customary professions of impartiality, was not always able to suppress his personal feelings about business before him in the Chair. At least twice, on 14 December 1770 and 7 April 1773, he read out motions in a contemptuous manner.[4] On 12 March 1771, too, he made

[1] B.M. Eg. MSS. 3711, pp. 66–81. H. Walpole, *George III*, IV, 37.
[2] B.M. Eg. MSS. 220, pp. 114–48.   [3] Harpton MSS., no. C. 49.
[4] B.M. Eg. MSS. 223, p. 514; 245, p. 274.

several comments on the obstructive tactics of some opposition members during the measures against the printers of newspapers containing reports of debates. Norton first remarked that he was 'tired with the proceedings'. Soon afterwards he deliberately explained that he meant 'not bodily fatigued, but hurt with the proceedings'. Barré at once asked if the Speaker meant to cast reproach on any members, and Norton disclaimed any such idea: 'Not a word escaped my lips that meant to throw blame upon either side.' But only a few minutes later he could not forbear to comment, 'This will go into the *Journals*. What will posterity say?'[1] Such partisan behaviour in the Chair was constitutionally a retrograde step: but that it resulted from Norton's temperament not from his deliberate policy was shown by an incident of 20 February 1771. The occasion was a debate on a bill to alter the Nullum Tempus Act, a subject of particular delicacy for Norton. It was he, acting for Sir James Lowther, who had discovered an apparent flaw in a grant of crown lands in Cumberland to the Duke of Portland that had given rise to the contemporary *cause célèbre* of the legislation and the proposed amendment.[2] When Sir William Bagot appealed for the opinion of the Chair on the effect of the bill, Norton therefore confessed, 'I feel myself extremely unhappy to be appealed to in anything relative to this question because the whole House knows the part I have taken in this matter. I am therefore mistrustful of myself.' Lord George Cavendish then spoke to order: 'Nothing is so great disorder as for the Speaker to deliver his opinion from the Chair.' Norton agreed: 'I honour myself that I am the servant of the House. I am, and happy too I have given no opinion.' Lord George Cavendish explained, 'I only thought it necessary in me to speak to order to object to what I thought the most disorderly proceeding I ever heard. To call upon the Speaker to give his opinion upon the point in debate is the most irregular thing that could be.'[3]

Apprehensions about the partisan conduct of Norton in the Chair had little real substance, and the fear that he would be a

---

[1] B.M. Eg. MSS. 226, pp. 72–80.

[2] Bonsall, *Sir James Lowther and Cumberland and Westmorland Elections 1754–1775*, p. 83.

[3] B.M. Eg. MSS. 225, pp. 63–4.

tool of administration proved to be entirely without foundation. There was never a personal relationship between Norton and Lord North comparable to that between Onslow and Sir Robert Walpole. North had not been responsible for Sir Fletcher's appointment; and the minister was unwilling to consult and too indolent to flatter the Speaker. As early as 17 March 1770 Norton complained to members of the opposition Grenville group that Lord North had left him 'totally uninformed of the intention to sit after Easter'.[1] Norton himself was too demanding and too outspoken. In 1771 he pressed a demand for a peerage by equivocal conduct in the Chair: Lord North was apprehensive, though wrongly, that in the main debate on the Falkland Islands crisis on 13 February the Speaker would deny administration the customary advantage of moving an Address of Thanks.[2] In 1772 one rumour put Norton's terms as 'the assurance of a peerage' and a place in the Admiralty for his son.[3] Pique at the refusal of government to grant him any favours led Norton in that year to embarrass the ministry by his interventions in the debates on the Royal Family Marriage Bill. He made twenty speeches on the bill during the Committee stage; and, although he was ostensibly a supporter of the measure, his legal sniping soon led the administration to regard him as an enemy. In a long speech of 13 March Norton pointed out various difficulties in the way of any definition of the royal family, and rose several times later to defend his views.[4] On 16 March, while purporting to defend the clause applying the bill to all descendants of George II, his comments on its extensive nature aroused so much uneasiness among members that he was attacked by Attorney-General Edward Thurlow.[5] On 18 March Norton successfully moved an amendment that royal consent should be formally signified by the Great Seal.[6] Finally, on 20 March, criticizing the penalty clause, he announced that it referred to a non-existent statute of Richard II's reign.[7] If Norton's behaviour was meant to force administration to buy him off,

---

[1] Malmesbury MSS., Memo. of 17 Mar. 1770.
[2] *London Evening Post*, 23 Feb. 1771.   [3] B.M. Add. MSS. 29133, fo. 94.
[4] B.M. Eg. MSS. 236, pp. 198–221, 234–7; 237, pp. 18–19, 41, 42.
[5] B.M. Eg. MSS. 237, pp. 237–70.   [6] B.M. Eg. MSS. 238, pp. 76–96.
[7] B.M. Eg. MSS. 238, pp. 251–78.

the manoeuvre was a disastrous failure. Here is Horace Walpole's comment for 20 March: 'The Speaker was grown a strong opponent . . . He wanted a peerage for his wife, a lieutenant-colonelcy for his son, and to be Chancellor himself, but lost the Court, was given up by the Opposition, and left alone the next day.'[1]

Norton encountered so much criticism after his speeches on this bill that he seldom spoke afterwards in Committee:[2] but he did express his opinions on the two important subjects that next came before the Commons. On 23 March 1773 he made three speeches expounding the view that the Crown had a right to the territories of the East India Company.[3] And on 28 March 1774 he voiced his approval of the American legislation proposed that year.[4] Moreover, when on 10 February 1775 Norton was apparently asked for his legal opinion on the colonial situation, he gave it in unequivocal terms: 'The law does not know the word *rebellion*. Levying war against the King is treason; so is endeavouring to wrest the sword out of the hands of the executive power.'[5]

By the general election of 1774 Norton's conduct had not yet raised any administration doubts over his continued tenure of the Chair, except perhaps his insatiable demands for reward. Horace Walpole heard the story that 'when Lord North proposed to him to be Speaker again, he said "And is that all?", intimating he expected a bribe for taking so great an office.'[6] Sir Fletcher Norton was re-elected Speaker without opposition on 29 November 1774, being proposed by Lord Guernsey and seconded by Lord Robert Spencer.[7] Two days earlier George III had heard a rumour that John Wilkes intended to propose for Speaker a former waiter just elected to the House, Robert Mackreth. The scandalized King wrote to North, 'this would appear impossible to be true if the author's character was not known to be so void of decency': but Wilkes did not push the joke any further.[8]

[1] H. Walpole, *Last Journals*, I, 62.   [2] Almon, *Parl. Reg.*, XVII, 320.
[3] B.M. Eg. MSS. 245, pp. 109–10.
[4] Fortescue, *Corr. of George III*, III, p. 87. H. Walpole, *Last Journals*, I, 433.
[5] Almon, *Parl. Reg.*, I, 174.   [6] H. Walpole, *Last Journals*, I, 410.
[7] Almon, *Parl. Reg.*, I, 3.
[8] Fortescue, *Corr. of George III*, III, p. 154.

The event that decided Sir Fletcher Norton's future career was his speech of 7 May 1777 when he presented the King with a 'Bill for the better support of His Majesty's Household, and of the Honour and Dignity of the Crown of Great Britain'. With reference to this payment of the Civil List Debt, the Speaker addressed George III in these words: 'In a time of public distress, full of difficulty and danger, their constituents labouring under burdens almost too heavy to be borne, your faithful Commons postponed all other business, and, with as much dispatch as the nature of their proceedings would admit, have not only granted to your Majesty a large present supply, but also a very great additional revenue; great, beyond example; great beyond your Majesty's highest expense.' Several witnesses stated that Norton had said 'wants' instead of 'expense', an even more offensive remark: but the Speaker denied this attribution, and the official version of the speech was that given above.[1]

Two days later Norton, from the Chair, drew the attention of members to criticism of him in the House that day by Paymaster-General Richard Rigby, who promptly rose and 'spoke of the Chair in terms very nearly bordering on disrespect. Insisted that he had a right to animadvert on the Speaker's speech, or on his conduct, within or without that House, if he thought it improper. . . . The Speaker was no more than another member, and he was as free to differ from the chair as from any other individual in that House. He proceeded to great heat, which seemed to make the treasury bench uneasy.' Charles James Fox perceived that Rigby had pressed the matter too far, and seized the chance to make political capital for the opposition. Announcing that he would take the sense of the House on a resolution 'which, if negatived, in his opinion the Speaker could not sit longer in that chair with reputation to himself or be further serviceable in his station, after being publicily deserted, bullied, and disgraced', Fox proposed the following motion. 'That the Speaker of this House, in his speech to his Majesty at the bar of the House of Peers on Wednesday last . . . did express with just and proper energy, the zeal of this House for the support of the honour and

---

[1] Almon, *Parl. Reg.*, VII, 152. *Commons Journals*, XXXVI, 478–9.

dignity of the crown in circumstances of great public charge.'

Norton then stated that he would not remain in the Chair if the motion was rejected, and the administration was in a dilemma. Passage of the resolution would involve approval of Norton's speech and, as Horace Walpole observed, 'consequently the condemnation of their own act'.[1] But ejection of the Speaker from office in such circumstances was unthinkable, as Sir Fletcher well knew. He was again exploiting, as on 16 February 1770, the virtual inability of the House to pass a vote of censure on the Chair. All ministerial evasion failed. Welbore Ellis suggested that the motion should be withdrawn, as Norton had probably spoken without notes. He was supported by Attorney-General Thurlow, who declared that the Speaker had merely expressed his own opinion. Rigby proposed to evade the question by an adjournment, but withdrew this motion on learning that the Speaker would then still resign. In the end Fox's resolution was carried 'without a division, almost unanimously', being followed by a vote of thanks to the Speaker.[2]

This incident severed the normal relationship of government and Speaker. In 1780 Norton declared that since 1777 Lord North had withdrawn 'even the appearance of all friendship and confidence'. The ministry rarely sent to him for advice, and seldom carried out any that had been given.[3] The Speaker apparently sought to heal the breach in the summer of 1778, for he then returned to town for an audience with the King. George III granted the interview, on 26 June, but assured Lord North beforehand, 'I shall very patiently hear him and certainly say as little as possible.'[4] Norton presumably learnt that there was no way back to favour; and he sided against administration in the few speeches he later made in Committee.[5] The highlight of the Speaker's opposition career was an episode of 13 March 1780, during a Committee on Edmund Burke's Establishment Bill. Charles James Fox called on Sir Fletcher Norton, 'as the highest legal authority in the

---

[1] H. Walpole, *Letters*, X, 51.   [2] Almon, *Parl. Reg.*, VII, 168–75.
[3] Almon, *Parl. Reg.*, XVII, 327–9.
[4] Fortescue, *Corr. of George III*, IV, p. 173.
[5] See, for example, Almon, *Parl. Reg.*, XI, 192; XIII, 509.

kingdom', to give his opinion on the competence of the House to control the Civil List expenditure. 'The Speaker's secretary rushed through the side gallery, and repaired instantly into the Speaker's chamber. Sir Fletcher Norton now made his appearance, and took his seat on the Treasury Bench.' From there he announced support of the bill, commenting that a stand over royal expenditure should have been made in 1777. Although interference in the King's own household needed strong justification, and he therefore disapproved of some clauses, it was right that Parliament should control 'that part of the Civil list appropriated to the special circumstances of government'. Norton said that he had been consulted on the bill, and the whole scene may well have been staged to win support for it: observer Horace Walpole expected that 'all the mercenaries will follow Sir Fletcher, and pretend it is the cry of the nation they follow.'[1]

At the end of his speech Norton made a direct attack on Lord North: 'He was not a friend to the noble Lord, and he had repeated proofs that the noble Lord was no friend of his.' The Speaker's motive was indignation at a rumour that Attorney-General Wedderburn was soon to be made Chief Justice of the Court of Common Pleas. This would be contrary to the arrangement of 1770 made when Norton had agreed to take the Chair, and of which he gave the House full details after North had denied all knowledge of that negotiation. Lord North thereupon said that 'he neither knew of the transaction at the time, nor looked upon himself bound when he did come into office by any such promise.'[2] This incident, a public wrangle between the Leader of the House and the Speaker about the bargaining behind the appointment to the Chair, was detrimental to the dignity of the House. Horace Walpole described it as 'a strange scene of Billingsgate between the Speaker and the minister'.[3] At the next meeting of the Committee, on 20 March, Norton rose to apologize to the House for his behaviour. He had introduced irrelevant matters, 'but maintained the truth of what he had asserted. He said he knew how much he had been abused in newspapers for what he had

---

[1] Almon, *Parl. Reg.*, XVII, 318–25. H. Walpole, *Letters*, XI, 142.
[2] Almon, *Parl. Reg.*, XVII, 327–33.   [3] H. Walpole, *Letters*, XI, 141.

said, but that he despised them, and only desired to excuse himself to the House.'[1]

Sir Fletcher Norton spoke against administration during two later debates in Committee that session. He supported Dunning's famous motion of 6 April on the influence of the Crown: and on 1 May he denounced Lord North's proposal to appoint non-Parliamentary Commissioners of Accounts as unconstitutional delegation of power to a committee of strangers.[2] By that time it must have been apparent to all political observers that Norton's retention of the Chair would not be countenanced by the ministry for longer than was necessary. On 14 April, when Norton hinted at resignation on the ground of ill-health, Lord North declared that 'he hoped the learned gentleman had no real thoughts of resigning; but if he had . . . he thought it would be very proper for the House to know it in time'.[3] This exchange may have been a hint by the Speaker that he would retire if offered a suitable inducement, and North's refusal to pay the price. George III was sceptical about Norton's state of health when replying to North's report of events: 'I have not the smallest doubt that the Speaker has pleaded illness to enable the Opposition to pursue the amusement at Newmarket the next week.'[4] Three days later Secretary at War Charles Jenkinson gave the King a detailed account of the situation: 'Though the present Speaker is ill, I am persuaded that he and his friends make him worse than he really is, and he will appear in the House of Commons on Monday next or not, as it will best answer his purpose.' Norton was negotiating with both Lord North and opposition leader Lord Rockingham, 'and he will act according to . . . the Bargain he is able to make with either Party.' Lord North himself was looking for a new Speaker. One member he had in mind was Jenkinson's own brother-in-law and cousin Charles Cornwall, who was a Lord of the Treasury: but Jenkinson believed that North's preference was for Frederick Montagu.[5] Political gossip also named Montagu, and correctly.[6] North's

---

[1] H. Walpole, *Last Journals*, II, 289.
[2] Almon, *Parl. Reg.*, XVII, 461–5, 618–19.
[3] Almon, *Parl. Reg.*, XVII, 528.
[4] Fortescue, *Corr. of George III*, V, p. 43–4.
[5] Fortescue, *Corr. of George III*, V, p. 46.
[6] H. Walpole, *Letters*, XI, 161.

choice overrode the fact that Montagu was a follower of Rockingham and M.P. for a borough, Higham Ferrers, of which the Marquess was patron. For he was also a personal friend and relative of Lord North himself, and a man greatly respected in the House. Lord Advocate Henry Dundas thought him 'a man of honour, candour and integrity . . . in his person both sides would concur in maintaining the decency, dignity, and order of the House'. Frederick Montagu possessed independent means; Parliamentary experience, having been a member since 1759; and legal knowledge, becoming a Bencher of Lincoln's Inn in 1782. Lord North was confident that his nomination would meet with unanimous support.[1] The projected change came to nothing in April because Norton retained the Chair, but North revived the plan after the general election in the autumn of that year. Montagu was offered the Chair in October, but despite pressure to accept from both North and Rockingham, he declined because of the probable strain on his health and the political delicacy of his position: a member so closely associated with opposition could not honourably accept an office bestowed by administration.[2]

A clash over the appointment of a new Speaker could not now be avoided. Norton's position gave the opposition a weapon too tempting to be disregarded when the administration choice fell on a partisan candidate. North put forward his second choice, Charles Wolfran Cornwall, who resigned his position as a Lord of the Treasury merely to take the Chair instead. When the new Parliament met on 31 October, Cornwall was proposed by Lord George Germain, Secretary of State for the Colonies, who referred to Norton's 'precarious state of health'. After Cornwall had been seconded by Treasurer of the Navy Welbore Ellis, opposition member John Dunning rose to express his astonishment that Norton had not been proposed. Declaring that the Chair was not vacant, he moved that 'Sir Fletcher Norton be continued Speaker', and was seconded by Thomas Townshend, the opposition nominee against Norton in 1770. Norton then announced that he had

---

[1] See the biography of Montagu in Namier and Brooke, *The House of Commons 1754–1790*, III, 153–5.
[2] Much of the relevant correspondence is printed by J. E. Tyler, op. cit., pp. 363–78.

already resolved not to be Speaker again, on grounds of ill-health, but that he had been disgracefully dismissed without the courtesy of any previous intimation. Charles James Fox declared that 'to appoint a successor in this way is not without a precedent, but extremely unusual.' The pretext of official concern for Norton's health was discarded by Paymaster-General Richard Rigby. He said that it was not 'part of the constitutional law of Parliament, that when a member was once elected to the Chair of the House, he was to sit there as long as he pleased', and even attacked Norton's capacity as Speaker. Rigby put the debate in terms of political simplicity. 'As to the mighty secret, the true cause of moving for a new Speaker by one side of the House, and supporting the old Speaker by the other, it was reducible to a very simple fact, and when put in plain English . . . was no more than this, "We'll vote for you if you'll be for us."' With the question a clear alignment between administration and opposition the ministry carried Cornwall's election by 203 votes to 134.[1]

A further opposition attempt to embarrass government on the question occurred on 20 November, when Thomas Townshend proposed a vote of thanks to the late Speaker. He put forward a simple motion, in a vain hope of unanimity, and did not copy the only precedent, the motion of thanks to Onslow in 1761 with its references to 'dignity, ability and impartiality'. His speech, indeed, was something of a back-handed compliment to Norton. The motion was opposed by six out of eleven speakers in the subsequent debate, and Colonel George Onslow compared the presenting-speeches of his uncle, which had merely expressed a desire for economy, with Norton's insult of 1777 both to the Commons and to the throne. A thin and unenthusiastic House carried the motion by 136 votes to 96.[2] Once again the administration did not care to slight the Chair. Here is Horace Walpole's comment on that 'odd interlude in the House of Commons. Some of the opposition proposed to thank the late Speaker, Sir Fletcher. Lord North had promised not to gainsay it. Neither side could admire such a worthless fellow; those he has left, less than those who have adopted him; and yet the vote of thanks passed

---

[1] Debrett, *Parl. Reg.*, I, 2–17.   [2] Debrett, *Parl. Reg.*, I, 103–16.

by a majority of forty—and so one may be thanked for being a rogue on all sides.'[1]

Sir Fletcher Norton was the first Hanoverian Speaker to resume his seat as an ordinary member of the House. After 31 October 1780 he did not attend again until 17 February 1781, when, in a formal exchange of courtesies, Speaker Cornwall addressed him on his entry into the chamber and Norton replied.[2] Sir Fletcher then resumed a normal role in debate, and his prestige as former Speaker gave his views added weight. 'The House was all attention' when he rose to speak on 26 March 1781 in support of an opposition motion.[3] Norton played a part in the final Parliamentary attack on the North ministry, speaking for the opposition in four important debates.[4]

As soon as the opposition took office the Rockingham group raised the question of a peerage for the former Speaker, a request clearly unwelcome to the King, for on 27 March 1782 Lord Shelburne told George III, 'I had a good deal of difficulty again last night to put off Sir Fletcher Norton's Peerage *for the present*.'[5] The idea was already current that service in the Speaker's Chair should be rewarded by a peerage. Lord Chief Justice William De Grey, pressing for a peerage in 1778, reminded Lord North that every Attorney-General of the reign had obtained one except Norton and himself, and 'that Sir Fletcher is in a situation that leads to a coronet'.[6] Norton himself had already applied for a peerage: so had Sir John Cust before him, and a tacit acknowledgement that a retiring Speaker had a claim to such an honour was given after Cust's resignation on 17 January 1770. Three days later Lord North sent for his elder son Brownlow Cust to give him a message from the Duke of Grafton, the First Lord of the Treasury. This was that the King was embarrassed by previous commitments on future peerages and so could not give one to Sir John Cust by himself. He would therefore be included in the first list of new peers to be made, or his son in the event of his death: in the interval Sir John was to have an office 'as a

---

[1] H. Walpole, *Letters*, XI, 319.   [2] Debrett, *Parl. Reg.*, I, 379.
[3] Debrett, *Parl. Reg.*, II, 366–8.
[4] Debrett, *Parl. Reg.*, V, 128–30, 418; VI, 329, 406–8.
[5] Fortescue, *Corr. of George III*, V, p. 420.
[6] Fortescue, *Corr. of George III*; IV, p. 95.

mark of his Majesty's approbation of his services, until he can be removed into the House of Peers'.[1] Sir John Cust died only four days afterwards: but the promise was redeemed when the commitments were cleared by a mass creation of peerages on 20 May 1776. His son then became Baron Brownlow; and the simultaneous creation of Arthur Onslow's son George as Baron Cranley doubtless helped to create the tradition that a peerage should recompense a Speakership, even though this latter honour was primarily earned by the recipient himself. Norton obtained his peerage, as Baron Grantley, on 9 April, after the Rockingham group had learned that Lord Shelburne had obtained one for his supporter John Dunning. Norton received prior notice of only a few hours, and the desire of Lord Rockingham and his friends for parity of patronage within the ministry was thought by contemporaries to have been a stronger motive for the step than Norton's own claims.[2] Posterity saw only that a former Speaker had been created a peer; and the tradition that a retiring Speaker should be entitled to a peerage was effectively established.

Dunning, when proposing Norton on 31 October, had disclaimed any personal objection to Cornwall; but the debate showed that some members regarded him as an unsuitable candidate. Cornwall was an open political careerist, not the man of independent means respected in the Commons. He had become an office-holder only by deserting the opposition in 1774 when Lord North's ministry was firmly established. Cornwall, too, did not even secure his own election to Parliament, for he represented the Treasury borough of Rye. Thomas Townshend therefore attacked Cornwall as an improper choice on the grounds of both office and constituency.[3]

It had in former times, he observed, been always customary to see the chair of the House of Commons filled by men who were independent, and men who represented either a large county, or some neighbouring borough. Mr. Onslow was no placeman. Mr. Cornwall held an office under the crown, disposal at the pleasure of the crown, and Mr. Cornwall was the representative of one of the

---

[1] *Cust Family Records*, III, 112.   [2] Wraxall, *Memoirs*, III, 13–15.
[3] Debrett, *Parl. Reg.*, I, 7.

Cinque Ports ... The office of speaker ought to be filled by a person free from all influence of the Crown. It was the first duty of the Speaker to guard the rights and privileges of the people, against the increased and increasing influence of the Crown.

The objection to a placeman in the Chair was not valid, for Cornwall had already resigned his Treasury post and accepted a legal sinecure identical to that held by Norton. The new issue of the Speaker's constituency was an attempt at a further extension of the Chair's independence from the Crown. The demand was not that the Speaker should be a self-returning member, and Rockingham had earlier made it clear to Frederick Montagu that he was expected to continue as M.P. for Higham Ferrers if he took the Chair. 'It would be strange that on your being elected Speaker by the House that you should be re-elected for any other place ... you could not change and come in for a *government borough*, without most rashly endangering your own character.'[1] The claim advanced by Townshend was merely that the Speaker should not owe his seat to the influence of the Crown, an issue hitherto absent in the Georgian period. Compton and Onslow had both been county members, representing Sussex and Surrey respectively. Cust had been returned on a family interest at Grantham, Norton by his own personal efforts at Guildford. It was Richard Rigby who countered the objections. He reminded members that Arthur Onslow had been Treasurer of the Navy while in the Chair, and dismissed the matter of Cornwall's constituency with the assertion that 'there was no local representation within these walls'.[2] The size of the majority for Cornwall shows that the constitutional issues raised by Townshend had little effect on opinion within the House.[3]

The apparent triumph of Arthur Onslow in establishing the political independence of the Chair had been limited. Although his own personal standing had enabled him to criticize as well as support ministers, the first of his successors who had ventured to do the same had been removed from office at the earliest

---

[1] Wentworth Woodhouse MSS. R 162, quoted Tyler, op. cit., p. 368.

[2] Debrett, *Parl. Reg.*, I, 14.

[3] The evidence on the political role of Cornwall when Speaker is too scanty to make possible any assessment for the Parliament of 1780.

opportunity. The ostensible reason for this step had been the attack on King and ministers in 1777 when Norton was acting in his official capacity as Speaker. But Sir Fletcher believed that he had also given offence by the expression of his political opinions in Committee. During the debate of 13 March 1780 in the Committee on Burke's Establishment Bill, he made this declaration:[1]

He said, since he had the honour of presiding in that chair, (pointing to it) he had on every occasion avoided as much as possible, giving any opinion respecting matters which came before that House. His duty and inclination led him to adopt that mode of conduct. His duty, lest from the respectable and honourable station be filled, his mixing in debate, without arrogating any thing to himself, might be supposed to create an improper influence, in some of his hearers; and his inclination forbad him, because he knew from experience that whatever he might support as an individual member, might be apt to bias his judgement in his other character, that of Speaker, when he came to preside in the House. It was true that the mode and order of proceeding did not preclude him from speaking in a committee: the House was now in one; consequently, within the most rigid rules of order, he was as much at liberty to deliver his sentiments as any other member, and he was ready to acknowledge that he had more than once, soon after he was called to his present honourable station, exercised that right. But he could not say for what reason, but so it happened, that he found whenever he had exercised it, that his conduct was liable to misinterpretation, and that whatever he offered, as arising from his own feelings and judgement, was deemed rather as taking a step out of the proper duties of his office, which were said to be a strict observance of whatever might tend to impress on the House the most strict impartiality and indifference.

He had not long presided in that chair when he discovered what was deemed the proper line of conduct for him to pursue. The House was in a Committee on a most important, and in his opinion, a most consequential bill [The royal marriage bill in the Year 1772]. . . . he had the misfortune at that time, by complying with the seeming wishes of the House, to give some persons very great offence, which he could assure them he by no means intended.

Thenceforward, he endeavoured to avoid as much as possible mixing in the debates, or of giving his sentiments, but when it seemed to be the united sense of the House . . . he was ready to

[1] Almon, *Parl. Reg.*, XVII, 319–21.

acknowledge, that he had experienced within himself a propensity to wish success to that side of the question which he had supported in the Committee, as soon as the House was resumed . . . consequently, though he might not be converted to the opinions of those who wished him to be silent upon every occasion, he was satisfied that the seldomer he mixed in debate, the more likely he would be to avoid giving offence to either side of the House.

Norton, however, then spoke on the bill, and he also spoke on two later occasions in Committee when still Speaker.[1] Later that year Rockingham assumed that Montagu would make known his political views in Committee if he became Speaker. 'Your sitting in the Chair of the House of Commons as Speaker, can have no more effect upon your vote as a member of Parliament, than your sitting upon any of the Benches: your opinions on the public measures which may be agitated, and the principles by which you direct your conduct will ever be your guide.'[2] Yet in his speech of 13 March 1780 Norton deliberately drew attention to the anomaly of the political situation of the Chair. He then announced to the House that he had been criticized for exercising the hitherto unquestioned right of the Speaker to make speeches in Committee. He had done so in the knowledge that his tenure of the Chair would soon be at an end, and his intention may have been to inhibit his successors from expressing political opinions. That was certainly the effect. Speaker Cornwall does not appear to have spoken in Committee, at least during his first Parliament; and although later incumbents of the Chair continued to speak and vote in Committees until 1870, known instances of speeches by Speakers are extremely rare—under a dozen occasions in a period of ninety years. Norton's pique virtually achieved the result sometimes wrongly attributed to Onslow's policy.[3]

Sir Fletcher Norton's career had shown that Speakers would not be allowed to criticize the King's government. They had freedom only to give general support to ministers, a privilege of little value and one that could tend only to detract from the prestige and reputation of the Chair. Already there was

---

[1] Almon, *Parl. Reg.*, XVII, 321-9, 461-5, 618-19.
[2] Wentworth Woodhouse MSS. R 162, quoted Tyler, op. cit., p. 368.
[3] Porritt, *Unreformed House of Commons*, I, 474-80. Dasent, *Speakers*, pp. 282-331.

evolving the opinion that any freedom for the Speaker to express his political views was incompatible with his position as an impartial Chairman of the House: for Norton's remarks were caused by contemporary criticism of his own behaviour. Complete abstention of the Speaker from politics would be a prerequisite for the genuine and permanent independence of the Chair.

16

MR. SPEAKER:
CHAIRMAN OF THE HOUSE

THE first business of the House of Commons at the meeting of each new Parliament was the election of a Speaker, without whom the House could not sit. The day began with strict formality, as James Harris, then a new member, recorded on 3 November 1761.[1]

> About one we assembled in the house to the number of about 350, the Speaker's Chair being empty, and the mace under the table. The door was shut and members took their places, when after a smart knock or two, the Gentleman Usher of the Black Rod was let in, who delivered his Majesty's message requiring our attendance in the House of Lords. We went. There his Majesty by his Chancellor informed us, that we should go and choose a Speaker, and present him on Friday next, the 6th instant.

The election itself was often also a set piece of ceremony, and the official candidate of government was usually the retiring Speaker. Whether or not the nominee was a new man, the administration choice was made known at a special Cockpit meeting held for this sole purpose on the day before the assembly of a new Parliament: this was a quite separate occasion from the pre-sessional Cockpit meeting of ministerial supporters every year for the reading of the King's Speech. Detailed accounts have been found of only two such meetings.[2] On 13 January 1735 Dudley Ryder noted that when Sir Robert Walpole proposed Onslow 'he set forth his qualities that made him fit for the office. After he had done, Mr. Onslow himself took notice of the pleasure it was to him to be thought of in so large an assembly.'[3] On 2 November 1761 James Harris heard Leader of the House George Grenville

---

[1] Harris Diary, 3 Nov. 1761.
[2] A third, in 1780, was mentioned in the debate on the election of the Speaker. Debrett, *Parl. Reg.*, I, 12.
[3] Harrowby MSS., doc. 7 P.

recommend Sir John Cust, 'who spoke a little, seemingly excusing himself'.[1]

When the members had returned from the House of Lords to their own House, the Clerk would point to any members who signified an intention to speak, and they addressed the Clerk by name.[2] After a candidate had been proposed and seconded, his election might follow at once or after he had been further commended by one or more other members: alternatively, another candidate might be proposed, and the House would vote on the choice. Whether or not a contest had taken place the successful candidate then made the 'disabling speech' customary for several centuries, declaring his own unfitness for the office. His protests would be ignored, and the Speaker-Elect was escorted to the Chair by his proposer and seconder, with a second conventional protest on the steps of the Chair itself. This custom of mock modesty had long fallen into disrepute. Speaker-Elect Compton, even when complying with the practice in 1715, remarked that 'excuses upon these occasions were generally so much suspected'. Many of Onslow's hearers must have remembered his acceptance of the Chair at the Cockpit the previous day when he performed the whole disabling procedure in the House on 14 January 1735.[3] It was Onslow who first abandoned the 'disabling speech' in 1741, and the token resistance on the way to the Chair in 1747. Sir John Cust revived both customs, at his two elections in 1761 and 1768: but in 1770 Sir Fletcher Norton became the only Speaker of the century to take the Chair without any disclaimer at his first election. He had announced this intention in his reply to his nomination: 'I shall not make an apology out of form, though agreeable to precedent. There is a ceremonial in that matter, in my opinion, which has disgraced the House.'[4] Even hostile Horace Walpole commended this break with tradition, recording that Norton 'with a manliness at least in his profligacy, took possession of his post, without acting those

---

[1] Harris Diary, 2 Nov. 1761.

[2] Details of the elections of Speakers may be found in the *Journals* of the House for the appropriate dates. The various speeches are not printed there from 1770. An account of the first election of Norton may be found in B.M. Eg. MSS. 3711, pp. 66–81; and that of Cornwall is recorded in Debrett, *Parl. Reg.*, I, 12–17.

[3] Harrowby MSS., doc. 7 P.

[4] B.M. Eg. MSS. 3711, pp. 76–8.

stale affectations of modesty with which other Speakers had been wont to get themselves forced into the Chair.'[1] In 1780 Charles Cornwall apparently made no disclaimer on his first nomination, but 'the self-denying farce was very faintly acted ... on ascending the Chair.'[2] This modified disabling procedure survived the century.

Thirteen of the seventeen elections of a Speaker between 1714 and 1800 were uncontested; but four out of the seven Speakers were opposed at their first nomination, Norton in 1770, Cornwall in 1780, and both Grenville and Addington in 1789. When a second name was put forward the House divided on the election of the first candidate proposed, who in each case was the administration nominee. On such occasions the same procedure was adopted as when the House was in Committee, members going to the right or left side of the Chair. The Clerk put the question, and appointed one teller on each side.[3]

When the new Speaker was seated in the Chair the Mace would be placed on the Table, to symbolize the full sitting of the House. There followed within a few days the presentation of the Speaker by the House to the sovereign, in the House of Lords. This involved a third stage in the traditional disabling procedure, a formal request to the King to recommend to the Commons that the House should make another choice. This act of assumed modesty in the royal presence was not performed by Onslow in 1747 and 1754, but Sir John Cust revived it. Norton did not adopt it in 1770 and 1774, but Cornwall again revived this piece of ceremonial, and it was also used by Henry Addington at his first election, in June 1789. The sovereign invariably ignored such pleas of incapacity, and the ceremony ended with the royal compliance with the Speaker's request for the customary privileges of the Commons. The Speaker then returned to the Lower House to report this grant of privileges, and concluded the procedure of his election with a speech of thanks.

At every election the proposer and seconder mentioned a

---

[1] H. Walpole, *George III*, IV, 37.   [2] Harris Diary, 31 Oct. 1780.
[3] Hatsell, *Precedents*, II, 224. For the method of voting in Committees see *supra*, pp. 278–9

list of the personal qualities desirable in a Speaker, a catalogue that hardly varied at all. In 1715 political loyalty to the new royal family was a quality much stressed, but this stipulation was gradually watered down in the ensuing era of stability to some such generalization as 'a firm attachment to the constitution'. The personal background of each candidate naturally involved some suitable adaptation. Compton, Onslow and Cust were credited with the advantages of respectable family and property, and Onslow's ancestral connection with the Chair was portrayed as a further point in his favour. Norton, and also presumably Cornwall, was commended for being a lawyer and for previous experience as an office-holder. Every candidate was endowed, so it was said, with ability, integrity, impartiality, knowledge of procedure, and zeal for the rights and privileges of the House. Stereotyped though these qualifications might have become, they still provided some indication of the duties and obligations of the Chair.

Defence of the prestige and privileges of the House against the Crown, the House of Lords and the common populace alike was by tradition the first task of the Speaker; but by the eighteenth century its importance had greatly diminished. Any member could draw the attention of the House at any time to an alleged breach of privilege; and it is clear that the Speaker's role as defender of the House in this respect was merely to be the member foremost in doing so. In practice this often meant only the observance of constitutional conventions. It must have been widely known, for example, that ministers sent reports of debates to the sovereign, but the fiction was retained of royal ignorance of proceedings in the House. Hence the indignation, real or assumed, when on 26 February 1757 Secretary of State William Pitt reported a message from George II that the execution of Admiral Byng had been postponed because 'a member in his place' had a statement to make. Henry Fox at once raised the question of privilege, 'the Crown being supposed to have no knowledge or cognizance of what is said there'. Speaker Onslow 'declared himself extremely hurt with the words, pronounced them wrong, and of most dangerous consequence'. As a message from the Crown it must be recorded in the *Journals*. 'The House may enter what it pleases, but it is a Message sent solemnly by the King and I never knew an instance of overlooking it.'[1] The message was printed in the *Journals*, but there immediately followed an entry drafted by the Speaker at Pitt's suggestion, a special paragraph stating that it should not be made a precedent.[2]

Relations with the House of Lords had to be conducted in a manner that implied the equality of the two Houses. Offence was taken whenever the Lords sent a resolution or bill with a statement that it had passed the upper House 'unanimously', for this implied an infringement of a free decision by the Commons. On 29 March 1764 Speaker Cust unthinkingly objected to a Lord's message that a Commons' resolution on franking had been agreed 'unanimously', until Jeremiah Dyson pointed out that the word was a compliment and not a constraint.[3] Objections were promptly made in the Commons on 7 May 1723 when the House of Lords requested the attendance of some M.P.s to answer questions on the evidence given to the Lower House with reference to Atterbury's attainder. 'The Speaker declared the old way was by messages and conferences between the two Houses, and that it was criminal in any member to divulge what had passed in the House.'[4] Messages had to be sent or received with appropriate ceremony and respect: delegations from the Lords appeared at the Bar of the Commons with heads uncovered. Conferences between representatives or 'managers' of the two Houses in the Painted Chamber were the official means of consultation. This was neutral ground, but Dudley Ryder's notes of conferences on 17 and 18 May 1737 show that formal equality was not observed at such confrontations: the members of the Commons stood with their hats off, whereas the Lords sat with their hats on.[5]

Complaints about the behaviour of the sovereign or the Lords were not common. Most cases of privilege arose from the actions of ordinary citizens. Alleged infringements involving individual members, their servants and their property formed the most frequent ground of complaint: but important issues arose over matters affecting the House itself, and the most

---

[1] H. Walpole, *George II*, II, 332–5.
[2] *Commons Journals*, XXVII, 738. B.M. Add. MSS. 32870, fos. 218–21.
[3] Harris Diary, 29 Mar. 1764.   [4] *Knatchbull Diary*, p. 23.
[5] Harrowby MSS., doc. 7 P.

significant concerned the press reporting of debates.[1] The century was punctuated by frequent and usually successful attempts of the House to preserve a veil of secrecy over its proceedings, and these were often instigated from the Chair. On 13 April 1738 Speaker Onslow not only drew the attention of the House to the printing of debates but also himself drafted the resolution comprehensively forbidding the practice.[2] It was Speaker Cust who on 3 March 1762 informed members that the *Dublin Journal* had printed their debates: but, despite a motion to take the printer into custody, the House decided merely to republish the order of 1738. Speaker Norton, however, refused to help the Onslow cousins when in February 1771 they began the prosecution of the newspaper printers which erupted into a famous clash between the Commons and the City of London that finally established the practical inability of the House to prevent Parliamentary reporting. 'He contemptuously clapt his hand on his backside and said, "No, Damme, If I do"', so Colonel George Onslow told James Harris a year later.[3] Yet during the debate of 12 March 1771 on the subject Norton from the the Chair made no secret of his hostility towards the minority obstruction of the actions of the House; and in April rumour said that he had threatened to resign the Chair if the Select Committee appointed to inquire into the episode made no report.[4] After 1771 contempt appears to have replaced prohibition as the official attitude of the House to newspaper reports. Here is Speaker Cornwall's advice on 20 December 1782 after Home Secretary Thomas Townshend had complained of accounts of debates in the press: 'The Speaker said a few words on the subject of taking notice of misrepresentations in public prints of expressions or arguments that had been delivered in that House; it was a practice which he would not recommend, as such a notice, and attempting to

[1] For the story of Parliamentary reporting in the eighteenth century see B. B. Hoover, *Samuel Johnson's Parliamentary Reporting*, pp. 1–32; F. S. Siebert, *Freedom of the Press in England 1476–1776*, pp. 346–52; my paper, 'The Beginning of Parliamentary Reporting in Newspapers, 1768–1774', *Eng. Hist. Rev.*, 74 (1959), pp. 623–36; and A. Aspinall, 'The Reporting and Publishing of the House of Commons' Debates, 1771–1834', *Essays Presented to Sir Lewis Namier*, pp. 227–57.
[2] Chandler, *Debates*, X, 278–87.
[3] Malmesbury MSS., memo. of 4 Apr. 1772.
[4] B.M. Eg. MSS. 226, pp. 1–84. H. Walpole, *George III*, IV, 213.

set the argument right, might perhaps be construed into an avowal of what was not contradicted.'[1] That members no longer acted in vigorous defence of their privileges was further shown the next month, by the surprising decision of the House to take no action when Speaker Cornwall on 28 January 1783 informed the Commons that forged letters in his name had been sent to newspaper proprietors forbidding publication of the provisional peace terms.[2]

The privileges and dignity of the House were enforced, if necessary, by two sanctions, commitment to custody and the lesser punishment of reprimand. As part of the attempt to prevent press reporting of debates in 1771 Lord Mayor Brass Crosby and Alderman Richard Oliver were committed to the Tower of London for the protection they had afforded as officials of the City of London to the printers of offending newspapers. The application of custody was arbitrary, as sometimes to offenders in election cases. The sheriff of Denbighshire was sent to Newgate for a wrongful return at the general election of 1741:[3] and some Middlesex J.P.s who had called in soldiers at the Westminster election of the same year were also committed to custody. Reprimands were administered by the Speaker, and received by offenders on their knees until 1772. Such treatment did not create respect: Horace Walpole noted of one offender, on 31 January 1751, that 'as he rose from the ground, he wiped his knees, and said "it was the dirtiest house he had ever been in".'[4] A few days later, on 6 February 1751, there occurred a memorable incident when an Alexander Murray refused to kneel for a reprimand as punishment for heading a riot at another Westminster election. He was committed to close confinement in Newgate on a motion made by a furious Speaker Onslow himself. When on 25 February Lord Egmont attacked this decision as lacking precedents, 'the Speaker made a warm and solemn speech for the honour of the House . . . and said the want of a precedent of such behaviour as Murray's did but conclude more strongly against him.'[5] The House had only the authority to order such imprisonments while it was sitting, and they ended with the close of a session:

[1] Debrett, *Parl. Reg.*, IX, 131–2.
[2] Debrett, *Parl. Reg.*, IX, 187–90.
[3] *Commons Journals*, XXIV, 89–92.
[4] H. Walpole, *George II*, I, 13–21.
[5] H. Walpole, *George II*, I, 28–31, 50.

this particular order against Murray was renewed at the beginning of the next session in November 1751, but he absconded.[1]

The prestige of the House also had to be defended against the
behaviour of its own members as private persons. A formal
reprimand from the Chair was sufficient retribution for incompetence or minor misdeeds, but expulsion from the House was
the method of dealing with members guilty of disreputable or
illegal conduct. The punishment was graded according to the
offence: in March 1732, after an investigation into the conduct
of three members appointed trustees under an Act of Parliament, two were expelled for deliberate malpractices, but the
third, guilty only of negligence, suffered merely a reprimand
by Speaker Onslow.[2] Expulsion was a decision of the whole
House, and the Speaker's role was usually formal; but such
action might be suggested by the Chair. Speaker Onslow gave
members a strong hint on 17 February 1757 when, after official
Admiralty notification to the House of the death sentence on
Admiral Byng, he 'produced a long roll of precedents for
expelling him before execution, lest his disgrace should reflect
on the House'.[3] Horace Walpole commented a fortnight
later: 'The Speaker would have had Byng expelled the House,
but his tigers were pitiful'.[4] And the Admiral was still an M.P.
when he was shot on 14 March.

Defence of the privileges of the House was therefore already
coming to be one of the formal functions of the Speaker. The
office also involved a great many routine duties, such as the
supervision of ballots for Select Committees, and the examination of witnesses at the Bar of the House. If the Speaker delivered reprimands, he also had the more pleasant task of
conveying the thanks of the House to members for meritorious
services to the state. It was the Speaker, accompanied by other
members, who carried Addresses, money bills and other
messages from the House to the sovereign, and who from the
Chair informed the Commons of royal replies and messages.
The Speaker, indeed, was the official channel of communica-

---

[1] H. Walpole, *George II*, I, 208–12. *Erthig Chronicles*, I, 320. On 16 March 1772
it was resolved that persons brought to the Bar of the House should receive
orders or reprimands standing, not on their knees. Clementson Diary, p. 36.
Commons Journals, XXXIII, 594.

[2] Chandler, *Debates*, VII, 238–40.   [3] H. Walpole, *George II*, II, 312.

[4] H. Walpole, *Letters*, IV, 38.

tion between the House and the outside world. He would read out letters sent to him concerning the House, although Norton reminded members of the Chair's discretionary power in this respect when refusing to make known a letter from John Wilkes on 20 March 1771.[1] The Speaker would also bring to the official attention of the House matters already of public knowledge that affected the functions, officials or rights of the House in any way.

The office of Speaker involved not only formal duties inside the House, but also assistance outside the chamber to private members who were intending to introduce Parliamentary business. Here the role of the Speaker was to make available to members his procedural knowledge. Speaker Onslow was often shown drafts of proposed bills and petitions for his approval, and he sometimes made alterations in them.[2] It is not clear when and to what extent these services of the Speaker were freely available to all members; but by the middle of the century the obligation of the Chair to give technical assistance to members on matters of private business appears to have been generally acknowledged. After his resignation Sir John Cust was particularly commended by Lord North on 22 January 1770 for his attention to 'bills of conveyance of great estates. If they had been his own, he could not have taken more care.'[3] Norton rationalized the process: within two months of his election to the Chair he had drafted specimen copies of the three most common types of private bills, those for turnpikes, enclosures and canals.[4]

One further obligation on Mr. Speaker outside the House was that of entertaining members to dinner. Recognition of this social duty was implicit in such perquisites as the provision of a service of plate and of an annual supply of claret.[5] Information on this subject is scanty. It is possible, for example, that it was customary for a Speaker to entertain every member during the lifetime of a Parliament, in so far as that was practicable; for one of Sir John Packington's complaints about Speaker Compton at his re-election on 9 October 1722 was

---

[1] B.M. Eg. MSS. 226, pp. 498–9.
[2] *H.M.C. Egmont Diary*, I, 92, 110, 273, 367, 370; II, 25; III, 102, 106–7, 195.
[3] B.M. Eg. MSS. 3711, pp. 66–72.
[4] Malmesbury MSS., memo of 17 Mar. 1770.   [5] See *supra*, p. 287N.

that he had never been invited by him to dinner all the previous Parliament.[1] There may have been a convention that new members were accorded priority, for it was during his first session that James Harris dined with the Speaker, his chaplain, and ten other members.[2] In 1770 the Speaker's receptions were held weekly, on Sunday evenings.[3] Before the end of the century the social obligation had become a formal institution, with the Speaker apparently providing receptions or dinners for members on every Saturday and Sunday during the session, and with precedents establishing which privy councillors, office-holders and other leading men of the House should attend the first, second or third dinner of the session.[4]

Contemporary assessments of a Speaker were not based on his performance of formal and routine duties, whether in the Chair or otherwise arising from his office. The basis of a Speaker's reputation was his management of the House during debates, involving both an ability to maintain order and the guidance of members on matters of procedure and practice. Hence, of course, came the need for the qualities of character, impartiality and Parliamentary knowledge: realization came during the century of the need of a further qualification, that of physical endurance.

The Speaker had to remain in the Chair throughout the proceedings of every day on which the House sat, unless it resolved itself into a Committee. Even then he was obliged to remain in attendance, usually in the gallery or in the Speaker's Room, so that he would be able to resume the Chair at once when the Committee ended or if any disorder arose there.[5] The House could not sit unless the Speaker was present, as John Hatsell stated.

During the Speaker's absence, whether from illness or any other cause no business can be done, nor any question proposed, except a question of adjournment, and that question must be put by the

---

[1] *Knatchbull Diary*, p. 2.   [2] Harris Diary, 2 Apr. 1762.
[3] *London Evening Post*, 20 Feb. 1770.
[4] Porritt, *Unreformed House of Commons*, I, 472.
[5] Hatsell, *Precedents*, II, 243 N. This obligation of continuous attendance may also have fallen on the Clerks and on the Speaker's chaplain. H. Walpole, *Letters*, VI, 3. *Cust Family Records*, III, 96.

Clerk. This has been often, and must always be a very great inconvenience, and it is grown much greater lately, from the quantity of business, and the length of sittings of the House of Commons: many proposals have been made, of having a Deputy Speaker, a Speaker pro tempore, etc: but nothing of this kind has yet taken place.[1]

No such suggestions have been found in contemporary debates, although when Speaker Norton was taken ill on 14 April 1780 General Conway expressed incredulity that there were not any precedents for appointing a temporary Speaker.[2] Clerk Hatsell was optimistic in his apparent assumption that some solution would soon be adopted: not until 1855 was provision made for a Deputy Speaker.[3]

This circumstance must be attributed to the remarkably good health of the Speakers as well as to the absence of any real pressure of time. Between 1714 and 1789, during the period of office of the first five Hanoverian Speakers, the customary days of business lost through actual ill-health of the Speaker averaged only about one day every two years.[4] It is impossible to assess, however, the other Parliamentary time lost through consideration for the Speaker's health. Sometimes the House adjourned early for this reason; on 23 November 1763 George Grenville informed George III that 'the Speaker appearing to be very much exhausted, it was impossible to go any further tonight.'[5] Many of the adjournments over the next day after a late sitting may have been due to the same motive. At the end of the long debate of 19 May 1773 on Lord Clive some members pressed to continue the next day, 'but the Speaker with his blunt and unceremonious frankness told them it was too much fatigue for him, and that they should not have his company, on which it was postponed till the 21st.'[6] Further inconvenience arose because a Speaker sometimes had other motives for requesting an adjournment of

---

[1] Hatsell, *Precedents*, II, 222–3.   [2] Almon, *Parl. Reg.*, XVII, 529–30.
[3] Redlich, *Procedure of the House of Commons*, II, 170–1.
[4] Some such adjournments given in the *Index* to the *Commons Journals* or in unofficial sources proved on investigation not to be due to this cause or not to have taken place at all; but, of course, there may have been other occasions of which no record has been found.
[5] Fortescue, *Corr. of George III*, I, p. 62.   [6] H. Walpole, *Last Journals*, I, 231.

the House: the one from 22 April to 29 April in 1779 was made because of the death of the Speaker's brother.[1]

For Speaker Compton only one possible instance of ill-health has been found: diarist Knatchbull recorded on 14 January 1723 that 'the House met after the Speaker's illness and the recess', but the previous adjournment had taken place on 21 December until that date, and a Christmas recess of three weeks was customary.[2] Speaker Onslow was 'immortal in the Chair', Horace Walpole observed in 1763 when discussing an illness of his successor.[3] Only four occasions have been found when an adjournment was caused by Onslow's ill-health, one in 1731, two in 1738 and one in 1748: they include the longest such interval during the century, from 17 February to 1 March 1738.[4]

Onslow's reputation for good health might well have suffered if he had continued in the Chair after 1761. Lengthy debates on John Wilkes undoubtedly help to explain Sir John Cust's recurrent illnesses. The session dominated by the *North Briton* case was broken by short adjournments in November 1763 and February 1764 when Cust was unable to take the Chair.[5] Thereafter Cust's health was a frequent cause of concern to his family and friends: in the autumn of 1764 he went to Spa, and he sought recuperation and rest in several subsequent recesses.[6] His fate was sealed by the long debates on the Middlesex election case in 1769. Sir John collapsed in the Chair at Prayers on 12 January 1770. Diarist Newdigate then blamed the strong smell of charcoal in the chamber, but six days later Horace Walpole was writing of a paralytic disorder.[7] Cust resigned the Chair on 17 January, and died a week later at the age of fifty-one. The historian of the Cust family had 'no doubt that Sir John Cust's premature death was caused by a complication of ailments in the digestive and other functional

---

[1] Harris Diary, 22 Apr. 1779.

[2] *Knatchbull Diary*, p. 10. *Commons Journals*, XX, 98. For contemporary references to the Speaker's illness see *H.M.C. Portland*, VII, 344–5.

[3] H. Walpole, *Letters*, V, 388–9. For the opinion that Onslow did not enjoy good health, however, see Vulliamy, *The Onslow Family*, p. 124.

[4] *Commons Journals*, XXI, 662; XXIII, 39–40, 158; XXV, 532.

[5] *Commons Journals*, XXIX, 673, 871.

[6] *Cust Family Records*, III, 73. *Erthig Chronicles*, II, 58.

[7] Newdigate Diary, 12 Jan. 1770. H. Walpole, *Letters*, VII, 353.

organs of his body, due to long periods of confinement in the Chair during the too frequent long sittings of the House of Commons, in addition to general exhaustion in the performance of his duties '.[1] On the very day of his death, 24 January 1770, the House made a first relaxation of the rule requiring the continuous presence of the Speaker. Here is a contemporary newspaper report of a decision not recorded in the official *Journals*.

An august Assembly agreed on Wednesday to a very prudent and humane regulation, purporting that it should be a standing rule for the Sp—r to deport the C—r whenever the usual calls of nature should require his absence, and that the H— should still continue sitting. The want of so provident a regulation is thought to have hastened the death of the late Sp—r.[2]

This alteration was probably made at the request of Sir Fletcher Norton, who had been elected to the Chair two days previously; for he was not a man to suffer in silence. On 24 April 1771 the House adjourned further business immediately after Norton had made this complaint: 'Will you have no mercy upon yourselves, or me.'[3] During the protracted proceedings against printers of newspapers earlier that session he had given vent to his feelings on at least two occasions. On 14 March, when a second successive night sitting developed over the attendance of printers, Norton declared from the Chair that it would be impossible to finish before six or seven o'clock the next morning, and asked the House to find 'somebody more able and fit'.[4] His complaint was ignored, and the sitting lasted until five o'clock.[5] On 20 March Norton could not resist the interjection, 'I have not dined this week, Sir', after a complaint that members had left the debate for dinner.[6] Only once did the ill-health of the Speaker result in any delay of business during Norton's first decade in the Chair; in 1773 his gout caused an adjournment from 4 February to 9 February;[7] but it was to be Norton's ill-health during 1780 that provided the excuse for his removal from the Chair.

---

[1] *Cust Family Records*, III, 112.
[2] *London Evening Post*, 27 Jan. 1770. The suggestion was made by Welbore Ellis. B.M. Eg. MSS. 3711, p. 82.
[3] B.M. Eg. MSS. 230, p. 99.   [4] B.M. Eg. MSS. 226, p. 105.
[5] B.M. Eg. MSS. 226, p. 137.   [6] B.M. Eg. MSS. 226, p. 473.
[7] *London Chronicle*, 6 Feb. 1773.

The first incident occurred on 15 February. 'Lord George Gordon rose to speak, but while he was on his legs the Speaker seemed to be suddenly taken ill. Colonel Barré then rose, and moved that the debate should be adjourned. A great confusion now arose, and after a few minutes the House adjourned.'[1] The House was obliged to meet the next day according to its own rules in the absence of a previous motion for a longer adjournment, but promptly adjourned again until 21 February.[2] On that occasion Lord North, after moving an amendment to an opposition motion, 'proposed, on account of the Speaker's health, to leave the motion, thus amended, on the table till next day, and to adjourn. The Speaker thanked the House for their kind attention, but he found himself so much better as to hope, that the business of the House would suffer no further interruption on his account.' The ensuing debate lasted until after midnight.[3] That Norton's health had not recovered was to be shown by his interruption of business on 14 April. It was again Lord George Gordon who was speaking when Sir Fletcher told the House that he was not well. After John Dunning had asked whether business should continue, 'the Speaker rose and informed the House that he was indisposed, and had been so for some time; but, notwithstanding that, he was ready to do his duty, sooner than impede or retard the public business.' Lord John Cavendish suggested an adjournment, and Norton rose again. He 'said that for the last day or two he had been extremely ill, and was far from being well for several months past. The constant attention to the discharge of his duty had greatly impaired his health ... He was advanced in years; he was in a bad state of health ... He much doubted whether his longer sitting in that chair would answer the expectations of the House.' Lord North was less sympathetic than the opposition members, suggesting an adjournment only until 19 April. 'There was a vast deal of business before the House, which it would be extremely detrimental to the public to postpone.' Dunning countered with a formal motion to adjourn until 24 April, and Norton gave an account of his illness. He had suffered a gouty complaint since February, although the Easter recess had made some recovery possible.

---

[1] Almon, *Parl. Reg.*, XVII, 128.   [2] *Commons Journals*, XXXVII, 606–8.
[3] Almon, *Parl. Reg.*, XVII, 132–42.

The House then adjourned for the period of ten days proposed by Dunning.[1] When the House met on 24 April the Speaker offered the customary thanks to members for their indulgence, announcing his intention to discharge his duty, at least for the rest of the session.[2] Horace Walpole believed that Norton was avowedly acting 'against the advice of his physicians'.[3] Altogether only nine customary days of business in 1780 had been lost through Norton's illness, but the circumstances gave administration a pretext for his removal from the Chair at the opening of the next Parliament on 31 October. Norton himself then admitted that he had already resolved not to be Speaker again on medical grounds, 'but he would be an idiot to think that the reason'. Although in town for the previous three days, he had not been consulted on the matter.[4] It was to be an ironic comment on the excuse that the new Speaker, Charles Cornwall, should die after little more than eight sessions in the Chair, on 2 January 1789 at the age of fifty-three—only one day after his predecessor, who had lived to be seventy-three.

It is my Business to take care that the Orders and Methods of Proceeding shall be regularly observed. In all Questions about Order I am to inform you, so far as consists with my Knowledge, of what has been formerly done in the like Cases; and I am to take care that all Decency and Order shall be observed, both in our Debates and Proceedings: This is my Duty, and this I shall always endeavour to perform as far as lies in my Power: In all Cases I am to observe those Directions that the House shall be pleased to give.

Contemporary opinion must have approved, as it was meant to, this exposition of the functions of the Chair by Arthur Onslow on 31 January 1733.[5] The Speaker was to maintain order in debate, and to derive both the rules of procedure and the methods of conducting business from precedents; but he was always to be subject to the will of the House. Practice did not accord with this theory. A major achievement of Onslow was the advance he made towards the creation of a case law

---

[1] Almon, *Parl. Reg.*, XVII, 527–30. For contemporary scepticism about Norton's illness see *supra*, p. 322.
[2] Almon, *Parl. Reg.*, XVII, 531–2.   [3] H. Walpole, *Last Journals*, II, 300.
[4] Debrett, *Parl. Reg.*, I, 8–10.   [5] Chandler, *Debates*, VII, 267.

of procedure.[1] In this he was foremost, but not unique: all Speakers necessarily made some contribution to the evolution of procedure by their decisions, knowledge and advice. Rulings from the Chair were usually understood to be based on the past practice of the House, and Speakers were sometimes given time to look into precedents:[2] but this professed reliance on precedent was often a mere convention, to enable a Speaker's decision to be founded on the alleged custom of the House rather than on his own unsupported authority. There may also have been the realization that undue concern with the precedents and rules of procedure might prove detrimental to the efficient conduct of business in the House. The view has been put forward that the contemporary concern with formality was a reflection of the basic conservatism of the age:[3] but this interpretation should not be pressed too far. During a procedural dispute on 13 March 1741 Henry Pelham, then Paymaster-General, made this comment: 'As all the Orders of the House are, doubtless, made for more easy and expeditious dispatch, if an Order be contrary to this end, it ought to be abrogated for the reasons for which others are observed.' This was a natural opinion to be voiced from the Treasury Bench: but it was backed by Speaker Onslow himself, the man often depicted as the chief champion of conservative and obstructive procedure. 'The importance of this affair seems not to be so very great as to require a rigorous observance of the rules; and it were to be wished, for the ease and expedition of our deliberations, gentlemen would rather yield points of indifference to one another, than insist so warmly on circumstances of a trivial nature.'[4]

Rulings from the Chair were sometimes ignored or disputed. Sir John Cust suffered most in this respect, and not without reason:[5] but other Speakers were not unchallenged. In a dispute on 16 March 1726 Compton conceded a point of order

---

[1] That this was his aim is evident from his notes and comments on procedure: for descriptions of them see Vulliamy, *The Onslow Family*, pp. 98, 126–7; and Laundy, *The Office of Speaker*, p. 264.

[2] See, for example, Chandler, *Debates*, VII, 313–15: B.M. Add. MSS. 32877, fos. 422–3.

[3] J. S. Watson, 'Parliamentary Procedure as a Key to the Understanding of Eighteenth Century Politics', *Burke Newsletter*, III (1962), p. 110.

[4] Chandler, *Debates*, XII, 293–4.   [5] See *infra*, p. 358.

to Sir Robert Walpole;[1] and on 16 May 1782 the House disregarded a suggestion by Cornwall on the correct procedure for altering a bill.[2] Even Onslow at the height of his prestige found a procedural ruling ignored when it proved unacceptable to the majority of members present; this happened over an election case on 28 January 1751 despite the evident desire of the ministry to abide by Onslow's decision.[3] The occasional arguments between members and the Chair on points of procedure were themselves strictly out of order, as Henry Dundas observed on 15 March 1782 when calling Thomas Powys to order for disputing a ruling by Speaker Cornwall. 'He said, if the honourable member doubted the authority of the chair, his way was not to argue upon it, but to take the sense of the House by a question.'[4] There is no instance during the century of any procedural decision by the Chair being overruled by a vote of the House: but that it remained a constitutional axiom that the Speaker was the servant of the House was shown by an incident on 3 March 1779. During a procedural dispute Lord North made this remark: 'The House is bound by the authority of the Chair in all cases whatsoever.' At once Charles James Fox moved for these words to be taken down by the Clerk, who noted them wrongly because of the noise. The incident ended when North, claiming that he had been interrupted, qualified his statement by adding, 'if the House should so determine'.[5]

Much of the procedural aspect of the Speaker's task involved advice and assistance to members in their conduct of business through the House rather than pronouncements on points of dispute. Speakers sometimes needed to remind members of the correct forms, as when Norton on 22 February 1773 said that an amendment must be put as 'a motion to explain and amend'.[6] The Chair gave help with the problems of legislation, provided guidance on rules, and offered suggestions on methods of avoiding technical difficulties. Remarkable even in this context of ready assistance was the desire of the House on 17 March 1773 that Sir Fletcher Norton should speak from the Chair as a lawyer, not as Speaker, to give his opinion on the

[1] *Knatchbull Diary*, p. 56.
[2] Debrett, *Parl. Reg.*, VII, 165.
[3] H. Walpole, *George II*, I, 16.
[4] Debrett, *Parl. Reg.*, VI, 464.
[5] Almon, *Parl. Reg.*, XII, 36–7.
[6] B.M. Eg. MSS. 244, pp. 153–4.

competence of a proposed witness. Norton complied with this request, but declined a similar one on 13 May 1774.[1]

Observance of the correct rules and forms of business depended on 'decency and order' in debate. The control of the Chair over members embraced two distinct tasks, the need to ensure that speakers observed the rules of debate, and the obligation to maintain silence and attention for the members speaking.[2] The powers that could be invoked by the Chair to discipline speakers were varied and extensive. Members who gave offence by their speeches were even liable to commitment to custody. On 5 April 1715 Sir William Wyndham attacked the proclamation issued by George I before the recent general election as 'of dangerous consequence to the very being of Parliaments'. A motion was made to commit him to the Tower. This was opposed by Robert Walpole, and Wyndham was instead reprimanded by Speaker Compton the next day.[3] Such censure from the Chair was the traditional punishment, after offenders had been called to the Bar to ask pardon of the House on their knees.[4] The eighteenth century saw the virtual disappearance of this practice, the House being almost always satisfied by an immediate apology and withdrawal of the offending words.

For a Speaker to prevent general noise and disturbance in the House, however, was often difficult and sometimes impossible. The Chair had been given a weapon for use against individual members on such occasions by a standing order of 22 January 1694: 'That Mr. Speaker do call upon the Member, "by name", making such disturbance, and that every such person shall incur the displeasure and censure of the House.'[5] It was not clear what the consequences of such action would be; both Onslow and Norton were reputed to have professed ignorance on the point.[6] Threats from the Chair to 'name' members do not appear to have been carried out until 15 December 1792, and its application then was half-hearted. Thomas Whitmore was 'named' after making continuous

---

[1] B.M. Eg. MSS. 245, pp. 23–4; 259, p. 47.   [2] See *supra*, Chapter 11.
[3] Chandler, *Debates*, VII, 15–8. For the commitment of William Shippen to the Tower in 1717 see *supra*, p. 215. He appears to have been the last M.P. to suffer imprisonment for words spoken in debate.
[4] *Knatchbull Diary*, p. 76.   [5] *Commons Journals*, XI, 66.
[6] Macdonagh, *The Speaker of the House*, p. 63.

interruptions. On the previous day as well he had so frequently and loudly interrupted a debate that the order of 1694 had been read. Whitmore was at once directed to leave the House. A motion was then made that he should be called in and reprimanded by Speaker Addington in his place. Another member informed the House that Whitmore had authorized him to make an apology on his behalf. On the suggestion of the Speaker, the motion for a reprimand was withdrawn, and Whitmore given permission to return.[1] The device of 'naming' individual members was in any case quite unsuitable for preventing the occurrences of noise or disorder that marred the decorum of debates: and a general suspension of business was a self-defeating and temporary measure rarely if ever adopted. Only by sheer force of personality, aided by constant attention and correct timing of interventions, could any Speaker maintain order in the House: and the ability to do so must form the basis of any assessment of the performance of individual Speakers.

Contemporaries were agreed on the talents of Speaker Compton. The hostile Sir John Packington even suggested at his re-election in 1722 that he was too clever a man to be Speaker: 'Took notice there was no necessity of having men of great parts in the chair, provided they had nothing in view but the service of the House, and that it was preposterous to go to plough with a razor etc.'[2] His successor Onslow thought that 'he was very able . . . in the chair'.[3] And this judgement a century later suggests that Compton fulfilled at least some of the exacting requirements of the Chair: 'To the maintenance of decorum, the Speaker's formal and solemn manner, set off with a majestic presence and sonorous voice, largely contributed, while they seemed to denote greater extent of knowledge and more profundity of wisdom than he could in reality claim. These useful attributes, to which might be added a strict application to business, a rigid observance of state ceremonial, and a punctuality to the minute in time of appointments'. All this made him a satisfactory Speaker in the opinion of

---

[1] *Commons Journals*, XLVIII, 13. Hatsell, *Precedents*, II, 231.
[2] *Knatchbull Diary*, p. 2.   [3] *H.M.C. Onslow*, p. 516.

George I and his ministers,[1] but historical assessment of Compton's role as Speaker has usually been coloured by the later recollection of John Hatsell that he did not regard it as part of his duty to prevent noise during debates.[2]

It is reported of Sir Spencer Compton, that, when he was Speaker, he used to answer to a Member, who called upon him to make the House quiet, for that he had a right to be heard. 'No, Sir, you have a right to speak, but the House have a right to judge whether they will hear you.' In this the Speaker certainly erred; the Member has a right to speak, and the House ought to attend to him; and it is the Speaker's duty to endeavour for that purpose, to keep them quiet; but, when the love of talking gets the better of modesty and good sense, which sometimes happens, it is a duty very difficult to execute in a large and popular assembly.

Negative evidence on such a matter must always be unsatisfactory: but it is certainly true that in the very scanty Parliamentary reports of the period no instance has been found of any intervention by Speaker Compton to prevent noise or general disorder in debate, whereas some information does survive on other aspects of his role as Speaker; on a few occasions, for instance, he interrupted speeches because of personal remarks about other members or adverse reflections on Parliamentary decisions.[3]

Compton has been overshadowed by his successor. Arthur Onslow's contemporary fame as Speaker was based more on his success as Chairman of the House than on the advance of the Chair towards political impartiality which is the chief basis of his posthumous reputation.[4] Even the admiring Hatsell, however, did not claim his complete success. 'All these rules [of debate] ... Mr. Onslow endeavoured to preserve with great strictness, yet with civility to the particular Members offending; though I do not pretend to say that his endeavours had always their effect.'[5] Courteous Onslow may

---

[1] Townsend, *House of Commons*, I, 230.

[2] Hatsell, *Precedents*, II, 108. Compton certainly made some such pronouncement, for Edmund Burke reminded the House of it in 1770. B.M. Eg. MSS. 220, p. 241.

[3] *Knatchbull Diary*, pp. 13, 21, 44.

[4] For a biographical account of Onslow see Vulliamy, *The Onslow Family*, pp. 87–154; and for a recent assessment of him as Speaker see Laundy, *The Office of Speaker*, pp. 261–73.

[5] Hatsell, *Precedents*, II, 236.

have been: but his dominance of the House was clearly based on a temper that made him feared and respected rather than liked. His interventions to restore order are often described as 'warm', and several commentators depict his behaviour as choleric. Horace Walpole recorded for posterity with evident delight an account of how as a young member he once baited Speaker Onslow into 'a great rage' in the House. And in 1764 he made this comment to Lord Hertford on Sir Fletcher Norton's notorious comparison of a resolution of the House of Commons with a decision of a group of drunken porters: 'Had old Onslow been in the chair, I believe he would have knocked him down with the mace.'[1] Thomas Lewis, who was an M.P. throughout Onslow's tenure of the Chair, recalled in 1770 that the passionate nature of the Speaker's outbursts had frequently silenced recalcitrant members. 'Great warmth I've often seen with Onslow'. Lewis also remembered that members 'had on both sides a respect for him as a man of family and great abilities in the station he held.'[2] Onslow's personal status as an independent gentleman, the immense knowledge he accumulated on procedure, and his evident pride in the House were obvious advantages in the task of maintaining order: but essentially it was strength of character that gave Onslow an initial authority that was later reinforced by his experience and by the mere passage of time. In 1761 there were only twenty members in the House who had sat under any other Speaker.

From his first session in the Chair, Onslow is found reproving members for language reflecting adversely on Parliament and Parliamentary decisions, the Crown, the House of Lords, and other members both collective and individual. He realized that for the Chair to command respect the Speaker must himself be no respecter of persons; and the lash of his tongue fell on such leading members as William Pulteney, Henry Pelham, William Pitt and Henry Fox as well as on many lesser men.[3] When the offender was Sir Robert Walpole himself, however, Onslow chose the method of a general reprimand to

---

[1] H. Walpole, *Letters*, I, xxxix; VII, 9.   [2] Harpton MSS., C 49.
[3] For some examples see N.L.W. MSS. 1352, fos. 66, 73, 110, 188: *Knatchbull Diary*, p. 76: *H.M.C. Egmont Diary*, I, 67, 220; III, 278: Chandler, *Debates*, VII, 166: H. Walpole, *Letters*, II, 438–9: H. Walpole, *George II*, II, 154, 325.

the House, such as this admonition on 4 February 1734:
'Gentlemen, it is no business of mine to appear on either side
of the question. But it is my duty to take notice, when gentlemen are disorderly. There is nothing more irregular than for
gentlemen to be personal in their debates, or to mention anything that has been said in a former session of Parliament, or
even only the very day before.'[1]

Instances of Onslow's control over members speaking could
be multiplied even from the sadly inadequate records of
Parliamentary proceedings during his tenure of the Chair.
So little information has survived that only two incidents in the
period of thirty-three years have been found to illustrate Onslow's
undoubtedly consistent policy of maintaining sufficient order
in debates for the members speaking to be heard. Onslow's
zeal in this respect sometimes defeated its own purpose, being
such as to upset inexperienced members trying to speak. Here
is John Campbell's story of an incident during the debate on
the Address on 16 November 1742: 'Sir John Rushout got up
to speak the first day, but was put out and he said the Speaker
trying to make the House quiet, put him out worse than anybody, and he scolded the Speaker as they speak aside in a play
and so that I heard him plainly and would have laughed
very heartily.'[2] On 30 April 1733 a complaint about Onslow's
failure to prevent disorder was made and answered. William
Glanville began a speech against the motion to pass a Stock-
jobbing Bill with these words: 'I would sooner have taken notice
of these things, but there happened to be such a noise and
disturbance in the House, both upon the second reading of
this bill, and likewise when it was in the Committee, that I
could not expect to be heard; and therefore I did not then
rise up to say anything against it.' Onslow's conduct was
promptly defended by Sir John Barnard in this account of
contemporary practice:[3]

I am, indeed, surprised to hear any gentleman say, that there was
upon any occasion such a noise in the House that he could not be
heard: it is true, when a bill is passing, which is thought to be a bill
of course, there are but few gentlemen give great attention to it;
and upon such occasions, when gentlemen are not otherwise

---

[1] Chandler, *Debates*, VIII, 64.   [2] N.L.W. MSS. 1352, fos. 130–1.
[3] Chandler, *Debates*, VII, 379–80.

employed, they will fall a talking with one another, which must occasion some little noise in the House. But every gentleman knows, that upon any such occasion, whoever inclines to speak to the bill in hand, may rise up and call to the Chair. It is then the duty of the Chair to order silence, and then the House will become attentive to the gentleman who is to speak. This is the method of proceeding in this House; and this, Sir, you have always taken a proper care to see punctually observed.

It is impossible to make any satisfactory assessment of Onslow's management of the House from the contemporary evidence of the debates. The best testimony to his triumph in the Chair is the unanimous acclaim of his fellow-members. His son George wrote these proud words about his father in 1771: 'He was allowed universally to be the best and ablest Speaker that ever filled the Chair. His whole delight was in his business, and his only aim to act uprightly and justly there, and with strict impartiality.'[1] Even more convincing is the testimony by Horace Walpole on Onslow's retirement in 1761, for Walpole had often reported the Speaker's actions with a cynical and critical pen.

The last day of the session, March 18th, was fixed for returning the thanks of the House of Commons to Mr. Onslow, their Speaker, who had filled the Chair with unblemished integrity during the whole long reign of George the Second, and who had the prudence to quit the scene before his years and growing infirmities made him a burden to himself and the public. No man had ever supported with more firmness the privileges of the House, nor sustained the dignity of his office with more authority. His knowledge of the Constitution equalled his attachment to it. To the Crown he behaved with all the decorum of respect, without sacrificing his freedom of speech. Against encroachments of the House of Peers he was an inflexible champion. His disinterested virtue supported him through all his pretensions: and though to conciliate popular favour he affected an impartiality that by turns led him to the borders of insincerity and contradiction—and though he was so minutely attached to form that it often made him troublesome in affairs of higher moment, it will be difficult to find a subject whom gravity will so well become, whose knowledge will be so useful and so accurate, and whose fidelity to his trust will prove so unshaken.

[1] *H.M.C. Onslow*, p. 520.

The Address of thanks to Onslow was moved by an independent member, Sir John Philipps, and seconded by the Chancellor of the Exchequer Henry Legge, and several other members then rose to add their praise of the Speaker.

The good old man sat over-powered with gratitude, and weeping over the testimonies borne to his virtue. He rose at last, and closed his public life in the most becoming manner; neither over-acting modesty, nor checking the tender sensibility which he necessarily felt at quitting the darling occupation of his life. His thanks to the House for their patient sufferance of his errors, and for their gracious acceptance of his endeavours to serve them, were shortly, but cogently, expressed; and his voice, and the tears he could not restrain, spoke still more forcibly how much his soul was agitated by laudable emotions.

Sir John Philipps had already assured the House that some pecuniary reward was intended. Sir George Savile declared that the Commons rather than the Crown should bestow this mark of esteem, and the Address finally voted to the King, after Onslow's protests had been overborne, contained an assurance that the House would reimburse George III for the cost.[1] An annuity of £3,000 was bestowed by the sovereign to continue for Arthur Onslow's life and also for that of his son George.[2] Onslow was the first Speaker to have a pension on retirement, and also the first to be voted the freedom of the City of London.[3] For Crown, Commons, and City to show simultaneous approval of the same man was unanimity rare in the eighteenth century.

Further testimony to Onslow's success as chairman of the House came after experience of his successors. Clerk John Hatsell made frequent and invariably favourable references in his *Precedents*, and tributes also came from members in the House. Thomas Townshend, an M.P. since 1754, when proposing a vote of thanks to Norton as the former Speaker on 20 November 1780, conceded that he could not place either Norton or Cornwall in the same class as Onslow: 'Mr. Onslow was a very singular and a very extraordinary character, a character which it fell to the lot of few men to resemble

---

[1] H. Walpole, *George III*, I, 39–41. *Commons Journals*, XXVIII, 1108–9.
[2] *Commons Journals*, XXIX, 244.   [3] *Annual Register*, 1761, p. 106.

perfectly.'¹ Richard Rigby, an M.P. since 1745, made a critical comparison of Speaker Norton with Onslow on 14 May 1777: 'When Mr. Onslow was Speaker, he would not let members stand on the floor, or by the chair, or behind the chair talking; and when the House was disorderly, he used to call out and say, he hoped the House would support him in keeping order.'² On 31 October 1780 it was again Rigby who, in another criticism of Norton's weakness, reminded the House of the contrast with the great Speaker:³

He remembered Mr. Onslow was remarkable for an opposite conduct, and was said to have too much buckram in his manner (to use a familiar phrase). The younger part of the House complained, that he carried matters with rather too high a hand; the fact however was, the House had then more dignity, its proceedings were more grave and solemn, and people without doors treated it more respectfully . . . though Mr. Onslow might be too pompous, the extreme opposite line of conduct was infinitely more liable to be attended with bad consequences.

There has long been a conventional assessment of the motive behind Onslow's determination to maintain order in the House. It centres on his much-publicized concern for the rights of the minority. Onslow's reputation in this respect is based on the recollection of his comments by John Hatsell:⁴

He said, it was a maxim he had often heard, when he was a young man, from old and experienced Members, that nothing tended more to throw power into the hands of Administration, and those who acted with the majority of the House of Commons, than a neglect of, or departure from, these rules. That the forms of proceeding, as instituted by our ancestors, operated as a check and controul on the actions of Ministers; and that they were in many instances, a shelter and protection to the minority, against the attempts of power.

This emphasis on the role of the Chair as the defender of the individual members against the executive stemmed from Onslow's desire for popularity. Undoubtedly the formal procedures of the House afforded members ample opportunities for debate and obstruction; but it should be remembered that

¹ Debrett, *Parl. Reg.*, I, 103–7.   ²Almon, *Parl. Reg.*, VII, 194.
³ Debrett, *Parl. Reg.*, I, 16.   ⁴ Hatsell, *Precedents*, II, 237.

the tactic of deliberately delaying business was rarely adopted at the time. A prime concern of Onslow, moreover, was always to ensure the passage of business with as much expedition and harmony as possible; and it was inevitably minority and individual opinions that suffered in this pursuit of efficiency and unanimity. Onslow's professions differ from his practice. In any case, administration control of a majority vote meant that ministers could, if necessary, have their own way in any procedural matter, great or small. Onslow's own memoirs, indeed, reveal that this professed concern for the minority was in reality embraced by a wider constitutional purpose:[1]

Let me say to you, as what an English gentleman should pride himself in and have ever before his eyes and deem the most valuable property he has, that by a seat in Parliament he has an opportunity to raise himself by his abilities and disinterested character there (the one as necessary as the other), to any height of true power and name with satisfaction to his own free heart (the only real comfort of greatness) and without going through that horrible course of servile dependence upon and yet more servile flattery to the will, caprice, insolence, and often the vices of a Prince or his ministers, and which is the general foundation of all eminence in arbitrary Governments.

This passage is the key to Onslow's career as Speaker. The rules of procedure afforded members an opportunity to discuss business, rather than to delay or defeat it. Onslow's insistence on the equitable treatment in debate of the opponents of government and of other individual members is explained by his conception of the role of the House of Commons in the constitution. Its debates he regarded as the vital part of the function of the House as a path to political power.

Onslow's concern for the prestige and privileges of the House arose from this belief in the value of its political importance, symbolic and actual. Hence, too, sprang his emphasis on the significance of his own office. His pomposity was so notorious that 'the person of dignity' was a newspaper synonym for the Speaker in 1752.[2] Hatsell recalled that it was Onslow's custom to insist that members entering or leaving the House should make a bow to the Chair, by calling out to those who failed to

---

[1] *H.M.C. Onslow*, p. 505.   [2] H. Walpole, *Letters*, III, 123.

do so.[1] Speaker Norton suggested that this courtesy should end during the first debate when he was in the Chair, on 24 January 1770: 'I wish to avoid the little salutations of gentlemen that pass, because it interrupts the attention.'[2] The practice nevertheless continued, although Carl Moritz in 1782 did not think it enhanced the dignity of proceedings: 'as often as any one wishes to go out, he places himself before the Speaker, and makes him his bow, as if, like a schoolboy, he asked his tutor's permission.'[3]

Sometimes when enforcing order Onslow would remind the House of the reason why members should avoid abuse. On 4 April 1733, after Sir Thomas Aston denounced the author of the Excise Bill as 'an enemy to his King and country . . . the Speaker took him down to order, and reproved him. He told him if such words were suffered to come out of any member's mouth, there was an end of all debating, and even of Parliament.'[4] On 13 March 1741 Onslow followed an intervention with this comment: 'My office obliges me on this occasion to remark, that the regard due to the dignity of the House ought to restrain every member from digressions into private satire, for in proportion, as we proceed with less decency, our determinations will have less influence.'[5] Onslow's concern for the dignity of the House, his maintenance of order and his insistence on strict observance of the rules of procedure were not merely ends in themselves: they were intended to preserve the House of Commons in the role of the cornerstone of the British constitution.

Onslow's rule over the Commons had helped to establish standards of Parliamentary behaviour: but his success in the Chair led contemporaries to underestimate the task of a Speaker.[6] The personal qualities required for the post do not seem to have been considered in the negotiations of 1761 over the choice of his successor. George Grenville's character and knowledge would have stood him in good stead, and

---

[1] Hatsell, *Precedents*, II, 233N.   [2] B.M. Eg. MSS. 3711, p. 99.
[3] Moritz, *Travels*, p. 53.   [4] *H.M.C. Egmont Diary*, I, 350.
[5] Chandler, *Debates*, XII, 299.
[6] J. S. Watson, 'Arthur Onslow and Party Politics', *Essays in British History*, p. 165.

Edward Bacon had considerable experience as a Chairman: but both Thomas Prowse and Sir John Cust were country gentlemen with no obvious aptitude for the office. Only the Duke of Newcastle recorded immediate doubts on the final choice of Cust.[1] Horace Walpole, later to be severe in his comments, made this remark at the time: 'Sir John Cust is Speaker, and bating his nose, the Chair seems well filled.'[2] Cust, however, was lacking in both procedural knowledge and the force of character necessary for Parliamentary storms that would have taxed Onslow at his prime. His rulings from the Chair sometimes went unheeded. In a discussion of 11 December 1761 on the use of the King's name in debate, it was the view of Solicitor-General Charles Yorke that prevailed, not that of Cust. On 11 April 1763 the House ignored the Speaker's objection to an amendment widening the scope of a bill at the report stage. Procedural expert Jeremiah Dyson flatly contradicted Cust's opinion on 10 February 1764 that a Committee of the Whole House was necessary for the repeal of any tax. On 24 November 1768 Hans Stanley disagreed with his views on the duty of M.P.s to present petitions.[3] The evidence on each of the incidents suggests that none of Cust's opinions were in accordance with previous Parliamentary practice. A Speaker so often wrong, and these are merely examples, could not command respect. The prevailing contemporary assumption of Cust's incompetence and the feebleness of his personal authority are both illustrated by an incident of 14 February 1764. Opposition members Henry Seymour Conway and William Pitt challenged the Speaker's claim that he had read out an amendment to a motion. 'Lord North supported the Speaker, called it an outrage on all decency to deny the Chair to his face.' Lord Strange then contrived to demonstrate that Cust was, in fact, right in his contention: but that such a scene should have occurred at all is itself a sign of Cust's lack of control.[4]

Cust's failure in the all-important task of maintaining order during debates is apparent from many reports of proceedings.

---

[1] B.M. Add. MSS. 32929, fo. 409.   [2] H. Walpole, *Letters*, V, 140.
[3] Harris Diary, 11 Dec. 1761, 11 Apr. 1763, 10 Feb. 1764. B.M. Eg. MSS. 215, pp. 239–40.
[4] Harris Diary, 14 Feb. 1764.

James Harris made frequent references to noise in his diary; on several occasions, for example, he noted laconically that members were 'seen to speak but not heard'.[1] During the discussion of the two Wilkes cases of the *North Briton* in the session of 1763–1764 and the Middlesex elections in that of 1768–1769 there was often general disorder in the House. That the reason was the mild and ineffectual nature of Cust's rule may be illustrated from the diary of Henry Cavendish. On 23 November 1768 Cust merely expressed the hope that the next person who got up would make a motion; and during later debates on Wilkes he resorted to general reproofs rather than direct action against individual members. On 8 December 1768 he declared that 'heat and violence is of no service'; and on 31 January 1769 he remarked that 'he was sorry to say that this House of Commons was more noisy than the former'. Cust was not equal to the task, and two days later a formal complaint was made by Rose Fuller. 'I shall be the man to know how the House was kept in order formerly.' Speaker Cust replied, 'the House will bear me witness how much I have endeavoured to keep order. One method is to name gentlemen.'[2] But he never carried out this threat.

Contemporary comment confirms the impression of Cust's weakness that is given by the direct evidence of the debates. George III had noticed his incapacity by 1763.[3] By the time that Horace Walpole came to write of the Speaker's election in his *Memoirs* Cust had been in the Chair for some years. Walpole's considered comment then was that Cust 'had nothing but industry; he was indeed a very poor creature'. And here is his judgement on the Speaker when he resigned in 1770. 'In no light was Sir John Cust a loss. His want of parts and spirit had been very prejudicial. He had no authority.'[4] Some historians have tried to redeem Cust's reputation by emphasis on his admirable qualities as a private individual:[5] but to have a pleasant character was a positive disadvantage for the role of Speaker. Lord North's eulogy of Cust at Norton's election is significant in that it did not claim for him personal qualities

[1] Harris Diary, 9 Dec. 1761, 13 Mar. 1763, 26 Mar. 1764.
[2] B.M. Eg. MSS. 215, pp. 198, 335; 216, p. 236; 217, p. 53.
[3] *Grenville Papers*, II, 165.　　　　[4] H. Walpole, *George III*, I, 68; IV, 33.
[5] H. Walpole, *George III*, I, 68N. *Erthig Chronicles*, II, 97–8.

essential for the Chair, and for the remark that 'his indulgence to us all, and readiness to assist us upon every occasion with his instruction; his benevolence, his every amiable quality are known to you, Sir, and to us all.'[1] The reputation Cust left behind him is shown by this comment of Nathaniel Wraxall, who did not enter the House until ten years later: 'The Chair of the House of Commons, during the whole course of the Eighteenth Century, was never filled with less dignity or energy, than by Sir John Cust.'[2]

The choice of Sir Fletcher Norton as his successor was a clear indication that government had learned the lesson of Cust's tenure of the Chair. Norton was a man formidable alike in learning and temper, a lawyer unpopular for his reputed lack of scruple in both his practice and his politics, and for his robust method of debating in the House. But even Horace Walpole recognized that he might serve the purpose well. 'Nothing can exceed the bad of his character even in this bad age, yet I think he can do less hurt in the Speaker's Chair than anywhere else. He has a roughness and violence, too, which will not suffer the licentious speeches of these last days, and which the poor creature his predecessor did not dare to reprimand.'[3]

Norton was involved in an argument with opposition members on 24 January 1770, the first day of business after his election to the Chair. His resolute action was commended by Leader of the House Lord North: 'You, Sir, whilst you are in that Chair, by the experience we have had this day, will take care that the artillery in this place shall observe the rules of war.' At the close of the debate the Speaker addressed the House on the difficulties of his office.

I do find, indeed, already, that this seat is not likely to be a bed of roses. It is the most irksome, the most painful task, I ever undertook in my life. If from no motive, but doing my duty, I stopped particular gentlemen, when I thought they were going out of the way, I am blamed. If gentlemen do say more than they ought, and I dont stop them, I am blamed for that. What shall I do? . . . I have sat still, painfully sat still, hearing on this side, and that side improper things. I durst hardly use my own judgement in putting

[1] B.M. Eg. MSS. 3711, pp. 66–8.   [2] Wraxall, *Memoirs*, I, 374.
[3] H. Walpole, *Letters*, VIII, 354.

a.stop to it. Unless the House will give me indulgence I dont know whether I shall be able to dare to do my duty.[1]

Norton's firm behaviour on this occasion aroused favourable comment: 'Their new Speaker began yesterday to show his Authority, and they say behaved extremely well. You know he has a capacity for that or anything else that he pleases to undertake.'[2] This comment from an outside observer was confirmed by the opinion of James Harris, who wrote to his son on 6 February 1770: 'Our new Speaker seems to keep order with becoming authority. He appears to stand like Virgil's Rock, and bid the waves defiance.' In another letter a week afterwards he made a similar comment: 'Our new Speaker Norton, seems to do well, and to maintain order, as far as order in such a place as where he presides can be maintained.'[3]

There is ample evidence that during his early years as Speaker Norton sought to rule the House with a firm hand, frequently intervening to maintain order and to enforce the rules of debate.[4] Norton prided himself on his knowledge of procedure, contradicting even Jeremiah Dyson on the subject.[5] Henry Cavendish noted on 13 April 1772 that he was 'very angry' with William Burke for having suggested, wrongly, that a ruling from the Chair was in error.[6] Norton made many pronouncements on Parliamentary practice, and his decisions appear to have been soundly based on precedent or common sense: one example was his ruling on 28 May 1778 that M.P.s who were prisoners of war released on parole could sit in the House. Solicitor-General Wedderburn had questioned the right of General Burgoyne to do so; but there was a clear precedent in the case of Lord Frederick Cavendish during the Seven Years' War, and Norton declared that 'it was not a matter of doubt.'[7]

This picture of Norton as a strong Speaker may need qualification: quite a different view was put forward by Paymaster-

[1] B.M. Eg. MSS. 3711, pp. 84–7, 91, 97–9.
[2] *H.M.C. 10 Report, Part I*, p. 419. E. Thompson to E. Weston.
[3] *Malmesbury Letters*, I, 192.
[4] Many instances of Norton's actions as Speaker from 1770 to 1774 may be found in Henry Cavendish's diary. B.M. Eg. MSS. 220–263, 3711.
[5] B.M. Eg. MSS. 226, p. 271.   [6] B.M. Eg. MSS. 240, p. 363.
[7] Almon, *Parl. Reg.*, IX, 260–1.

General Richard Rigby in the debate of 31 October 1780 over the election of Cornwall as his successor. Rigby then gave Norton's lack of control over the House as one reason for his removal from the Chair: 'One part of his conduct had often appeared to him extremely wrong, and that was his relaxation of the rules of proceeding with the ordinary business of the House, and his want of strictness in observing order, and keeping gentlemen within due bounds. This he had spoken of to the late Speaker more than once.'[1] Certainly in a debate of 14 May 1777 Rigby complained that 'a less good-natured man would keep order better.'[2] During his last years as Speaker Norton may have been less in command of the House, as a result of deteriorating health and the increasing realization that his tenure of the Chair would end with the Parliament. But no contemporary evidence to substantiate Rigby's assertions has been found: and the contention of incapacity might have been merely another excuse for a political decision about which the administration had some constitutional qualms. Certainly there is no reason to dispute the safe verdict of Nathaniel Wraxall that Norton 'possessed eminent Parliamentary Knowledge as well as legal Talents. Far from suffering in his Capacity of Speaker, by a Comparison either with his immediate Predecessor or Successor in that high office, he must be considered as very superior to both.'[3]

Wraxall never sat in the House under Speaker Norton, but he left an unflattering verdict on Charles Cornwall after first-hand experience: 'Cornwall possessed every physical quality requisite to ornament the Place, a sonorous Voice, a manly as well as imposing Figure, and a commanding Deportment. . . . After his Election Cornwall gave little Satisfaction, and had recourse to the narcotic virtues of Porter, for enabling him to sustain its Fatigue; an Auxiliary which sometimes becoming too powerful for the Principal who called in its Assistance, produced Inconveniences.' This picture of the Speaker in a drunken torpor is, of course, that conveyed by the *Rolliad* in 1784, the relevant part of which Wraxall himself quoted:[4]

> There Cornwall sits, and ah! compelled by Fate,
> Must sit for ever through the long Debate,

---

[1] Debrett, *Parl. Reg.*, I, 15.   [2] Almon, *Parl. Reg.*, VII, 194.
[3] Wraxall, *Memoirs*, I, 374.   [4] Wraxall, *Memoirs*, I, 374–5.

Save when compelled by Nature's sovereign Will,
Sometimes to empty, and sometimes to fill . . .
Like sad Prometheus fastened to the Rock,
In vain he looks for pity to the Clock;
In vain the Powers of strengthening Porter tries,
And nods to *Bellamy* for fresh Supplies.

Wraxall could not find a good word for Cornwall even on his death in 1789. 'Never was any man in public situation less regretted, or sooner forgotten, than Cornwall!' This silent condemnation appears to have been universal, for Wraxall noted that during the debate over the choice of a successor 'I believe not a word of regret, or even of approbation, was expressed for the character and services of the deceased Speaker, from any part of the house. In truth, he little deserved such recognition of his official merit.'[1]

Wraxall's comments are invariably cited in studies of Speaker Cornwall, and form the basis of his reputation for incompetence. The evidence of his first Parliament suggests that it is unfair. He appears in reports of debates as a vigorous and well-informed Speaker, frequently intervening on his own initiative to stop altercations and other unparliamentary language and behaviour, and to insist that the House must have a motion to debate.[2] On many occasions he gave advice to members on procedure, and expounded and explained the rules of the House.[3] If no member paid testimony to Cornwall in the customary manner, the writer of his obituary in the *Gentleman's Magazine* found a compliment to pay: 'As Speaker, he uniformly conducted himself with an affability, dignity, and rectitude of conduct highly becoming his elevated situation.'[4]

There is less substance than has usually been supposed in the conventional opinion that Arthur Onslow's successors failed to maintain the position he had established for the Chair.

[1] Wraxall, *Memoirs*, VII, 251. For confirmation of the absence of any mention of Cornwall in that debate see Cobbett, *Parl. Hist.*, XXVII, 904–7; and Debrett, *Parl. Reg.*, XXV, 155–8.

[2] Debrett, *Parl. Reg.*, I, 103, 112; II, 47; V, 192; IX, 164. Wraxall, *Memoirs*, II, 277, 300, 354, 421; III, 126–7.

[3] Debrett, *Parl. Reg.*, II, 214; VI, 308, 464; VII, 79, 261, 272–3; IX, 65, 312, 466, 498; X, 1–2, 565–6; XII, 94, 127–8.

[4] *Gentleman's Magazine*, 1789, I, 87.

Cust's tenure of the office brought a prompt realization that the holder of the post needed to be a man of positive character and of a certain competence in Parliamentary business. Such men were sufficient to continue the momentum of the habits and practices established under Onslow: at the very least they could and did cite his precedents and opinions. The eighteenth century was for the House of Commons 'the age of Onslow'.

SELECT BIBLIOGRAPHY

PRIMARY SOURCES

A. *Manuscripts*

i. *In the British Museum*

Eg[erton] MSS. 215–263, 3711. The Parliamentary Diary of Henry Cavendish 1768–1774.[1]

Add[itional] MSS. 6839. Sir Andrew Mitchell Papers.

Add. MSS. 29132–29194. Warren Hastings Papers.

Add. MSS. 30865–30896. John Wilkes Papers.

Add. MSS. 32686–33072. Newcastle Papers.

Add. MSS. 35349–36278. Hardwicke Papers.

Add. MSS. 38190–38468. Liverpool Papers.

MS. Facs. 340 (1–4). John Robinson Papers in the possession of the Marquess of Abergavenny at Eridge Castle.

ii. *In other repositories*

Baker of Bayfordbury MSS. Hertfordshire County Record Office. (By permission of Mr. W. L. Clinton-Baker.)

Bettisfield MSS. National Library of Wales.

Parliamentary Diary of Matthew Brickdale 1770–1774. 11 Vols. Bristol University Library. (Cited as Brickdale Diary.)

Chatham MSS. Public Record Office. (Cited as P.R.O. 30/8.)

Cholmondeley Houghton MSS. Cambridge University Library. (By permission of the Marquess of Cholmondeley.)

Parliamentary Diary of John Clementson 1770–1804. House of Lords Record Office. (Historical Collections, House of Commons. Cited as Clementson Diary.)

Dashwood MSS. Bodleian Library, Oxford. (By permission of Sir Francis Dashwood.)

Harpton MSS. National Library of Wales.

Parliamentary Diary of Narcissus Luttrell 1691–1693. 2 vols. Codrington Library, All Souls College, Oxford. (By permission of the Librarian. Cited as Luttrell Diary.)

---

[1] References are made by page, not folio. The triple pagination in Eg. MSS.222 is indicated by the respective letters, A, B, C.

Newdegate MSS. The personal diary (1751–1780) and other papers of Sir Roger Newdigate. Warwickshire County Record Office. (By permission of Mr. Humphrey Fitzroy-Newdegate. Diary cited as Newdigate Diary.)

Stackpole Letters. N.L.W.MS.1352. National Library of Wales.

Wentworth Woodhouse MSS. Sheffield City Library. (By permission of Earl Fitzwilliam.)

iii. *In private possession*

Harrowby MSS. Diaries and papers of Sir Dudley Ryder (1691–1756) and Nathaniel Ryder, 1st Baron Harrowby (1735–1803). In the possession of the Earl of Harrowby.

Ley MSS. In the possession of the late Mr. O. C. Williams.

Malmesbury MSS. The Parliamentary Diary (1761–1780) and political memoranda of James Harris. In the possession of the Earl of Malmesbury. Diary cited as Harris Diary.

B. *Printed Sources*

i. *Contemporary Correspondence and Memoirs*

HISTORICAL MANUSCRIPTS COMMISSION (Cited as *H.M.C.*)

   10 Report, Part I (1885), pp. 199–452. Weston Underwood MSS.

   12 Report, Part X (1891), pp. 168–428. Earl of Charlemont MSS.

   14 Report, Part IX (1895), pp. 458–524. Onslow MSS. (Cited as *H.M.C. Onslow*).

   15 Report, Part VI (1897), pp. 13–756. Earl of Carlisle MSS.

   Duke of Portland MSS. Vol. VII (1901).

   Diary of John Perceval, 1st Earl of Egmont (3 vols., 1920–3. Cited as *H.M.C. Egmont Diary*).

Correspondence of John, fourth duke of Bedford, selected from the originals at Woburn Abbey, with an introduction by Lord John Russell (3 vols., 1842–6. Cited as *Bedford Papers*).

The Correspondence of Jeremy Bentham (ed. T. L. S. Sprigge, 2 vols., 1968, in progress).

Boswell's London Journal 1762–1763 (ed. F. A. Pottle, 1966).

The Correspondence of Edmund Burke (ed. T. W. Copeland and others: 8 vols., Cambridge, 1958–69, in progress. Cited as *Burke Correspondence*).

Bishop Burnet's History of His Own Time by G. Burnet (7 vols., Oxford, 1823. Cited as Burnet, *History*).

Sir Henry Cavendish's Debates of the House of Commons during the Thirteenth Parliament of Great Britain (ed. John Wright, 2 vols., 1841–3. Cited as *Cavendish Debates*).

Correspondence of William Pitt, earl of Chatham (ed. W. S. Taylor and J. H. Pringle, 4 vols., 1838–40. Cited as *Chatham Correspondence*).

Records of the Cust Family, vol. 3 (ed. Lionel Cust, 1927).

The Parliamentary Diary of Sir Edward Dering 1670–1673 (ed. B. D. Henning, New Haven, 1940).

The Political Journal of George Bubb Dodington (ed. J. Carswell and L. A. Dralle, 1965).

The Life of John Elwes, by E. Topham, 1790.

Chronicles of Erthig on the Dyke (ed. A. L. Cust, 2 vols., 1914. Cited as *Erthig Chronicles*).

Memorials and Correspondence of Charles James Fox (ed. Lord John Russell, 2 vols., 1853).

The Correspondence of King George the Third from 1760 to December 1783 (ed. Sir John Fortescue, 6 vols., 1927–8. Cited as Fortescue, *Corr. of George III*).

The Letters of Edward Gibbon (ed. J. E. Norton, 3 vols., 1956).

Autobiography and Political Correspondence of Augustus Henry, Third Duke of Grafton (ed. Sir William R. Anson, 1896).

The Grenville Papers; being the correspondence of Richard Grenville, Earl Temple, K.G., and the Right Hon. George Grenville, their friends and contemporaries (ed. W. J. Smith, 4 vols., 1852–3).

Additional Grenville Papers 1763–65 (ed. J. Tomlinson, Manchester, 1962).

Some Materials Towards memoirs of the reign of King George II. By John, Lord Hervey (ed. R. Sedgwick, 3 vols., 1931. Cited as Hervey, *Memoirs*).

Letters on Certain Proceedings in Parliament, during the Sessions of the Years 1769 and 1770, written by John Hope, Esq. (ed. J. Almon, 1772. Cited as *Hope Letters*).

The Parliamentary Diary of Sir Edward Knatchbull 1722–1730 (ed. A. N. Newman, Camden Third Series, Vol. XCIV, Royal Historical Society. 1963. Cited as *Knatchbull Diary*).

Leicester House Politics 1750–1760 (ed. A. N. Newman, *Camden Miscellany XXIII*, pp. 85–228. Camden Fourth Series, Vol. VII, Royal Historical Society, 1969).

A Series of Letters of the First Earl of Malmesbury, His Family and Friends (ed. James Howard Harris, Third Earl, 2 vols., 1870. Cited as *Malmesbury Letters*).

Travels of Carl Philipp Moritz in England in 1782 (ed. P. E. Matheson, 1924. Cited as Moritz, *Travels*).

Memoirs of the Marquis of Rockingham and his Contemporaries (ed. George Thomas, Earl of Albemarle, 2 vols., 1852).

The Parliamentary Papers of John Robinson 1774–1784 (ed. W. T. Laprade, Camden Third Series, Vol. XXXIII, Royal Historical Society, 1922).

The Parliamentary Diaries of Nathaniel Ryder 1764–1767 (ed. P. D. G. Thomas, *Camden Miscellany XXIII*, pp. 229–351. Camden Fourth Series, Vol. VII, Royal Historical Society, 1969. Cited as *Parliamentary Diary of Nathaniel Ryder*).

The Letters of Horace Walpole, Fourth Earl of Orford (ed. Mrs. Paget Toynbee, 16 vols., Oxford. 1905. Cited as H. Walpole, *Letters*).

Memoirs of the Reign of King George the Second by Horace Walpole (ed. Henry Fox, Lord Holland, 3 vols., 1847. Cited as H. Walpole, *George II*).

Horace Walpole. Memoirs of the Reign of King George the Third (ed. G. F. Russell Barker, 4 vols., 1894. Cited as H. Walpole, *George III*).

The Last Journals of Horace Walpole, during the Reign of George III from 1771–1783 (ed. A. F. Stewart, 2 vols., 1910. Cited as H. Walpole, *Last Journals*).

Historical and Posthumous Memoirs of His Own Time by Sir N. W. Wraxall, Bart. (7 vols., 1836. Cited as Wraxall, *Memoirs*).

ii. *Parliamentary Proceedings and Procedure*

The Journals of the House of Commons (cited as *Commons Journals*).

J. ALMON, *The Debates and Proceedings of the British House of Commons from 1743 to 1774,* 11 vols., 1766–75 (cited as Almon, *Debates*).

J. ALMON, *The Parliamentary Register . . . 1774 to . . . 1780.* 17 vols., 1775–80 (cited as Almon, *Parl. Reg.*).

R. CHANDLER, *The History and Proceedings of the House of Commons . . . 1660 to . . . 1743.* 14 vols., 1741–4 (cited as Chandler, *Debates*).

W. COBBETT, *Parliamentary History of England from . . . 1066 to . . . 1803.* 36 vols., 1806–20 (cited as Cobbett, *Parl. Hist.*).

J. DEBRETT, *The Parliamentary Register . . . 1780 to . . . 1796.* 45 vols., 1781–96 (cited as Debrett, *Parl. Reg.*).

T. C. HANSARD, *Parliamentary Debates . . . from 1803 . . .*

J. HATSELL, *Precedents of Proceedings in the House of Commons.* 4 vols. (4th edit. 1818. Cited as Hatsell, *Precedents*).

C. STRATEMAN, ed., *The Liverpool Tractate, an eighteenth century manual on the procedure of the House of Commons* (New York, 1937).

iii. *Contemporary Periodicals*

    Adams Weekly Courant (Chester)
    Annual Register
    Gazetteer
    General Evening Post
    Gentleman's Magazine

Lloyd's Evening Post
London Chronicle
London Evening Post
London Magazine
Middlesex Journal
Morning Chronicle
Morning Herald
Morning Post
North Briton
Public Advertiser
Public Ledger
St. James' Chronicle

SECONDARY WORKS

(a) *Books*

BEATSON, R., *A Chronological Register of Both Houses of the British Parliament from . . . 1708 to . . . 1807* (3 vols., 1807).

BOND, M. F., *A Short Guide to the Records of Parliament* (1963).

BOND, M., *The Records of Parliament* (Canterbury, 1964).

BONSALL, B., *Sir James Lowther and Cumberland and Westmorland Elections 1754–1775* (Manchester, 1960).

BROWN, P. *The Chathamites* (1967).

CAMPION, SIR GILBERT, *An Introduction to the Procedure of the House of Commons* (2nd ed., 1950).

CHRISTIE, I. R., *The End of North's Ministry, 1780–1782* (1958).

COXE, W., *Memoirs of the life and administration of Sir Robert Walpole, earl of Orford* (3 vols., 1798. Cited as Coxe, *Walpole*).

DASENT, A. I., *The Speakers of the House of Commons, from the earliest times to the present day* (1911. Cited as Dasent, *Speakers*).

EHRMAN, J., *The Younger Pitt: The Years of Acclaim* (1969).

FOORD, A. S., *His Majesty's Opposition 1714–1830* (1964).

GIPSON, L. H., *The British Empire Before the American Revolution* Vol. X (New York, 1961).

HAIG, R. L., *The Gazetteer 1735–1797* (Carbondale, 1960).

HASTINGS, M., *Parliament House* (1950).

HOOVER, B. B., *Samuel Johnson's Parliamentary Reporting* (Los Angeles, 1953).

HOWARTH, P., *Questions in the House* (1956).

KEMP, B., *King and Commons 1660–1832* (1957).

LAUNDY, P., *The Office of Speaker* (1964).

MACDONAGH, M., *The Reporters' Gallery* (1913).

MACDONAGH, M., *The Speaker of the House* (1914).

MANTOUX, P., *Notes Sur Les Comptes Rendu Des Séances Du Parliament Anglais au XVIIIe Siècle conserves aux Archives du Ministère Des Affaires Etrangères* (Paris, 1906).

MAY, SIR THOMAS E., *A Treatise on the law, privileges, proceedings and usage of Parliament* (14th ed., 1946. Edited by Sir Gilbert Campion).

NAMIER, SIR LEWIS, *The Structure of Politics at the Accession of King George III* (2nd ed., 1957).

NAMIER, SIR LEWIS, and BROOKE, JOHN, *The House of Commons 1754–1790. The History of Parliament* (3 vols., 1964).

PARGELLIS, S., and MEDLEY, D. J., eds., *Bibliography of British History. The Eighteenth Century, 1714–1789* (Oxford, 1951).

PLUMB, J. H., *Sir Robert Walpole* (2 vols., 1956, 1960).

PORRITT, E., and A. G., *The Unreformed House of Commons* (2 vols., Cambridge, 1909).

REDLICH, J., *The Procedure of the House of Commons. A Study of its History and Present Form* (3 vols., 1908).

REID, L., *Charles James Fox. A Man for the People* (1969).

SIEBERT, F. S., *Freedom of the Press in England 1476–1776* (Urbana, 1952).

STANHOPE, PHILIP, 5th Earl, *Life of the Right Honourable William Pitt* (4 vols., 1861–2. Cited as Stanhope, *Pitt*).

THOMSON, M. A., *A Constitutional History of England 1642 to 1801* (1938).

TOWNSEND, W. C., *History of the House of Commons, from the Convention Parliament of 1688–9 to the Passing of the Reform Bill in 1832* (2 vols., 1843–4. Cited as Townsend, *House of Commons*).

VULLIAMY, C. E., *The Onslow Family 1528–1874* (1953).

WARD, W. R., *The English Land Tax in the Eighteenth Century* (1953).

WILLIAMS, O. C., *The Historical Development of Private Bill Procedure and Standing Orders in the House of Commons* (2 vols., 1948).

WILLIAMS, O. C., *The Clerical Organisation of the House of Commons 1661–1850* (Oxford, 1954).

(b) *Essays, articles in periodicals and occasional publications*

ASPINALL, A., 'The Reporting and Publishing of the House of Commons' Debates, 1771–1834', *Essays Presented to Sir Lewis Namier* (ed. R. Pares and A. J. P. Taylor, 1956), pp. 227–57.

BELLOT, H. H., 'General Collections of Reports of Parliamentary Debates for the Period since 1660', *Bulletin of the Institute of Historical Research*, 10 (1932–3), pp. 171–7.

BOND, M. F., 'Acts of Parliament', *Archives*, 3 (1957–8), pp. 201–18.

EDWARDS, SIR GORONWY, 'The Emergence of Majority Rule in the Procedure of the House of Commons', *Transactions of the Royal Historical Society, Fifth Series* Vol. 15 (1965), pp. 171–84.

FRASER, P., 'The Growth of Ministerial Control in the Nineteenth Century House of Commons', *English Historical Review*, 75 (1960), pp. 444–63.

GIBBS, G. C., 'Parliament and the Treaty of Quadruple Alliance', *Williams III and Louis XIV: Essays 1680–1720 by and for Mark A. Thomson* (ed. Ragnhild Hatton and J. S. Bromley, Liverpool, 1968), pp. 287–305.

GIPSON, L. H., 'The Great Debate in the Committee of the Whole House of Commons on the Stamp Act, 1766, as reported by Nathaniel Ryder', *Pennsylvania Magazine of History and Biography*, 86 (1962), pp. 10–41.

LAMBERT, S., 'A Century of Diplomatic Blue Books', *Historical Journal*, 10 (1967), pp. 125–31.

LAMBERT, S., 'Printing for the House of Commons in the Eighteenth Century', *The Library*, 23 (1968), pp. 25–46.

LAMBERT, S., ed., *List of House of Commons Sessional Papers 1701–1750* (List and Index Society Special Series. 1968).

NAMIER, L. B., 'The Circular Letters; an Eighteenth Century Whip to Members of Parliament', *Eng. Hist. Rev.*, 44 (1929), pp. 588–611.

RANSOME, M., 'The Reliability of Contemporary Reporting of the Debates of the House of Commons, 1727–1741', *Bull. Inst. Hist. Res.*, 19 (1942–3), pp. 67–79.

THOMAS, P. D. G., 'The Beginning of Parliamentary Reporting in Newspapers, 1768–1774', *Eng. Hist. Rev.*, 74 (1959), pp. 623–36.

THOMAS, P. D. G., 'Sources for Debates of the House of Commons 1768–1774', *Bull. Inst. Hist. Res. Special Supplement No. 4* (1959).

THOMAS, P. D. G., 'John Wilkes and the Freedom of the Press (1771)', *Bull. Inst. Hist. Res.*, 33 (1960), pp. 86–98.

THOMAS, P. D. G., 'Check List of M.P.s Speaking in the House of Commons, 1768–1774', *Bull. Inst. Hist. Res.*, 35 (1962), pp. 220–6.

TYLER, J. E., 'John Roberts, M.P., and the first Rockingham Administration', *Eng. Hist. Rev.*, 67 (1952), pp. 547–60.

TYLER, J. E., 'Lord North and the Speakership in 1780', *Parliamentary Affairs*, 8 (1954–5), pp. 363–78.

WATSON, J. S., 'Parliamentary Procedure As a Key to the Understanding of Eighteenth Century Politics', *Burke Newsletter*, 3 (1962), pp. 108–28.

WATSON, J. S., 'Arthur Onslow and Party Politics', *Essays in British History Presented to Sir Keith Feiling* (ed. H. R. Trevor-Roper, 1964), pp. 139–71.

(c) *Unpublished Works*

THOMAS, P. D. G., 'The Debates of the House of Commons 1768–1774', (Ph.D. Thesis, Univ. of London, 1958).

WILLIAMS, O. C., 'The Topography of the Old House of Commons', (1953. One copy of this monograph is available in the House of Lords Record Office).

INDEX